Being Good in a World of Need

UEHIRO SERIES IN PRACTICAL ETHICS

General Editor
Julian Savulescu, University of Oxford

Choosing Children
The Ethical Dilemmas of Genetic Intervention
Jonathan Glover

Messy Morality
The Challenge of Politics
C. A. J. Coady

Killing in War
Jeff McMahan

Beyond Humanity?
The Ethics of Biomedical Enhancement
Allen Buchanan

Ethics for Enemies
Terror, Torture, and War
F. M. Kamm

Unfit for the Future
The Need for Moral Enhancement
Ingmar Persson and Julian Savulescu

The Robust Demands of the Good
Ethics with Attachment, Virtue, and Respect
Philip Pettit

Why Does Inequality Matter?
T. M. Scanlon

Why Worry About Future Generations?
Samuel Scheffler

Fellow Creatures
Our Obligations to the Other Animals
Christine M. Korsgaard

How to Count Animals, More or Less
Shelly Kagan

Being Good in a World of Need
Larry S. Temkin

Being Good in a World of Need

LARRY S. TEMKIN

OXFORD
UNIVERSITY PRESS

OXFORD
UNIVERSITY PRESS

Great Clarendon Street, Oxford, OX2 6DP,
United Kingdom

Oxford University Press is a department of the University of Oxford.
It furthers the University's objective of excellence in research, scholarship,
and education by publishing worldwide. Oxford is a registered trade mark of
Oxford University Press in the UK and in certain other countries

© Larry S. Temkin 2022

The moral rights of the author have been asserted

First Edition published in 2022

Published in the United States of America by Oxford University Press
198 Madison Avenue, New York, NY 10016, United States of America

British Library Cataloguing in Publication Data
Data available

Library of Congress Control Number: 2021942495

ISBN 978-0-19-284997-7

DOI: 10.1093/oso/9780192849977.001.0001

Printed and bound in Great Britain by
Clays Ltd, Elcograf S.p.A.

To all those who have been dealt a cruel hand, whether by man or Fate. Those whose plight is sickening, infuriating, heart-wrenching, and deeply unfair.

Also, to Peter Singer, Angus Deaton, and Derek Parfit.

And, as always, to my family. Especially, Bud, Lee, and Meg.

Contents

Preface

The Dinner Party. On April 3, 2016, my wife Meg and I hosted a small dinner party at our home. The guests included Holly Smith, a major moral philosopher and former Executive Dean of the Faculty of Arts and Sciences at Rutgers; Jeff McMahan, one of the world's leading philosophers on the ethics of killing and just war theory; Alvin Goldman, widely regarded as the greatest living philosopher of knowledge; Derek Parfit, regarded by many as the best living moral philosopher; Angus Deaton, winner of the 2015 Nobel Prize in Economics for his work on international development; and Patrick Byrne, the billionaire founder of *Overstock.com* who has been called the "most hated man on Wall Street."

Inviting Byrne had been something of a mistake. Knowing that his father was a distinguished Rutgers alum, and having met Byrne on campus on several occasions, I stupidly assumed that he lived in New Jersey. In fact, he lived in Utah. As luck would have it, however, Byrne was scheduled to fly from Utah to London the evening of the dinner party. When he learned who else would be there, he decided to have his plane stop in New Jersey for four hours before continuing on his way—just long enough for him to attend the dinner.

The event was everything Meg and I had hoped it would be, and then some. The conversation moved easily and quickly across a wide range of fascinating social, political, and ethical topics. It was, if I may say so, the most interesting dinner party I have ever been a part of, whether as host or guest. One particularly memorable moment occurred when Byrne relayed a conversation that he had had with the leader of a tribal faction in Afghanistan some four or five decades earlier. The leader—a warlord, in fact—was expressing great frustration that the United States and other Western powers were tying his hands, and not allowing him to ruthlessly expunge every man, woman, and child of a rival faction. The leader boldly predicted that one day the West would regret its "squeamishness" on the matter.

As it turned out, that day arrived on September 11, 2001, when the world became acutely aware of the name of the faction that the warlord had wanted to eradicate—*the Taliban.* For, as the world soon learned, it was the Taliban which, for many years, had played a central role in supporting and protecting Al Qaeda, the terrorist organization that perpetrated the infamous events of 9/11.

You can imagine the conversation that ensued regarding the morality of the warlord's position. (A real-world variation of the stock ethical dilemma: if you had the chance to kill Hitler when he was a baby, knowing what he would do as an adult, should you do so? Would you?)

As we neared the end of the meal, the conversation turned to the topic of global poverty and inequality. Deaton, who is a large man with an outsized personality, pushed himself back from the table, and began presenting some of the key claims from his book *The Great Escape: Health, Wealth, and the Origins of Inequality*.[1] In brief, Deaton suggested that global inequality was to some extent the natural and predictable result of the fact that, due to a wide range of social, political, cultural, and historical factors, human progress takes place at an uneven rate throughout the world. That is, global inequality is the unavoidable flipside of uneven human progress. Accordingly, insofar as human progress is greatly desirable, rightly worthy of celebration, and inevitably uneven, at least practically, there is less cause for handwringing than most people assume regarding global inequality.

Predictably, Deaton's view produced an outpouring of responses. On the other side of the table, as well as the issue, Parfit and McMahan spearheaded significant pushback. Longtime supporters of Oxfam, and more recently the Effective Altruism Movement, Parfit and McMahan insisted that even if inequality *was* the natural byproduct of uneven global progress, there was no reason for it to persist to the massive degree that it does. More particularly, Parfit and McMahan contended that there was much that those who were well off could, and should, do to improve the lot of the world's worst off. In support of their view, Parfit presented a version of Peter Singer's famous *Pond Example*, which was intended to establish that just as we have a moral obligation to save a child drowning in a pond, even if doing so will ruin our clothes and our expensive shoes, so we have a moral obligation to help those in need on the other side of the world who will die if we don't send them aid, and this is so even if the cost to us of sending aid is the equivalent of the price of a new outfit and a pair of shoes, or more.

Deaton was unconvinced. To the contrary, he contended that Peter Singer, and others like him, had actually done more harm than good, by urging millions of people to donate to charities operating directly in the world's poorest regions. Parfit and McMahan found this claim preposterous. They simply could not believe that Singer and his followers had done more harm than good, by contributing to, and urging others to contribute to, effective aid

---

[1] Princeton University Press, 2013.

agencies like Oxfam. Deaton countered that aid agencies like Oxfam were almost certainly less effective than Parfit and McMahan presumed. More importantly, Deaton contended, even where such agencies had significant successes, they were almost always outweighed by significant indirect negative effects that the aid agencies produced while operating in many of the world's poorest regions. Among the worst of these effects, according to Deaton, were the ways in which aid agencies tended to prop up autocratic and totalitarian regimes, weaken democratic principles and institutions, and undermine the responsiveness of local governments to their citizens. Underlying Deaton's position was his conviction that the responsiveness of a government to its citizens is fundamentally important for a nation's long-term social, political, and economic progress.

Again, Parfit and McMahan were incredulous. They found it almost impossible to believe that international development agencies like Oxfam had the negative effects that Deaton was attributing to them, and even more difficult to believe that any negative effects that they had might be sufficient to outweigh the enormous amount of good that such agencies produced.

The discussion continued long after the dessert plates were cleared. Although he had been quite vexed during the exchange, Parfit found some consolation in the thought that his dispute with Deaton was more practical than theoretical. More particularly, Parfit insisted that even if Deaton were right regarding most of his claims—which Parfit highly doubted—this wouldn't undermine the truth of Effective Altruism. It would simply point out the importance of finding other paths to helping the world's neediest people. This might require identifying or creating aid organizations that were even more effective than Oxfam—organizations that could be counted on to do more good than harm, perhaps, in part, by strengthening democratic principles and institutions, or improving the responsiveness of local governments to their citizens.

Long after our guests had departed and we had cleaned the dishes, I found myself reflecting on the evening's discussions. In particular, I couldn't stop thinking about the exchanges regarding our obligations to the needy, since that has been a topic close to my heart for as long as I can remember. Deaton and I had discussed his views on several previous occasions: once when we were together at a conference in Geneva, once when we met for lunch in Princeton, and another time at a dinner party at his home. On each of those occasions, I had reacted almost *exactly* as Parfit and McMahan had on this occasion—indeed, at some points, it seemed as if their responses were almost word-for-word how I had previously responded to Deaton. Normally, that fact would have substantially buttressed my conviction in the truth of our position. After all, Parfit and McMahan were on a very short list of the moral philosophers that I most admired, with Parfit being at the very top of that list. But that night, as I listened to the exchanges between Deaton, on the one side, and Parfit and McMahan, on the other, the arguments that I, myself, had made on multiple previous occasions struck me very differently. More particularly, I found there to be something deeply troubling, methodologically, about the confidence that Parfit, McMahan, and I all had that *surely* Deaton was wrong.

After all, Deaton was a distinguished development theorist—a Nobel Laureate, no less—who had spent vast amounts of time immersed in the largely empirical realm of economics, a realm replete with data and statistical analyses about foreign aid. By contrast, Parfit, McMahan, and I were all paradigmatic examples of armchair philosophers who had spent a great deal of our lives thinking about the normative issues relevant to foreign aid—such as the badness of global suffering and inequality, the importance of giving priority to those worse off, and the nature and strength of the obligations that well-off people have to aid the needy. However, Deaton wasn't disputing the normative fact that the suffering of millions in the world's poorest regions is really bad. Nor was he disputing the normative fact that if we could effectively help such people at relatively little cost to ourselves or others we ought, morally, to do so. Deaton was making a largely empirical claim that *in fact* international aid agencies in many of the world's poorest regions do more harm than good, and thus that Peter Singer, and others, do more harm than good when they contribute to such agencies, and urge millions of others to do likewise.

Given Deaton's background, training, and area of expertise, versus ours, how could Parfit, McMahan, and I be *so* confident, as we all were, that Deaton *must* be wrong in making his empirical claims? Moreover, even if we were right, how could we be so *certain* that we were, given the nature of the claims in dispute? On reflection, it suddenly seemed clear to me that we should be much less confident than we were in our position. And since I was one of those people who had been contributing to international relief agencies for most of my life, as well as urging thousands of students over the years to do likewise, this sudden realization shook me to the core. What if I was wrong? What if Deaton was right? Was it possible that, however well-intentioned, I had actually been doing more harm than good for most of my life in my attempts to aid the needy?

That night, I couldn't sleep. I tossed and turned the whole night thinking about Peter Singer's famous Pond Example, wondering whether or not the fact that we had to save the drowning child really did imply, as so many of us had long believed, that we should be donating to international relief agencies like Oxfam. I begin to think about variations of Singer's example. Many variations. Suppose that the child was drowning in a pond, but before we could save him we had to cross a bridge occupied by a thug. He would only let us save the child if we first killed one of his enemies. Should we save the child then? What if we "only" had to cut off the hands of one of his enemies? What if the thug demanded a gun before he would let us cross the bridge, or ammo for a gun? What if we knew that he would use that gun, or that ammo, to kill some other innocent people? Even though it would then be *he* that was killing others, and not *we*, would we be required, or even permitted, to give in to his demands, in order to save the drowning child? What if the thug only demanded money? But we had good reason to believe that he would use that money to support his gang members, who were terrorizing their community. Should we still give him the money, in order to save the drowning child? What if the thug had thrown the child into the water, so as to extract concessions from us, in exchange for his then saving the child, or allowing us to save the child?

My mind went round and round, generating one scenario after another, in the way that philosophers are prone to do. Each scenario represented a variation of Singer's original Pond Example. Each was intended to illuminate the broader question of under what conditions one would be permitted, required, or forbidden from aiding someone in need.

By the time I drifted off to sleep, sometime near dawn, I had generated more than twenty variations of Singer's original Pond Example. As it turned out, in most of them, it seemed clear that it would morally wrong to save the drowning child. In a few of them, it seemed clear that it would be morally right to save the child. In some, it seemed permissible, but not required, to save the child. And in others it simply wasn't clear what we should do about the drowning child. The question, of course, is whether in the world's poorest regions, where aid is often most needed, the situation is more like the scenarios where we shouldn't save the drowning child, as Deaton clearly believed, or more like the scenarios where we should save the drowning child, as Singer clearly believed, and as I, Parfit, and McMahan had always assumed.

In June of 2015, I had been invited to deliver the Uehiro Lectures. Prior to our dinner party, I had been planning to write my lectures on issues in population level bioethics connected with longstanding concerns of mine about justice, fairness, and equality. However, by the morning following our dinner party I had a new topic. I realized that I needed to think much more deeply than I ever had about how to be good in a world of need. This was a topic about which I had long had firm, and settled, convictions. But I was no longer confident that those convictions were well founded, or even true.

The result is the volume that you now hold in your hands. This volume doesn't settle the worries that kept me up all night, following our dinner party. To the contrary, if anything it exacerbates them. But it does so in a way that I believe is valuable, about a topic of extraordinary global importance. Perhaps, by the end, you will agree.

East Brunswick, New Jersey
May, 2020

Postscript. The above Preface is the one that I had long planned for this book. However, it was written in New Jersey at a time when New Jersey and New York were the epicenter of a global pandemic the likes of which the world hadn't seen in 100 years. It is my sincere hope that by the time you are reading these words effective vaccines and treatments will have been developed and globally distributed, and that the worst of the epidemic will be well behind us. But as I am typing these words, such developments still appear to lie significantly in the future; and pain, suffering, and death on a massive scale still lie in store before that day arrives.

As this book was already undergoing final revisions when the pandemic struck, and it was already long overdue to the publisher, I decided not to revise it in light of the global impact of the coronavirus. Still, I would like to add just a few thoughts prompted by the pandemic.

I am, by nature, an inveterate optimist. Even as a horrifying death grip overwhelmed my part of the world, the optimist in me couldn't help but look for positives associated with the pandemic. And sure enough, there were positives to be found.

As people remained in their homes, to avoid Covid-19, death and suffering from the flu, and other communicable diseases, decreased. Likewise, crime rates significantly decreased. Emergency room visits due to automobile crashes, barroom brawls, accidents from active sports and outdoor activities dramatically decreased. And as the global economy slowed to a crawl, and oil consumption dropped to lows unseen in the modern era, pollution decreased, nature flourished, and the drivers of negative climate change were substantially reduced.

Socially and politically, there was a strong, and partly successful push for a moratorium on scores of deadly local conflicts in regions throughout the world. There was a massive global effort to find effective vaccines, and effective treatment options, with scientists, businesses, countries, and countless volunteers around the world teaming up in pursuit of a common goal. And those efforts were fueled by boundless energy as well as nearly limitless resources. Everywhere one turned one heard, and felt, the sentiment that we are all in this together; and that the world needs to unite, perhaps as never before, to fight the common deadly enemy that threatened every country, and every way of life.

Indeed, in the face of the massive harms caused by Covid-19 in the United States, Great Britain, Russia, China, Iran, and (possibly) North Korea, there was reason to hope that even longtime geopolitical rivals and enemies might put aside their differences and band together long enough to defeat the deadly scourge. I confess that the optimist in me hoped that this might lead to further, lasting breakthroughs in the relations between those countries.

There has also been a massive outpouring of love, support, appreciation, and funds for those most affected by the disease, as well as for large numbers of people who play crucial roles in our societies, but whose efforts are typically overlooked. These include: those who died, or are struggling to survive, often separated from their loved ones; those who lost their loved ones, and who were unable to hug them, kiss them, or even be in the same room with them to look them in their eyes, and tell them, face-to-face, how much they loved them; the doctors, nurses, physicians' assistants, and other staff doing the best they can to provide care and comfort, but lacking the tools to do so effectively, or the protections they need for their own safety and that of their families; the first responders; the faceless thousands in our food and delivery chains; caregivers of the young, the aged, and those who are mentally or physically challenged; teachers; those who have lost their jobs due to the pandemic; foodbank and other charity workers; psychologists, social workers, artists, and religious leaders, each of whom, in their own way, do their part to address the terrible damage that the coronavirus has done to so many people's mental and spiritual health; and so on.

In sum, if one is looking for silver linings, even amid an utterly horrible global catastrophe, there are linings to be found. At the top of the list, for me anyway, is the spirit of cooperation, appreciation, and concern for others that the global pandemic has provoked; together with the sense that we are all in this together, and the "there but for the grace of God go I" attitude which each of us *should* have when regarding those who are badly off, but which far too many lack. For many, the massive damage wrought by Covid-19—an invisible, silent, deadly disease that recognizes no geographical boundaries and is utterly blind as to its victims' race, religion, nationality, gender, sexual orientation, or class—has served as a stark reminder of our common fragility, our common mortality, and our common humanity. This is, I believe, a very good development to come out of a very tragic situation, and my hope, of course, is that that outlook will persist and dominate our thinking toward others, and especially toward those less fortunate than ourselves, long after the virus has been defeated.

Unfortunately, having said all that, there is another side of me that sees my optimism as rather naïve and sadly mistaken. That side is part realist, part pessimist, and part cynic. If one looks closely one sees that the "we're all in this together" attitude may have been more apparent, than real. Or, however real it may have been in the beginning, it was short-lived. In my own country, the United States, longstanding geopolitical divisions reared their ugly head, as the worst hit areas in terms of death (as I type these words, this is subject to change, of course) were so-called "blue" states: New York, New Jersey, Illinois, California, Massachusetts, Pennsylvania, and Michigan. After the initial shock and horror of hearing that thousands of their fellow citizens were dying of the coronavirus daily, many residents in so-called "red" states began to wonder how much sacrifice they should be willing to undergo to aid those whose social, political, and cultural values were often so opposed to their own.

Similarly, as more data poured in, we learned that while the coronavirus was an equal opportunity illness in terms of the nature of its transmission, its impact varied substantially along several dimensions. In particular, we learned that those most likely to be adversely affected by the virus were overwhelmingly elderly, or people with certain preexisting medical conditions, and that the latter group were disproportionally members of socially and economically disadvantaged groups—especially blacks and Latinos. Sadly, with that knowledge came a predictable response—why should those who were young, healthy, well-off, and predominantly white lose their jobs, make substantial sacrifices, or radically change their lifestyles for the sake of those at much greater risk from exposure to the virus?

Likewise, as the coronavirus raced across the U.S. and the world, rich states and countries competed with poorer ones for scarce medical supplies, with predictable results. Prices for ventilators and high-quality personal protective gear skyrocketed, and they were disproportionately scooped up by rich countries, states, businesses, sports teams, and individuals. To be sure, this brought to market vast quantities of health gear and equipment that did not exist prior to the pandemic, and some of these valuable supplies would later be available to poorer areas when they were no longer needed by richer areas. But the fact is that as the coronavirus initially began to speed across the globe, the poorest people in the poorest areas—already the least prepared to deal with a major health crisis—were left in a woefully precarious position if they were affected by the virus.

Understandably, the wealthiest countries were focusing on their own national emergencies and prioritizing their own citizens, largely leaving the world's poor to fend for themselves and creating a heated market for scarce medical resources in which the poor could not successfully compete. Far from the communal spirit of "we're all in it together," the actual dynamic smacked of "every country, region, state, and person, for itself or herself".

Similarly, while it may seem heartening that seemingly unlimited resources are available to find effective vaccines and treatments for this global scourge, surely it is no coincidence that of the ten richest countries in the world, eight of them are among the fifteen worst impacted countries in terms of deaths due to Covid-19 (as of this moment): the United States, the United Kingdom, Italy, France, Germany, Canada, China, and India.[2] Does anyone think for a moment that anywhere near such resources would be available to find effective vaccines and treatments if most of the devastation caused by the coronavirus were located in the world's poorest countries?

The preceding question is rhetorical. Still, let me note the following. In the roughly *four months* since the first coronavirus deaths were reported in the United States in early February, 2020, the United States government, alone, has committed over six *trillion* dollars to combat the financial crisis caused by the coronavirus and the U.S. response to it. As I write these words, the U.S. death toll from the virus is 101,359.[3] By contrast, the *entire world* spent a total of 40.4 *billion* dollars in the *seventeen year* span from 2000 to 2016 to combat malaria,[4] during which time it is estimated that 13,917,548 people died from malaria.[5] The overwhelming majority of the malaria deaths during those years occurred in sub-Saharan African (~ 89 percent) and South Asia (~ 9 percent).

---

[2] For a ranking of the 10 richest countries in the world, as of 2020, see https://www.visualcapitalist.com/richest-countries-in-world/, accessed May 27, 2020. For a ranking of the counties with the most deaths due to the coronavirus, as of May 27, 2020, see https://www.worldometers.info/coronavirus/, accessed May 27, 2020.

[3] As per https://www.worldometers.info/coronavirus/country/us/, accessed May 27, 2020.

[4] This figure is calculated from data available at http://www.healthdata.org/news-release/global-malaria-spending-2-billion-short-who-target-stifling-progress-toward-eliminating, accessed May 27, 2020.

[5] This figure is based on estimates of the Institute for Health Metrics and Evaluation that can be found at https://ourworldindata.org/malaria, accessed May 27, 2020. In particular, the figure was derived from year-by-year information available from the chart *Malaria deaths by region: 1990–2017*.

Of course, one can always argue about the numbers,[6] or suggest that I am comparing apples—money spent addressing the financial fallout from a disease—to oranges—money spent trying to eradicate or treat a disease. Still, the natural and plausible conclusion to be drawn is that vastly more resources are available to fight deadly diseases and their impact when they adversely affect the rich, than to fight deadly diseases and their impact when they predominantly impact the poor.

This is not a novel conclusion. Bioethicists and others have long pointed out how pharmaceutical companies focus their attention on rich-country diseases, rather than poor-country diseases, even when the morbidity and mortality costs of the latter are substantially greater than those of the former. Nor it is surprising. After all, given current market incentives, there is far more profit to be made by treating rich-country diseases than poor-country diseases. Even so, for some, including the author and, I presume, most readers of this book, the conclusion in question is both disturbing and sad.

Relatedly, the United States is already committing billions to ensure that as soon as safe and effective vaccines become available, their citizens will have access to them. Presumably, other rich countries are taking similar steps. Now, as it happens, in this instance this development does not seem inappropriate. After all, as of this writing, the United States has some 30 percent of the world's cases of coronavirus, and 28.8 percent of the world's deaths due to the virus. Still, I cannot help but believe that the United States and other rich countries would be similarly jockeying to ensure that their citizens were the first to receive necessary life-saving vaccines and treatments, even if, contrary to fact in this instance, the disease were ravaging poor countries even more.

On May 14, 2020, the *Wall Street Journal* ran a story titled "U.S. Says Chinese, Iranian Hackers Seek to Steal Coronavirus Research."[7] Similar stories ran in the *New York Times*, the *Washington Post*, the *Independent*, and the *BBC*. Such stories raise an obvious question. In the face of a dangerous global pandemic, why should China, Iran, or any other country have to hack anyone's computers to get information that might be relevant to defeating the disease? Why isn't every scrap of information pertinent to fighting the disease instantly available to anyone, anywhere, who could make good use of it?

---

[6] For example, the models used to estimate total deaths due to malaria by the Institute for Health Metrics and Evaluation and those used by the World Health Organization differ, with the former yielding a larger number of deaths than the latter.

[7] Available online at https://www.wsj.com/articles/chinese-iranian-hacking-may-be-hampering-search-for-coronavirus-vaccine-officials-say-11589362205, accessed May 28, 2020.

I am not naïvely asking such questions. I understand the real-world impediments to the free flow of information when billions of dollars and national prestige are at stake. But the stories in question belie the rosy picture painted previously, of the world working as one in a spirit of full cooperation to defeat a dangerous common enemy. For all the lip service that has been given to countries setting aside their differences, their egos, their national pride, and worries about profit, the truth is that such considerations remain in play, inevitably slowing the disease's defeat, at untold costs to global health and the world's financial systems.

Finally, those concerned about the global needy have long noted how hard it is to get the world's well-off to pay attention to the plight of the world's badly-off. Except in the case of sensational events—massive natural disasters, devastating famines, genocides, or rape being used as a weapon of war—the well-off have grown weary of the never-ending string of stories about poverty, hunger, and sickness afflicting low-income countries. Like the three monkeys—who see no evil, hear no evil, and speak no evil—we avert our eyes, close our ears, and remain silent, both in word and deed, in the face of much of the world's suffering.

As the world has been overwhelmed by the spread of the coronavirus, the world's needy have been pushed out of the daily news cycle almost entirely. We read and hear of the Covid-19 death toll in the United States, Great Britain, Italy, France, and Spain. And in anywhere else where the coronavirus is rearing its ugly head. But during this time of international crisis, the ongoing ravages of lower respiratory tract infections (such as tuberculosis), HIV, diarrhea, ischemic heart disease, parasites, and vector-borne diseases (such as malaria) fail to register so much as a blip on our collective radar. Yet, it is worth bearing in mind that so far, at least, the very worst day, globally, in terms of deaths due to the coronavirus was April 17, 2020, when it is estimated that 8,429[8] people died from the virus. By contrast, recent mortality estimates released by the World Health Organization, UNICEF, the United Nations Population Division, and the World Bank Group, suggest that a child under the age of 15 dies every five seconds around the world, the overwhelming majority of whom are under the age of five and die from preventable or treatable causes.[9] This comes to 17,280 children dying per day.

---

[8] https://www.worldometers.info/coronavirus/worldwide-graphs/#total-deaths, accessed May 28, 2020.

[9] https://www.who.int/news-room/detail/18-09-2018-a-child-under-15-dies-every-5-seconds-around-the-world-, accessed May 28, 2020.

The daily death toll due to the coronavirus is horrifying and shocking. But even more horrifying and shocking is the daily death toll due to preventable and curable diseases. Or, rather, the latter *should* be even more horrifying and shocking. That in fact it is not—we tend to respond to the latter fact with a collective yawn—is, in my judgment, an indication of how far short we still are from being guided by the better angels of our nature.

Today, as I write these words, people around the world are desperate for a return to "normalcy" that they hope will accompany the widespread distribution of effective vaccines or treatment options for the coronavirus. The pessimist in me suspects that when that day arrives, the fortunate among us will return to our previous inward-looking ways, largely ignoring those who have been dealt a cruel hand by man or Fate. The optimist in me hopes for a genuinely new and better normal. One where we really do take the viewpoint that we are all in this together, and where our reaction to the downtrodden is not to avert our eyes, but to take seriously the thought that "there but for the grace of God go I."

Unfortunately, even after many years of thinking about this topic, and completing this book, it *still* is not clear to me how to be good in a world of need. However, I *am* confident that ignoring the needy is not a morally acceptable option. Somehow, we must find a way to live our lives in a way that appropriately responds to that simple, but important, truth.

L.S.T.
May, 2020

Acknowledgments

This book is based on my 2017 Uehiro Lectures sponsored by the Oxford Uehiro Centre for Practical Ethics.[1] I would like to express my sincere appreciation to everyone who made those lectures possible, and who helped to make them one of the highlights of my academic career. This includes my audiences, for their enthusiasm and excellent questions; Miriam Wood and Rachel Gaminiratne, for their great efforts organizing the series, and making my visit as smooth as possible; and the Uehiro Centre Lecture Committee, for selecting me to give the lectures. It especially includes Julian Savulescu, Founder and Director of the Uehiro Centre for Practical Ethics, who played a pivotal role in inviting me, graciously hosted me during my visit, and has been an incredibly patient and understanding Editor as a series of life events, both good and bad, delayed this book's completion. In addition, I would like to express my deep appreciation to the Uehiro Foundation for its creation and generous support of the Oxford Uehiro Centre for Practical Ethics and the Uehiro Lectures. Without the Uehiro Foundation, the Uehiro Lecture and Book Series, and this book, would not exist.

I would also like to thank everyone at Oxford University Press who has played a role in this book's production. This includes Editorial Assistant, Sarah Posner; Senior Assistant Commissioning Editor, Jenny King; my extremely efficient and understanding Project Manager, Vasuki Ravichandran; my outstanding Copyeditor, Joanna North; and, most of all, the Senior Commissioning Editor for Philosophy, Peter Momtchiloff.

Most of this material was written specifically for the 2017 Uehiro Lectures and this book. However, I have been lecturing on these topics, and related ones, for many years, and this book has been influenced by the thinking that went into those lectures and the responses they prompted from their audiences. Unfortunately, in most cases I never knew the names of those I was interacting with, and in others my memory is too poor to give appropriate credit. Accordingly, I would like to give a general, if inadequate, note of thanks to everyone who has provided me with the opportunity to lecture on topics related to this one, or provided me with feedback on those topics.

---

[1] Available online at https://www.practicalethics.ox.ac.uk/uehiro-lectures-2017.

Among others, this includes countless undergraduate and graduate students at Rice, Rutgers, Princeton, Oxford, and Harvard. Also, the organizers and audience members of my lectures "Being Good in a World of Need," "Being Good in a World of Need: Some Empirical Worries and an Uncomfortable Philosophical Possibility," "Universal Health Coverage: Solution or Siren? Some Preliminary Thoughts," "Obligations to the Needy: Some Empirical Worries and Uncomfortable Philosophical Possibilities," "Obligations to the Needy," "Obligations to the Needy: Singer's Pond Example versus Supporting International Aid Organizations—Some Disanalogies and their Normative Significance," "A Few Concerns about the Effective Altruism Movement," "Global Poverty: Why Should We Care?" "Thinking about the Needy, Justice, and International Organizations," "Development Assistance: Acting Justly or for Reasons of Justice," "Thinking about the Needy," "Welfare, Poverty, and the Needy: A Pluralistic Approach," "Why Should We Care?" and "Why Should America Care?" These various lectures were delivered to Harvard's Edmond J. Safra Center for Ethics (2021), the Effective Altruism Group, Cambridge University (2020), the Oxford Effective Altruism Group (2018), the University of St. Andrews Philosophy Society (2018), the University of Edinburgh (2018), Frances Kamm's Kennedy School Graduate Seminar, Harvard (2018), the Harvard Effective Altruism Chapter (2015), the Centre for Applied Philosophy and Public Ethics, the Australian National University (2015), the Harvard High Impact Philanthropy Group (2013), the Society for Applied Philosophy Annual Lecture, Corpus Christi College, Oxford (2013), the Program in Ethics and Health Eighth Annual Conference, *Universal Health Coverage in Low-Income Countries: Ethical Issues*, Harvard (2013), Steve Macedo's Ethics and Public Policy Class, Princeton (2012), The Birmingham Chapter of Giving What We Can (2012), the World Bank, Washington, DC (2011), the Rutgers Chapter of Giving What We Can (2011), The Princeton Chapter of Giving What We Can Chapter (2011), the School of Advanced Study's Institute of Philosophy, University of London (2006), the Kline Colloquium on Equality, Poverty, and Global Justice, University of Missouri (2004), a Symposium on *Welfare and Poverty*, Fifth International Conference of the Gesellschaft für Analytische Philosophie (GAP), Bielefeld, Germany (2003), the Global Justice Conference, Columbia University (2001), the Houston Philosophical Society (1998), and the Institute on World Affairs, Iowa State University (1998).

A symposium based on my third Uehiro Lecture appeared in *The Journal of Practical Ethics*, Volume 7. I am grateful to Julian Savulescu, Editor of this Series, and Peter Momtchiloff, Senior Editor of Oxford University Press, for permission to publish some of the material committed to this book in that symposium, as the article "Being Good in a World of Need: Some Empirical Worries and an Uncomfortable Philosophical Possibility."[2] I am also grateful to the Editor of *The Journal of Practical Ethics*, Thomas Douglas, for his role in bringing that symposium to fruition, as well as to the other contributors to that symposium—Matthew Clark and Theron Pummer, Theodore M. Lechterman, Alida Liberman, and William MacAskill—for their thoughtful responses to my article. Although many of the claims that I make in my third Uehiro Lecture survive in this book, I have substantially revised and clarified my views in light of the useful feedback that I have received from many people on that material.

At various points in this book, I present or draw on claims and conclusions argued for previously in my articles "Thinking about the Needy, Justice, and International Organizations,"[3] "Thinking about the Needy: A Reprise,"[4] "Universal Health Care Coverage: Solution or Siren? Some Preliminary Thoughts,"[5] "Welfare, Poverty, and the Needy: A Pluralistic Approach,"[6] and "Why Should America Care?"[7]

Some of my views about helping the needy have also previously appeared online.

I am grateful to David Edmonds and Nigel Warburton for interviewing me in 2018 for their *Philosophy Bites* Podcast, "Larry Temkin on Obligations to the Needy";[8] to Katrien Devolder for the 2017 Uehiro Centre interview "Larry Temkin on Peter Singer, Effective Altruism, and Aiding the Needy";[9] to Boris Yakubchik for organizing a Rutgers Giving What We Can session with me and Toby Ord, entitled "Global Poverty: Why Should We Care? What Can We Do about It?";[10] and to Waleed Aly and Scott Stephens for their interview "What Do We Owe Those in Need?" which aired on February 6, 2019 on their Australian Broadcasting Corporation award winning radio show *The Minefield*.[11]

---

[2] *Journal of Practical Ethics* 7 (2019): 1–23.   [3] *Journal of Ethics* 8 (2004): 349–95.
[4] *Journal of Ethics* 8 (2004): 409–58.
[5] *Journal of Applied Philosophy* (2014): 1–24; doi:10.1111/japp.12050.
[6] In *Philosophie und/als Wissenschaft* (*Philosophy-Science-Scientific Philosophy: Main Lectures and Colloquia of GAP.5*), ed. Christian Nimtz and Ansgar Beckermann, 147–63, Paderborn: Mentis Press, 2005.
[7] *Ag Bioethics Forum* 11 (1999): 9–15.
[8] Available online at http://hwcdn.libsyn.com/p/4/8/a/48a779ee34e742f3/Larry_Temkin_on_The_Obligations_to_the_Needy.mp3?c_id=20122623&cs_id=20122623&expiration=1528400956&hwt=c749f11752aba948008dd8e4d201d391.
[9] Available online on the Uehiro Centre's Practical Ethics Channel at https://www.youtube.com/watch?v=l68pi6_alt0.
[10] Available online at https://www.youtube.com/watch?v=HcZkXq2C40I.
[11] Available online at https://www.abc.net.au/radionational/programs/theminefield/what-do-we-owe-those-in-need/10774518.

This is a book published in a Series on Practical Ethics. The audience for this book is intended to be wider than that of the typical book published by academic philosophers for a narrow audience of professional philosophers. I have written this book accordingly. This means, among other things, that I have tried to present views that any intelligent person might find interesting and worthwhile about a fundamentally important topic, while avoiding, as much as possible, the jargon and other intellectual wrappings of a so-called scholarly work. Given that, unless explicitly indicated otherwise, everything in this book is original with me—*in the sense* that the claims and arguments in support of those claims are my own. However, I do not claim originality *in the sense* of arguing for views for which no one has previously argued, though I certainly hope, and believe, that that there is some of that going on in this book as well.

Accordingly, I freely acknowledge that many of my claims may have been previously made by others. Where I am aware of that fact, I acknowledge it. However, the literature on poverty, development, and helping the needy is overwhelmingly vast and, except as noted below, I have made no attempt to canvas it here. So, I sincerely apologize, in advance, to anyone who has published similar claims to those I make here that I have not acknowledged. I assure you that this is not a sad case of my presenting your claims as my own, but the happier case of two people independently coming to the same view— which hopefully makes it more likely to be true—with the second person being unaware of the first person's work. In this, I take some small comfort in the words of André Gide, which Shelly Kagan used as the epigraph of his first book, *The Limits of Morality*,[12] "Everything has been said before, but since nobody listens we have to keep going back and beginning all over again."

Before proceeding to other acknowledgments specifically related to this book, I'd like to take a moment to thank my former teachers, many of whom, sadly, have passed away. My Princeton graduate school professors: Paul Benacerraf, John Burgess, Tom Nagel, James Ward Smith and, my personal favorites, Gil Harman, Michael Frede, David Lewis, Margaret Wilson, and, especially, Tim Scanlon. As importantly, my University of Wisconsin undergraduate professors, who first sparked my interest in Philosophy, and encouraged me to become a philosopher at a point when, frankly, I had no clue what that really meant: Mike Byrd, Robert Hambourger, Zane Parks, Marcus Singer and, especially, Fred Dretske and Dennis Stampe.

---

[12] Oxford: Clarendon Press, 1989.

At various points this book draws on information from the field of global health. Some of my knowledge of this field stems from a wonderful year I spent at the National Institutes of Health in the Department of Clinical Bioethics. I am most grateful to Zeke Emanuel for making that year so enjoyable and stimulating. Much of the rest of my knowledge of global health is owing to a series of intellectually interesting and rewarding relationships that I have had, over the years, with the World Health Organization, the Brocher Summer Academy in Global Population Health, the Institute for Health Metrics and Evaluation, and the Harvard School of Public Health's Program in Ethics and Health. All of these relationships were initiated, and fostered, by Dan Wikler, and I am deeply indebted to him for that.

Over the years, many people have commented on my talks on this topic, or on a draft chapter of my Uehiro Lectures. I am grateful to each of them. These include Hilary Greaves, Nicole Hassoun, Michelle Hutchinson, Tyler John, Ole Martin, Kieran Oberman, Theron Pummer, Connor Rochford, and Teru Thomas.

A few people sent me comments on the entire draft of my Uehiro Lectures, or an entire draft of this book. I am deeply indebted to each of them. These include Nick Beckstead, Will MacAskill, Jake Nebel, and Ingmar Persson.

The members of my reading group, Shelly Kagan, Frances Kamm, and Jeff McMahan have given me feedback on just about every draft I have written on this topic over the last twenty years. Their criticisms and suggestions are consistently among the most powerful and helpful I receive, and they have improved my thinking about this topic, and many others, immeasurably. However, my debt to them goes well beyond their feedback on my work. Our regular meetings have been a tremendous source of intellectual stimulation and pleasure.

A few people deserve special mention. Jan Narveson and I publicly debated the topic of our obligations to the needy both at the Institute on World Affairs, in 1998, and at the Fifth International Conference of the Gesellschaft für Analytische Philosophie, in 2003. We also published lengthy articles on this topic, and replies, in a special two-person symposium in *The Journal of Ethics* in 2004. I am grateful to Jan for the collegial spirit that he brought to our debates, even as he forcefully presented his own views, and pushed me to further develop and defend my own. (I am also grateful to J. Angelo Corlett, then Editor of *The Journal of Ethics*, for organizing the symposium, and encouraging us to take as much space as we needed to fully develop our views and reply to each other. Unrelatedly, let me also belatedly acknowledge that it was on a typewriter of Jan's—temporarily left in Derek Parfit's possession and lent to me when my own typewriter broke down—on which I typed the earliest draft of *Inequality*,[13] way back in 1978–9. Thanks to Jan for that as well.)

Peter Unger's book, *Living High & Letting Die: Our Illusions of Innocence*,[14] is one that I have long used in my introductory ethics courses. It is powerful and provocative, and it forces both students and teachers to question their views about our obligations to the needy. However, my greatest debt to Unger is that he was the one who recommended that the Institute on World Affairs invite me to debate Jan Narveson, when he, himself, was unavailable. Up until then, I had long worried about the plight of the needy personally, and I regarded it as an important and useful topic to address pedagogically, but I had never thought deeply about it philosophically, or lectured or published on the topic professionally. That changed, thanks to Unger, starting in 1998, for which I am most grateful.

Terrence Wood is a development economist at the Australian National University. He sent me many pages of comments on an earlier draft, as well as empirical data and many citations to work in the development literature relevant to this book's claims. I have not been able to follow all of the leads with which he provided me, or to do full justice to his many excellent suggestions. However, I am extremely grateful for his feedback, support, and encouragement. While Wood had worries about some of my claims, at least as originally stated, I was comforted by the fact that he found most of my claims to be compatible with, and supported by, the development literature.

Brian Oosthuizen served as my research assistant. With a background in International Development, keen intelligence, a great work ethic, and a passion for the issues discussed in this book, Brian was an ideal research assistant. I tasked Brian with wading through some of the development literature to see if my claims were supported by that literature, and if not, how I might need to revise my claims. Brian performed that task cheerfully and efficiently and provided me with many of the citations to non-philosophy that appear in this work. Brian also gave me many useful comments and did much of the initial work on the references. I am extremely grateful to him.

Others also helped with typescript preparation. Adam Gibbons compiled the initial index, and Jimmy Goodrich put the index in final form. Anyone who has constructed a useful index knows what an important, and difficult, task that is. To both Adam, and Jimmy, I am most grateful. Also, I am very grateful

---

[13] Temkin, Larry, *Inequality*, New York: Oxford University Press, 1993.
[14] New York: Oxford University Press, 1996.

to Tyler Chang, Lucy Huang, and Steven Hernandez for putting the citations and references in proper form.

Roger Crisp deserves separate mention. He sent me many useful comments on an early draft. Then later, he again sent me many useful comments on my penultimate draft, as a reader for Oxford University Press. His thoughtful and judicious comments were most welcome.

My debts to Leif Wenar are many. His book, *Blood Oil: Tyrants, Violence, and the Rules That Run the World*,[15] is a powerful book on a closely related topic from which I have greatly benefited. And I was pleased to learn that Leif shares many of my views about this topic when, after reading a draft of this book, he humbly sent me a copy of his excellent article "Poverty is No Pond: Challenges for the Affluent,"[16] which I had not previously seen. Leif has also given me many useful comments, both in discussions and correspondence. Like Crisp, he provided me with valuable comments on both an early draft, and on the penultimate draft, as a reader for Oxford University Press. As importantly, Leif has enthusiastically supported this project by providing me with a rich set of resources and contacts outside of Philosophy. It was Leif who put me in contact with Terence Wood and Brian Oosthuizen. It was also Leif who introduced me to the important writings of the development economist Roger Riddell, whose book, *Does Foreign Aid Really Work?*,[17] is a model in terms of its comprehensive and balanced approach to assessing the benefits and shortcomings of foreign aid, and its keen recognition of the limits of our current state of knowledge regarding this topic.

I have already mentioned the pivotal role that Angus Deaton played in prompting the writing of this book, in my Preface. His book, *The Great Escape: Health, Wealth, and the Origins of Inequality*,[18] is interesting, troubling, and very important. Through our discussions, together with his book, Angus has given me one of the greatest gifts that one academic can give to another. To paraphrase Kant, he awakened me from my dogmatic slumbers. Using a rare combination of insight, argument, intelligence, patience, good will, and conviction, Angus has forced me to seriously rethink views that I had held firmly, without question, for virtually my entire life. Although this has been deeply unsettling—and I am still not sure, even now, to what extent I agree with Angus—I shall always be profoundly grateful for that.

---

[15] New York: Oxford University Press, 2017.
[16] In *Giving Well: The Ethics of Philanthropy*, ed. P. Illingworth, T. Pogge, and L. Wenar, New York: Oxford University Press, 2011, pp. 104–32.
[17] Oxford: Oxford University Press, 2007.   [18] Princeton: Princeton University Press, 2015.

In many ways, Peter Singer is the foil for this book. But he is also its hero. He has employed the powerful tools of Philosophy to shine a searing light on one of humanity's darkest problems. And his compassion for the least fortunate, and deep commitment to *doing* something about their plight, is a potent example for others to follow. I have no doubt that Peter is on the side of the angels in his commitment to helping the world's downtrodden. However, I also believe that Deaton is on that side, and I sincerely hope that I am, as well. Although I raise many worries, throughout this book, about what actually follows from Singer's famous Pond Example, my admiration for him, and debt to him, cannot be overstated.

Derek Parfit's immediate role in sparking this book was noted in the Preface. However, my debt to him goes much deeper than that. Derek was my teacher, my thesis advisor, my mentor and, later, my Editor, colleague, and longtime co-teacher. He was the best philosophical interlocutor I ever knew, a rich source of insight, a model philosopher in every respect, and my closest philosophical friend. It is no exaggeration to note that any modest successes that I have achieved in Philosophy, I owe to him. Indeed, were it not for his enthusiastic and unwavering support, I think it highly likely that I would have left Philosophy long ago.

I end with some acknowledgments unrelated to Philosophy. I want to thank my grandparents, siblings, aunts, uncles, and other relatives, for providing me with an unbelievably nurturing and supportive family environment. I especially want to thank my immediate family, for filling my life with meaning, pride, joy, and love. My children, Daniel, Andrea, and Rebecca; their spouses, Qing, Jason, and Jeff; and, as of now, my grandchildren, Kate, Weston, and Cora.

My parents, Bud and Lee, smothered me with every imaginable form of love and support from the day that I was born until the days they died, and the impact of that will remain with me for as long as I remain conscious. My parents provided me with living examples of good people living good lives. It was they who, by both word and deed, instilled in me my lifelong concern for the less fortunate. I have tried to emulate them in my own life, and to pass along their example to my own family, as well as my students.

Finally, my wife, Meg, has been with me since the end of our sophomore year in high school. We met on a 31 mile hike, raising money to feed the hungry, and our shared values have provided the unbreakable bond that connects our lives together. To say that I owe Meg everything does not begin to express the depth of my gratitude to her. For all that she has made possible in my life, and all that she continues to make possible, I thank her, and love her.

Any man's death diminishes me, because I am involved in Mankind; And therefore never send to know for whom the bell tolls; it tolls for thee.

John Donne

1

Introduction

1.1 A Rich World with Pockets of Devastation

We live in an amazing age. Events and objects that would have been regarded as pipedreams, or even miracles, a scant 50 or 100 years ago are now mundane, every day, realities: transcontinental air flights, computers, cell phones, the internet, and so on. I once owned a portable computer whose 198 kilobyte floppy disk had greater memory power than the *entire five floors* of the Pentagon's computer banks in the 1950s. Today, a 30-gram two terabyte (that's two *trillion* bytes) flash drive memory stick is available for less than $30!

Advances in medicine are no less breathtaking. Entire diseases have been wiped out, and previously crippling maladies are now treatable. Triple by-pass surgeries are now routine, as are kidney, liver, and artificial heart transplants. Moreover, we can now improve the human condition itself, via a wide range of pharmaceutical and genetic enhancements.

Globally, the last sixty years have seen substantial increases in literacy and life expectancy, coupled with substantial decreases in birth rates and infant mortality. Moreover, while even in the most "enlightened" societies there remains substantial room for improvement with respect to disadvantaged groups in attitudes, mores, and the legal arena—as recent events spurring the Black Lives Matter and Social Justice movements starkly remind us—in many countries, the treatment of women, blacks, native peoples, people with physical or mental disabilities or illnesses, religious, ethnic, or racial minorities, the elderly, people with different genders or sexual orientations, and so on, is better than it has ever been.

In short, in many respects, this is the "golden age" of human development, as literally billions of people are living better than virtually all our human predecessors.[1] Indeed, almost certainly, most of those living in countries with

---

[1] Many people have observed this. Among them Angus Deaton, in *The Great Escape: Health, Wealth, and the Origins of Inequality* (Princeton: Princeton University Press, 2013), and Steven Pinker in *The Better Angels of Our Nature: Why Violence Has Declined* (New York: Viking Books, 2011), and *Enlightenment Now: The Case for Reason, Science, Humanism, and Progress* (New York: Penguin Books, 2018).

Being Good in a World of Need. Larry S. Temkin, Oxford University Press. © Larry S. Temkin 2022.
DOI: 10.1093/oso/9780192849977.003.0001

advanced economies are living longer, healthier, better lives than the kings and queens of yore. However, while billions have escaped lives in the "state of nature" that Thomas Hobbes memorably described as "solitary, poor, nasty, brutish, and short,"[2] not everyone has been so fortunate. To the contrary, large pockets of humanity have been left behind—indeed, shockingly large pockets. Worse yet, in many cases people have not merely been *left* behind, they have, as it were, been *pushed* behind.[3]

Here, are a just a few pertinent facts. First, in 2014, more than three billion people lived on less than $2.50 per day; of these, more than 1.3 billion people lived on less than $1.25 per day, which the United Nations regards as the threshold of *extreme poverty*.[4] Second, in 2013, the world's wealthiest countries possessed 76 percent of the world's Gross Domestic Product (or GDP), but less than 14 percent of the world's population; and the world's 500 billionaires possessed more than twice as much of the world's GDP as the 2.4 billion members of the world's low-income countries combined.[5] Third, the world's seven richest people possessed more of the world's GDP than all 567 million people of the world's poorest 41 countries.[6] Fourth, as noted in the Preface, it has been estimated that, in 2018, a child under the age of 15 died every five seconds around the world, the overwhelming majority of whom were under the age of five and died from preventable or treatable causes.[7] This came to 17,280 children dying per day. Note, this is a substantial *improvement* from the thirty-year period from 1965 to 1995, during which it is estimated that, on average, at least 27,000 children died each day from readily preventable causes.[8] Fifth, more people died from hunger and remediable diseases in

---

[2] *Leviathan*, 1651, Part 1, Chapter 13.

[3] For an excellent depiction of the basic situation noted in this paragraph, and some of the key factors accounting for it, see Leif Wenar's powerful *Blood Oil: Tyrants, Violence, and the Rules that Run the World* (New York: Oxford University Press, 2017).

[4] Most of the facts in this paragraph were taken from "11 Facts about Global Poverty," *DoSomething. org*, URL: https://www.dosomething.org/us/facts/11-facts-about-global-poverty, accessed June 15, 2020. The article cites the United Nations 2014 Human Development Report as the source of its facts. Specifically, "Sustaining Human Progress: Reducing Vulnerabilities and Building Resilience," Human Development Report 2014, United Nations, available at http://www.who.int/healthinfo/statistics/ChildCOD_method.pdf   https://www.dosomething.org/us/facts/11-facts-about-global-poverty#fnref1, accessed February 25, 2015.

[5] See Shah, Anup, "Poverty Facts and Stats," *Global Issues: Social, Political, Economic and Environmental Issues That Affect Us All*, URL: https://web.archive.org/web/20200901010445/https://www.globalissues.org/article/26/poverty-facts-and-stats, accessed August 31, 2020.

[6] Shah, "Poverty Facts and Stats."

[7] These mortality estimates were released by the World Health Organization, UNICEF, the United Nations Population Division, and the World Bank Group. See https://www.who.int/news-room/detail/18-09-2018-a-child-under-15-dies-every-5-seconds-around-the-world-, accessed May 28, 2020.

[8] This claim is based on one presented by Peter Unger in his important book *Living High & Letting Die: Our Illusion of Innocence* (New York: Oxford University Press, pp. 4–5).

the twenty years from 1990 to 2010—some 360 million people—than died in the whole of the 20th century from wars and repressive regimes—less than 250 million people.[9]

The preceding facts, and others like them, reflect this book's starting point. We live in a period of enormous wealth, the likes of which the world has never seen before. Billions of people are extraordinarily well off, at least materially. Yet ours is a world marked by massive inequality and poverty, whose impact is at the same time both devastating and seemingly avoidable.

This raises this book's central question: What is involved in being good in a world of need? Unfortunately, this book will not, in the end, provide an answer to that question. It will, however, discuss many issues relevant to answering that question. More particularly, my aim is to call attention to some important considerations which, I believe, have too often been ignored or overlooked; including by many generous and well-intentioned people who genuinely want to help those who have been dealt a cruel hand by man or Fate.

1.2 The Audiences for This Book

This book has multiple audiences in mind. Its intended audiences include, at different points: development economists, aid workers, experts on global aid, followers of Peter Singer, many Effective Altruists, professional philosophers, and commonfolk who care about the needy. This makes the writing of this book difficult in many ways, since material that will be new and exciting for some, will be old news for others. Furthermore, I am acutely aware that issues that philosophers find interesting and important, others find bewildering or pointless. This raises tricky questions of presentation. How do I succeed in reaching some members of my intended audience, without losing others?

Unfortunately, there is no perfect solution to this dilemma. The best I can do, I think, is to be upfront about what I am doing, from the outset, and to offer useful signposts along the way to guide the reader.

---

[9] See Martiner, Ramon, "Causes of Death in the World. 1990, 2005, 2010," *Health Intelligence*, URL: https://web.archive.org/web/20200901011600/http://publichealthintelligence.org/content/causes-death-world-1990-2005-2010, accessed August 31, 2020. In his book, *Death By Government* (New Brunswick, NJ, Transaction Publishers, 1994) R.J. Rummel estimates that just under 170,000,000 people were murdered by governments in the 20th century, while Milton Leitenberg suggests that "for the full twentieth century, approximately 231,000,000 people died in wars and conflict" (see his "Deaths in Wars and Conflicts in the 20th Century," Cornell University Peace Studies Program, Occasional Paper #29, 3rd Edition, 2006, available online at https://www.clingendael.org/sites/default/files/pdfs/20060800_cdsp_occ_leitenberg.pdf, accessed June 15, 2020).

I believe that this book has some important new contributions to make even for those experts who have steeped themselves in the philosophical or economics literature on poverty, aid, and development. This is so throughout the book, but especially so, perhaps, in Chapters 12–14. However, since this is a book in a series on Practical Ethics, which aims to reach a general audience, those experts are not this book's *primary* target. Rather, my target audience is the *non-experts* who are not familiar with the vast literature on the topic, but who are deeply concerned about the sickness and suffering pervading our world, much of which seems avoidable or treatable in a world as rich as ours. More particularly, my primary target is those people who take it for granted that the well-off have a responsibility to aid the badly-off, and that, ultimately, this responsibility requires them to contribute to effective aid organizations that operate directly in the world's poorest regions to aid the worst-off members of those regions. Having non-experts in mind as my primary target impacts both the style and content of the book. Among other things, I have adopted a more informal style than I otherwise would have were I only addressing professional philosophers. In addition, I have included a lot of material that is likely to be familiar to experts, but unfamiliar, interesting, and important to non-experts.

The primary target audience for this book includes many philosophers. However, it also includes many academics outside of Philosophy, many non-academics in a wide range of fields, and many ordinary citizens throughout the world—including, in particular, any non-expert who has been moved to contribute to international aid organizations working in the world's poorest regions, or who has urged others to make similar contributions on behalf of the world's needy.

In writing this book, I have, near the top of my mind, the countless students I have met over the years in my classes, or while lecturing to Effective Altruism groups, who have devoted time, effort, and resources to supporting international aid organizations like Oxfam, UNICEF, CARE, Doctors Without Borders, and the International Red Cross or Red Crescent—or whom I have encouraged to do so. And, of course, it is not only the students I have personally met that I have in mind here, but the millions of students and others like them who have been similarly encouraged by their teachers or motivated by the plight of the world's needy to address that plight by supporting international aid organizations like those just mentioned.

Also near the top of my mind are those who feel that they have to do something in support of worthy causes, but they aren't sure which causes to support, the form of the support, or how much support is required. There are endless charitable organizations clamoring for support, and endless volunteer opportunities that one might take on. It can all be bewildering and perhaps, in some cases, paralyzing. My hope is that this book might be helpful to those who find themselves in this position, as well.

Having said that, I am a philosopher, and I think it is important to respond to many of the worries that my peers have raised, or could be reasonably expected to raise, to my claims. Where it would be useful to my main audience, and not too disruptive to the flow of my argument, I have considered such worries in the main text. However, where dealing with such worries is unduly complicated, theoretical, recherché, or discipline specific, I have addressed them in the footnotes. Being relegated to a footnote does not imply that a worry is less important than one addressed in the main text; merely that it is unlikely to bother most readers, or that the answer may be more trouble than it's worth for a general audience.

There are a few footnotes that non-philosophers are particularly likely to find useful. I have marked those with an "*". The rest of the notes are most likely to be of interest to professional philosophers and aid experts. Others should feel free to skip them, skim them, or delve into them more carefully, depending on their interest in the particular issue addressed in the footnote.

Throughout this book, I will be addressing a key example of Peter Singer's, as well as a certain segment of the *Effective Altruism Movement* (about which I will say much more in Section 1.6). Still, consistent with my earlier remarks, I want to be clear that most of the concerns I raise regarding Singer's example and Effective Altruism are *not* directed at Singer himself, or the leaders of the Effective Altruism Movement. Those individuals are experts in the field, who are acutely aware of most (though not all) of the concerns this book raises. Rather, my concern is with the followers of Singer, or the rank-and-file members of Effective Altruism, or those who teach the topic of global poverty or hunger in an introductory class, but who are not, themselves, experts in the field.

In sum, while I believe this book makes some important contributions to the debate about global aid that should be of interest to philosophical, economic, and aid experts, such experts are not my *main* audience. This book is aimed principally at those who work on behalf of, or contribute to, international aid organizations, but who have not read widely, or thought deeply, about this book's issues. Or, perhaps those who have thought deeply about the topic, but who have approached it with presuppositions that gave rise to certain blind spots in their thinking, such that they failed to even consider many of the issues this book raises. Many such people have firm views about aiding the needy that are based mainly on what they learned in church or at home; from movies, commercials, the internet, or other media; from discussions with family, friends, or peers; or perhaps from a single powerful philosophy paper that they were introduced to at some point in their lives—most likely, Peter Singer's classic article, "Famine, Affluence, and Morality."[10] For such people, I believe there is much in this book that will be new and important, and much to be learned about being good in a world of need.

Finally, every author wants his or her book read in its entirety. Each chapter, and section, has a purpose. So, I want to recommend that everyone read the book in the order in which it is written. Still, if a non-philosopher or non-expert begins to find a section pointless, impenetrable, or mind-numbing, I encourage him or her to just skim it, or skip it and go on to the next section. For non-experts, the core of the book is contained in Chapters 2, 4–11, and 15–16. Chapters 3 and 12–14 are among the book's most original and important contributions, but they are also the most difficult and philosophical chapters. Some material has been relegated to appendices, as likely to be of interest and significance mainly to philosophers, Effective Altruists, or Expected Utility Theorists.

1.3 Methodological Remarks and Preliminary Comments

In this section, as well as Sections 1.4–1.7, I will say a bit about my methodological approach, offer a number of preliminary comments, introduce some terminology, explain some of my background assumptions, and specify a particular subgroup of the Effective Altruism Movement with whom this book engages. This material will clarify what I am doing and why I am doing it. Hopefully, it will also forestall some objections that might otherwise arise in the minds of some readers.

Throughout these sections, I will be briefly discussing concerns that some experts have raised to earlier drafts. I believe that every reader might benefit from these sections. However, these sections contain a lot of stage setting, and some of the issues raised by the experts would likely not occur to or be of much interest to many members of my target audience. Accordingly, readers eager to get to the meat of the book may want to read the following four paragraphs, and then simply skim, or skip, to Section 1.8.

---

[10] *Philosophy and Public Affairs* 1 (1972): 229–43.

Thought experiments have long been a staple of philosophy. From Plato's Cave,[11] to Descartes's Evil Demon,[12] to Putnam's Twin-Earth,[13] philosophy has often moved forward via the use of striking, memorable, examples. Contemporary moral philosophy is filled with examples that have been carefully crafted to both capture our imagination and persuade our reason: Foot's Trolley Problem,[14] Thomson's Violinist Case,[15] Nozick's Experience Machine,[16] Parfit's Repugnant Conclusion,[17] Williams's Jim and the Indians Case,[18] and so on. Of course, good philosophers take pains to carefully interpret their examples, and to provide clear arguments in support of whatever conclusions their examples are intended to illustrate. However, the reality is that for most people, including many philosophers, it is often the key examples that are doing much of the heavy lifting in convincing people to accept the conclusions of the accompanying arguments.

Powerful examples typically work by focusing the readers' attention on certain key factors that the authors deem relevant to thinking about the issues they are discussing. When an example "works," it elicits an intuition, or judgment, in the reader in support of the relevance of the factors to which the author is trying to draw the reader's attention, of which the reader might have been previously unaware, or to which the reader may have previously paid insufficient attention.

For example, for a long time, many people just assumed that the key question in the abortion debate was whether the fetus was or was not a person—if it was, then abortion would be impermissible, because surely a fetus was innocent, and it was just assumed that killing an innocent person was wrong. However, Judith Thomson cast doubt on this assumption, by asking us to consider a case where one was kidnapped, and hooked up to an innocent violinist who needed the use of one's kidneys to survive. Thomson argued that one would have no moral obligation to remain hooked up to the violinist, if doing so threatened one's own life, or would require a significant sacrifice of one's own wellbeing. Most readers share Thomson's view about this case.

[11] Plato, *The Republic*, translated by B. Jowett, 3rd Edition, Oxford: Oxford University Press, 1892.

[12] Descartes, René, *Meditations on First Philosophy*, translated by Donald A. Cress, 2nd Edition, Indianapolis: Hackett Publishing Company, 1988.

[13] Putnam, Hilary, "The Meaning of 'Meaning'," in *Language, Mind, and Knowledge, Minnesota Studies in the Philosophy of Science*, Vol. 7, Minneapolis: University of Minnesota Press, 1975, 131–93.

[14] Foot, Philippa, "The Problem of Abortion and the Doctrine of Double Effect." *Oxford Review* 5 (1967): 5–15.

[15] Thomson, Judith Jarvis, "A Defense of Abortion." *Philosophy and Public Affairs* 1 (1971): 47–66.

[16] Nozick, Robert, *Anarchy, State, and Utopia*, New York: Basic Books, 1974.

[17] Parfit, Derek, *Reasons and Persons*, Oxford: Clarendon Press, 1984.

[18] Williams, Bernard, "A Critique of Utilitarianism," in *Utilitarianism For and Against*, by J.J.C. Smart and Bernard Williams, Cambridge: Cambridge University Press, 1973, 77–150.

That is, most readers agree that even if the violinist were an innocent person, the kidnapped person would not be acting wrongly if she unhooked herself from the violinist, even if this meant killing him, if this were the only way for the kidnapped person to save her own life, or to avoid a significant sacrifice of her own wellbeing. In this way, Thomson's Violinist Case led many people to recognize that what they may have previously assumed to be the case was mistaken; even if one were to grant that the fetus was a person, that would not be enough, by itself, to establish the immorality of abortion.[19]

A powerful example is, like the proverbial picture, worth a thousand words. One example that has had a significant impact is Peter Singer's famous Pond Example, which originally appeared in his 1972 landmark essay "Famine, Affluence, and Morality." Arguably, the roots of the modern Effective Altruism Movement, at least among philosophers, can be traced back to the power and influence of that example. In this book, I will be extensively scrutinizing Singer's Pond example, in part by considering and contrasting it with some examples of my own, to see whether it can bear the weight that many people, including me, have put on it over the years. In doing this, I shall be presenting several worries that others have raised against Singer and the uses to which his work has been put, worries that have a bearing on the real-life recommendations and practices of Singer and his followers, as well as those of certain followers of Effective Altruism. As noted in my Preface, my thinking about this topic has been heavily influenced by Angus Deaton, the 2015 Nobel Laureate in Economics.[20] However, I shall present my own examples and arguments in support of the worries that Deaton and others have expressed.

Some readers may be puzzled why I spend so much time focusing on Singer's Pond Example, while essentially ignoring the large corpus of writing that Singer has published on this topic since publishing his pioneering article. My answer to this is fourfold. First, Singer's original article is undoubtedly one of the most influential and widely-cited Philosophy articles in the fields of ethics of the past fifty years, and, for many, the Pond Example is the key and most impactful element of that article.[21] Second, although Singer has

---

[19] See Thomson's "A Defense of Abortion."

[20] From various conversations we have had over the years in Geneva, Princeton, my home, and his home; and also from his writings, especially his book, *The Great Escape*.

[21] In the article, "List of Important Publications in Philosophy," *Wikipedia* cites "Famine, Affluence, and Morality" as one of only eight articles in the fields of Ethics and Value Theory that make the list of the fifty important publications in Philosophy. See, https://en.wikipedia.org/wiki/List_of_important_publications_in_philosophy#Ethics_and_value_theory, accessed June 21, 2020. Looking up each of the listed articles on *PhilPapers: Online Research in Philosophy* (available online at: https://philpapers.org/), "Famine, Affluence, and Morality" was the most cited of the post-1970 articles.

continued to develop his position on famine relief in a number of subtle and sophisticated ways, he has never abandoned or substantially revised his view about the Pond Example, and its relevance for thinking about our obligations to the needy.[22] Third, anecdotally, I have met many students over the years who have become convinced that they should contribute to international aid organizations like Oxfam, or become Effective Altruists, because of Singer's Pond Example. Finally, and most importantly, whatever Singer's own views regarding the limitations and/or implications of the Pond Example, and whatever Singer's other, or more developed, views on the topic, it is by closely examining what his original Pond Example does and doesn't show, that I can illuminate many of this book's main points.

This last point is also relevant to why I largely ignore many other important works on the topic, such as Peter Unger's *Living High and Letting Die: Our Illusions of Innocence*.[23] There is much in Unger's book with which I agree, and also much with which I disagree. Still, while I shall refer to Unger's book at various points, for the most part I don't need to engage with Unger's arguments to make the points I want to make in this book.[24] Accordingly, such engagement would unnecessarily clutter my presentation, making it more pedantic and less accessible to my audience. So, I leave such engagement out. Likewise, for engagement with other authors who have written on this topic. Unless engagement with another author is necessary for simplifying, clarifying, or otherwise advancing my argument, I have left it out.

In a similar vein, one notable philosopher has suggested that this book relies too heavily on the views of Angus Deaton, which he regards as outliers among those held by development economists. Several points about this. First, Angus Deaton's stature as one of the world's leading development economists was cemented long before he was awarded the Nobel Prize. In addition to a host of major academic contributions to development economics, he has served on

---

[22] For example, Chapter 1 of Singer's *The Life You Can Save*, begins with an expanded version of his original Pond Example (New York: Random House, 2009). I also personally saw Singer present versions of his Pond Example when helping to launch the Rutgers chapter of the Effective Altruist Group Giving What We Can, on December 2, 2010, and when he and I together helped launch the Birmingham, England chapter of Giving What We Can on October 12, 2012.

[23] New York: Oxford University Press, 1996.

[24] While Unger does a masterful job of undermining a lot of bad reasons that people offer for thinking that they have a moral obligation to save a nearby drowning child, but no moral obligation to save a distant child dying of hunger or disease, he considers virtually none of the issues raised in this book—"internal" corruption within aid organizations, "external" corruption in regions where aid is most needed, possible unintended negative side-effects, internal or external "brain drain," undermining government responsiveness, and so on. More importantly, while relevant to the positions he considers, Unger's claim that *salience explains* but does not *justify* people's differing attitudes towards helping a nearby drowning child versus helping a distant child dying of hunger or disease has no bearing on this book's arguments.

important governmental advisory committees in the United Kingdom, China, and the United States. Furthermore, he has been an influential voice in several major international organizations, including the World Health Organization, the International Monetary Fund, the Organisation for Economic Co-operation and Development (OECD), and the World Bank. Thus, Deaton has earned the right to have his views taken seriously where they are directly relevant to this book's topic. Second, while I grant that Deaton's views are at odds with those of most development economists, I strongly reject the view that all *minority* views are *outliers*. As will become clear as the book unfolds, Deaton's views are hardly idiosyncratic. Plenty of economists, journalists, government officials, and aid workers hold views similar to Deaton's. Besides, if we have learned anything from the history of ideas, it is that minority views (and outlier views as well, for that matter) are not necessarily false—sometimes they are just difficult to grasp, hard to believe, or ahead of their time. Third, since some of Deaton's most plausible claims have implications that are both surprising and disturbing, they warrant scrutiny. Fourth, and most importantly, I believe that the full significance of Deaton's views has not been widely understood, and that there is much to be learned from a careful consideration of his views.[25] So, while I reject the claim that Deaton's views are outliers, from my perspective, the question of whether or not Deaton's views are outliers is irrelevant. What matters is whether assessing Deaton's views advances our understanding of this book's issues. I believe that it does.

The preceding is related to a methodological point that Aristotle made over two thousand years ago.[26] Aristotle believed that each virtue was a mean between two extremes. So, for example, the virtue of courage lay between the extremes of cowardliness on the one hand, and rashness on the other, and the virtue of generosity lay between the extremes of miserliness on the one hand and profligacy on the other. He further believed that if someone has a natural disposition towards one extreme, one may have to push her towards the other extreme for her to end up in the middle, virtuous, position where she belongs. Now Aristotle's point was practical, rather than theoretical.[27] Still,

---

[25] See Chapters 11–13. In Chapter 12, I offer an argument in support of one of Deaton's boldest claims that he hadn't previously considered, and that even he failed to fully appreciate when I first presented it to him. As we will see, it is an argument with particularly troubling implications.

[26] The positions ascribed to Aristotle in this paragraph appear in the *Nicomachean Ethics*, Books II–V (in *The Basic Works of Aristotle*, edited by Richard McKeon, New York: Random House, 1941).

[27] Roger Crisp suggested that I explicitly recognize this, and thus make it clear that I am extending Aristotle's methodological insight beyond the practical domain into the theoretical, or intellectual, domain.

whatever one believes regarding Aristotle's view of the virtues, I believe there is something to be said for his methodological point in both practical and theoretical domains. This book reflects that fact.

This book also reflects a second methodological point of Aristotle's; namely, his *principle of dialectic*. Roughly, this principle holds that in addressing a problem, you must get any competing views of experts on the table, and then work through each of them to arrive at the truth.[28]

As noted in the previous section, my book's target audience is those people—like me, for most of my life—who take it for granted that the well-off have a responsibility to aid the poorly-off, and who just assume that this requires them to contribute to effective aid organizations that operate directly in the world's poorest regions. Many of those people may be acquainted with the pro-aid views of people like Peter Singer, Peter Unger, Toby Ord, Will MacAskill, Thomas Pogge, and Jeffrey Sachs, but know little, if anything, about the anti-aid views of people like William Easterly, Alex de Waal, David Rieff, Michael Maren, Helen Epstein, Dambisa Moyo, Linda Polman, Thomas Dichter, and Angus Deaton.[29] So, following Aristotle, in this book, given my target audience, I mainly focus on *worries* about aid, or certain *forms* of aid. I do this not because I believe the aid skeptics are right, but because I believe there is reason to take their views seriously, and not simply ignore them or dismissively sweep them under a rug, as, say, "outlier views" not worthy of rebuttal.

On this topic, as with many moral topics, I believe the truth is complex, multi-faceted, and obscure. But this is a topic which, among philosophers, at least, has tended to focus on only one side of the debate. Or, perhaps more

---

[28] See Book VII, Section I of the *Nicomachean Ethics*. I am grateful to Roger Crisp for reminding me of Aristotle's principle of dialectic, and its relevance to my approach.

[29] See Singer, *The Life You Can Save*; Unger, *Living High & Letting Die*; Ord, Toby, *The Precipice: Existential Risk and the Future of Humanity*, New York: Hachette Books, 2020; MacAskill, William, *Doing Good Better: How Effective Altruism Can Help You Help Others, Do Work that Matters, and Make Smarter Choices about Giving Back*, New York: Avery, 2016; Pogge, Thomas, *World Poverty and Human Rights*, Cambridge: Polity Press, 2008; Sachs, Jeffrey D., *The End of Poverty*, New York: Penguin Books, 2005; Easterly, William, *The White Man's Burden: Why the West's Efforts to Aid the Rest have Done So Much Ill and So Little Good*, New York: Penguin Press, 2006; de Waal, Alex, *Famine Crimes: Politics & the Disaster Relief Industry in Africa*, Oxford: James Currey and Bloomington: Indiana University Press, 1997; Rieff, David, *The Reproach of Hunger: Food, Justice, and Money in the Twenty-First Century*, New York: Simon & Schuster, 2015; Maren, Michael, *The Road to Hell: The Ravaging Effects of Foreign Aid and International Charity*, New York: The Free Press, 1997; Epstein, Helen, *Another Fine Mess: America, Uganda, and the War on Terror*, New York: Columbia Global Reports, 2017; Moyo, Dambisa, *Dead Aid: Why Aid Is NOT Working and How There Is a Better Way*, New York: Farrar, Straus and Giroux, 2009; Polman, Linda, *The Crisis Caravan: What's Wrong with Humanitarian Aid?*, New York: Metropolitan Books, 2010; Dichter, Thomas W., *Despite Good Intentions: Why Development Assistance to the Third World has Failed*, Amherst: University of Massachusetts Press, 2003; and Deaton, *The Great Escape*.

accurately, it is a topic on which only one side seems to have received a widespread and enthusiastic hearing. This book aims to give the other side a full hearing. My hope, of course, is that by pushing the line I do in this book, my readers will ultimately end up with a more thoughtful, balanced, defensible view regarding how to be good in a world of need.

As noted in my Preface, I first began questioning my standard assumptions about the "obvious" desirability of contributing aid to people in great need, by considering variations of Singer's Pond Example, where it was no longer "obvious" that we should help. This then raised the question as to whether the situation of people in need in the world's poorest countries was more like that of the child in Singer's original Pond Example, or more like that of those in need in my variations of his example. Shelly Kagan pointed out, in discussion, that I could skip the intermediate step, and look directly at possible disanalogies between aiding a drowning child in a pond, and aiding people in need in different real-world contexts. This seemed to me right, and often that is what I have ended up doing. However, in some cases I have simply considered variations of Singer's original example, to illuminate some factor that may be relevant to the desirability of aid.

Having said that, I hasten to add that when I identify some factor that is present (or lacking) in Singer's original example, but not present (or lacking) in some variation of his example, or in certain real-world cases of people in need, I am *not* contending that that factor is, by itself, relevant to whether one should, or should not, offer aid if one can. For reasons that Kagan, Frances Kamm, Joseph Raz, and I have all discussed, and that Kamm has usefully called the *Principle of Contextual Interaction*, factors may have different moral significance—varying in both valence (positive, negative, or neutral) and degree (strong or weak)—depending on the presence or absence of other factors in the contexts in which those factors arise.[30]

Unfortunately, this makes moral reasoning very messy, and prevents me from decisively concluding that some factor supports or undermines the case for aid, or for a particular form of aid. However, I believe the factors that I have identified are at least potentially relevant, perhaps in conjunction with other factors depending on the context, to the desirability of aid efforts. I am afraid that in this book that is often the best I can do. For the most part, I must leave

---

[30] See Kagan's "The Additive Fallacy," *Ethics* 99 (1988): 5–31; Kamm's *Morality, Mortality, Vol. I: Death and Whom to Save From It*, New York: Oxford University Press, 1993; Raz's *The Morality of Freedom*, Oxford: Clarendon Press, 1986; and my *Rethinking the Good: Moral Ideals and the Nature of Practical Reasoning*, New York: Oxford University Press, 2012.

it to others to judge just how much, if at all, such factors, in combination, impact the moral desirability of aiding those in need.

Some readers will think that I have too many references to the development literature. Others will think that I have too few. This is, perhaps, unavoidable. This is, first and foremost, a philosophy book. It is filled with hypothetical cases and examples. And its arguments are often highly abstract and theoretical. By doing this, I can successfully identify various factors that I believe are often overlooked in discussions about aiding the needy. However, my theoretical arguments do not establish whether the factors I have identified are present in the real-world contexts where aid is desperately needed, and they are no substitute for the detailed empirical work necessary to determine that— empirical work for which sociologists, anthropologists, and development economists are well suited, but not I. However, I, and my research assistant, have now read enough of the literature by development economists and aid workers to be satisfied that this book's concerns are not merely the phantasms of a philosopher's mind, but are, indeed, relevant to many real-world practical contexts.

When I first started reading the economics and aid literature, I made a mark in the margin of each page where claims were made that were compatible with, or directly supported, the views I argue for here. I ended up with literally thousands of marks spread across virtually every book and article that I looked at. I soon realized that I couldn't possibly include all of the relevant citations, without overwhelming my readers and transforming this book into a massive, unwieldy, literature review that was much less interesting, readable, or philosophically important. Therefore, I have opted to include just enough references to some of the economics and aid literature to suggest that my central claims are compatible with the empirical evidence, but no more. Unsurprisingly, then, this book doesn't pretend to be, nor is it a substitute for, a work in development economics, nor it is based on the on-the-ground experiences of an aid worker. Interested readers are encouraged to read those literatures, which are both eye-opening and important.

Having said that, many development economists have come to the view that the empirical data regarding aid effectiveness is, in many ways, incomplete and inconclusive. Moreover, many have also come to the view that some of the data we desperately need in this domain is particularly difficult, if not impossible, to come by.[31] As we will see, ultimately this book supports both these

---

[31] See, for example, Roger Riddell's important book, *Does Foreign Aid Really Work?* Oxford: Oxford University Press, 2007, and also Deaton's *The Great Escape*. I shall return to this point later.

views, even as it points towards some of the areas for which we need more, and better, empirical data, if we can get it.

One concern raised by Angus Deaton, to an earlier draft, is that the abstract, theoretical examples that I employ to establish the possible downsides of aid efforts are too "bloodless," and pale in comparison with the real-world examples of where aid efforts have gone spectacularly wrong. In essence, the criticism is that this book doesn't do enough to "shock the conscience of my readers" with blood and guts, and the worry is that readers can't truly appreciate the position of aid skeptics, if they don't have a fully accurate picture of the horribly negative consequences that aid sometimes has.

In response to Deaton, I have now offered, in Section 7.5, an account of the events in Goma, of (what is now) the Democratic Republic of the Congo, where aid efforts went spectacularly awry with tragic consequences. Notwithstanding the inclusion of that section, Deaton's criticism remains a fair one that readers should bear in mind as they proceed. While this book aims to alert the reader to ways in which aid efforts can go awry, I *am* guilty of underselling the negative consequences that aid efforts have sometimes had in the real world. Still, let me briefly note three reasons for my approach.

First, there are already many accounts, written by journalists, economists, and former aid workers, that provide graphic details of instances where aid efforts have produced horrendous consequences.[32] I have no new accounts of my own to reveal, or valuable details or insights to add to the powerful accounts that have already been given. Thus, those interested in such accounts should read the already available literature that provides them.

Second, there is an old saying in the legal profession that hard cases make bad laws. I am reluctant to focus attention on the very worst outcomes that aid efforts have had, when trying to think about the factors that we need to pay attention to generally in assessing the desirability of different kinds of aid efforts. Though I recognize the importance of knowing just how badly things can go in the worst cases, I also fear that the graphic details of the very worst cases may have a distorting influence on our thinking. In this book, I aim to identify factors that are relevant to the desirability of certain forms of aid, but which, in my judgment, are often overlooked. Perforce, it remains to be determined, on a case-by-case basis, when these factors are present, how important they are, and how much of an impact they might have in the context in question.

---

[32] See, for example, the books by de Waal, Dichter, Easterly, Epstein, Maren, Moyo, and Rieff, cited in note 29 of this chapter.

Finally, as noted previously, this book was written by a philosopher. And, at the risk of offending rhetoricians with a caricature of their position, the difference between a philosopher, and a rhetorician, is that a rhetorician tries to get her audience to accept a particular conclusion any way she can, most notably, through the power of imagery and emotion; while a philosopher tries to get her audience to accept a particular conclusion through the power of arguments and reason.

This book's topic is one about which one *should* be passionate. If, when thinking about the plight of the world's worst-off, one is not emotional—if one doesn't feel anger, resentment, sympathy, and pity—there is, I believe, something deeply wrong with you. Even so, if one wants to get at the *truth* of how we should respond to the plight of the world's needy, I think it is important to step back from the emotions one feels, and to reason about the topic as carefully, reflectively, and even, as much as possible, dispassionately as one can. Admittedly, this is not always easy to do, but hopefully this helps to explain this book's rather abstract, theoretical, "bloodless" tone.

It isn't because I don't care about this topic. There are few topics, if any, about which I care more. It is, simply, because I am committed to trying to determine the truth regarding how to be good in a world of need. The approach taken in this book is, I believe, conducive to that goal. (This is not to say that our emotional responses have no role to play in alerting us as to where the truth may lie, or that emotions don't play a crucial, and even indispensable role in the fully human life.)

One last point regarding this. It is common for certain anti-abortion groups to display graphic pictures of bloody and mangled fetuses outside of abortion clinics. It is also common for certain charitable organizations to display graphic pictures of little babies with distended bellies and flies crawling in their eyes and nose (what is sometimes disparagingly called *poverty porn*). In both instances, the gut-wrenching pictures promote a visceral reaction in many, and no doubt they have been deemed effective at motivating some people to act as their displayers intend. However, while such pictures accurately display very real effects of certain abortions, or certain instances of poverty, hunger, and disease, they are, in my judgment, deeply problematic, and they hardly settle the question of how best to respond to an unwanted pregnancy, or poverty, hunger, and disease. The same is true, I believe, of the most graphic accounts of spectacular aid failures. Those accounts, too, display very real effects of certain aid efforts; but they, too, in my judgment, are problematic, and they hardly settle the question of how best to respond to the world's needy.

But make no mistake. This book's worries are not merely theoretical. They have practical analogues in the real world. And in some cases, at least, those practical analogues have been much worse in terms of genuine human impact, than anything this book describes.

1.4 Intuitions

Let me next address the role that intuitions play in my arguments. This is, in fact, a point about methodology, but it is important enough to warrant its own section.[33]

We have intuitive judgments about particular cases, actual or hypothetical, as well as about general principles. In addition, we have both initial, pre-theoretical, intuitive judgments, and firm, considered, ones. According to Henry Sidgwick, and many others, such intuitive judgments provide the starting point for moral theory.[34] For Sidgwick, the task of moral philosophy is largely one of seeking a coherent, systematic, and non-ad hoc way of accommodating and explaining many of our pretheoretical intuitive judgments as well as most of our firm, considered, ones. Moreover, ideally, the method sought should offer a plausible and principled way of assessing, and where appropriate revising, people's intuitive judgments about both particular cases and general principles. John Rawls's view about the desirability of seeking a state of *reflective equilibrium* with respect to one's pre- and post-theoretical intuitions and judgments, expresses a position that is similar to Sidgwick's in its essential methodological tenets, even if it differs in its details.[35]

There are serious questions about Sidgwick's methodological approach. One of the most important concerns the normative status of its results. Why should we believe that any results yielded by such a methodological approach correspond with the truth about morality, if there is such a thing, rather than merely cohere with most of our initial beliefs? Presumably, if there is an answer to this question, it lies with a position that might be called rational intuitionism. Roughly, on such a view, there are moral facts; these moral facts provide reasons to believe certain things; a fully rational person is, in the right circumstances, responsive to all the reasons that there are; a fortiori, a fully

---

[33] The remainder of this section is taken, verbatim, from my book *Rethinking the Good*, pp. 6–8.
[34] See Sidgwick's *The Methods of Ethics*, 7th Edition, London: Macmillan, 1907.
[35] See Rawls's *A Theory of Justice*, Cambridge, MA: Harvard University Press, 1971.

rational person will, in the right circumstances, form appropriate beliefs in response to the reasons provided by the moral facts; and finally, these appropriately formed beliefs either constitute or generate at least some of our moral intuitions and judgments. I confess that I am tempted to some version of rational intuitionism, so construed. But I will not try to defend such a view, as doing so would require another book, and there is nothing in this book that commits me to such a position.

A second important question about Sidgwick's approach concerns whether the task he has in mind is achievable. It seems reasonable to *seek* a coherent, systematic, and non-ad hoc method of accommodating and explaining many of our pre-theoretical intuitive judgments and most of our firm considered ones; but this doesn't mean that there is good reason to expect that we will actually *arrive* at such a method. Indeed, Sidgwick himself was acutely aware that his approach failed to reconcile some of our deepest beliefs about the nature of rationality and morality with what he regarded as a fundamental desideratum for moral theory.[36] So, it is an important and open question how to respond to our moral intuitions, if we are unable to arrive at a method for dealing with them of the sort that Sidgwick seeks.

I agree, then, that serious questions can be raised about Sidgwick's methodological approach. But I share his conviction that our moral intuitions about both particular cases and general principles are the starting point for moral theory. Our moral intuitions provide the data, as it were, with which moral theory must concern itself. Accordingly, in this book there is a lot of attention paid to identifying our moral intuitions about a host of actual and hypothetical cases, as well as our intuitions about various general moral or practical principles and ideals.

Some people may hope to "do away" with the role of intuitions in normative theory. But I believe that this is a fool's quest. In my judgment, appeal to intuitions is an indispensable staple of normative theory. Thus, it is no accident that such appeals appear in the most important writings of many of

---

[36] Derek Parfit writes that "When asked about his book [*The Methods of Ethics*], Sidgwick said that its first word was *Ethics*, and its last *failure*" (*Reasons and Persons*, p. 443). Sidgwick's response reflected his belief that moral theory had to provide an answer to Glaucon's challenge, "Why should I be moral?" (from Plato's *Republic*), and that to do this successfully moral theory had to establish that either prudence and morality never conflicted, or that if they did, one ought to act morally insofar as one was rational. But Sidgwick believed that his masterpiece couldn't answer this fundamental problem for moral theory, because it couldn't reconcile his beliefs about the nature of individual rationality—including his belief that it was always rational (even if not uniquely so) to act in one's own best interest—with his beliefs about what morality demanded of us—including his belief that morality sometimes required us to act contrary to our best interests.

the best contemporary moral and political theorists.[37] Of course, we must be prepared to subject our intuitions to critical scrutiny, and to revise or reject them in the light of such scrutiny. Ultimately, however, I believe that all plausible normative theories rely on intuitions.

In sum, I take our intuitive judgments seriously, as features of our response to the world that need to be understood, explained, and, where possible, accommodated. Getting clear on our intuitions is not the last step in moral theorizing; but it is a crucially important step, and one that must come very near or at the beginning of such theorizing.

1.5 Terminology

For this book's purposes, I shall often refer to the people whom we hope to help via aid as the "needy." I am well aware that objections to this term might be raised, to some of which I am quite sympathetic. Unfortunately, there is no perfect terminology in this domain. Some divide the world into "North" and "South," or "West" and "Non-West," but, of course, these terms are geographically misleading. Australia and New Zealand, for example, are both part of the

---

[37] This point will be obvious to anyone with even a passing acquaintance with the literature of the last forty years. See, for example, the writings of: G.A. Cohen, Philippa Foot, Thomas Hurka, Shelly Kagan, Frances Kamm, Jeff McMahan, Thomas Nagel, Robert Nozick, Derek Parfit, John Rawls, Joseph Raz, Thomas Scanlon, Amartya Sen, Judith Thomson, and Bernard Williams. (I trust that those whom I have not named here will forgive me, as I couldn't possibly list all of the excellent philosophers who have made significant appeals to intuitions in their work.)

Some philosophers decry the use of theorizing in approaching ethical issues. A fortiori, such philosophers will have little use for intuitions in normative theory. Such philosophers might favor approaching each real-life moral issue and deciding how to respond to that issue based on *phronesis* or practical wisdom, or, equivalently, based on what "the good person" would do in such a situation. Others might think that one must decide each real-life case based on its merits without any prior preparation or guidance that a normative theory might provide. Some might think that the particularities of the situation we find ourselves in will generate an "aesthetic intuition" about how we should respond, or in some other way determine our response. Still others will say that our decisions as to how to live our lives must be guided by the ethics and mores of our societies, and not the moral theories of philosophers. (Advocates of such views might appeal to Aristotle (see the *Nicomachean Ethics*), Sidgwick (see *The Methods of Ethics*), Jonathan Dancy (see *Ethics Without Principles*, Oxford: Clarendon Press, 2006), or Bernard Williams (see *Ethics and the Limits of Philosophy*, Cambridge, MA: Harvard University Press, 1985). Though Aristotle and Sidgwick were themselves moral theorists par excellence, and Williams is famous for using provocative examples to produce powerful intuitions in support of his anti-utilitarian and anti-Kantian approach to ethics.) I reject the anti-theory approach to ethics, but cannot defend my position here. Instead, let me simply note my belief that such approaches do *not* lessen the importance of intuitions for ethics; rather, they simply shift the point and way in which intuitions enter and influence ethical decision making, from prior periods of normative theorizing to in-the-moment practical actions. I should add that I believe that intuitions play an important role in *both* normative theorizing *and* in-the-moment decision making. (I am grateful to Roger Crisp for suggesting that I might want to say something about what the possible alternatives might be to appealing to intuitions in normative theory.)

Southern Hemisphere! More importantly, many people in the so-called South or Non-West don't need our aid, while some living in the so-called North or West would be perfectly appropriate aid recipients. Similar objections can be raised to identifying the people with whom this book are concerned in terms of their membership in the "third world" as opposed to the "first world," or "developing countries" as opposed to "developed countries," or "non-industrial societies" as opposed to "industrial or post-industrial societies."

Better divisions, for our purposes, are between the "poor" and the "rich," or the "disadvantaged" and the "advantaged," or simply the "worse-off" and the "better-off," and I shall occasionally employ these distinctions, especially the latter. However, these distinctions are also, each in their own ways, problematic. For example, although their usages can be extended, "poor" and "rich" are principally monetary terms. But many people might be candidates for aid not because they are poor, but because they live in countries that deprive them of their basic human rights, or where infant and maternal mortality is high and life expectancy is low, or because they have been the victims of horrible sectarian violence, or rape as an instrument of war. Likewise, "disadvantaged" and "worse-off" are relative terms that apply across a multitude of dimensions. Someone with a normal IQ of 100 may be seriously disadvantaged or worse-off in applying to schools or jobs in comparison with someone with an IQ of 130, and virtually everyone is substantially disadvantaged or worse-off in terms of physical or musical ability in comparison with pro athletes or concert pianists. But those are not the people with whom this book is concerned.

I often employ the term "needy" because it reflects the thought that we should try to help those "in need," where this is quite naturally understood in terms of people whose most basic or fundamental needs are wholly, or largely, unmet. Basic or fundamental needs include the need for food, water, shelter, safety, economic security, healthcare, and the like. Roughly, then, the basic needs are those elements of the human condition that must be met to a sufficient degree, for someone to live even a minimally decent life, let alone to flourish.

So, to be clear, when I refer to people as "needy," I am not suggesting, in any way, that such people are whiny, wheedling, dependent, cloying, clingy, or anything of the sort. Although such notions may be associated with some uses of the term in common parlance, in this book referring to someone as "needy" merely recognizes that some of their most basic, fundamental needs are wholly or largely unmet.

Also, as the preceding implies, despite my use of the definite article, "the," "the needy" does not refer to a monolithic group. To the contrary, "the needy" refers to an extraordinarily diverse group of people who may vary in virtually every way imaginable: including, but not limited to, race, religion, gender, sexual orientation, nationality, caste, class, and location, as well as their social, political, economic, and cultural histories, institutions, and situations. Each needy person's predicament is specific, and may require a response reflecting that specificity. Thus, the only generalization that can safely be made of people who are needy, as I am using that term, is that one or more of their basic needs have not been met to such a degree that it is difficult for them to lead even a minimally decent human life.

With those caveats in mind, I hope that linguistically sensitive readers will not be put off by my use of the term "the needy." Any readers who still find the term distasteful, even when so understood, are welcome to substitute their own favorite terms for the population in question throughout this book.

On another note, in this book, I shall use the terms "charities," "organizations," and "agencies" interchangeably in describing various groups whose goal is to help the needy. Similarly, I will use various combinations of "aid," "relief," and "development" in describing their goals. Sometimes, I will make it explicit that I am referring to an international aid group, but often I will drop the word "international" when referring to such groups. Moreover, most of what I have to say will also apply, and is intended to apply, to local and national groups whose goals are to aid the needy. Thus, unless there are contexts where it is important to distinguish between them—in which case I will explicitly make this clear—I will refer to any group whose aim is to aid the needy as an "international relief charity," an "aid organization," an "aid agency," a "development agency" or any combination thereof.

In this book, when I talk about aid agencies I shall mostly be focused on what might be called *on-the-ground aid agencies* operating directly in the world's poorest regions. But it is important to recognize that there are many different kinds of aid agencies within that broad category. Aid agencies can be unilateral, bilateral, multilateral, governmental, non-governmental, religious, secular, large, small, etc. Also, aid agencies can have markedly different aims; for example, poverty reduction, education, disease treatment or prevention, female empowerment, and so on. In addition, aid can generally be lumped into one of two categories, humanitarian or developmental. Given this, it is important not to paint one's picture of the effectiveness of aid agencies with too broad a brush, or to presume that all agencies share the same strengths and weaknesses. Nevertheless, I believe that most of the worries I raise in this book regarding on-the-ground aid agencies can be legitimately raised with respect to different kinds of aid agencies with different aims. However, as we will see, some of my empirical worries are particularly relevant to development aid rather than purely humanitarian aid. I will return to the significance of this point at the end of the book.

Other terminology will be introduced, as needed, throughout the book.

1.6 The Assumption of Innocence

In thinking about the needy, most people implicitly assume that those in need are "innocent." For the most part, I shall follow that assumption, though at various points I shall make this explicit. For this book's purposes, we can make do with a rough, intuitive, notion of "innocent." To wit: roughly, a needy person is *innocent* if she isn't responsible for her plight, doesn't have a vicious character, and isn't guilty of heinous acts. In many philosophical discussions about the morality of aiding the needy, the paradigmatic examples of people in need are women, children, and infants. Infants clearly meet the suggested criteria for being innocent, as do the overwhelming majority of women and children.[38]

A host of philosophically interesting and important questions can be raised about the assumption of innocence. There is an important biblical tradition according to which "all children of Adam"—which is to say all humans—are sinners.[39] While such claims will seem strained to many contemporary ears when applied to infants and small children, they may sound more plausible applied to others. On the other end of the spectrum, some believe that we lack the kind of free will necessary to ascribe moral responsibility to people, so that, in the morally relevant sense, no one is responsible for their actions, character, or predicament. On the former view, *no one* past childhood is "innocent," on the latter view *everyone* is, at least in the sense employed in this work.

Some people believe that questions of innocence are wholly irrelevant to whether people in need should be aided. This view is particularly plausible when one is talking about basic humanitarian aid such as feeding the hungry

---

[38] Jonathan Glover points out that the overwhelming percentage of killers and mass murderers are men in his monumental book *Humanity: A Moral History of the Twentieth Century*, New Haven: Yale University Press, 2001. Paula Casal echoes this claim, and suggests what we might do about it, in her provocative article "Sexual Dimorphism and Human Enhancement," *Journal of Medical Ethics* 39 (2013): 722–8.

[39] See "For all have sinned, and come short of the glory of God" ("Romans 3.23–24," *Bible*, URL: https://www.bible.com/bible/compare/ROM.3.23-24, accessed August 31, 2020), and "He that is without sin among you, let him first cast a stone at her" ("John 8.7," *BibleGateway*, URL: https://www.biblegateway.com/passage/?search=John%208:7&version=KJV, accessed August 31, 2020).

or easing suffering. This perspective is reflected in the rich tradition of the Red Cross and Red Crescent. It is part of the core principles of such organizations to provide needed care and comfort to *all* soldiers and victims of armed conflict, without regard to questions of guilt or innocence, or on which side of the conflict someone is.[40]

I cannot take on the mare's nest of free will in this book, and for the most part will eschew entering the various debates just noted. However, I will return to these issues briefly in Sections 7.1 and 7.5, where I note that the conviction that we should aid the needy may depend, in part, on one's views about whether the people in question are innocent or responsible for their plight. Unfortunately, in some cases, at least, these are controversial issues about which reasonable people can disagree.[41]

1.7 Effective Altruism

Many people who look at the issues raised in this book, do so through the lens of *Effective Altruism*. This is a powerful lens which magnifies and illuminates a particular way of thinking about the needy. However, like other lenses, it can be distorting if it isn't properly employed, and, in my judgment, its single-minded focus makes it ill-suited to understanding the full range and complexity of factors relevant to being good in a world of need.

Although this book isn't about Effective Altruism, per se, it has much to say that is relevant to assessing Effective Altruism. In this section, I will introduce Effective Altruism; distinguish between different groups of Effective Altruists; clarify the subset of Effective Altruists with which this book engages; and note, in advance, some of the implications that this book has for Effective Altruism.

Altruists are people who are concerned about others, and who act on that concern to promote their welfare. Arguably, *Effective Altruists* are people who seek to use reason and evidence to efficiently promote—or, ideally, to most efficiently promote—the welfare of others. I say arguably, because some would claim that Effective Altruists are people who are determined to find the most efficient way to make the world better, or people who seek to use reason

---

[40] This position is elaborated on, and critiqued, throughout Polman's *The Crisis Caravan* (see pp. 1–2, 7–11, 15, 21–2, 26, 32, 42, 43, 47, 51, 55, 103, 119, 121, 144, 173–4, and 192–3).

[41] The preceding paragraphs were sparked by a query of Tyler John's. In response to my use of the expression "innocent people," John wrote, in correspondence, "who is truly innocent?" I am grateful to John for prodding me to clarify the sense in which I am using the term "innocent," and, as importantly, for prompting me to recognize some of the ways in which it is controversial to even bring questions of innocence into any discussion about the morality of aiding the needy.

and evidence to do the most good. Stated in such terms, Effective Altruism appears to be either equivalent to, or a close kin of, utilitarianism or consequentialism.[42*] And, in fact, I think it is fair to say that the philosophical roots of Effective Altruism lie in the utilitarian/consequentialist tradition.[43]

However, Effective Altruism has become a somewhat amorphous philosophical and social movement which includes many non-consequentialists, and which aims to convince many people of the desirability of addressing important concerns in a certain manner regardless of their general moral approach and commitments. As I will soon note, Effective Altruism includes people with different goals, but its members typically share a commitment to using reason and evidence, as much as possible, to determine the most efficient

---

[42*] *Consequentialism* is a type of moral theory, of which there are many forms. *Utilitarianism* is one form of consequentialism, of which there are many versions. For the purposes of this book, I shall use the term *consequentialism* to refer to those moral theories that are concerned with the goodness of outcomes, and that hold that an act is right if, and only if, it brings about the *best* available outcome (or, more accurately, any outcome which is such that no other available outcome is better than it). Here, the best available outcome is understood as the one that *maximizes* the total amount of good in the world while *minimizing* the total amount of bad in the world, in such a way that the difference between the world's total good and its total bad is as large as possible if there is more good than bad, and as small as possible if there is more bad than good.

The version of utilitarianism discussed in this book is one that might be called *total utilitarianism*. On this view, an act is right if and only if it brings about the best available outcome, where each outcome's overall goodness depends solely on the *wellbeing*, or quality of lives, of its sentient (conscious) members. Wellbeing is measured as a function of the difference between the total amount of good in a person's life and the total amount of bad in her life, and the aim is for that difference to be as large as possible if there is more good in her life than bad, and as small as possible if there is more bad in her life than good. The view then measures an outcome's overall goodness as an additive function of the wellbeing of each of its sentient members. Thus, total utilitarianism seeks to maximize the world's value by maximizing the total overall value, or wellbeing, of its sentient members.

Non-utilitarian versions of consequentialism give weight to other factors, or ideals, besides, or in addition to, individual wellbeing in determining the best outcomes. For example, some consequentialists give independent weight to ideals such as equality, justice, or perfection, in assessing the goodness of outcomes. Likewise, some consequentialists give independent weight to environmental concerns, such as clean air, soil, and water; preserving the natural beauty of a mountain range, barrier reef, or arctic tundra; or having a healthy and diverse biosphere that is teeming with non-sentient flora and fauna. By *independent weight*, I mean that such factors are valued for their own sake (*non-instrumentally*), and not merely because they contribute to the wellbeing of an outcome's sentient members (*instrumentally*).

[43] Among the figures who have some claim to founding, or co-founding, the Effective Altruism Movement are Peter Singer, William MacAskill, and Toby Ord. Singer has long been identified with the utilitarian/consequentialist tradition, and MacAskill and Ord were not only influenced by Singer in their own thinking, their early writings on Effective Altruism also drew on, and reflect, the utilitarian/consequentialist tradition. That said, all three, and MacAskill in particular, are prepared to acknowledge that there may be deontological constraints that limit the ways that one can permissibly promote the goals of Effective Altruism. A similar point is true of Nick Beckstead, who co-founded the first U.S. chapter of the Effective Altruist organization Giving What We Can, and who subsequently worked at Oxford's Future of Humanity Institute and GiveWell, before moving, in 2014, to another Effective Altruist organization, the Open Philanthropy Project. When Beckstead started out, his approach to Effective Altruism was very much influenced by the utilitarian/consequentialist perspective, though he now tempers that approach with other normative considerations, including certain deontological ones.

morally permissible way of achieving those goals.[44] In doing this, most Effective Altruists appeal to a version of *Expected Utility Theory* which holds, roughly, that for any goal that one is pursuing, one should choose among those morally permissible options in such a way that the *expected value* of one's choice is maximized in terms of the realization of one's goal.[45]

The "morally permissible option" qualification is what allows non-consequentialists, as well as consequentialists, to sign on to Effective Altruism. So, for example, while both utilitarian and deontological Effective Altruists might generally subscribe to the goal of benefiting as many people as much as possible, they would put markedly different constraints on the morally permissible means of achieving that goal. Thus, for example, utilitarian and deontological Effective Altruists might disagree as to whether one could kill one innocent person to save five other innocent people. Still Effective Altruists would all agree that if one could permissibly support one NGO (Non-Governmental Organization) and the expected value of one's action would be equivalent to the expected value of saving one innocent life, or one could permissibly support another NGO in the same manner and to the same extent, and the expected value of one's action would be equivalent to the expected

---

[44] Insofar as this book is navigating terrain that is occupied by both philosophers and development economists, it is worth drawing attention to relevant analogies between issues described here, and issues that are more broadly recognized within the development literature. Just as it is true that Effective Altruists are brought together under a shared name and objective while often having quite divergent aims, it is also true that "development assistance" is often talked about as one unified and homogeneous activity, and yet there are massively disparate applications of it. Accordingly, just as any objections I raise about certain positions associated with Effective Altruism shouldn't be construed as warranting a wholesale rejection of Effective Altruism, so, any criticisms I make regarding the effects of certain types of development assistance shouldn't be construed as warranting a wholesale rejection of efforts to aid the needy. Since it is important not to lose sight of this, I shall reiterate it at various points in the book.

My position, here, is similar to that of many in the development community. See, for example, Riddell, *Does Foreign Aid Really Work?*; Glennie, Jonathan and Andy Sumner, *Aid, Growth and Poverty*, London: Palgrave Macmillan, 2016; and Ravallion, M., "On the Role of Aid in the Great Escape," *Review of Income and Wealth* 60 (2014): 967–84.

[45] Each action that we do may result in a host of different possible outcomes $O_1, O_2, O_3, \ldots, O_n$, each of which will occur with some probability $p_1, p_2, p_3, \ldots, p_n$. Let $V(O)$ represent the overall value obtaining in outcome O in terms of the realization of one's goal (giving due weight to each of the respects in which O is good in terms of one's goal, and each of the respects in which O is bad in terms of one's goal). Then we can represent the Expected Value (EV) of action A in terms of one's goal by the formula $EV(A) = p_1(V(O_1)) + p_2(V(O_2)) + p_3(V(O_3)) + \ldots + p_n(V(O_n))$. It is important to note that one's goal can be extremely complex and broad, or simple and narrow. The goal of promoting education among the needy is a worthwhile goal, but narrower than the goal of promoting the interests of the needy, which would include, among other things, a concern for their monetary and health interests as well as their educational interests. And, of course, the goal of promoting the interests of the needy will be narrower than the goal of promoting the interests of all humans, which in turn will be narrower than the goal of promoting the interests of all sentient beings.

value of saving five innocent lives, then, other things equal, there would be compelling or decisive reason to do the latter, and thus one ought to do so.[46]

Some Effective Altruists differ in their scope of moral concern. So, for example, some Effective Altruists are principally concerned about the effects of their choices on humans, others on rational beings, others on sentient beings, and so on. Similarly, the concrete focus of Effective Altruism varies. Some people believe that Effective Altruists should focus their attention (including their time, effort, and money) on aiding non-human animals. Others believe that Effective Altruists should focus their attention on existential risks to humanity or to sentient life on Earth. Others believe that Effective Altruists should focus their attention on promoting the Effective Altruism Movement itself. Others believe that Effective Altruists should focus on increasing knowledge about what options are, in fact, most likely to produce the most overall good (taking full account of both the positive and negative effects of each option). Still others believe that Effective Altruists should focus their attention on aiding the world's needy.

One important divide among Effective Altruists is whether the group should be mainly a research group—one committed to doing the research necessary to determine how to do the most good—or an advocacy group—one advising people as to what they ought to do in order to do the most good, including, for example, advising them as to which charities they should contribute. And, of course, some Effective Altruists may focus on some combination of these concerns, and others as well.

With that as background, in this book, whenever I discuss Effective Altruism, I shall be concerned, unless explicitly indicated otherwise, solely with that portion of the Effective Altruism Movement that focuses on aiding the world's needy. In addition, I shall be especially concerned about the advocacy wing of that group. We might refer to the position I have in mind as Global Aid Effective Altruism, to distinguish it from the other wings of the Effective Altruism Movement. However, given this book's subject matter, I hope it will not be confusing if I usually just refer to the position in question as *Effective Altruism*, for short.

While there is room for disagreement within this movement, let me note a number of key, related positions that are commonly associated with (Global Aid) Effective Altruism:[47]

---

[46] See *The Effective Altruism Handbook*, edited by Ryan Carey, Oxford: Centre for Effective Altruism, 2015, p. 119.

[47] Whether or not each of these positions should be, or are fairly, associated with this movement is an important issue to which I shall return to later.

1. There are strong reasons to aid those in need as long as there is a morally permissible way of doing so, and doing so would not require a substantial sacrifice on one's part.[48,49] Given this, affluent people globally—which includes most people in countries with developed industrial or post-industrial economies—have strong reasons to help the world's needy. For some Effective Altruists, these reasons are often seen as decisive, or sufficiently compelling, to make it the case that the affluent have a duty to help the needy.

2. In the context of much work regarding Effective Altruism, the notion of "the world's needy" is, at least for practical purposes, typically understood as primarily involving those people in the world's poorest countries facing premature death or severely debilitating conditions due to poverty, famine, war, tyranny, ignorance, or disease. This is an important subgroup, but only a subgroup, of the global needy as characterized previously—namely, those whose most basic or fundamental needs are wholly or largely unmet. (Still, it remains true that, as we will see later, the members of this subgroup are incredibly diverse along virtually every possible dimension.)

3. Although there are many organizations that do worthwhile work, not all organizations are doing equally important work, in the sense of promoting ends of equal value. Other things equal, there are stronger reasons to support organizations doing more important work, than organizations doing less important work. Therefore, other things equal, insofar as one chooses to give to an organization with the aim of doing good, one should give to an organization doing more important, rather than less important, work.[50]

---

[48] Some Effective Altruists would contend that when there is enough at stake, we have a positive duty to aid even if it would require a substantial sacrifice on our part. This is the view that Singer most favors in "Famine, Affluence, and Morality." It is also the view favored by Peter Unger in his book, *Living High & Letting Die*. I am here considering a weaker, and therefore more broadly held, Effective Altruist position.

[49] The moral imperative to aid the needy is widely recognized, and not only by Effective Altruists. So, too, is the thought that the moral case for administering development assistance depends, in part, on its efficacy. So, for example, Glennie and Sumner write: "On the one hand, there is, to most, a clear moral obligation to help poorer countries and people. On the other hand, there is a concern that financial transfers either do not work very well or even undermine broader development efforts" (*Aid, Growth and Poverty*, p. 1). The recognition that the strength of the reasons to aid varies with the efficacy of the aid is embodied in Effective Altruist thinking, and reflected in the third, fourth, and fifth points noted hereafter.

[50] This statement is only an approximation of the view in question. A more nuanced statement would recognize that many aid organizations undertake a host of projects of greater or lesser importance. Insofar as it is possible, one would want to earmark one's support for the most important projects. I am grateful to Brian Oosthuizen for suggesting that I add this clarification. A similar clarification applies, mutatis mutandis, to the following points, as well.

4. Likewise, although there are many organizations doing important work, not all organizations are equally efficient. Other things equal, there are stronger reasons to support organizations that are more efficient, than organizations that are less efficient. Therefore, other things equal, insofar as one chooses to give to an organization, with the aim of doing good, one should give to a more efficient organization that is doing important work rather than a less efficient organization that is doing equally important work.

5. Recognizing that not all ways of supporting organizations are equally efficient, other things equal, insofar as one chooses to support an organization with the aim of doing good, one should do so in the most efficient manner possible.

6. Even if we believe that aiding the needy is a matter of "charity" and not a (strict) duty, for those people who *do* decide to give to charity with the aim of doing good, other things equal, they ought to give in the most effective manner to the most effective charities that are doing the most important work. (This position is suggested, though not strictly implied, by 2, 3, and 4. Note, it assumes that the most effective charities doing the most important work will be sufficiently effective that the overall good resulting from one's supporting that charity will be greater than the overall good that would result from one's supporting the most effective charity doing less important work.)

7. One needs criteria for determining the most effective organizations that are doing the most important work (henceforth, "the best organizations" for doing good). Roughly, the criteria will need to take appropriate account of quality—in the sense of the kinds of ills that are being addressed and the nature of the improvements that the organization makes in beings' lives; of quantity—in the sense of both the number of beings positively affected by the organization's efforts and the duration of the positive effects on beings' lives; and of cost—in the sense of the value of the total resources that the organization spends to produce the results that it does.

8. In supporting effective charities, one's goal should be to do the most good, compatible with not acting wrongly, and this means improving the outcome as much as possible. To do this, one needs to do whatever will most improve people's lives or make people better off, among the morally permissible options. This view reflects the *welfarist assumption* of many economists, that an outcome's goodness is solely a function of the *welfare* or *wellbeing* of its members. On this view, the only way to

improve an outcome is to make people better off, and the only way to do the most good is to improve the quality of people's lives as much as possible.

9. Since we live in a world of uncertainty, we can never be sure whether or not our action will in fact do the most good. Accordingly, in choosing which charities to support, rationality requires that we let Expected Utility Theory guide our actions. This is because Expected Utility Theory is the dominant and, many believe, the most plausible theory of rational choice under conditions of uncertainty. In essence, this means that in supporting effective charities, one's goal should be to maximize the expected utility of one's contributions.

10. So far as possible, one should seek hard, scientific, evidence regarding which organizations are, in fact, the best organizations. Although much more work needs to be done in this important area, several groups already exist that are doing the important work of gathering and assessing the relevant data, and on that basis identifying the (likely) best organizations to choose from insofar as one seeks to fulfill one's duty to aid others, or wants to give to charity so as to do (the most expected) good.[51] The results of this crucial work can be found on the websites of these groups, or on the websites of various other groups that draw on their work, and other sources, to list the organizations that are deemed to be the "best" insofar as one seeks to fulfill one's duty to aid the needy, or to donate to charity for the sake of "doing good." For many Effective Altruists, the most reliable websites are thought to include:[52]

---

[51] Some people wholeheartedly agree with the important point that one needs evidence regarding which aid agencies are most effective, but point out that the *kind* of evidence that is collected and assessed is key here. They worry that Effective Altruists are not actually gathering the evidence that is necessary to make the determinations they seek to make. This is the view of Angus Deaton, for example (conveyed in correspondence), which is why he does not support the current Effective Altruist Movement despite being sympathetic to its overall aim. Much of this book can be seen as indirectly supporting Deaton's view on this matter. Unfortunately, for a variety of complex reasons that are both practical and theoretical in nature, accurately accumulating the evidence that would be necessary to confidently make the determinations that Effective Altruists want to make is exceedingly difficult. Much more so than most philosophers or followers of Effective Altruism have realized, I believe. (Though, in fairness, I think many of the philosophical leaders of the Effective Altruism Movement *are* acutely aware of the difficulties in question.)

[52] These are the most pertinent Effective Altruism websites for those concerned with aiding the needy. Other Effective Altruism websites for those with other concerns include: Animal Charity Evaluators—https://animalcharityevaluators.org/; Effective Altruism Fund—https://app.effectivealtruism.org/funds; and the Open Philanthropy Project—https://www.openphilanthropy.org/.

GiveWell—www.givewell.org
The Life You Can Save—www.thelifeyoucansave.org
Giving What We Can—www.givingwhatwecan.org

11. Although many thousands of charities promote valuable causes—such as providing shelters for abandoned animals, glasses for people with vision problems, mental health benefits for veterans, hot meals for the elderly, preservation of the environment, protection of endangered species, research for cancer, toys for poor children, scholarships for college students, books for libraries, mentors for at-risk students, funding for the arts, wish-fulfillment for cancer victims, and so on— in fact, (Global Aid) Effective Altruists believe, the best charities, understood as the most effective charities doing the most important work, are some of the international relief and development charities. These are the charities that can be counted on to be among the very best in terms of doing the most expected good with the resources they expend and, hence, these are among the organizations that can be counted on to give the most expected "bang for the buck" for one's contributions. Other things equal, then, these are the charities there is most reason to support.

In sum, in this book, when I refer to Effective Altruists, I am referring to those (Global Aid) Effective Altruists who believe that there are strong reasons to aid the needy, and that, other things equal, they often provide affluent people with decisive or compelling reasons to aid the needy. Some Effective Altruists believe that such reasons are often sufficiently strong that the affluent have a duty to help the needy. Others believe that even if aiding the needy is a matter of charity, rather than a duty, insofar as we are going to give to charity, there are strong, compelling, or decisive reasons to effectively give to the best charitable organizations, where these will be the most effective organizations that are doing the most (expected) good. These Effective Altruists believe that in fact certain organizations can be counted on to be the among the (most likely) best charitable organizations, ideally having been identified as such after being subjected to rigorous empirical scrutiny by certain groups that can be counted on to carefully, impartially, and reliably assess and rank different charitable organizations.[53] Finally, unless someone has some reliable empirical

---

[53] Nick Beckstead points out that some Effective Altruists acknowledge that, for now, this is more of an aspirational goal rather than a reality, and that we may not have the kind of hard, empirical data in this domain that we would like, ideally, to have. So, unfortunately, there may be no substitute for careful

reasons to believe that there are other charitable organizations that are even better in the relevant respects, then, other things equal, one ought to give to the particular international relief and development organizations listed on the relevant websites noted previously (in point ten) insofar as one is seeking to fulfill one's duty to aid the needy, or insofar as one is choosing to give to charity with the primary aim of doing good.[54]

To be clear, I am not claiming that *every* Effective Altruist whose primary concern is with aiding the world's needy subscribes fully to each of the points noted above precisely as I have framed them. Different Effective Altruists would want to add or subtract from the points I have listed or frame their positions in more nuanced ways. But I hope, and believe, that the position that I have roughly sketched is a sufficiently fair and accurate characterization of the general position of many of those Effective Altruists whose primary focus is on aiding the world's needy.

Strikingly, some of the most important leaders of the Effective Altruism Movement are no longer focused on aiding the world's needy, though they once were. This is so, for example, of Toby Ord, co-founder of the Effective Altruism organization *Giving What We Can*; Nick Beckstead, co-founder of the first U.S. chapter of Giving What We Can; and Will MacAskill, co-founder

---

reflection on the limited evidence we have, and then relying on our intuitions, or most reasonable judgments, regarding which organizations are best. GiveWell, a leading organization in the Effective Altruism Movement, acknowledges as much in its discussion of Cost-Effectiveness, where it writes: "We seek charities that are 'cost-effective' in the sense of *saving or improving lives as much as possible for as little money as possible*" but then immediately acknowledges that "**There are many limitations to cost-effectiveness estimates, and we do not assess charities only—or primarily—based on their estimated cost-effectiveness.**" Expanding on this disclaimer, GiveWell notes that "**Our cost-effectiveness estimates** include administrative as well as program costs and generally look at the cost per life or life-year changed (death averted, year of additional income, etc.). However, there are many ways in which they do not account for all possible costs and benefits of a program." Also, "**Our cost-effectiveness estimates** rely on a number of inputs for which we have very limited data on which to base our estimates as well as informed guesses and subjective value judgments, such as the likelihood that a charity's implementation of an intervention will have the same effect as measured in a separate study of that intervention, or how one weights increasing income relative to averting death." See https://www.givewell.org/how-we-work/our-criteria/cost-effectiveness, accessed December 17, 2018 (all italics and bold print in the above quotes are as they appear on the website). GiveWell deserves much credit for the honesty and relative transparency reflected in such remarks. Though, it is also the case that one must explore their website carefully—following links from their home page, to "HOW WE WORK," to "Criteria," to "Cost-Effectiveness"—to actually find this admission of the limitations of their claims to the purported cost-effectiveness of their recommended charities. In any event, much of what follows in this book supports, or is a vindication of, this modest appraisal of the current situation in identifying the most effective international relief organizations.

[54] Of course, often charitable contributions are not made with the primary aim of doing good. Often people give to charities primarily to honor someone or to respect their wishes. Likewise, often people have particular projects, commitments, or personal relations that make giving to certain charities especially appropriate. Still, many give to charity because they feel an overwhelming need to help others and to do good, unconnected with any projects or commitments that are near to their heart. For such people, Effective Altruists believe, it would be a mistake if they gave to a charity that did less good rather than to one that did more good, assuming it was equally easy and possible to do either.

of both Giving What We Can and another Effective Altruist organization, *80,000 Hours*, and author of the influential Effective Altruist book *Doing Good Better*.[55] Ord, Beckstead, and MacAskill are already independently aware of many of the worries this book raises, and would accept many, though certainly not all, of them. However, they are less concerned about these worries than I am, because they have already shifted their attention to research and public advice concerning existential risks—that is, global catastrophic risks that threaten all human or sentient life on Earth, such as biological, AI, nuclear, and extreme climate change risks.

For example, in personal correspondence, MacAskill informed me that it was his view that thoughtful efforts to reduce global catastrophic risks "have a better cost-effectiveness than organizations like AMF [*Against Malaria Foundation*, long rated as one of the top global aid charities by GiveWell and The Life You Can Save], even if we just consider the potential deaths of people over the next 100 years—I [MacAskill] think that 10 billion of carefully targeted philanthropy would reduce extinction risk by at least a percentage point." Accordingly, insofar as Ord, Beckstead, and MacAskill no longer believe that people concerned with doing the most good should focus on aiding the needy, they are *not* my target when I am discussing Effective Altruists in this book, even though they clearly *are* Effective Altruists (in the broader sense of the term) and helped launch, and continue to help set the agenda for, the Effective Altruism Movement.

Nevertheless, Effective Altruism has become a large and influential global movement. And many of its rank-and-file members were attracted to the Effective Altruism Movement in the first place, and remain committed to it, precisely because of their deep concern about the world's needy.[56] Moreover, as noted previously, many people are concerned about helping the needy, whether they are Effective Altruists or not, and this explains the rise of large numbers of well-funded NGOs whose mandate is to aid the global needy. Thus, as one author observed, "The non-governmental organizations (NGOs)

[55] New York: Avery Press (an imprint of Penguin Random House), 2015.

[56] In a recent survey of the Effective Altruism community, "poverty was overwhelmingly identified as the top priority among respondents." Given nine different categories—Animal Welfare, Cause Prioritization, Environmentalism, AI, Non-AI Far Future Existential Risk, Poverty, Rationality, Politics, and Meta—"601 EAs (or nearly 41%) identified poverty as the top priority, followed by cause prioritization (~19%), and AI (~16%). Poverty was also the most common choice of near-top priority (~14%)..." and "There were very few people who did not want to put any EA resources into cause prioritization, poverty, and meta causes." See "EA Survey 2017 Series: Cause Area Preferences," by Eve McCormick, a project of *Rethink Charity*, posted September 1, 2017 and available on the Effective Altruism Forum at https://forum.effectivealtruism.org/posts/xeduPnHfCQ9m9f3go/ea-survey-2017-series-cause-area-preferences, accessed December 18, 2018. I am grateful to Tyler John for bringing this site to my attention.

have at their core the purpose of reaching the disadvantaged. Such organizations come into being in direct response to human need and exist to address it. Their mandates are philanthropic, including efforts to address long-term poverty by means of development.... Between them, three of the largest international NGOs—CARE, Oxfam, and Save the Children—mustered combined funds of over 3.2 billion in 2013."[57]

Given this, it makes perfect sense for Effective Altruist organizations to try to identify and recommend the most effective aid organizations *even if* the leaders of such organizations do not themselves believe that supporting aid organizations is the most effective way of doing the most expected good that one can with one's charitable contributions. After all, if many millions of people are concerned about aiding the needy, and are contributing billions of dollars each year to charitable organizations in support of that goal, doesn't it make sense, from an Effective Altruist perspective, to try to sway such donors to contribute to the aid organizations with the most effective aid efforts?[58] Accordingly, there is good reason that some of the most important Effective Altruism organizations, including GiveWell, The Life You Can Save, and Giving What We Can, have websites that are mainly devoted to how best to aid the world's needy. It is to the many advocates, admirers, and followers of Effective Altruism who *are* mainly concerned with how best to aid the needy, and to the countless social, political, and business leaders, as well as commonfolk, who turn to Effective Altruism websites for advice on how best to aid the needy, that my discussion of Effective Altruism is directed.

Before going on, let me say a bit more about how to think about the considerations I will be offering relevant to (Global Poverty) Effective Altruism. Much of this book will be highlighting certain factors that many Effective Altruists have, in my judgment, not paid sufficient attention to in assessing the desirability of contributing to international aid organizations.

---

[57] Black, Maggie, *International Development: Illusions and Realities*, Oxford: New Internationalist Publications, 2015, p. 44.

[58] To get some sense of the scope of charitable giving on a global basis, which is truly massive, see the "CAF World Giving Index 2018: A Global View of Giving Trends" available at https://www.cafonline.org/docs/default-source/about-us-publications/caf_wgi2018_report_webnopw_2379a_261018.pdf, accessed August 24, 2019. Of course, not all of the charitable giving tracked by the Charities Aid Foundation is directed towards the needy, as defined in this work. Still, as Sir John Low, Chief Executive of CAF observes in his foreword to the 2018 report, "The levels of generosity we see in countries is truly humbling, particularly when it shows huge support for others in countries which have suffered years of conflict, war or instability. That really demonstrates our shared human values shining through." Though the report does not cite a given number of contributors to aid the needy, its data suggests that the number of people who are concerned about the needy is easily in the hundreds of millions, and may be well more than a billion.

This material is fully compatible with Effective Altruism, and, if true, could readily be accepted by its followers.

Much of what I argue for is compatible with the spirit of Effective Altruism, but not with each of its specific elements. So, for example, while I believe that to a large extent Effective Altruists have their hearts in the right place, I think it is a mistake for them to rely so heavily on Expected Utility Theory to guide their actions. Relatedly, I reject any approach that judges the goodness of outcomes as a simple additive function of how good those outcomes are for each of their members. Likewise, as we will see, I believe that we need a wider, more pluralistic, conception of the good, one that recognizes more factors as relevant to the goodness of outcomes, than merely the welfare, or wellbeing, of the members of those outcomes.[59] These points are, I believe, very important. However, they could all be viewed as friendly amendments to Effective Altruism. In particular, these points are all compatible with what I take to be the most fundamental commitment of Effective Altruism; namely, that in giving to charity, one should aim at doing as much (expected) good as one can, given one's resources, compatible with one's not acting wrongly in so doing.

Accordingly, I believe that most of what I say in this book, relevant to Effective Altruism, could be accepted by Effective Altruists, if they are willing to accept a pluralistic conception of the good, and a more holistic, non-additive view of outcome goodness that doesn't rely solely on Expected Utility Theory in ranking the desirability of different prospects. However, the book does raise deep concerns about the scope of Effective Altruism, for those who want to combine Effective Altruism with a non-consequentialist outlook. After all, a basic tenet of non-consequentialism is that "thou shalt not do evil that good may come of it."[60] That is, in general, one cannot act wrongly, even for the sake of some greater good that might come of it. However, this raises serious questions about interventions to aid the needy in conditions where we have good reason to believe that such interventions may also lead to serious rights violations of others. Unfortunately, as we will see, those are precisely the conditions that obtain in many of the situations where aid is most needed.

Further, while there are many practical prescriptions of Effective Altruism that I endorse, ultimately, I reject the narrow "do the most good" approach that underlies their prescriptions, even when it is constrained by deontological considerations. As I will argue, there is more to being good in a world of need,

---

[59] I say more about this later. However, for a much more detailed discussion of these issues, and their importance, see my books *Rethinking the Good* and *Inequality* (New York: Oxford University Press, 1993).

[60] This view is often attributed to St. Paul, and referred to as the *Pauline Principle*.

than simply doing the most good that one can, consistent with acting rightly. (Here, and often throughout the book, I drop the qualifier "expected" for stylistic reasons; so, instead of writing "expected good" I simply write "good.")

Finally, I want to be clear that while Effective Altruists who focus on concerns other than helping the needy are *not* my main target, that does not mean that I agree with them, or that this book's considerations have no bearing on their views. I believe that Ord, Beckstead, and MacAskill are clearly right to be concerned about existential risks. We would be fools to ignore the enormous import that such risks have. However, I believe that they, and others, go off the rails to the extent that they focus on that issue more or less to the exclusion of a concern for the current needy. This is, I believe, a grave mistake; one driven by a commitment to the "do the most expected good" approach embodied in Expected Utility Theory.[61] I believe that Expected Utility Theory is a powerful and important model which can often be effectively used in the service of our most pressing moral issues. But we go awry, I believe, when we let that model dictate to us which of our moral issues *are* most pressing. Many of my reasons for holding this view have been developed, at length, in my book *Rethinking the Good*,[62] and I cannot repeat them here. However, I say a bit more about how Expected Utility Theory can drive us off the rails in Appendix A, especially as it pertains to the issue of existential risk.

1.8 Overview of the Book

In Chapter 2, I note that I have long been concerned about helping the world's needy and have long been sympathetic with the aims of Singer and the Effective Altruism Movement. However, I argue in favor of a *pluralistic* approach to aiding the needy, according to which there are a host of normative reasons that have a bearing on the nature and extent of our obligations to the needy,

---

[61] Strictly speaking, the Effective Altruists I have in mind here have an unrestricted sense of "do the most good" meaning that they want to produce the most good possible, regardless of where, when, or to whom that good occurs. This involves a commitment to a *neutralist* or *impersonal* conception of the good. By contrast, many people are attracted to *person-affecting views*, which limit the focus of our concern to those people or sentient beings who actually exist presently, or to those people or sentient beings who do or will actually exist now or in the future, *independently of our choices*. On the distinction between person-affecting views and non-personal affecting views, and their importance for morality, in general, and future generations and existential risk, in particular, see Derek Parfit's *Reasons and Persons* and my *Rethinking the Good*. (I am grateful to Roger Crisp for suggesting that I clarify this point.)

[62] Temkin, Larry, *Rethinking the Good: Moral Ideals and the Nature of Practical Reasoning*, New York: Oxford University Press, 2012.

including outcome-based reasons, virtue-based reasons, and deontological-based reasons.

In Chapter 3, I discuss Peter Singer's famous Pond Example, which helped give rise to the Effective Altruism Movement. I show that while our intuitive reactions to Singer's example are compatible with Effective Altruism, they are also compatible with my pluralistic approach. Furthermore, I offer several arguments and examples to show that we should, in fact, adopt a pluralistic approach to thinking about the needy, rather than the narrow, monistic "do the most good" approach of Effective Altruism. I suggest that in responding to the needy a truly decent person must be open to the full range of moral considerations relevant to the situation; among other things, this will involve being *virtuous* and acting *rightly or permissibly*, as well as promoting as much good as one can.

In Chapter 4, I note several possible disanalogies between saving a drowning child and giving to an international relief organization. These include whether those needing help are members of one's own community, whether one's aid requires the assistance of many intervening agents, and whether one is actually saving lives as opposed to helping to defray any of the legitimate costs incurred by aid agencies. I suggest that the last two factors may have a bearing on the nature of one's obligation to aid someone in need.

In Chapters 5 through 7, I discuss the dark side of humanity. This discussion points to further important disanalogies between saving a drowning child and supporting international aid agencies. Among other things, I discuss reasons to worry about internal corruption—corruption within aid agencies themselves; and also reasons to worry about external corruption—corruption external to aid agencies themselves, but with which aid agencies may become enmeshed. I argue that both kinds of corruption must be taken seriously. I note that in some cases we may have to just "learn to live" with certain kinds of corruption, in order to aid the needy. However, I also note that the line between man-made and natural disasters is often blurred in ways that limit the scope of the "we must learn to live with it" response.

I further argue that the case for aiding the needy may depend, in part, on whether those needing assistance are innocent or not responsible for their plight, whether the needy are victims of an accident or social injustice, and whether anyone stands to benefit from one's intervention other than the needy themselves.

In addressing these topics, I argue that we must be attuned to the many direct and indirect ways in which international aid efforts may inadvertently benefit the perpetrators of grave social injustices, incentivizing such injustices.

Similarly, we must be aware of the possibility that our aid efforts may end up rewarding corrupt leaders whose policies have contributed to hybrid natural/-man-made disasters, thus encouraging such disastrous policies. These questions are related to the problem of dirty hands, and raise both consequentialist and deontological concerns regarding aid efforts which must deal, directly or indirectly, with warlords, tyrants, or corrupt regimes.

Furthermore, I note that aid organizations have every incentive to look for and emphasize all the good that they accomplish, and much less incentive to look for bad effects from their interventions. Even worse, I point out that well-intentioned people will often fail to report, or even cover up, the corrupt behavior of others, or the negative impacts of their aid efforts, to protect an aid agency to which they are committed. Unfortunately, this is often the case even for people who are, themselves, above reproach in their personal conduct. I suggest that these factors often make it difficult for independent agencies to accurately assess the overall impact of aid agencies.

Together, the factors discussed in Chapters 5 through 7 make the case for contributing to international aid agencies much less clear than the case for saving the drowning child in Singer's famous example. Indeed, in Chapter 7, I present the case of Goma, where aid efforts went terribly, tragically, awry. Goma starkly reminds us that this book's considerations are not mere, abstract, possibilities; they have real-world counterparts of great normative significance.

In Chapter 8, I discuss marketplace distortions in human capital that can arise when aid agencies outbid the local market to hire highly qualified local workers to promote their agendas. I claim that this can lead to both internal and external "brain and character drains." I argue that when this happens on a large scale, it may have substantial, unintended, negative consequences elsewhere in the society. This is because it may divert highly talented people of great character from jobs that are crucial for a poor country's social, political, or economic development. Whether or not such consequences ultimately outweigh the positive effects of aid interventions, they certainly need to be considered in assessing the overall desirability of such interventions.

In Chapter 9, I discuss some of the difficulties of identifying aid efforts worthy of support. I note that it is often difficult to determine whether an aid effort has been a success, because often aid efforts may have indirect or long-term negative consequences that are difficult to identify or anticipate. I also point out that each aid context is unique, so that aid efforts that are highly successful in one local context may utterly fail in another local context.

Similarly, highly successful local projects may not always be replicable on a much larger regional or national scale.

I consider an example from the area of education to illustrate how even the best-laid plans of highly talented, highly motivated, and well-intentioned individuals with virtually unlimited resources can spectacularly fail for unforeseen reasons. Moreover, this can be so even for a local project in one of the world's wealthiest, and most highly educated, countries. Given this, it should not be surprising if it is difficult to confidently predict success for projects in the world's poorest and less educated regions, where the conditions of success are likely to be far from ideal, and where the possibilities of misunderstandings and missteps are high due to social, cultural, political, historical, and, often, language differences. I acknowledge that this chapter's worries may apply to a lesser extent to some of GiveWell's top-rated charities, but provide reasons to believe that they don't disappear entirely, even for such charities.

In Chapter 10, I argue that foreign interventions often involve psychological attitudes that are morally problematic; that they often fail to show sufficient respect for the local people, customs, and ways of life; and that they are prone to undermining the interests, priorities, and autonomy of the local people. Accordingly, I suggest that even if aid efforts avoid some of the most damaging and objectionable elements of colonialism, they often raise worries about ethical imperialism and Western hegemony that are reminiscent of colonialism.

In Chapters 11 through 13, I discuss Angus Deaton's controversial claim that international aid efforts are doing more harm than good. In particular, I discuss his contention that international aid efforts ultimately undermine the responsiveness of local and national governments to their citizens in ways that are crippling for substantial long-term social and economic progress. I also consider Jeffrey Sachs's approach to global poverty, and various lessons we can learn from the Millennium Villages Project.

Most people find it very hard to believe that in supporting international aid organizations they might be doing more harm than good. In part, this is because it seems clear, to many, that their contributions may substantially improve the quality of lives of some, while having only a negligible impact on a government's responsiveness to its citizens. In light of this common reaction to Deaton's claim, I discuss the possibility that aid efforts may exemplify an *Each/We Dilemma*, where there is a conflict between what is *individually* moral and what is *collectively* moral. Specifically, I raise the troubling possibility that advocates of international aid may be correct to insist that there are many international relief organizations that do more good than harm, and that each of us, individually, has strong moral reason to support such organizations; and yet, Deaton may nevertheless be correct in contending that if each of us does that, we, together, will be doing more harm than good. Thus, collectively we may be acting wrongly, in supporting international aid organizations, even though, as individuals, each of us is acting rightly in doing so.

Each/We Dilemmas have profound implications for contemporary society, and are notoriously difficult to resolve. I argue that global aid may be an instance of an especially intractable form of Each/We Dilemmas. If so, it may be clear that each of us ought, individually, to support international aid efforts; and also clear that we, together, ought not to do so. Moreover, there may be no clear way of reconciling these conflicting prescriptions.

I also consider several possible responses to Deaton's concern. I suggest that some of them only strengthen his position, and that others are open to plausible objections. In addition, I suggest that Deaton's worry raises deontological concerns about global aid efforts, as well as the consequentialist concerns on which he focuses.

I don't claim that Deaton is ultimately right in his view that international aid efforts do more harm than good. However, I think that his worry must be taken seriously. If there is even a chance that he is right, and I think there is, then that may have substantial implications for how, if at all, we should try to aid the global needy.

With that said, I note that even if Deaton is right that, overall, international aid efforts do more harm than good, that does not settle the question of whether we should support such efforts. Given this book's pluralistic approach, it is possible that we should aid the needy even if, by the lights of the consequentialist approach favored by most Effective Altruists and development economists, we ought not to.

In Chapter 14, I discuss Thomas Pogge's claim that for most people in the world's richest countries aiding the needy is a duty, and not merely an optional act of charity, because we are partly responsible for their plight, in that our actions directly and indirectly harm them in ways that violate their rights. I also argue that considerations of fairness, justice, and equality are relevant to how we should respond to the plight of the needy. I note that these issues raise a host of complicated questions which are not easily answered. Together, these considerations offer further support for the view that the topic of global need is extremely complex, both normatively and empirically; and that we need a pluralistic approach if we are to have any hope of determining how to be good in a world of need.

Chapter 15 takes stock of many of the book's main results. It notes that despite its importance and widespread influence, Singer's famous Pond

Example, and the larger argument of which it is a part, offers us little guidance as to how we should respond to global need. In particular, it does not support the conclusion that we should be supporting international aid organizations like Oxfam.

Chapter 15 also notes that there are important differences between my view and that of Effective Altruism. Still, I urge that it is important not to overstate these differences. I note that most of this book's claims are compatible with Effective Altruism. I also note that the differences between my view and Effective Altruism can be reduced—though not removed entirely—if Effective Altruism moves to a wider conception of the good than welfare (narrowly understood in terms of the quality of people's conscious mental states or the satisfaction of their preferences).

I note that some Effective Altruism organizations, like GiveWell, offer concrete recommendations as to which aid organizations are deserving of support. I contend that this book's results suggest that such recommendations may be premature. I also note that there is a big difference between being confident that one's aid contributions have positive expected utility, and being confident that they do more good than harm. This point is especially important to bear in mind, I suggest, for those who contend that people should contribute to "effective" aid organizations even to the point where this involves substantial sacrifices of their own wellbeing, or that of their loved ones.

Chapter 15 also presents several important clarifications, qualifications, and implications of this book's claims. Among other things, I note that many of this book's worries only apply to on-the-ground aid efforts in countries with weak or corrupt governments, or in countries with weak or small economies. So, for example, many of my worries would not arise for aid efforts in many middle- or upper-income countries. This is important, I suggest, since we should be concerned about aiding poor people, rather than poor countries, per se, and since many poor people live in countries that are not particularly poor or corrupt.

Chapter 15 also emphasizes that this book's worries are serious and should not be ignored. This is especially so for anyone who believes, as most Effective Altruists do, that one needs to consult Expected Utility Theory in deciding which aid efforts to support. I contend that if there is even a small chance that some of this book's worries are right, this should alter the expected utility of many international aid efforts. I note, in particular, how this might impact the expected value of the four deworming charities that are currently listed among GiveWell's eight top-rated charities.

In Chapter 16, I summarize the book's main claims. I acknowledge that I have serious doubts about whether this book may ultimately harm the very people I am concerned to help. However, I now believe that there may be even greater danger for the global needy in my previous one-sided approach in support of global aid. I note that I have had to leave many complex and difficult questions open, and I indicate some important paths, suggested by this book, that require further exploration. Finally, I address the question of where one might go from here, in light of this book's results. These remarks are aimed at those who find this book's arguments persuasive, but who, like me, remain concerned about the needy, and remain committed to trying to determine how to be good in a world of need.

The book also includes two appendices. In Appendix A, I argue that Expected Utility Theory is a useful model, but that it must be employed carefully. I maintain that an obsessive commitment to following the dictates of Expected Utility Theory can drive us off the rails. In Appendix B, I argue that the issue of whether spatial and temporal proximity are themselves irrelevant from the moral point of view is much more complicated than most people have assumed. Appendices A and B are likely to be of most interest to philosophers, Effective Altruists, Development Economists, and other specialists.

1.9 Final Remarks

In his thoughtful, and comprehensive book, *Does Foreign Aid Really Work?*, Roger Riddell writes the following:

> The moral case for providing aid is not solely dependent upon the existence of acute human suffering and widespread poverty which aid funds have the potential to address, and the ability of donors to provide the resources required. For many, also, it is self-evident that the moral case for aid also critically depends upon the ability of the aid provided to contribute effectively to the alleviation of human suffering and the reduction of poverty.
>
> (p. 128)

Most philosophers and many Effective Altruists take it as a given that there are effective international aid agencies that alleviate human suffering and reduce poverty. Moreover, this is undoubtedly true on the local level and in the short term, as there is a massive amount of data that shows that most aid projects *are* successful in achieving their immediate goals. Unfortunately, however, there is much less hard data showing that aid agencies are successful in achieving a net gain in the reduction of human suffering and poverty in the long run, taking account of all of the indirect and unintended consequences that their efforts have.

About this issue, development economists are divided. While many, and perhaps most, believe there has been a positive, though perhaps weak, overall impact of aid efforts on suffering and poverty reduction, some are convinced that the overall effects of aid have been negative, and others are agnostic about the issue.

Riddell, who has perhaps thought about this topic as carefully and thoroughly as anyone, has much to say about it. He is worth quoting in some detail:

Assessments of the impact of aid are only as good as the information on which they are based. Yet there are problems, many of them serious, with the accuracy of large amounts of data from which confident conclusions are drawn.

Does aid make a difference at the national level, or even more widely, at the international level? Tracing the overall relationship between aid and its impact at the national and international levels requires accurate, reliable and consistent data over time and across countries of both the amounts of aid provided and the different variables against which the relationship with aid is to be tracked, especially changes in poverty levels, and differences in overall growth rates. There are problems on both counts.

Take aid data first.... [T]here are serious questions about the accuracy of some official aid data, and usually significant differences between amounts of ODA [Overseas Development Aid] recorded by donors and the amounts of aid that recipient governments receive....

It is not only the accuracy of aid data which creates problems for assessing relationships between aid and expected outcomes. If aid is meant to have a positive impact on the overall growth of a recipient economy, then data on growth needs to be accurately assessed. Even in industrialized economies national accounts data are known to be inaccurate. They will be even less accurate in underdeveloped countries, one of the characteristics of most poor countries being the poor quality of their national accounts statistics....

Even greater problems arise in relation to trying to pinpoint the numbers of people who are poor and trends in poverty over time. In spite of massive efforts to improve data-gathering in recent decades, we still do not know accurately across the poorest countries of the world the number of poor people, changes in the number of people living in poverty, those living in permanent or chronic poverty, and those for whom poverty is more of a temporary or transitory problem than a permanent feature of their lives. Much of the poverty data that are used, and widely quoted, are based on estimates—some extremely crude.... According to the United Nations, for over 65 countries (mostly the poorest) there are no data on the number of people living in poverty; for almost 100 countries, no data which record changes in poverty over time; and for 115 countries, no data are collected which monitor changes in child malnutrition (as recorded by weight) a key indicator of poverty....

Against the backdrop of these sorts of data-gaps and data problems, we should be wary of studies which make bold assertions about aid's overall impact on growth and poverty, especially at the country and cross-country level.[63]

Riddell draws on a vast amount of literature and data to arrive at his conclusion, and my own limited reading of the literature, together with the considerations adduced in this book, leads me to side with Riddell on this issue. As matters stand today, I do not believe that we have sufficiently hard and clear data to conclude one way or the other regarding the overall, long-term, impact of global aid efforts. I know what I hope to be the case, but I don't in fact know whether those hopes have been realized, or are likely to be realized in the near future.

Leif Wenar believes

the upshot of the empirics is that our epistemological situation as donors may be worse than EA [Effective Altruism] often paints it, and in fact may be bad enough to call into question how much specific action-guiding can be

---

[63] *Does Foreign Aid Really Work?*, pp. 166–7. Note that Riddell scrupulously cites many sources for his claims, including: Degnbol-Martinusses, John and Poul Engberg-Pedersen, *Aid: Understanding International Development Cooperation*, London: Zed Books, 2003; Clemens, M.A., S. Radlett, and R. Bhavnani, *Counting Chickens When They Hatch: The Short Term Effect of Aid on Growth*, CGD Working Paper No. 44, Washington, DC: CGD, 2004; White, H. "The Case for Doubling Aid," *IDS Bulletin* 36 (2005): 8–13; Morgenstern, Oscar, *On the Accuracy of Economic Observations*, 2nd Edition, Princeton: Princeton University Press, 1963; Szekely, M., N. Lustig, J.A. Meijia, and M. Cumpa, *Do We Know How Much Poverty There Is?*, Washington, DC: Inter-American Development Bank, 2000; Ruggeri Laderchi, C., R. Saith, and F. Stewart, *Does It Matter That We Don't Agree on the Definition of Poverty? A Comparison of Four Approaches*, QEH Working Paper No. 107, Oxford: Queen Elizabeth House, 2003; and McKay, A. and B. Baulch, "How Many Chronically Poor People are There in the World? Some Preliminary Estimates," Chronic Poverty Research Centre Working Paper No. 45, Manchester: University of Manchester, 2004.

expected from Expected Utility Theory. EAs [Effective Altruists] are strongly suggesting that ordinary people make significant changes, in their careers, or not spending money on their families . . . . [In doing so,] they are making the empirical assumption that they *know* . . . [that if we follow their advice we will be] doing the most good, or more good than harm, but have they disposed the burden of proof that lies on them to show that there is empirical justification for their prescriptions? It seems not.[64]

Of course, Effective Altruists will insist that they do not have to know whether global aid efforts have been effective *on the whole* in reducing suffering and poverty; they only have to know that the particular aid agencies they urge us to support are effective at reducing overall suffering and poverty. Admittedly, that is a much lower bar to pass. Even so, given the issues about data and methodology raised by Riddell and others, and given the considerations I will be presenting in this book, I am not convinced that Effective Altruists have the information they need to pass even that, much lower, bar. Moreover, for reasons given in Chapter 13, ultimately, it may not be enough, to defend the Effective Altruist's position, to simply pass the lower bar, especially if they are urging people to make substantial changes in their life plans, lifestyles, or personal priorities.

Before proceeding, let me confess to a certain trepidation regarding this book. As I have already indicated, and will detail further in Chapter 2, I have long been concerned about the world's needy. Accordingly, even when I have had doubts about the cogency of my arguments or the efficacy of the policies that I have advocated, I have been reluctant to express them publicly, much less to go into print with them, for fear that doing so would aid the forces of parochialism, selfishness, apathy, and skeptical resignation that dominate much of the world when it comes to the matter of aiding the world's needy.

Still, throughout my philosophical career, I have been deeply inspired by Derek Parfit's uncompromising commitment to pursue the truth, and to follow the arguments wherever they lead, even if sometimes they lead to unsettling conclusions. In this book, I have tried to follow Parfit's example to the best of my limited abilities.

Unfortunately, I believe that too many well-intentioned philosophers— including me for most of my life—have been blinded by deeply held and longstanding practical and ideological commitments when it comes to the topic of global aid. Many of us have been too quick to dismiss, without

---

[64] Personal correspondence.

argument, the worries that have been raised about efforts to aid the world's needy, confident in the seemingly a priori position that such objections *must* be wrong. I am certain that such reactions are unwarranted, philosophically. They may also be tragically mistaken, practically. This is, I now believe, a possibility that must be taken seriously.

My aim in this book is not to prove that my worries are compelling. To the contrary, I raise them in the sincere hope that someone will convincingly show that they can, indeed, be laid to rest. However, I believe that that important work has not yet been adequately done. And it needs to be. If it can't be done, then I, and others, may need to drastically revise our recommendations regarding how best to aid the world's needy.

Finally, let me remind the reader of the important methodological point previously noted in Section 1.3. In this book, I will be emphasizing a side of the global aid debate that, I believe, has received insufficient attention from many philosophers, Effective Altruists, and ordinary people struck by the huge disparities that exist between the world's best-off and the world's worst-off. I want to give that side a full and fair hearing. I do this in the hopes of opening the eyes of those, like me, who have always had firm views about the topic of global aid, without fully appreciating just how complex, and murky, the topic really is.

Though I am currently agnostic about whether, in the long run, aid efforts reduce suffering and poverty overall, that does not mean that I am an opponent of aid. To the contrary, as I will make plain in my concluding chapter, despite all the worries this book raises, I remain convinced that those of us in a position to do so must somehow find a way to do much more than we normally do on behalf of the needy. Thus, I remain, at my core, a strong proponent of aid. Unfortunately, however, it is much less clear to me now, than it once was, to whom aid should be directed, the form that aid should take, and how to trade off between the complex and often competing considerations relevant to being good in a world of need.

2

Global Need

My Longtime Commitment and Earlier Views

This chapter is divided into two sections. In Section 2.1, I present some autobiographical remarks, regarding my lifelong concern about the needy. In Section 2.2, I present some of the key claims I have made in the past in support of that commitment. In doing this, I argue for a pluralistic approach to thinking about the needy.

2.1 A Lifelong Concern about the Needy

There is a rich tradition in philosophy which holds that if one wants to know the moral truth about a given matter, one needs to adopt a disinterested, impartial, rational perspective.[1,2] As implied in Section 1.3, I believe there is

[1] This tradition dates back at least to Kant (see Kant's *The Metaphysics of Morals*, edited by Mary J. Gregor, Cambridge: Cambridge University Press, 2013 and also his *Groundwork of the Metaphysics of Morals*, edited by Mary J. Gregor, Cambridge: Cambridge University Press, 1998), and has had numerous supporters, including many contemporary utilitarians, Kantians, and contractualists. However, there has also been a lot of pushback against the "hegemony" of rationalism in moral thinking that dates back at least to Hume (see Hume's *A Treatise of Human Nature*, edited by L. Selby-Bigge, Oxford: Clarendon Press, 1896), including from many contemporary virtue theorists, care theorists, and feminist philosophers.

[2] There is also a tension within much of the development literature between the emotional side of development, which is famously leveraged by large charities and NGOs in advertisements, and the more rational and critical side that is often deployed by development economics. That said, it is important to note that while development economics presents itself as prima facie more rational and defensible, many conclusions that are drawn in the development literature seem to be driven more by emotion—or one's ideological commitments—than the data itself. Thus, as one development economist observed, "Although the issue of aid effectiveness, the impact of aid on growth, has attracted considerable research attention, there is no consensus view. It is not unusual for different researchers using the same data and econometric approach to arrive at dramatically different conclusions by altering a specific modelling choice" (Morrissey, O., "Why Do Economists Disagree so much on Aid Effectiveness? Aid Works (in Mysterious Ways)," initial draft paper for presentation at the IMF-CFD Conference on Financing for Development, Geneva, 2015, p. 1). Likewise, one study found that according to two different definitions of poverty, the figure for those living in poverty in Latin America ranged from 17 to 77%! (See Laderchi, C.R., R. Saith, and F. Stewart. "Does it Matter that we do not Agree on the Definition of Poverty? A Comparison of Four Approaches." *Oxford Development Studies* 31 (2003): 243–74, URL: https://www.academia.edu/8302026/Livelihoods_and_Poverty_Approved_Public_Version_of_Chapter_13_of_the_Working_Group_II_contribution_to_the_IPCC_Fifth_Assessment_Report, accessed August 24, 2019.)

Being Good in a World of Need. Larry S. Temkin, Oxford University Press. © Larry S. Temkin 2022.
DOI: 10.1093/oso/9780192849977.003.0002

much to be said for that tradition (though also much to be said against it). Unfortunately, to the extent that tradition is correct, then I must confess that I am not well-placed to discern the truth about our obligations to the needy. This is because I was raised by both my parents to be concerned about the less fortunate; taught by my religious tradition that we have an obligation to help the poor and the hungry; and have, as long as I can remember, been touched by the plight of the needy and felt the need to do something about it. Let me briefly expound on these remarks.

My mother was a liberal democrat, who taught English as a second language at a city technical school, as a way of helping our city's disadvantaged. Her adult students were overwhelmingly poor, immigrants, and people of color. My father was a patriot, a veteran, and a conservative republican. When I was young, he and his brother worked seven days a week in a two-person foundry. However, my father was every bit as concerned about the needy as my mother. After his business had become fairly successful, he would send his vendors and valued customers a card during the holidays explaining that rather than sending them a gift that they didn't need, his company had "adopted" a poor child in another country—usually in South America or Africa—helping to pay for that child's school supplies. Often my father received a picture of the child, along with a letter written by the child's teacher, indicating how much of a difference their contribution had made in the child's life.

My parents also raised me to be a member of "the clean plate club." Why? Because of all the starving children in China and India! I knew full well, as did my parents, that my cleaning my plate would do nothing to relieve the hunger of children elsewhere. But they believed firmly, as I still do, that there is something deeply wrong about wasting food in a world where so many people die of starvation, are seriously malnourished, or go to bed hungry each night.

In Sunday School, I was taught the tradition of *Tsedakah*. Tsedakah is a Hebrew word literally meaning justice or righteousness, but it involved a weekly collection for the poor and the needy. Moreover, importantly, giving to Tsedakah was considered a duty, not merely an option. As a small boy, with a weekly allowance of a quarter, it always seemed to me *right* to give a nickel or a dime, each Sunday, to those less fortunate than I. When my allowance eventually rose to a dollar a week, a quarter seemed more appropriate.

On Halloween, my siblings and I would "trick or treat" for UNICEF. We would carry around small orange and black UNICEF milk cartons, hoping that our neighbors would help fill them with spare change to aid the world's needy children. At the end of a long night, I would swell with pride as I counted up the nickels, dimes, quarters—and even the occasional dollar!—that my efforts had produced.

When I was ten, my family visited New York for the 1964 World's Fair. I'll never forget the experience of coming up from the subway and seeing a young African-American woman sitting on a blanket, surrounded by a bevy of very young children—perhaps as many as ten, all younger than me—with a baby nursing at her breast, a look of desperation in her eyes, and her hand stretched out begging for money. I remember an overwhelming sense of pity for the mother and children. And, even more than that, an overwhelming sense of anger and shame that hundreds of seemingly well-to-do people—including my own family—streamed past her. The vast majority of them didn't give her a penny. They didn't even slow down. They simply ignored her; deftly avoiding her blanket, her eyes, and her hand, as if she didn't even exist. Of course, as an adult, I now recognize the many reasons why giving money to a beggar on the street might be problematic.[3] Still, as a ten-year-old, that scene left an indelible mark on my psyche, and it helped bring into focus in a vivid and visceral manner a set of concerns that have remained with me to this day regarding injustice, inequality, unfairness, and our obligations to the needy.

In 1970, as a high school sophomore, I collected sponsors from friends and family—typically at the rate of a nickel or dime per mile—to support me on a 31-mile "hunger hike" whose proceeds were earmarked to help alleviate world hunger.[4*] I also began arguing with my father and uncles about the immorality of America's ethos of "conspicuous consumption" in a world where so many

---

[3] For a popular article that gives expression to some of these reasons, see Caroline Fiennes's "Help the homeless—don't give them spare change." *The Financial Times*, April 19, 2017, URL: https://www.ft.com/content/f2e25252-1b8b-11e7-a266-12672483791a, accessed December 18, 2018. For a contrary view of the issue, see Mark Horvath's "Giving Money to Homeless People is Okay." *Huffpost*, March 31, 2017, URL: https://www.huffingtonpost.com/entry/giving-money-to-homeless-people-is-okay_us_58de9ef7e4b0ca889ba1a57b, accessed December 18, 2018.

[4*] This hunger hike preceded, by a year, the May 8, 1971 "Walks for Development" which were coordinated by the American Freedom from Hunger Foundation with the goal of fighting global hunger. The 1971 event was the United States's largest nationally coordinated walkathon to date, with over 150,000 people walking over two million miles, raising over $1.2 million to fight hunger. No doubt the size of the 1971 walkathon was significantly impacted by the unfolding horrors in East Pakistan/Bangladesh (noted next, in the text).

Given the deeply personal character of this section's remarks, I can't resist noting that the city with the largest number of participants in the famous 1971 nationwide hunger hike was my hometown of Milwaukee, Wisconsin, with an estimated 20,000 people walking along the 31-mile route (https://en.wikipedia.org/wiki/Walkathon).

I also can't resist noting the following. It is commonly claimed that helping others is one of the best ways of helping yourself. This may or may not be true for most people, but it was certainly true for me. It was on the 1970 Milwaukee hunger hike that I met Meg Grimm, who was similarly hiking to feed the hungry. We began dating soon afterwards, got married in 1975, and have been happily together ever since. This is, of course, no doubt another reason why my attitude towards aiding the needy is not altogether unbiased.

people were dying of hunger and disease. In particular, I rankled at how much my own family had begun engaging in such a lifestyle, as my father's business began to take off, and we rose from working class, to middle class, to upper middle class. These arguments increased in 1971, as the horrors of the East Pakistan/Bangladesh civil war became public and gripped the world's attention.[5] As we now know, the toll of the nine-month civil war involved some three million people dead, some 300,000 women becoming victims of sexual violence, and some ten million refugees seeking asylum in India.[6] Then, a scant three years later, as I was a senior in college, Bangladesh once again caught the world's attention, as an estimated 450,000–1.5 million people died, between July 1974 and January 1975, as a result of starvation and diseases such as cholera and diarrhea.[7]

In graduate school, I studied at Oxford for a year, and it was there that I first learned about the work of Oxfam. It was during my graduate school days that I became convinced that people should devote most of their charitable contributions to effective international development and relief organizations. While there were countless charitable organizations that supported causes that I believed in—many of which I had contributed to, or volunteered for, in high school or college—I came to the view that, ultimately, most of those causes were less urgent, and less important, than aiding the world's neediest members. Here, in essence, I was adopting the perspective of Effective Altruism, long before that movement existed.

As a young Assistant Professor, I began to teach a contemporary moral problems class. The issues covered in the class often varied from year to year. But one topic in that class remained constant from the very beginning to my last class, and that was the topic of our obligations to the needy. That was also the only topic in the class where I dropped any pretense of neutrality. I tried, as with all the topics I covered, to give the strongest arguments I could on behalf of both sides of the issue. However, on that topic, alone, I conveyed my own view of the matter, taking a stand as to where I thought the strongest arguments lay, and what I thought we should do given those arguments. Among

---

[5] See Kagy, Gisella, "Long Run Impacts of Famine Exposure: A Study of the 1974–1975 Bangladesh Famine." Preliminary Draft, University of Colorado, 2012, URL: https://www.dartmouth.edu/~neudc2012/docs/paper_289.pdf, accessed September 4, 2016.

[6] See Hoque, Mofidul, "Bangladesh 1971: A Forgotten Genocide." *Bangladesh—Audacity of Hope*, March 5, 2013, URL: https://mygoldenbengal.wordpress.com/2013/03/05/bangladesh-1971-a-forgotten-genocide/, accessed September 4, 2016. These were the horrors that Peter Singer memorialized for subsequent generations of philosophy students, and others, in the opening sentences of "Famine, Affluence, and Morality" (*Philosophy and Public Affairs* 1 (1972): 229–43).

[7] See Kagy's "Long Run Impacts of Famine Exposure."

other things, at the end of the "obligations to the needy" section of the class I would have my TAs take up a collection, with all proceeds going to effective international relief or development organizations.

I emphasized that contributions were strictly voluntary, and it was done in such a way that, together with my "blind" grading system, students could be confident that their class grade would not depend in any way on whether they contributed to the collection or the size of their contribution if they chose to give. I also promised that in addition to the amount that my wife and I give each year to such organizations, I would match student contributions one-for-one up to three thousand dollars. On several occasions the class, in combination with other Department members who also chose to contribute to our efforts, raised over $10,000. And I would estimate that since I first began teaching in 1980, my classes have raised a six-figure amount devoted to aiding the world's needy.

In addition, as a young faculty member at Rice University, I helped launch, and served as an advisor to an Oxfam student club, devoted to raising student awareness of, and funds for, Oxfam. Activities of the club included a Thanksgiving-related "Hunger Banquet," which raised both consciousness and money on behalf of the world's hungry. The club also organized a university-wide Oxfam Meal Skip Program where, once a week, students could swipe their meal card, but not take a meal, with all proceeds that would have gone to paying for their meal going to Oxfam, instead.[8]

In 1998, I was asked to debate the topic of obligations to the needy with Jan Narveson for the Institute on World Affairs.[9] That led to several publications on the topic,[10] lectures to a wide range of audiences,[11] and my helping to launch several chapters of the charitable organization Giving What We Can.[12]

---

[8] Alas, this program lasted less than a year, before the university ended the program for bureaucratic reasons that, frankly, made no sense to me. Also, as is often the case with student-led groups, the Rice Oxfam Club eventually ended when the students in my class who originally founded the club graduated, and no one else stepped up to lead the club. This was partly due to a major, high visibility university-led effort to get Rice students actively involved in helping the local, Houston, community.

[9] At Iowa State University.

[10] "Why Should America Care?" *Ag Bioethics Forum* 11 (June 1999): 9–15; "Thinking about the Needy, Justice, and International Organizations," and "Thinking about the Needy: A Reprise." *The Journal of Ethics* 8 (2004): 349–95 and 409–58.

[11] From economists and poverty specialists at the World Bank, to mostly philosophy graduate students and faculty at Columbia University, the University of Missouri, the University of London, and the Fifth International Conference of the Gesellschaft für Analytische Philosophie (GAP at Bielefeld, Germany), to mostly undergraduates and the general public at Princeton, Harvard, and Rutgers.

[12] At Princeton (along with Jeffrey Sachs), and at the University of Birmingham, UK (along with Peter Singer). I have also spoken to the Rutgers Chapter of Giving What We Can, the Harvard Effective Altruism Group, and the Harvard High Impact Philanthropy Group.

Finally, let me conclude this section by expanding upon, and briefly commenting on, the point of these distinctively non-philosophical autobiographical remarks. Each year, since our marriage in 1975, my wife and I have contributed to a decent number of charitable organizations that we deem worthwhile, with the greatest proportion of our donations going to international development and relief organizations, including Oxfam, Doctors Without Borders, and several of GiveWell's top rated charities. Additionally, I try to exercise daily, and when I do, I open the *Charity Miles* app on my phone, and select Nothing But Nets as the charitable organization to which a contribution will be made for each mile that I walk or bike. Even so, I live in a large home, drive a luxury car, take obscenely expensive vacations, and spend, on an ongoing basis, ridiculous amounts of money on myself and my family. So, I have no illusions about my efforts on behalf of the needy. The plain fact is that I do not do nearly as much as I could, or should, to benefit those less fortunate than I. Still, given this book's content, I thought it might be worthwhile to point out that my concern about those less fortunate is deep and longstanding, and that many of the worries I will be raising are worries that apply with equal, or even greater, force against the positions that I have long held on this topic, as against the views of others.

Unfortunately, we live in an era where there is a great tendency, even among philosophers, to simply dismiss the views of those "on the other side" of positions we hold, or those with different starting points than our own. The main point of my autobiographical remarks is to try to convey to those who support aiding the needy that I really *am* on the same side as they are, and that we share the same starting point. Yet, despite this, I have come, grudgingly, to have grave worries about certain of the assumptions that I have blithely held for more than three decades. My hope is that all of us who share the same starting point and concerns about the importance of aiding the world's needy will take these worries seriously, and collectively determine the best response to them, both theoretically and practically.

2.2 A Pluralistic Approach to the Needy—and the Ease of Giving

In this section, I briefly summarize the key claims that I have previously argued for in my lectures and publications regarding our obligations to the needy. I stand by virtually all these claims, and they continue to provide the background and framework for how I approach the topic. Here are the key claims I have previously made:

1. We should think about our relations to the needy, as we should think about other normatively significant issues, pluralistically.[13] In particular, I claim that there are at least three different sources of moral reasons: outcome-based reasons, virtue-based reasons, and deontological-based reasons. Each of these gives rise to an appropriate type of moral concern. Hence, I claim that the "fully moral life—the fully *human* life—requires that we pay attention to *each* of these concerns: to what *happens*—whether as a result of what we do or fail to do; to the kind of *person* we are—whether virtuous or vicious; and to our [deontological or agent-relative] *duties*—to ourselves and others."[14] When one does this, I argue, it is clear that there are outcome-based reasons, virtue-based reasons, and deontological-based reasons to aid the needy.

2. Regarding outcome-based reasons, I claim that "if you ask which *outcome* is better, one in which many innocent[15] people painfully die of easily avoidable causes, or one in which affluent people eat out less, and have fewer toys, clothes, or appliances, surely on any plausible theory of the goodness of outcomes, the latter outcome would be better than the former."[16]

3. Regarding virtue-based reasons, I contend that "among the most central and important virtues are the virtues of beneficence, sympathy, compassion, and generosity. But then, if one takes seriously the notion of having a good *character*, and being a *virtuous person*, surely at some point one must give priority to the easily preventable hunger, illness, and suffering of people, over

[13] The literature in development economics is massively diverse in its approaches, its judgments about aid effectiveness, and its recommendations about what, if anything, we should do to aid the needy. Increasingly, sophisticated development economists have emphasized that the issue of aid is enormously complex, and one that requires a nuanced approach that is sensitive to the particularities of each unique aid environment. I believe this lends further support to my pluralistic approach. Roughly, this is because it is deeply implausible to believe that all but one of the diverse views one finds in the development literature is completely wrong. Much more plausible, I believe, is the view that different factors, or different weightings of factors, underlie the diverse views that one finds in the development literature. Thus, on my view, there is something importantly right about most of the views in the development literature, and only a pluralistic approach has any hope of capturing that fact.

[14] See my "Thinking about the Needy, Justice, and International Organizations," p. 355.

[15] I have already addressed the assumption of innocence in this work in Section 1.6. As noted there, some people believe that *all* people are "innocent" in the sense of not being responsible for their character or actions. If one believes that, then one should simply regard the locution "innocent people" as redundant. However, many people believe that many war criminals, rapists, murderers, and thugs are not innocent, or not *as* innocent as most of their victims, and that we have greater obligation to help their victims than their victimizers. For such people, there is reason to distinguish between those needy who are innocent and those who are not.

[16] Again, see my "Thinking about the Needy, Justice, and International Organizations," p. 355.

further acquisition of goods that one does not need, may hardly use, and would not miss if one didn't have. For the truly virtuous person aiding the needy is not an option."[17]

4. Regarding deontological-based reasons, I hold that even if one grants, for the sake of argument, that people do not have a positive right to be aided, and that "[a]s such, we do not violate anyone's rights, or act unjustly, if we fail to aid the needy.... Even so, it seems clear our duties and obligations extend significantly beyond merely respecting rights, and that people can and often do act deeply *wrongly* even if they do not act *unjustly*."[18] I further argue that we do have a positive duty to aid the needy, that such positive duties can be every bit as strong, or even stronger, than many negative duties, that our positive duty to aid the needy will often require us to give priority to addressing more urgent needs over less urgent needs, and that there can be strong *reasons of justice* to aid the needy even if failing to aid the needy need not involve our *acting unjustly*.[19,20]

---

[17] "Thinking about the Needy, Justice, and International Organizations," p. 355.

[18] "Thinking about the Needy, Justice, and International Organizations," pp. 355–6. I recognize that some people may use the notions of "duty" and "obligation" interchangeably, and also see both as the flip side of "rights." While people can use such terms as they see fit, I prefer to distinguish between these notions. Specifically, I prefer to use a strong notion of *obligation*, corresponding to what one has *decisive* reason to do, or to what one *ought* to do *all things considered*. By contrast, I prefer a weaker notion of *rights* and *duties*, corresponding to certain types of prima facie or pro tanto reasons for acting, that may disappear or be outweighed by other moral considerations depending on the context. Also, as I use the terms, while rights may always give rise to correlative duties, the reverse need not obtain. So, for example, if you have a right against me that I keep my promise to you, (perhaps) I have a corresponding duty, reflecting a prima facie or pro tanto reason, to respect that right by keeping my promise. However, on my view, the fact that I may have a duty to express gratitude to you for having treated me generously, does not entail that you have a right to such gratitude from me, which I would violate if I failed to express my gratitude. With that said, I have only noted all this to avoid confusion in the minds of any readers who use the terms "rights," "duties," and "obligations" differently than I. None of this book's substantive claims depend on my usage.

[19] "Thinking about the Needy, Justice, and International Organizations," pp. 355–76. On the distinction between *acting justly* and acting *for reasons of justice* see, especially, pp. 368–70. For the importance of that distinction regarding our obligations to the needy see pp. 365–8 and 370–6.

[20] It is important to recognize that virtue-based reasons and deontological-based reasons reflect different kinds of considerations that might lead one to act. The former rest on the value of being a certain kind of person (for example, it is good to be someone who is generous and trustworthy). The latter rest on the value of standing in a particular kind of relation with those who will be affected by one's actions (for example, the relation of equals between two rational agents, each of whom is deserving of, and is owed, respect in their interactions with other rational agents; or the relation that arises between any two beings who are equal in the sense that they are both capable of having similar kinds of interests (such as, an interest in experiencing pleasures and avoiding pains), and both have an interest in their lives going as well as possible. Such common interests give rise to reasons that cannot be simply disregarded by anyone on pain of irrationality (specifically, on pain of failing to be fully responsive to all the reasons that there are). In some cases, these reasons may be sufficiently strong to constitute a deontological duty).

Note, while virtue-based reasons and deontological-based reasons will often support the same action—as they often do regarding the needy—they may also come apart. For example, someone

5. Regarding the plethora of worthy causes that one might support, I suggest that "ultimately, fulfilling our positive duties to others will almost certainly require most of us to address the easily preventable deaths of innocents, before contributing to the arts, scenic improvements, or—dare I say it—higher education!... [21] Thus, absent special agent-relative duties, or our deepest projects and commitments requiring otherwise, perhaps we may permissibly give to such causes only after first fulfilling our positive duty to respond to the most urgent needs of others."[22]

6. I point out that most affluent people in countries with industrial or post- industrial economies, including, for example, virtually everyone in the middle or upper classes of a country like the United States are, at least in economic terms, extraordinarily well off by global standards. I further point out how much money well-to-do people extravagantly spend on items that seem frivolous in a world where millions of people go to bed hungry each night: on fancy cars, massive homes, sporting events, large-screen TVs, toys (just how many dolls or stuffed animals does one child need?), kitchen

who is generous and compassionate may spend so much time and money helping people in need, that she is no longer able to fulfill all of her deontological duties, say, to keep her promises or to honor her contracts. Likewise, one may have to choose between fulfilling one's duty as a law-abiding citizen, by turning in a friend who has committed a crime, or acting in accordance with the virtues of friendship and loyalty. So, while virtuous people will generally act rightly, that will not always be the case. Similarly, while those who act rightly will often be virtuous, that, too, will not always be the case. Virtue and duty are distinct elements of the normative domain, each of which are important in their own way. (I am grateful to Roger Crisp, for suggesting that I say a bit more about the virtue/deontology distinction.)

[21] When I originally made this claim, I was referring to contributions that wealthy people often make to their alma maters in the developed world, and what I had in mind was contributions to support athletic programs, undergraduate or graduate prizes, lecture series, named chairs, new auditoriums, arenas, buildings, and so on. However, as I shall note in my concluding chapter, targeted contributions to basic research in certain STEM fields (Science, Technology, Engineering, and Medicine) may be a promising long-term way of helping the needy.

Moreover, there is a growing consensus within the development literature that development must be addressed holistically and along multiple dimensions. Indeed, the notion of *human development* has arisen to reflect the view that one should be as much concerned with access to education, healthcare, employment, opportunity, and so on, as with material gain. Accordingly, supporting education at all levels within the poorest regions has an important role to play in such development (though, perhaps in the near term, most importantly at the primary, middle, and high school levels). See, for example, Nussbaum, Martha C., *Creating Capabilities: The Human Development Approach*, Cambridge, MA: Harvard University Press, 2011; Sachs, Jeffrey D., *The End of Poverty*, New York: Penguin Books, 2005; Attanasio, Orazio et al., "Human development and poverty reduction in developing countries." Department for International Development, UK, 2016; and Alkire, Sabina and Maria Emma Santos, "Multidimensional Poverty Index." Oxford Poverty and Human Development Initiative, 2010, URL: https://www.ophi.org.uk/wp-content/uploads/OPHI-MPI-Brief.pdf, accessed September 6, 2018.

In sum, while I stand by the intent of my original claim, I recognize that a more nuanced way of putting my point is in order. (I am grateful to Brian Oosthuizen for suggesting this clarification.)

[22] "Thinking about the Needy, Justice, and International Organizations," pp. 358–9.

gadgets and appliances, clothes, fancy meals, luxury vacations, etc.[23] In concrete terms, I have observed that in 2009, individual Americans gave a total of 8.9 billion dollars to international aid. That same year, individual Americans spent 380 billion on tobacco products, 435 billion on alcohol, more than 300 billion on soft drinks, candy, chips, and other snack food, 2.6 trillion on eating out, and 2.7 trillion on entertainment. This means that individual Americans would have to contribute as much as they spent in 2009 on international relief for more than 720 years, before they would have spent as much as they spent in 2009 alone on tobacco, alcohol, snack food, entertainment, and eating out.[24]

7. Drawing on the preceding figures, I have noted that if Americans had cut their 2009 consumption of junk food, restaurant food, tobacco, and alcohol by 25 percent, and spent that money on international aid instead, this would have increased the amount that they spent in 2009 on international relief by more than 104 times, from 8.9 billion dollars to over 928 billion dollars. Moreover, I suggested, this would not only have been much better for the starving masses of the world, it would also have been much better for many people in the United States, as "presumably fewer Americans would die from stroke, heart disease, lung cancer, car accidents, and other factors related to our unhealthy eating, drinking, and smoking habits."[25] Thus, certain steps that might be taken to aid the needy might not only be good for those who are provided development assistance, it also might be good, at least on the whole, for those whose contributions make such assistance possible.

8. I have pointed out that the ability to help those less fortunate is not merely available to the rich or superrich; it is available to a large majority of ordinary citizens living in wealthy countries. Consider, for example, the situation of many typical undergraduates or graduates, many of whom think of themselves as "merely poor students." I note that if they are willing

---

[23] For the purposes of this book, I think of individuals living in so-called "developed" countries as being materially better off than those in so-called "developing" countries. Of course, I recognize that there exists vast income inequality within most so-called "developed" countries, including the United States. Accordingly, many in these countries will themselves fall into the category of the "world's needy." Likewise, many in so-called "developing" countries are very affluent. That said, for this book's purposes it is useful to maintain this general distinction.

[24] Most of the figures in this paragraph were gleaned from the 2012 U.S. Statistical Abstract, which was the most recent Abstract available the last time I lectured on this material, in 2015. I have updated these figures numerous times since 1981, and over the years there has been fairly little change in the relative amounts that individual Americans spend on such categories.

[25] "Thinking about the Needy, Justice, and International Organizations," p. 363.

to wait until just a few days after Christmas, or are careful to take advantage of pre-Christmas sales, they could buy the very same Christmas presents that they are going to buy anyway at a substantial savings. Similarly, many of those students buy a large daily coffee at a place like Starbucks. They might, instead, buy a medium-size coffee, or buy their coffee at the local convenience store, or make coffee at home and put the coffee in a thermos. Likewise, it is striking how many supposedly poor students nevertheless manage to buy designer jeans, purses, shirts, and shoes at retail stores, when the very same items can often be found at outlet stores 25–50 percent off—not to mention the possibility of wearing "no-name" brands at a fraction of the price that are similar in look, wear, and comfort, but that lack the distinctive "brand-name" logos. Many students go to the movies on Friday or Saturday nights. If, instead, they went to a matinee showing, they would see the very same movie at maybe 25 percent less. Countless students go out for food numerous times a week. They might, instead, go out one less time per week, or order water with their meal instead of soda, wine, or beer. Often students will get together for an evening of fun. If, as a general rule, people brought three beers to a party, instead of a six pack, there would still be plenty of booze for people to get a good buzz on. And for those students who smoke a pack of cigarettes a day, think of how much they could save each year if they cut their tobacco consumption by 25–50 percent.

I could go on and on. But I take it the point here is plain enough. It is easy for people to say something like, "I'm just a poor student, what can I do to help the world's needy?" But the reality is that there are countless ways in which the overwhelming majority of people in affluent countries could make small changes in their consumption patterns. Over the course of a year, the total amount of money saved from making a series of such changes could add up to a fairly substantial amount, which could then be sent to an effective international development organization. In this manner, one could, either alone or in conjunction with the efforts of others, have a very real impact on the quality of life of some of the world's neediest members.

Moreover, it is worth emphasizing that I have been suggesting changes in one's lifestyle and consumption patterns where, in a short time, one probably wouldn't even notice the difference in one's life—like if one ordered a smaller coffee each day, or started wearing "no-name" brands—or where there needn't even *be* a difference in the quality of one's experiences from owning or consuming a particular object of desire—like if one was careful to buy one's clothes, shoes, and accessories at outlet stores, or one's Christmas presents on sale[26]—or where there *would* be a difference in one's life, but where that change would almost certainly be *better* for one—like if one cut down on how much one smoked, drank alcohol, or dined out.

In sum, I believe that we should adopt a pluralistic approach to normative issues, and that on a pluralistic approach most of those who are in a position to do so—which includes most of those who are in a middle to upper income or wealth bracket in the West, as well as those who are similarly well-to-do in non-Western countries—should do much more than they do to aid the world's needy.[27] One "should do this for consequentialist reasons—to make the world better; for virtuous reasons—because that is the kind of person one should be; and for deontological reasons—because aiding the needy is not likely to be simply an option, but a duty, and one that may be every bit as strict as... [one's] duties to respect rights and act justly."[28,29]

---

[26] The word "needn't" in the preceding phrase is an important qualification. It tracks the fact that often in seeking to own something what we primarily want are the qualitative experiences which any token of that type of object can equally well provide due to its internal features. For example, we might want to own a particular bike, purse, or pair of shoes, because we like the bike's smooth ride, the purse's convenient features, or the shoes' comfort level. For such purposes, any two qualitatively indistinguishable objects will satisfy our preferences equally well. However, I am not denying that some objects have *relational* properties that *also* matter to us. The pleasure I receive from an object given to me by a loved one, acquired on a memorable trip, or purchased from a fancy store need not be solely a function of the object's internal qualitative features. Still, *often* what we want in acquiring an object *is* just a set of experiences that *any* numerically distinct object with qualitatively indistinguishable internal features could equally well provide. It is for *such* cases that I am claiming that there wouldn't even *be* a difference in the quality of one's experiences if one bought a given object on sale.

[27] By "us" here, I don't just mean wealthy individuals in wealthy countries. I maintain that there is a positive duty to help those in need for all of those in a relative position of privilege, including those who live in "developing" countries.

[28] "Thinking about the Needy, Justice, and International Organizations," p. 359.

[29] In correspondence, Tyler John suggests that a lot of deontologists would "get off the boat" when I claim that aiding the needy is a duty that may be every bit as strict as our duties to respect rights and act justly. He writes "if our duties of aid are equally as *strong* as our duties to respect rights, then it seems that we should be morally indifferent between (violate a serious right, donate to charity) and (fail to violate a serious right, fail to donate to charity). But that doesn't seem to be in the spirit of deontology." I think that John has misunderstood my position, and also that of most deontologists.

First, my claim that we have a duty to aid the needy doesn't imply anything at all about a duty to give to charity. Second, John's talking about violating a *serious* right introduces an element that was not part of my original claim, and importantly so. Part of my point is that not all rights, and not all rights violations are equally "serious." Indeed, even among rights violations of the same kind, some will be very serious, and some much less serious. And the same is true about any duties that we may have to aid the needy. So, for example, though both violate your right to private property—a very serious and important right for many deontologists—there is a big difference between someone's stealing a piece of your chocolate, and someone's emptying your bank account. Though both actions would be wrong, the latter would be much worse, even from a deontological perspective, than the former. Likewise, the duty to aid the needy can be very strong, as when I am the only person who can save a drowning child, or much weaker, as when I am one of many who could provide a poor family with some marginally better games.

It is sufficient for my claim to be true that *some* duties to aid, such as the duty to save the drowning child, may be every bit as strict as *some* duties to respect rights or act justly, such as the duty not to unjustly steal a piece of candy to which someone else has a right. Surely, most deontologists would accept this.

Reflecting on points 1–8, I once wrote the following:

The degree to which we are morally blameworthy for not aiding someone in need is partly a function of how dire the need is, and partly a function of how much it would cost us to do so—not only monetarily, but in terms of humanly valuable projects, relationships, responsibilities, and commitments. But surely, by such criteria, we are open to serious moral criticisms when we basically ignore—as most of us do—the tragic plight of innocent people suffering from easily preventable causes.... it is clear that each of us could do *vastly* more than we do to help the needy, without making a *dent* in our affluent lifestyle. And I, for one, have no doubt, that when the necessary arguments have been adduced, they will support what most of us, in our heart of hearts, already believe; namely, that the extent to which we neglect the needy is a serious moral failing.[30]

To a large degree, I stand by most of the preceding claims. However, as we will see, I now believe that matters are not as simple as my discussion of these issues has previously suggested. More particularly, I no longer believe that there is a straight line to be drawn from the truth of the claims I previously made, to how we should respond to the plight of the world's needy. Unfortunately, much more work needs to be done, both empirically and theoretically, to determine the true nature and extent of our obligations to the needy.

---

[30] "Thinking about the Needy, Justice, and International Organizations," p. 365. Again, "we" here refers to anyone who is affluent by global standards, and not just to wealthy people in the United States or the West.

3

Singer's Pond Example and Some Worries about Effective Altruism

In this chapter, I present Singer's original Pond Example, and I begin an examination of what follows from the example.[1] I note that our intuitive reaction to the example is compatible with various competing approaches to thinking about the needy, including both Effective Altruism and my own preferred pluralistic approach. I offer several variations of the Pond Example, together with other considerations, in support of my approach.

More specifically, in Section 3.1, I present Singer's original Pond Example, and offer two variations of it.

In Section 3.2, I present several lessons to be learned from the two variations of Singer's example. I suggest that my variations support a pluralistic approach to thinking about aid, and provide reason to worry about strict utilitarian versions of Effective Altruism. I also emphasize that we need to consider the impact of aid efforts on *everyone* impacted by those efforts, not merely the impact on the donors and recipients of aid. I point out that these lessons were already recognized and anticipated by Singer in his original article, though their importance has, I believe, been underappreciated.

In Section 3.3, I question whether Singer's Pond Example supports a non-utilitarian version of Effective Altruism. I suggest that while Singer's Pond Example is *compatible* with a non-utilitarian version of Effective Altruism, it doesn't *support* such a version. I offer one example where the "do the most good" approach of Effective Altruism seems particularly plausible. However, I also offer a new variation of the Pond Example that puts pressure on accepting any "do the most good" version of Effective Altruism, even a non-utilitarian one.

In Section 3.4, I argue that there are circumstances in which a virtuous person won't act so as to promote the most good, and won't even *entertain* the thought of looking for an alternative that might produce more good. This suggests that being virtuous, which is part of *being* good, can be at odds with

---

[1] Singer, Peter, "Famine, Affluence, and Morality." *Philosophy and Public Affairs* 1 (1972): 229–43.

Being Good in a World of Need. Larry S. Temkin, Oxford University Press. © Larry S. Temkin 2022.
DOI: 10.1093/oso/9780192849977.003.0003

the "do the most good" approach of Effective Altruism, even in a non-consequentialist form. On reflection, this should not be surprising. Unless one is a committed consequentialist, one recognizes that there is more to *being* good, than simply *doing* good. After all, an evil person can, on occasion, do good, but that isn't enough to make it the case that he or she is good.

In Section 3.5, I argue that just as there can be general agent-neutral duties to aid anyone in need, there can also be agent-relative duties to aid people with whom one is in direct contact, and that this can be so for strangers, as well as those with whom one has close, personal relations. Relatedly, I argue for the ethical significance of direct confrontation with another in need, as one is forced to immediately come to terms with the stark reality of another's fragility, mortality, and humanity (or perhaps sentience).

In Section 3.6, I note that dramatic rescues, and typical human responses to large-scale disasters reflect important human values and sentiments that are easily captured by the broad pluralistic approach to aiding those in need championed in this book. By contrast, such endeavors, which are often both noble and inspiring, will generally be at odds with the narrow "do the most good" approach of Effective Altruism.

In Section 3.7, I discuss the views of some Effective Altruists, regarding cases of "inefficient" personal involvement in aiding others, the *Earning to Give* approach of career choosing, and the appropriateness of "cutting corners" or mistreating others for the sake of aiding others. I argue that Effective Altruism's narrow focus on *doing* good, ignores the importance of *being* good.

In Section 3.8, I broach a topic I will return to later; namely, that many forms of aid reflect inegalitarian relations of power, money, status, and so on. This is, I believe, an issue that requires careful thought, in order to avoid both the Scylla of underestimating its importance, and the Charybdis of exaggerating its importance, both of which can be detrimental to the needy.

In Section 3.9, I argue that there is an important distinction to be made between events that lie *within* one's *personal* domain and events that lie *outside* of one's personal domain, some of which lie within a *political domain*. There are, I suggest, important factors relevant to how individuals must respond to events lying within their personal domains that are not relevant to how individuals must respond to events lying outside of their personal domains. I then point out that in Singer's original Pond Example the drowning child lies within the personal domain of the passerby. If that is right, I argue, then we can't generalize from our reactions to Singer's example to how someone must respond to the plight of a needy person outside of her personal domain.

Section 3.10 concludes by considering the upshot of this chapter's results for Singer's original Pond Example and Effective Altruism. I end by suggesting that while Effective Altruism's aim of maximizing expected welfare is *one* desirable goal to have in aiding the needy, achieving that goal is not *all* that matters. Many more factors are relevant to being good in a world of need.

This chapter addresses a lot of issues of importance, and I believe most readers will find the discussion illuminating. However, this chapter is deeply philosophical both in style and content, and it is likely to be of most interest to philosophers, and followers of Peter Singer or Effective Altruism. Accordingly, while non-experts are encouraged to read this chapter, they should feel free to skim or skip any sections where they find themselves bogging down or losing interest in the intricacies of the arguments.

3.1 Singer's Pond Example and Two Variations

In 1972, Peter Singer presented the following case in his now classic article "Famine, Affluence, and Morality":

> *The Pond Example*: if I am walking past a shallow pond and see a child drowning in it, I ought to wade in and pull the child out. This will mean getting my clothes muddy, but this is insignificant, while the death of the child would presumably be a very bad thing.[2]

It is, I believe, difficult to exaggerate the seismic impact on global consciousness that Singer's deceptively simple Pond Example has had. As noted in Section 1.3, "Famine, Affluence, and Morality" is one of the most influential Philosophy articles of the past fifty years and, for many, the Pond Example lies at the heart of that article. More particularly, in the forty-plus years since it was first introduced, countless people have been introduced to the Pond Example, or variations of it, and have concluded, largely on the basis of that example, that they ought to aid the world's needy.

Arguably, the roots of the Effective Altruism Movement can be traced to Singer's "Famine, Affluence, and Morality," and long after that original article was published the Pond Example continued to influence the thinking of

---

[2] "Famine, Affluence, and Morality," p. 231.

Effective Altruists, and to attract countless people to the Effective Altruism Movement.[3] But does the Pond Example actually support Effective Altruism? Does it, for example, support the view that if we are going to act on behalf of the needy, our main consideration should be to act so as to most efficiently address the most urgent and important needs so as to produce the most good? I think not. What the Pond Example seems to establish—but only "seems," as we will see later—is that if we can directly help another person in need at little significant cost to ourselves we should do so. But that position is compatible with a number of approaches regarding the nature, extent, and moral bases of our obligations to the needy, including the "do the most good" approach of Effective Altruism, but also including my own favored pluralistic approach.

Consider two variations of the Pond Example.

The Pond and Arm Example: I am walking by a deep pond, where a child is drowning. The child is just outside of my reach. As it happens, the only way for the child to be saved is if I cut off the arm of an innocent passerby and extend it to the drowning child. The passerby will be fine, but for the loss of his arm! What should I do?

The Pond and Bridge Example: On my way to a session of skeet shooting, I see a pond in the distance. There are five children drowning in the middle of it, and no one nearby to help. High above the pond is a railing-less bridge that a woman is crossing. I am an expert shot and can shoot very close to the woman's foot. This will startle the woman causing her to fall into the pond. She will break her neck and die from the fall, but her body will float, and the children will be able to safely hang onto her body until help arrives. What should I do?

---

[3] See, for example, "How to do the most good possible: The 'effective altruism' movement thinks it has some answers," The Economist Explains, *The Economist*, 2018, URL: https://www.economist.com/the-economist-explains/2018/06/07how-to-do-the-most-good-possible, accessed June 9, 2018. See also Derek Parfit's address to The Harvard Effective Altruism Group on April 21, 2015, available at https://www.youtube.com/watch?v=q6glXJ7dVU0, accessed June 8, 2019; Peter Singer's address at Rutgers University on December 2, 2010, where he helped launch the first U.S. chapter of the Effective Altruist organization *Giving What You Can*, available at https://www.youtube.com/watch?v=q6glXJ7dVU0, accessed June 8, 2019; and the opening paragraph of Chapter 1 of Peter Singer's Effective Altruism supporting book *The Life You Can Save* (New York: Random House, 2009). The Pond Example also appeared at the beginning of Chapter 1 of the first edition (though not the second) of *The Effective Altruism Handbook* (CreateSpace Independent Publishing Platform, 2015) edited by Ryan Carey with an introductory chapter by Peter Singer and Will MacAskill. The first edition's table of contents can be found at https://www.lesswrong.com/posts/WdWgQv9QXrF6uc9BB/the-effective-altruism-handbook, accessed June 8, 2019.

The Pond and Arm Example and the Pond and Bridge Example raise a host of questions from familiar debates regarding the relative moral importance of acts versus omissions, harming versus not helping, deontology versus utilitarianism, and so on. It is not my intent to rehash those debates here. Instead, I will simply note that whereas virtually everyone agrees that it would be immoral not to help the drowning child in Singer's original case, there would be much less agreement that it would be immoral not to help the drowning child, or children, in my two cases. Indeed, while some people, notably strict utilitarians, would claim that, other things equal, we *should* save the drowning child, or children, in my two cases, many people, and probably most, would insist that it would be immoral to help the child, or children, in my cases, in the ways described.

3.2 Support for Pluralism—Reasons to Worry about Strict Utilitarian Versions of Effective Altruism and Important Limits on the Pond Example's Implications

My cases suggest several lessons. First, those who are attracted to Effective Altruism, but who are not strict utilitarians, will need to find a foundation for Effective Altruism other than strict utilitarianism. So, while they may think that in aiding the needy there will always be good (utilitarian) reasons to want to do so in a way that promotes the most good, they will also need, and want, to recognize that the aim of producing the most good is likely to require balancing against competing moral considerations. Once one recognizes this, this opens the door for adopting my pluralistic approach for understanding the nature and extent of our obligations to the needy.

Second, we now see that the tempting initial conclusion to draw from Singer's original example—namely, that if we can directly help another person in need at little significant cost to ourselves, we should do so—was much too quick. In my examples, I have set up the cases in such a way that we *can* directly help another person in need, and, moreover, we can do so in a way that has little significant cost to ourselves—at least in self-interested terms. Still, in my examples, I may have to impose costs on others, violate the rights of others,[4] or act immorally, in order to effectively aid the needy, and that may

---

[4] Deaton gives an example to illustrate the case of development assistance indirectly contributing to the violation of people's rights. He notes that "in 2010, Robert Mugabe's Zimbabwe received ODA [Overseas Development Assistance] worth more than 10% of its national income, or nearly $60 per person." Deaton suggests that such assistance helped to enrich Mugabe and/or keep him in power, even

make it impermissible for me to do so even if the outcome in which one life is saved but an arm is lost would be better than the outcome in which the life is lost but the arm is preserved, and even if the outcome in which one life is lost but five lives are saved would be better than the outcome in which five lives are lost but one life is preserved.

Importantly, Singer anticipates these kinds of worries in "Famine, Affluence, and Morality," where he presents two possible action-guiding principles bearing on our obligations towards the needy, a strong principle and a weak one. The strong principle is:

Preventing Bad without Comparable Moral Loss: if it is in our power to prevent something very bad from happening, without thereby sacrificing anything of comparable moral importance, we ought, morally, to do it.[5]

The weak principle is:

Preventing Bad without Moral Loss: if it is in our power to prevent something very bad from happening, without thereby sacrificing anything morally significant, we ought, morally, to do it.[6]

Now, in fact, Singer holds the stronger principle himself. However, he claims that the weaker principle—which his Pond Example is offered as an application of—is sufficient to support the judgment that people who are reasonably well-off ought to aid those who are dying from famine or easily preventable diseases.[7]

Clearly, Singer's weaker principle, Preventing Bad without Moral Loss, provides ample room to accommodate most people's intuitions about my two Pond cases, since in such cases saving the life or lives *would* require sacrificing something morally significant. By contrast, in Singer's original Pond case, there is just me and the child in the pond, and there is no issue about my imposing costs on another, violating anyone's rights, or in any other

---

as he ran a repressive government that was frequently accused of violating people's rights. See Deaton's *The Great Escape: Health, Wealth, and the Origins of Inequality* (Princeton: Princeton University Press, 2013), p. 279. Mugabe has been a frequent target of *Human Rights Watch* for running a government fraught with rights abuses and repression. See, for example, "Zimbabwe: One Year On, Reform a Failure." *Human Rights Watch*, February 12, 2010, URL: https://www.hrw.org/news/2010/02/12/zimbabwe-one-year-reform-failure, accessed August 27, 2019.

[5] "Famine, Affluence, and Morality," p. 231.   [6] "Famine, Affluence, and Morality," p. 231.

[7] "Famine, Affluence, and Morality," pp. 234–5.

way acting wrongly, if I freely choose to make the small sacrifice of getting some of my clothes dirty to save the child's life.

So, the actual principle Singer uses the Pond Example to illustrate can handle our intuitions about my two cases. Moreover, Preventing Bad without Moral Loss is a principle that I, and I believe most other people, find deeply compelling. Indeed, it is hard to see how anyone who is not a total moral skeptic could reject such a principle. However, as will become clear later, I believe that Prevent Bad without Moral Loss is a much weaker principle than most people have thought, and that it cannot bear the weight that many people have implicitly put on it, when they have appealed to variations of the Pond Example in support of a host of concrete prescriptions as to what people ought to do if they want to aid the needy.

What about Singer's stronger principle, Preventing Bad without Comparable Moral Loss? Would that principle capture most people's intuitions about my two cases? That depends, of course, on what counts as a "comparable" moral loss. Singer glosses that notion as follows: "By 'without sacrificing anything of comparable moral importance' I mean without causing anything else comparably bad to happen, or doing something that is wrong in itself, or failing to promote some moral good, comparable in significance to some bad thing that we can prevent."[8] Thus, if, as many believe, cutting off someone's arm would be wrong, even for the sake of saving another person's life, and if, as many also believe, startling someone and causing them to break their neck and die would be wrong, even for the sake of saving five other people's lives, then even Singer's stronger principle would have the resources to capture most people's intuitions about my two Pond cases.[9]

Notice, as Singer has glossed the notion, what counts as a "comparable" moral loss will vary depending on one's substantive moral views about what makes actions right or wrong. So, for example, advocates of the *Doctrine of*

---

[8] "Famine, Affluence, and Morality," p. 231.

[9] In correspondence, Ingmar Persson notes that Singer might have done better to advocate for a more moderate principle that was stronger than Preventing Bad without Moral Loss, but weaker than Preventing Bad without Comparable Moral Loss. For example, Singer might have advocated for *Preventing Bad without Much Moral Loss*: if it is in our power to prevent something very bad from happening, without thereby sacrificing anything of much moral significance, we ought, morally, to do it. I agree that such a principle could capture our intuitions about Singer's original Pond Example, as well as our intuitions about my two cases. In addition, it could, in theory, avoid both the main objection to Preventing Bad without Moral Loss—namely, that it is too weak to be of much use—and the main objection to Preventing Bad without Comparable Moral Loss—namely, that it is too strong to be plausible. Of course, all the hard work would then revolve around fleshing out what constitutes "much" moral loss. The lower the bar is set for a loss to count as "much" moral loss, the less controversial it will be, but the more it will face objections akin to those faced by Preventing Bad without Moral Loss; while the higher the bar is set before a loss counts as "much" moral loss, the more controversial it will be, and the more it will face objections akin to those faced by Preventing Bad without Comparable Moral Loss.

Double Effect, distinguish between *intending* some harm for the sake of a greater good—which they think is wrong—and doing some good that results in a lesser harm that is foreseeable, but unintended—which may be permissible. Accordingly, such people might believe that it is wrong to kill someone, intending her death in order to save five others, but permissible to provide aid that saves five people, but foreseeably leads to the unintended death of a sixth person in a hospital as a consequence of corruption fostered by one's aid.[10] So, for the deontologist, unlike the consequentialist, whether the death of one person would be of "comparable moral significance" to saving five lives could, perhaps, depend on *who* produced the death, *how* it was produced, and the *intentions* of the agent in performing the act that led to the outcomes in question.

We see, then, that Singer's Pond Example was never intended to support a simple utilitarian version of Effective Altruism that would have all efforts towards aiding the needy be guided by the simple principle of doing the most good. Instead, the Pond Example was merely offered in support of the view that we should prevent bad whenever that would involve no sacrifice of moral significance; though, in fact, Singer holds the stronger view that we should prevent bad whenever that would involve no sacrifice of comparable moral significance.

3.3 Implications of Pond Examples for Non-Utilitarian Versions of Effective Altruism

Does the Pond Example support a non-utilitarian version of Effective Altruism? On the basis of the Pond Example, can we safely conclude that efforts to aid the needy should be guided by the principle of doing the most good, except in cases where doing so would involve our acting wrongly, (directly) harming someone, violating someone's rights, etc.? This is, to my mind, a much more plausible version of Effective Altruism. But even so, it is hard to see how the Pond Example supports such a view—though it is compatible with it. More importantly, depending on how broadly or narrowly one construes the various qualifications or restrictions on doing the most good, it seems that either the position is still problematic in certain important respects, or that it has strayed pretty far from the spirit of the "do

---

[10] I am grateful to Nick Beckstead for this observation which, as he rightly notes, may have a bearing on some people's intuitive reactions to concerns about corruption that I discuss later.

the most good" Effective Altruism Movement. To see this, let us consider several more examples.

Good PR Charity versus Poor PR Charity: For some time, Nick has been thinking that he should be doing more on behalf of others than he does. He is not especially rich, at least not by U.S. standards, but he has a comfortable, U.S. middle-class lifestyle. His only real luxury item is a valuable Rolex watch, worth $5,000 on the resale market, which was bequeathed to him by a favorite uncle. Nick enjoys owning the watch, but he realizes that he could make do perfectly well with a twenty-dollar watch, and he resolves to donate the watch to charity. As it happens, two brochures have recently arrived at his home from different relief charities.

One, from Good PR Charity, is a shiny brochure, addressed directly to Nick, by name, with a glossy picture of a small black toddler from Somalia. The toddler is a girl, with a sad face, a distended belly, and a plethora of flies crawling in and around her ears, eyes, and nose.[11] The brochure gives the child's name, Aamuun, and describes in heart-wrenching detail the child's life story, including how she came to be an orphan as a result of the Somalian Civil War, and that she is now dying from a combination of dysentery and starvation. The brochure claims that if Nick contributes $5,000 in the next two weeks to Good PR Charity, the money will be used to save Aamuun's life; while if Nick fails to contribute, Aamuun will die.

The second brochure, from Bad PR Charity, is rather plain, and it comes addressed to "occupant." There are no pictures, no names, no sad details about anyone's history or current predicament. There is just a matter of fact claim that there are many around the world in urgent need of assistance, and the assurance that if one contributes $5,000 to Bad PR Charity, that money will be used wisely to save the lives of three desperately ill children.

Nick is moved by the plight of Aamuun, and he would like to help her. However, he has read Peter Singer and Peter Unger, and he worries that perhaps he is just being manipulated by Good PR Charity's effective

---

[11] Such ads, which are common on late-night television as well as the print media, are often referred to as *poverty porn*. Many critique such ads, rightly in my judgment, for insensitively presenting the needy in demeaning and disempowering ways. Arguably, a similar critique might apply to my use of such an ad in my example. It is, of course, not my intent to portray the needy in demeaning or disempowering ways, but merely to accurately convey the visceral appeals that certain aid agencies make in seeking funds, and the real-world choices that people must make in deciding whom to aid. Still, I apologize if my example contributes in any way to negative stereotypes that some well-off people have about some of the world's least fortunate members. I am grateful to Tyler John, whose gentle prodding about my example led me to include this note.

advertising, which has succeeded in making Aamuun's plight especially salient to him.[12] He reasons that the three desperately ill children that would be saved by Bad PR Charity would be just as needy and deserving as Aamuun, even if he doesn't know their names and hasn't seen their pictures. After researching both companies carefully, and determining that they are legitimate and would, in fact, deliver on their promises, he sells his Rolex for $5,000, and sends the money to Bad PR Charity. Having done so, Nick takes great satisfaction in knowing that he has saved three innocent, desperately ill children.

Sudden Epiphany: Mark is not rich, at least by U.S. standards, but he leads a comfortable U.S. middle-class life. He has not trained in moral philosophy, has never heard of utilitarianism, or Effective Altruism, and has never considered, or argued with friends or neighbors about, how best to aid the needy so as to do the most good. For the most part, his charitable contributions have involved modestly giving to his alma mater, his religious institution, his PTA, occasionally dropping some money into the buckets of charities at his local grocery store, and supporting the fundraising efforts of his children, neighbors, and friends.

Mark's only real luxury item is a non-waterproof Rolex watch given to him by a favorite uncle. Because of the value of the watch, it has an elaborate set of safety clasps that require two hands to do and undo. So, on those days when Mark decides to wear his watch, he needs his significant other to put it on his wrist in the morning, and to take it off his wrist at night.

One day, as Mark is walking to work, wearing his Rolex, he passes by a pond where there is a small child drowning. No one else is around to intervene, and the only way for Mark, who is an excellent swimmer, to help the child is for him to dive into the water and save him. Mark's first thought is that he must dive into the water and save the child. Mark's second thought is that if he does so, his Rolex will certainly be ruined, but that he won't be able to take it off and still save the child. Mark's third thought is that as much as he loves owning, and wearing, his favorite uncle's watch, that is of no significance in comparison with the life of a child. So, Mark decides to dive in and save the child.

Just as Mark is about to do so, he has a sudden epiphany. He realizes that he could sell his Rolex for $5,000, and that there are effective charities, such as Bad PR Charity, which could use $5,000 to save three children who are no

---

[12] For an insightful and provocative discussion of the role that salience plays in explaining common intuitions about when one is required to aid someone in need, see Peter Unger's *Living High & Letting Die: Our Illusion of Innocence* (New York: Oxford University Press, 1996).

less deserving than the drowning child. Telling himself that the drowning child's flailing arms, desperate cries for help, and gasps for air are simply making his imminent death more salient than the deaths of the three children who might be saved by Bad PR Charity, Mark resolves to preserve and sell his Rolex, and to give the proceeds to Bad PR Charity.

Mark figures that there is no point in his just standing by the pond and watching the child drown, so he calls 911, reports the location of the drowning child, and then continues on to work. Mark is fully aware, as he does this, that by the time the emergency personnel arrive, all they will be able to do is recover the body and contact the family of the dead child.

Later that week, Mark sells his Rolex for $5,000 and he donates the money to Bad PR Charity. Sometime later, three innocent, desperately ill children on the other side of the world are saved by Bad PR Charity, because of Mark's actions.

What should we say about these examples? First, I will indicate how I respond to them. Then, in the next two sections, I will say more in defense of my response, and consider some of the broader implications of my view.

Regarding Good PR Charity versus Bad PR Charity, I believe that Nick would be right to respond the way he does. This is the sort of case where Effective Altruism's basic intuition seems most compelling. Nick wants to aid the needy. In doing this, it seems that he ought to support the charity that will do the most good. In particular, it seems that he is right to give to Poor PR Charity rather than Good PR Charity, and right to ignore the special salience that Good PR Charity's glossy brochure gives to Aamuun's tragic predicament. Notice, however, that in this case, the main factor that seems to have a morally relevant bearing on what Nick ought to do is the consequentialist question of which charitable action would, in fact, do the most good. I suggest, then, that this is the sort of case where the standard "do the most good" approach of Effective Altruism seems most plausible.

Regarding Sudden Epiphany I feel rather differently. I recognize that due to his acting the way he did, Mark will have in fact brought about the best outcome.[13] Just as in the preceding case, involving Nick, Mark will have

---

[13] Jake Nebel questions this, suggesting that the best option would be for Mark to save the child, and then donate $5,000 to the charity that will save three lives anyway, using sources of funding available to him other than selling off his Rolex watch. Now, in fact, in my example, I was presupposing that this "have your cake and eat it too" response was not an available option for Mark. But note, even if Mark did have access to other funds that he could send to the effective charity, this would not fundamentally alter his predicament. After all, in the real world, there are lots of children whom the effective charity could benefit. Accordingly, Mark would *still* face the choice of saving the drowning child and some

saved three lives, rather than merely one, by acting the way he did. Nevertheless, I feel that there must be something "wrong" with Mark for him to be able to act the way that he did.[14] Moreover, I'm inclined to say that not only is there something "wrong" with *him*, but that, all things considered, he probably *acted wrongly* by turning his back on the drowning child and doing what he did, even though his ultimate motive for doing so was the laudable one of wanting to do the most good that he could by saving three lives instead of just one.[15]

3.4 Being Virtuous and Avoiding One Thought Too Many

There are many factors influencing my judgment about Sudden Epiphany. I discuss several of them in this section, and others in the following one. First,

---

number, k, of other children by using his "extra" available funds, or letting the child drown and saving k + 3 other children, by using *both* his "extra" available funds *and* the proceeds from selling the undamaged Rolex.

[14] It is arguable that Maggie Black holds a similar view. See, for example, her book *International Development: Illusions and Realities* (Oxford: New Internationalist Publications, 2015). Black favors the direct attempt to benefit people by reducing poverty, over indirect approaches such as nation-building or debt relief, contending that the former is far superior to the latter "in people terms" and that there is "no other way to save people than one by one" (*International Development*, p. 45).

[15] Ingmar Persson agrees that there would be something wrong with Mark, if he didn't feel strong compassion for the drowning child that he had to steel himself against in order to do the most good. However, he also believes that a morally good person *should* be able to distance themselves from such spontaneous emotions, and realize that they can be outweighed, as they are, Persson thinks, in this case. A slightly weaker version of Persson's position would hold that while *some* morally good people will be able to overcome the strong compassion that they should feel for the drowning child, in order to save three children rather than one, not *all* morally good people will be able, psychologically, to do so. Presumably, however, on this version of Persson's view, the morally good person will recognize their inability to overcome their compassion as a form of *akrasia*, which is to be regretted, rather than lauded. Another possibility would hold that a good person might, without moral regret, act on their compassion and save the drowning child, but they might, also without moral regret, steel themselves to resist their compassion for the drowning child in order to save three others. On this view, compassion for the drowning child should strongly motivate a morally good person to save that child, but a morally good person could reasonably allow herself either to act in accordance with that motivation, or to overcome it for the sake of the greater good.

Note, the range of views suggested here mirrors a similar range of views regarding how one should act when deontological and consequentialist considerations conflict. In such cases, on some views, one acts rightly only by following the dictates of deontology; on others, one acts rightly only by following the dictates of consequentialism; and on still others, while it may be permissible to do what deontology requires, it is never impermissible to do what consequentialism prescribes. Kant held a view of the first kind (*Groundwork of the Metaphysics of Morals*, edited by Mary J. Gregor, Cambridge: Cambridge University Press, 1998); Mill held a view of the second kind (*Utilitarianism*, Indianapolis: Hackett Publishing Company, 1979), and Sam Scheffler and Derek Parfit have held views of the third kind (Scheffler, *The Rejection of Consequentialism*, Oxford: Clarendon Press, 1982; Parfit, *Reasons and Persons*, Oxford: Clarendon Press, 1984; and Parfit, *On What Matters*, Vols. 1 and 2, Oxford: Oxford University Press, 2011). On my version of pluralism, in some cases where deontology and consequentialism conflict one must follow the dictates of deontology, in others one must follow the dictates of consequentialism, and in still others it is permissible to follow either.

to borrow a famous expression from Bernard Williams, I think that Mark had "one thought too many" in his deliberations about what to do.[16] In my judgment, Mark's initial thought was the correct one—that he "*must* dive in and save the child." I don't fault Mark for having his second thought. It would be natural enough for him to think, as he was about to dive in, that doing so would ruin his Rolex. But then he should immediately think, as he did, that ruining his Rolex is of no significance in comparison with the child's life and, in my judgment, that thought should have been his final thought on the matter. That is, if Mark were a decent human being, his deliberations should have come to a halt at that point, there should have been no further thinking that led to his epiphany, and he should have simply dived in and saved the child. Or so I believe, anyway.

My view about Mark is related to my view about virtues, and the importance of being virtuous. Aristotle famously claimed that virtue is a disposition acquired by habit.[17] This meant that one becomes virtuous by repeatedly acting virtuously—that is, by doing what a virtuous person would do, over and over again. Eventually, one acquires the habit of acting virtuously, meaning that one will be "automatically" disposed to do the virtuous thing whenever an appropriate occasion for exercising the virtue presents itself. Moreover, and importantly, psychological dispositions are not the sort of attributes that can be turned on and off like a spigot, nor are they easily fine-tuned.[18] So, for example, if one has truly acquired the virtue of honesty—that is, the psychological disposition of being honest—and one is asked a question, one doesn't pause to consider the pros and cons of answering honestly, one simply answers honestly. Similarly, if one has acquired the virtues of loyalty or faithfulness, one won't even consider engaging in a dalliance with someone other than one's partner, even if an opportunity arises to which others, who lack the virtues in question, would readily succumb. And so on.

Of course, I do not intend to suggest that a virtuous person has literally lost her autonomy, or her capacity for rational reflection. Hence, there may be circumstances where compelling reasons not to act virtuously are so evident,

---

[16] See Bernard Williams's "Persons, Character, and Morality," in *Moral Luck: Philosophical Papers 1973–1980* (Cambridge: Cambridge University Press, 1981, p. 18).

[17] See Book Two, Chapter One, of the *Nicomachean Ethics* (in *The Basic Works of Aristotle*, edited by Richard McKeon, New York: Random House, 1941).

[18] This point is emphasized by Robert Adams, in his excellent article "Motive Utilitarianism," *Journal of Philosophy* 73 (1976): 467–81, and by Derek Parfit, in Part One of *Reasons and Persons*.

that a virtuous person who is also rational won't be able to help attending to them, and may even determine that, on that occasion, she ought, all things considered, not to "automatically" do what she is normally disposed to virtuously do. However, I do believe that a person of great virtue will not even entertain certain thoughts to which a less virtuous person might readily consider and respond.

Now I believe that among the moral virtues are the virtues of sympathy, caring, kindness, compassion, and generosity, and that all those virtues would be powerfully "activated" in the presence of a child who was drowning right before one's eyes. Together, such virtues are capable of giving rise to power-fully motivating emotions and reactive attitudes that would, and should, conspire to lead Mark to immediately respond to the child's plight in the circumstances described. This is why I claimed that Mark had "one thought too many," and that there must be something wrong with Mark, to deliberate and act as he did. For Mark to have responded as he did, at least if he were a typical human being, he would have had to lack the virtues of sympathy, caring, kindness, compassion, and generosity.[19]

The preceding view is controversial along numerous dimensions. Unfortunately, a complete rejoinder to each possible objection would require another book, and carry me far afield from this book's central claims. In lieu of that, let me simply note a few of the main objections, and gesture towards how I would respond to them, without attempting to fully develop and defend my responses.[20] Readers who share my view regarding Mark, can skip the remainder of this section, and go directly to Section 3.5.

---

[19] Note, one might argue, in defense of Mark, that he was being responsive to the virtues in question, but with respect to the three people that he was hoping to save by acting as he did. But there are several responses to this, which I shall note, but not try to defend here. First, as indicated, I don't think that, at the moment when Mark was confronted by the drowning child, he should have even paused to think about what else he might do, that would eventually lead to three people being saved instead of just one. Second, I don't believe that the moral virtues that human beings generally teach and learn license Mark to do what he did. Third, I am not convinced that someone like Mark would actually be more virtuous, or a more decent human being, than someone who saved the drowning child. Finally, fourth, even if we could teach and learn a set of virtues that supported Mark's actions, I am not convinced that, on the whole, doing so would actually promote the best overall outcome, for reasons of the sort that Williams presented in his famous defense of the claim that utilitarianism would "usher itself from the scene." (See Williams, Bernard, "A Critique of Utilitarianism," in *Utilitarianism For and Against*, by J.J.C. Smart and Bernard Williams, Cambridge: Cambridge University Press, 1973.)

[20] Together, the following worries were raised by Jamie Dreier, Peter Singer, Tyler John, Nick Beckstead, Tim Campbell, and Ingmar Persson. I am grateful to them for pushing me to say a bit more about my "one thought too many" view, even if what I present must, perforce, be only a partial response to their important challenges.

I begin with a clarificatory remark. Many philosophers have objections to the specific way in which Williams employs his "one thought too many" claim. Although I am quite sympathetic to Williams's view, it is not my intention to defend *his* position here. It is enough if I can make *my* use of the "one thought too many" position plausible. With that in mind, I turn next to some key objections to my position, and the gist of my responses to those objections.

Some people object that we are not responsible for the thoughts that pop into our heads, so we shouldn't really blame Mark if, just as he is about to jump into the water, it pops into his head that he could do more good by letting the child drown. This view may seem analogous to recognizing the important political right of freedom of thought, which holds that people have the right to think whatever they want, and that the state is only permitted to punish people for their actions, not for their thoughts.

Although I think the first claim is open to some subtle, but important pushback, I readily grant that, overall, there is much to be said for these views. However, I believe they are largely orthogonal to my claims. The relevant question for my purposes is not whether someone should be blamed or punished for their thoughts, but whether their thoughts may reveal something about their character. And I think that often we can appropriately judge someone's character, and criticize or think less of them, on the basis of the type of thoughts that arise in them in certain contexts. Of course, in saying this, we must be keenly attuned to the fact that such judgments are fallible, and careful about how such judgments influence our actions.

So, for example, if, when one sees a three-year-old, it pops into one's head how much fun it would be to have sex with the child, that says something about one, even if one never acts on that thought; similarly, if, when one sees a young animal, one wonders what it would be like to slowly tear the skin off of it; similarly, if, when one sees a frail person, one thinks how easy it would be to overpower them and take their money; and so on. To repeat, I am not making any claim here about whether we should blame someone who has such thoughts. Perhaps they cannot help themselves—perhaps such thoughts just "pop" into their heads like unwelcome intruders. Nor am I making any claim about whether we should punish someone who has such thoughts if they never act on them. Still, I think it is not inappropriate to suspect that there is something "wrong" with someone who has such thoughts. In general, if not invariably, such thoughts do not just pop into the heads of decent people. Rather, for the overwhelming majority of decent people, on the overwhelming majority of occasions, such thoughts would never arise.

Of course, I am not claiming that the content of the thought "I should save three innocent children rather than one" is akin to the contents of the thoughts "Wouldn't it be nice to have sex with a three-year-old, or to flay a young animal alive, or to steal from a frail person" in terms of their moral valence. Under most circumstances, the content of the former thought is perfectly respectable, while the contents of the latter thoughts are heinous. But my question concerns the conditions under which such thoughts would arise. My claim is that there are almost no circumstances in which the latter thoughts will arise in decent people, and that while there are many circumstances in which the former thought would arise in decent people—Good PR Charity versus Poor PR Charity being one such circumstance—Sudden Epiphany is not one of them.

Some people might claim that it couldn't ever reflect poorly on one's character for a thought to pop into one's head, as long as the content of the thought focused on whether one would be promoting the most good by acting in a certain way. This claim has an initial ring of plausibility and will strike some moral philosophers as uncontroversial. However, on reflection, I think this claim is much less plausible than it may seem and is quite likely false.

Suppose my mother or daughter is drowning in a pond, and before jumping in to save her the thought pops into my mind that perhaps I could do more good if I didn't save her. Even if that thought were true, I think its coming to mind before I saved my loved one *would* reflect poorly on me. As I put it previously, I think that there would typically (I'll not claim invariably) have to be something "wrong" with anyone who had such a thought at the crucial moment where the life of a loved one was at stake, and where there was no other overwhelming reason immediately at hand *not* to do the "obviously right" thing of jumping in and saving her. (It might be different, of course, if one's mom were drowning on the left side of the boat, and two of one's children were drowning on the right side of the boat, and one could only save the people on one side of the boat; or if one's mom were drowning on one side of the boat, and the only person who could stop a nuclear explosion from killing millions were drowning on the other.)

However legitimate and worthwhile it might be to question even the most "obvious" assumptions and "fundamental" truths in the comfort and safety of the philosopher's room, there is a proper time, and place, for everything. In the real world, I submit, watching your loved one go under the surface of the water is *not* the time and place to wonder whether saving them would promote the most good!

Again, the question here is not whether one should somehow be held responsible, blamed, or punished if, at that crucial moment, such a thought did suddenly pop, unbidden, into one's head. The question, rather, is whether there would typically (again, I'm not claiming invariably) be something "wrong" with someone who found themselves thinking such a thought as their loved one was drowning. I think there would be.

Analogously, I don't think the content of the thoughts: "I wonder if I would promote the most good by having sex with a three-year-old, or flaying a young animal alive, or taking money from a frail person" would be enough to assuage our worry about anyone who had such thoughts pop into their head when they spotted a three-year-old, a young animal, or a frail person. This is because, in the real world, there *is* typically (though not necessarily) something "wrong" with people who have such thoughts, whether or not they are responsible for such thoughts, and whether or not they act on them.

Some philosophers are upset with my claim because it strikes a little too close to home. They think that if they found themselves in Mark's predicament, they might well have the thought that they could do more good by letting the child drown, and donating the proceeds from selling their Rolex to an effective aid charity. And they don't believe that this shows that they are not decent.

Here, it is important to recall the details of my example. I don't deny that someone who has been trained in moral philosophy, or who has thought extensively about how to promote the best outcome, or who, after much reflection, has come to the view that utilitarianism is the correct moral view, or that they should be Effective Altruists, might, if they found themselves in Mark's circumstances, have the thought pop into their head that perhaps they should let the child drown, in order to be able to save three other innocent children. For such people, I will grant that the "one thought too many" charge is less plausible, and I'd be less inclined to think that the mere having of such a thought was good reason to think them not decent.

However, in my example, I stipulated that Mark wasn't trained in philosophy, hadn't heard of utilitarianism or Effective Altruism, and hadn't previously considered how best to aid the needy so as to do the most good. For Mark, and the countless people like him, I think the "one thought too many charge" *is* plausible, and that there would typically (though not invariably) have to be something "wrong" with him for such a thought to pop into his mind at such a critical life and death moment.

I add that while I am willing to grant that for a relatively small, and special, subset of people, the mere having of the thought in question wouldn't lead me to question their decency, I *would* still think that they had a questionable character if they were able to act on such a thought in such circumstances. This is because, as noted already, I think that they would have to be substantially lacking in terms of the virtues of sympathy, caring, kindness, compassion, and generosity to be able to walk away from a drowning child, even if their motive for doing so was to do the most good.[21]

Finally, in defense of Mark, it might be argued that he *was* being responsive to the virtues of sympathy, caring, kindness, compassion, and generosity in acting as he did. On this view, those virtues would prompt him to save the drowning child, but they would also prompt him to save three other innocent children. So, on balance, the virtues would tell in favor of leaving the child to drown, and donating the proceeds from the sale of his preserved Rolex to Bad PR Charity.

This position might be plausible if Mark confronted a drowning child in one part of the pond, and three other drowning children in another part of the pond, or in a nearby pond. It is also arguable that it might be plausible if Mark were confronted with the drowning child in front of him, and a live computer feed of the desperate condition of the three children he could save only if he let the one child drown. However, I don't find the position plausible with respect to Sudden Epiphany as I presented it.

Let me simply note four responses to this position, without further elaboration or defense. First, as already indicated, in the case as I presented it, I don't think that, at the moment when Mark was confronted by the drowning child, he should have even paused to think about what else he might do to save even more lives than that of the one child who desperately needed his help right then and there. Second, I don't believe that the moral virtues that human beings actually teach and learn would license Mark to do what he did, even after the possibility had occurred to him that he could save three other children by letting the one child drown. Third, I am not convinced that

---

[21] In correspondence, Nick Beckstead observes that were he in Mark's position he probably *would* think that perhaps he should let the child drown, to save three others. But he also admits, grudgingly, that he probably would not do it. This remark is both honest and revealing. Nick is one of the most committed Effective Altruists I know. He is also a person of great moral character. For Nick, his longstanding commitment to Effective Altruism might well lead him to have the thought in question. However, his moral character would almost certainly prevent him from acting on that thought. Being the good person that he is, Nick almost certainly would not be able to bring himself to leave the child to drown, even for the sake of the greater good that he could thereby promote.

No doubt some utilitarians and Effective Altruists would criticize Nick. They would regard his character as flawed, and find fault with his inability to use reason to rein in his virtue-related emotions when they overstep their bounds. They might even offer an evolutionary explanation for why it is so difficult for Nick, and others, to do what they ought to do in such cases.

I understand such claims and admire many of those who make them. However, I believe they are deeply mistaken. In my judgment, Nick's character is *not* flawed; his virtue-related emotions would *not* be overstepping their bounds (which is not to say that such cases do not ever arise); and Nick would be doing precisely what he *ought* to in saving the drowning child.

someone like Mark would actually be more virtuous, or a more decent human being, than someone who saved the drowning child. In fact, I'm pretty convinced the reverse is true. Finally, fourth, even if we could teach and learn a set of virtues that supported Mark's actions, I am not convinced that, on the whole, doing so would promote the best overall outcome, for reasons of the sort that Williams famously presented in defense of his claim that utilitarianism would "usher itself from the scene."[22]

Sudden Epiphany prompts several other responses besides the one that I have been focusing on to this point. Setting aside any further objections and responses to my "one thought too many" claim, let us turn to those next.

3.5 Agent-Relative Duties to Aid and the Ethical Significance of Direct Confrontation with Another in Need

It is common to think of obligations to the needy as part of a general *agent-neutral* duty of beneficence.[23*] On reflection, however, I believe that circumstances can give rise to particular *agent-relative* duties of beneficence between two strangers.[24*] Prior to seeing the child in the pond, Mark has a general duty to aid the needy, as does any person. However, I believe that when Mark finds himself face-to-face with a drowning child, as he does in Sudden Epiphany, where he is the only person who can save that child, and can do so at no significant cost to himself, a new, agent-relative, duty arises that provides a strong *pro tanto reason* for Mark to save the child.[25*] Moreover, I believe that that duty can take precedence over Mark's general duty to aid the needy, in the same way that Mark's other agent-relative duties can take precedence over his

---

[22] Williams's "A Critique of Utilitarianism," especially Part Six, pp. 118–35.

[23*] *Agent-neutral* duties are duties that everyone has to act in certain ways. So, for example, we all have an agent-neutral duty to respect other people's rights. This does not mean that such duties are *absolute*. In some cases, perhaps, the duty to respect another person's rights could be outweighed by competing duties or other moral considerations. Agent-neutral duties can vary in strength, depending on the nature of the duty in question.

[24*] *Agent-relative* duties are duties that one person has to another, in virtue of a particular relation that holds between them. For example, a teacher has agent-relative duties to his or her students, that others do not have, and a parent has agent-relative duties to his or her children that others do not have. Like agent-neutral duties, agent-relative duties need not be absolute, and they can vary in strength depending on the nature of the duty in question.

[25*] A *pro tanto* reason is a reason with some independent weight, or force, that counts in favor of acting in a certain way or wanting something to be the case. A pro tanto reason might be an agent-neutral reason, or an agent-relative reason; it might vary in strength depending on the nature of the reason; and it need not be absolute. Pro tanto reasons may or may not provide *decisive* reason to act in a certain way, or to want something to be the case, depending on what other reasons, if any, are relevant to one's choice situation.

general duty to aid the needy.[26] So, for example, it is not only the case that Mark's agent-relative duty to take care of his children would require him to save his daughter, rather than to save the lives of three strangers, it is also the case that Mark's agent-relative duty to someone whose car he borrowed would require him to return the car rather than to save the lives of three strangers by selling it and donating the proceeds to an effective charity. This is part of the reason why I claimed that in Sudden Epiphany there would not only be something "wrong" with *Mark* but also be something wrong with what Mark *did*.

Next, let me say a bit more about the relevance, if any, of the "face-to-face" nature of the situation in which Mark finds himself. First, it is not literally important that Mark be face-to-face with the drowning child, for him to have an agent-relative duty to save him. Presumably, Mark would have the same duty, and it would be equally strong, if, while the child was drowning, it was facing away from Mark. Second, I agree with Peter Singer, and most moral philosophers, in thinking that mere difference in spatial location is not, itself, morally significant.[27] Thus, someone who lives on the other side of the world is no less valuable, morally, than someone who lives close to me.

Nevertheless, there are philosophers who have claimed that the quintessential ethical moment arises when two human beings directly confront each other, and each recognizes that the "other" is, in fundamentally important respects, a "subject" just like oneself.[28] On this view, this ethical moment, involving mutual recognition between two subjects of consciousness, serves as the basis for the moral enterprise, which requires us to recognize and respect the interests and rights of others who are, in important relevant respects, just like us. Now, I don't want to exaggerate the role that such personal interactions play in grounding the nature and scope of morality, but I do believe that there

---

[26] Some development economists, from across the political spectrum, believe that governments should focus on alleviating poverty in their own countries, before addressing poverty in other countries. Although the precise reasons for this vary, the thinking underlying such views often parallels my position here. In particular, many believe that governments have special obligations to their own citizens that warrant giving them greater priority over non-citizens in terms of meeting their needs (though greater priority doesn't mean *lexical* priority, which is to say that the smallest interest of even a single citizen will always outweigh the greatest interests of any number of non-citizens).

[27] However, as we will see in Section 4.1, Chapters 9 and 10, and Appendix B, as important as this point is, it may not have either the theoretical or the practical implications that many have assumed it has.

[28] I am not presenting, here, the position of any particular philosopher, but see, for example, Buber, Martin, *I and Thou*, Mansfield Centre: Martino Publishing, 2010, and Levinas, Emmanuel, *Ethics and Infinity: Conversations with Phillipe Nemo*, Pittsburgh: Duquesne University Press, 1995. Jonathan Glover makes similar claims about the importance of recognizing the humanity of another that can arise when one person directly confronts the plight of another up close and personal (see *Humanity: A Moral History of the Twentieth Century*, New Haven: Yale University Press, 2001, pp. 37–8, 52–3, and 408–9).

is something deeply important for morality about personal one-on-one inter-actions, where one is confronted, in a stark and undeniable form, with the reality, fragility, mortality, and humanity, of another. It is, I believe, largely in those moments, where one's own character and humanity are both formed and revealed.[29]

Moreover, I believe that much of what is most important about such direct interactions can arise even when the recognition is one-sided, so that the element of *mutual* recognition is lacking.[30] This explains why analogs of the quintessential ethical moment can arise when one is in direct contact with an infant, a feeble-minded person, someone suffering from dementia, a person who may not even be aware of one's presence (maybe, as they are drowning, they are facing away from one), or perhaps even sentient animals who are like us in certain crucially relevant moral respects, even if they lack our most advanced cognitive capacities. Coming in direct contact with another who is sufficiently like us that we can see ourselves in them, and see them as relevantly like us, pushes us to treat them with dignity and respect, and as we would want to be treated by someone like us were we in their predicament.

Thus, on this view, whether or not there is *mutual* recognition, much of the push and pull of morality rightly arises whenever one is directly confronted in a stark and undeniable form with the reality, fragility, mortality, and humanity—or perhaps sentience—of another. Again, I do not want to exaggerate the importance of such personal interactions for morality. They only represent a part of the large, complex, messy, pluralistic story that is morality.

---

[29] In correspondence, Ingmar Persson writes "I would agree that face-to-face encounters are central for the *formation* of our moral reactions as children, but that is compatible with holding that in our fully developed outlook, the reactions formed should only play a peripheral or subordinate role. I'm inclined to hold that in our present highly technological and globalized world, in which our powers of acting at a distance are so extensive, it's imperative to be ready to set these spontaneous reactions aside more frequently than ever." Persson's view here is representative of many philosophers who have thought about the topic of aiding the needy, as well as many Effective Altruists.

I agree with Persson's modestly stated conclusion, that we should "be ready to set these spontaneous reactions aside more frequently than ever." But I doubt that we should set them aside nearly as often as Persson and others who share his outlook suppose. For reasons this book hopes to make clear, I believe that Persson and most other philosophers who have written on this topic have an overly optimistic view of the nature and efficacy of our "highly technological and globalized world."

I could easily imagine a much more technically advanced world than ours, where we really could be as "immediately and intimately" connected with someone on the other side of the world, as with someone five feet from us, and where there really *would* be no difference in the direct and indirect impact of our efforts to aid someone on the other side of the world than someone five feet from us. In such a world, the quintessential moments where our character and humanity are formed and revealed might be very different than they are now, and so, too, might be the nature and scope of morality. However, I believe that many philosophers have vastly underestimated the size of the gap between such a world, and our current one, and that talk about how "highly technological and globalized" our world is, which is common among such philosophers, is deeply misleading.

[30] I am grateful to Tyler John who prompted me to clarify this point.

However, it is, I believe, a significant part of that story in terms of its impact on the nature and scope of our moral rights, responsibilities, and permissions.

There is an old joke which goes: "I love humanity, it is people I can't stand." There is, as the joke implies, something wrong with anyone who makes such a claim. If you find yourself in one-on-one contact with another human being whose very survival, at that crucial moment, depends on you, and you could easily help them at no risk or significant cost to yourself, then, I believe that any decent human being would and should help that person.[31] Moreover, I believe that that is true whether the person in question is a friend, a family member, or a total stranger. We *do* have a general, agent-neutral, duty to help others in need, and other things equal that duty directs us to help more people in need rather than less people in need. But that general duty does not, I believe, trump the other moral considerations that arise for Mark in the case of Sudden Epiphany.

Finally, let us consider a variation of Sudden Epiphany, in light of the preceding considerations.

Well-Intentioned Donor: Tim is comfortably well off, but by no means rich. One day, he receives brochures from two charities that operate in his city, Good PR Charity and Bad PR Charity. The brochures indicate that each charity is open on Saturday afternoons, during which time one can bring cash, checks, or valuable items to donate. Tim glances at the brochures, thinks to himself that both look like they are doing important work, and then promptly files them away. As luck would have it, the following Monday, Tim receives a valuable Rolex from a recently deceased uncle, and while Tim is delighted that his uncle remembered him in his will, he also feels that he is perfectly happy with his $20 watch, and that the Rolex could be put to much better use if he donates it to an effective charity. Recalling the recently received brochures, he does some internet research on each charity and the value of his uncle's Rolex, and realizes that if he donates the Rolex directly to Good PR Charity, he can save Aamuun's life, while if he donates the Rolex directly to Bad PR Charity, he can save the lives of three unidentified, but equally deserving, children.

Despite being greatly moved by Aamuun's plight, Tim decides that given his desire to help the needy, it makes most sense to donate the Rolex where it

---

[31] There are, of course, always exceptions to such general claims involving so-called "catastrophe cases" (for example, cases where unless one lets the drowning child die, the entire city or nation will perish). But the important point is that these really are the exceptions rather than the rule for thinking about such cases.

will do the most good. So, he decides that he will wear the Rolex for the remainder of the week—partly for the once-in-a-lifetime experience of doing something that is normally reserved for the rich and famous, and partly in honor of his uncle—and then he will take it over and donate it to Bad PR Charity the following Saturday. As (bad) luck would have it, on Thursday, Tim finds himself walking by a pond in which a young child is drowning, and his only choices are either to dive in and save the child, but at the cost of destroying the Rolex's value, or to let the child drown.

Basically, I would respond to Well-Intentioned Donor in the same way that I respond to Sudden Epiphany, except that in this case it would be hard to find fault with Tim for having "one thought too many." Given that Tim had already spent a lot of time consciously reflecting on whether to donate to Good PR Charity or Bad PR Charity, it would be appropriate for him to entertain similar thoughts as he contemplated saving the drowning child. As he was about to dive in, he might wonder what makes this case different than the case of Aamuun. He might appropriately worry that perhaps he was letting the salience of the drowning child's plight cloud his judgment. Still, in the critical ethical moment that Tim finds himself in, where one human being finds himself directly confronting another in a life-or-death moment, I believe that if he were truly virtuous, Tim would quickly dismiss his worries and jump in. I also believe that Tim would have a particular agent-relative duty to save the drowning child that would outweigh his general agent-neutral duty to do as much good as he can in aiding the needy.

The preceding discussion is not exhaustive, and it is not intended to settle the questions we are addressing. However, I believe the considerations presented lend support to the pluralistic approach that I advocated in Section 2.2. In some cases, such as that exemplified by Good PR Charity versus Poor PR Charity, it may well be that the main considerations relevant to our obligations towards the needy involve the general agent-neutral duty to help the needy, if we can do so at little or no risk or cost to ourselves, together with the general agent-neutral duty of beneficence to act in such a way as to promote the most good. This is the kind of case where the approach of Effective Altruism seems most pertinent and plausible. However, in other cases, such as those exemplified by Sudden Epiphany and Well-Intentioned Donor, a host of other factors seem relevant to our assessment of the agent, and his or her actions, and the simple approach of Effective Altruism seems inadequate. In such cases, virtue-based considerations, particular agent-relative duties to aid someone in need, and the special ethical moment that arises when two subjects of experience come into direct contact all seem relevant, and they provide reasons for believing that in such cases a decent and virtuous human being would, and should, aid a stranger in need even if this means providing less overall good than they otherwise could for the world's needy.

3.6 Dramatic Rescues, Large-Scale Disasters, and Effective Altruism

The preceding discussion has a bearing on two related issues. First, it is notable that humans have a remarkable propensity to engage in dramatic rescues. They also have a remarkable propensity to galvanize on a massive scale in the face of large-scale disasters. When some children are trapped in a cave, climbers are lost on a mountain, miners are entombed underground, or sailors are lost at sea, an entire state, country, or the world may get caught up in their plight, and seemingly no effort or expense will be spared to save them. Similarly, when a nuclear reactor melts down, a tsunami hits, or a massive earthquake strikes; food, supplies, equipment, and highly trained emergency crews may fly in from around the world to do everything they can to assist.[32] Among other things, destroyed buildings will be painstakingly combed through for days, as the world watches, with bated breath, hoping to find anyone who might still be alive after a week without water and food.

From the standpoint of Effective Altruism, such efforts, however well-intentioned, are almost always deeply misguided. And, I confess, there is a big part of me that shares that view. When I think of all the time, effort, attention, and resources that went into saving a single, white, 18-month-old toddler trapped at the bottom of a well,[33] I can't help but think of all the other toddlers who could have been saved instead—most of them non-whites in

[32] Though it should be noted that the world does not always, or even generally, react to major disasters, whether natural or man-made. It is a common complaint of aid workers and those facing dire circumstances that the world only reacts to emergency situations that manage to squeeze their way into the crowded nightly news programs and that have something about them that enables them to capture and retain the world's attention for more than a moment. The factors that account for this are many, and are often unrelated to the scope of the emergency and the extent of the need. I am grateful to Angus Deaton for reminding me, in correspondence, of this well-known fact. When we address this book's central issue—how to be good in a world of need—it is important to bear in mind that those who actually capture our attention on the nightly news are only a small portion of those whose desperate conditions warrant our attention.

[33] I am here alluding to the famous case of "Baby Jessica." In 1987, 18-month-old Jessica McClure was trapped in a well in her aunt's backyard. The event caught the world's attention, and the whole world watched breathlessly as monumental efforts were made to save her. As a quick skim of the internet reveals, the story of Baby Jessica has been intensely chronicled and revisited often over the years. See, for example, https://www.bing.com/search?q=baby+jessica+rescue&form=EDNTHT&mkt=en-us&httpsmsn=1&plvar=0&refig=3c0149cb8d064b4ba8696c534a355219&sp=4&qs=AS&pq=baby+jessica&sk=LS1AS2&sc=8-12&cvid=3c0149cb8d064b4ba8696c534a355219&cc=US&setlang=en-US, accessed August 28, 2019.

Asia, Africa, and South America—if only a comparable amount of time, effort, attention, and resources had gone into supplying needy toddlers with cost-effective oral rehydration salts (for diarrhea), Vitamin A capsules (to boost the immune system), antibiotics (for pneumonia), vaccines (for measles, whooping cough, diphtheria, tetanus, and polio), bed nets (for malaria), or food packets (for chronic starvation and malnourishment).

At first blush, extravagant expenditures to save a single child's life seem obscene, and tragically wasteful. Yet, on reflection, I am no longer as confident as I once was that we should want it any other way.

There is, ultimately, something heroic, uplifting, and noble, about dramatic rescues. When someone is pulled out from the rubble of a collapsed building five days after an earthquake strikes, that is a powerful reminder of the extraordinary value of each individual life. Kant famously claimed that each life has infinite value, and while that is surely a mistake, there is something deeply attractive about Kant's position to which our "no cost is too high" approach to dramatic rescues gives voice.[34] There is also something inspiring and valuable about the way in which an entire country that is otherwise deeply divided can sometimes come together in the face of a national tragedy, or in which a world that is tragically parochial and constantly at odds can sometimes come together in the spirit of cooperation to aid the victims of a natural disaster.

Dramatic rescues remind us of our common humanity, and prompt us to act in light of that common humanity, in a way that few, if any, other events do. Clearly, such dramatic rescues are rarely, if ever, cost-effective in terms of maximizing the lives saved, or the people helped for the resources expended. Accordingly, I suspect that they must almost always be opposed by any clear-thinking, hard-headed, Effective Altruist. Yet there are other values that would be lost if we stopped engaging in dramatic rescues, values that need to be given weight when we consider when, and how, to aid the needy.

Williams famously pointed out that in order to be the sort of people who could always act so as to promote the most good, humans would need to abandon many of the features of human life that make our lives so valuable—such as love, friendship, loyalty, honesty, reliability, and trustworthiness. This, Williams claimed, would produce a worse outcome.[35] Similarly, I believe that human life would, overall, be sadder, bleaker, colder, less valuable, and less

---

[34] See Kant's *Groundwork of the Metaphysics of Morals*.

[35] Given this, Williams famously claimed that utilitarianism would "usher itself from the scene," adding that "If that is right...then I leave it for discussion whether that shows that utilitarianism is unacceptable, or merely that no one ought to accept it" ("A Critique of Utilitarianism," pp. 134–5).

praiseworthy, if we lacked the virtues and spark of humanity that propel us to make costly dramatic rescues despite the inefficiencies of such rescues. So, once again, I suggest that our efforts to aid the needy should not simply be guided by the monistic aim of doing as much good as we can. Rather, we need a more nuanced, pluralistic view that gives due weight to our full normative reality in determining how we should respond to the plight of those in need.[36]

3.7 Effective Altruism, Personal Involvement, and Integrity

Some Effective Altruists believe that the goal of doing as much good as possible has implications not merely for *which* charities one should support, but for *how* one should support the needy. Consider, for example, the view that "checkbook charity" is not enough, and that one should also actively volunteer on behalf of the needy. Many people hold such a view, believing that it is important for people to volunteer in their local communities, perhaps by delivering food to homebound seniors, helping build a home with Habitat for Humanity, working at a local soup kitchen, or volunteering for Big Brothers and Big Sisters. Still, depending on one's abilities and earnings capacities, many Effective Altruists would scoff at such claims, regarding such activities as misguided and self-indulgent.

Many agree with Williams's important insight that in order to be the sort of people who could always act so as to promote the most good, humans would need to abandon many of the features of human life that make our lives so valuable—such as love, friendship, loyalty, honesty, reliability, and trustworthiness—and that, on the whole, it would be worse for people if they did this. They further agree that this shows that utilitarianism may well have to "usher itself from the scene," in the sense of advising us to *not* become the sort of people who, on each occasion, are guided by the utilitarian principle of acting so as to maximize the good. However, some deny that this shows that there is a fatal flaw in utilitarianism. (For powerful considerations in support of this position, see Part One of Derek Parfit's *Reasons and Persons*.)

[36] The theoretical issues here are too complex to deal with in this book. However, the bottom line is that Effective Altruists could agree that if, in fact, our lives would be worse, overall, if we were always guided in our efforts to aid the needy by the aim of doing the most good, then we shouldn't be solely guided by that aim. Thus, the Williams line I am suggesting here is compatible with the *spirit* of Effective Altruism. Even so, adopting this line would require Effective Altruists to recognize much more complexity than they often do in advising people what they need to bear in mind in thinking about how best to respond to the plight of the world's needy. In fact, it would require them to advise people to make themselves the sort of people who will often *not* do what they *ought* to do by the lights of Effective Altruism. However, since anyone who follows their advice will have had good Effective Altruist reasons for having done so, they ought not to be *blamed* when they later often fail to do what is right by the lights of Effective Altruism. Non-Effective Altruists, by contrast, will typically insist that dramatic rescues and "inefficient" efforts in the face of large-scale disasters are not merely blameless, they are typically praiseworthy and *not* wrong.

For a detailed discussion of the complexities surrounding this issue, see Part One of Parfit's *Reasons and Persons*.

If, for example, one was a high-powered lawyer, who was paid by the hour, Effective Altruists might point out, correctly, that one could do far more good if, instead of spending one's valuable hours ladling food at the local soup kitchen, one did legal work during those hours, and donated one's earnings to effective charities. Concretely, suppose that one was prepared to work at the local soup kitchen for four hours each Saturday, 40 weeks each year, but could instead earn $300 an hour during those times working as a lawyer. Over the course of the year, the opportunity costs of ladling soup instead of doing legal work would come to $48,000. With that money, one could easily hire two people to work at the soup kitchen who would be just as helpful as oneself, for, say, $15 per hour each and a total of $4,800, and this would leave one with $43,200 to give to the most effective international relief organizations. Given this, the Effective Altruists suggest, it would be both selfish and crazy for one to insist on ladling the soup oneself, since one could do much more good both for the downtrodden at the local soup kitchen and innocent people dying of hunger or easily treatable diseases by just using one's time, and resources, more wisely.[37]

Likewise, there are many highly intelligent individuals who feel the "calling" to aid the needy, who wonder whether they should become an aid worker, or perhaps a doctor, ministering to the needy in a poverty-stricken country. Here, again, some Effective Altruists have practical advice to offer, what has been called the *Earning to Give* approach to career choices. They note that if one is capable of doing so, one could become a high paying corporate lawyer, or an investment banker, or a venture capitalist, make a ton of money, and by donating, say, merely half of one's yearly earnings do much more good for the world's needy than by attempting to personally alleviate their plight.[38]

---

[37] Tyler John points out that the Effective Altruist is not, of course, saying that such a person is being "selfish and crazy" relative to someone who does *nothing*—only relative to someone who uses their time much more effectively. I agree. Also, I grant that while there is nothing to be said for the former claim, there is something to be said for the latter one. Still, ultimately, I believe the latter claim reflects an unduly narrow approach to how a good person should respond to the world's needy.

[38] The *Earning to Give* approach to aiding the needy was originally emphasized, and popularized, by the Effective Altruism organization *80,000 Hours*, co-founded by Will MacAskill and Benjamin Todd. In recent years, some leaders of Effective Altruism have come to think that perhaps it was a mistake to emphasize Earning to Give as much as they did as one of the most effective ways for certain highly talented people to do good. In a July 6, 2015 blog post, Will MacAskill notes that a straw poll of the 80,000 Hours team suggests that members of the team now think that "only" 10–20% of "altruistically motivated graduates from a good university, who are open to pursuing any career path, should aim to earn to give in the long term" ("80,000 Hours thinks that only a small proportion of people should earn to give long term." *80,000 Hours, Centre for Effective Altruism* blog, July 12, 2015, URL: https://80000hours.org/2015/07/80000-hours-thinks-that-only-a-small-proportion-of-people-should-earn-to-give-long-term/, accessed June 20, 2019).

However, it is important to note that presumably members of the 80,000 Hours team would still recommend Earning to Give over becoming an aid worker, or a doctor, and personally ministering to

Some Effective Altruists would go even further. Suppose that the most lucrative jobs that one could land and be successful at "required" one to "cut corners" in various respects. Suppose, for example, that while one could certainly earn a decent wage as an investment banker—say, $300,000 per year—to earn the really big bucks—say, $5,000,000 per year—one had to engage in a combination of lies, half-truths, distortions, misleading information, illegal or gray area activities, legal but immoral activities, and so on. Suppose, further, that if one wasn't prepared to engage in the corner-cutting activities, one's accounts would be given to someone less scrupulous, who would readily engage in such behavior, and then some. Then, for some Effective Altruists, as long as one would donate a significant portion of one's salary to especially effective charities, one ought to take on the high paying job of being an investment banker and engage in the behaviors in questions, since doing so wouldn't be much, if any, worse for one's clients, and doing so would allow one to donate vastly greater sums to aid the needy, especially over the entire course of one's working lifetime.[39]

the needy in a poverty-stricken country. It is just that they now believe that there are even *more* effective avenues than Earning to Give for "altruistically motivated graduates from good universities" to pursue, if they hope to maximize the expected value of the good in the long term. In the blog post just cited, MacAskill suggests that these include "doing things like politics, policy, high-value research, for-profit and non-profit entrepreneurship, and direct work for highly socially valuable organizations." (This note was prompted by Tyler John, who rightly observed, in correspondence, that Effective Altruists do not believe that we should *all* pursue the Earning to Give option for promoting the most expected good that we can. Of course, I never claimed that they did. Only that, for certain people, they offered it as a more promising way of aiding the needy than becoming on-the-ground aid workers.)

[39] For considerations supporting this position, and even more controversial claims regarding the moral permissibility of stealing from, or harming, some to aid others, see Unger's *Living High & Letting Die*, especially Chapters 3 and 6.

The question of who does, or does not, count as an Effective Altruist is, I have found, controversial. Sometimes this is for theoretical reasons, sometimes it is for practical reasons, and sometimes, alas, it is mainly for reasons of ego and "turf" (who gets credit for being the "founder of Effective Altruism," who gets to decide who is, or isn't, in the "club", etc.). *Living High & Letting Die* was inspired by, and self-consciously written to advance the message and arguments of Singer's "Famine, Affluence, and Morality." In my judgment, it deserves a place in the "canon" of Effective Altruism, and there is every reason to count Unger as an Effective Altruist.

With that said, let me acknowledge that I am not aware of any generally recognized leaders of Effective Altruism who have publicly advocated for the views discussed here. Indeed, if anything, they have conveyed sentiments rejecting such a position. (For representative Effective Altruism texts, see Benjamin Todd's *80,000 Hours: Find A Fulfilling Career That Does Good* (Oxford: Centre for Effective Altruism, 2016); William MacAskill's *Doing Good Better: How Effective Altruism Can Help You Help Others, Do Work that Matters, and Make Smarter Choices about Giving Back* (New York: Avery, 2016); Peter Singer's *The Life You Can Save* (New York: Random House, 2009); and Singer's *The Most Good You Can Do* (New Haven: Yale University Press, 2015).) However, given the philosophical roots of Effective Altruism, which lie largely in the utilitarian/consequentialism tradition, together with their general commitment to Expected Utility Theory, I believe that, if pressed, most leaders of Effective Altruism would have to admit that their view commits them, at least in principle, to the kind of position expressed in this paragraph, and endorsed by Unger in *Living High & Letting Die*. They might argue, however, that, in fact, such actions are unlikely to maximize the expected good of one's actions, in the

In one important respect, the Effective Altruist is surely right. Insofar as one's aim in giving to charity is to do the most good that one can on behalf of the needy, one has strong reason to do extra hours of legal work and donate the proceeds to charity rather than to spend those hours serving in a soup kitchen; one has strong reason to take on a high paying job and donate a substantial portion of one's salary to an effective charity rather than to serve as an on-the-ground aid worker; and one even has strong reason to "cut corners" rather than serve one's clients honestly, assuming that one wouldn't be caught, and that doing so would significantly increase the size of one's donations to effective charities without leaving one's clients substantially worse off than they would otherwise be (recall that if one didn't treat them that way someone else would, and would likely treat them even worse). That is, I readily grant that there would be many cases where acting in the ways in question *would* do the most to benefit the needy, and would also bring about the best outcome, so that the general duty of beneficence or reasons to promote utility would militate in favor of such actions.

Nonetheless, as indicated previously, I believe there are other normatively significant factors that also have a bearing on such cases. Arguably, there is much more to being a genuinely good and decent human being than merely working in a high paying job and opening one's checkbook for effective charities, even if one's motivation in pursuing the high-paying life is the noble one of helping others. Arguably, there is something to be said for engaging in a morally praiseworthy life where one has the courage, at least at times, to directly confront other human beings in need, one-on-one, and to respond, appropriately, to their plight. Arguably, there is much to be said for living a life of great virtue and integrity, and of genuinely earning and retaining a good name, and the respect and admiration that comes with it.

By assumption, the highly paid corner-cutting investment banker will have done much more good in the world than the on-the-ground aid worker, and she will have done it for morally good reasons and with the best of intentions. Moreover, in a real sense, she will have sacrificed her good name for the sake of others less fortunate, and certainly there is something noble and praiseworthy about that. Even so, by assumption, she will have betrayed, for the sake of the

---

long run, because of the probability that in the long run such actions might be discovered and the adverse consequences that would ensue were that to happen.

Moreover, whatever their actual theoretical commitments, in principle, there are strong moral and practical reasons for leaders of the Effective Activism Movement to publicly disavow such actions, because of the misinterpretations, misuses, backlash, and damage to Effective Altruism that might ensue were they to do so.

greater good, a host of virtues in her day-to-day dealings with others who are *counting* on her to act on their behalf. Among the many virtues she will have abandoned are the virtues of honesty, trustworthiness, dependability, reliability, and integrity. To my mind, such a life may produce a lot of good, but it is not a good life, and it is not one in which I would wish anyone I deeply cared about to engage.[40]

Note, by the way, how we would feel about the Nazi guard who helped put little children in the oven, despite being repulsed by what he was doing, on the grounds that it was the highest paying job he could find, he was donating half of his income to effective charities, and that if *he* didn't do it someone else surely would. He might even have added, perhaps correctly, that his personal participation in the killings was better for his victims, since anyone who would have replaced him would likely have treated his victims more callously and brutally than he. Even if all this were true, I doubt it would be enough to support the conclusion that the Nazi guard was both acting rightly and a good person.

3.8 Morally Problematic Relations in Aid Giving

Before proceeding, let me add the following. Some people will have noted that there are further approaches to aiding the needy than the two I have focused on in this discussion. So, for example, in addition to the Effective Altruist approach of distant giving via effective aid organizations, and the face-to-face approach of the soup-ladling kind, there are improvements in underlying social, political, and economic conditions that might be brought about via political action and campaigning. Furthermore, some progressives might argue that there is much to be said in favor of the third approach over either of the other two. In particular, they might claim that the third approach to aid giving is compatible with aid givers and recipients recognizing and treating each other as equals, while the first two approaches involve inegalitarian relations of power, money, and status that make it difficult, if not impossible, for aid givers and recipients to genuinely relate to each other as equals. More generally, some will object to the first two forms of aid giving as distasteful,

---

[40] My thinking about these topics is significantly influenced by Williams's discussion in *Utilitarianism For and Against*. See, also, Susan Wolf's paper "Moral Saints" (*The Journal of Philosophy* 79 (1982): 419–39), for other important considerations with a bearing on this issue.

patronizing, inegalitarian, undemocratic, and so on, and claim that the third approach can avoid these features.[41]

There is, I believe, much to be said for the worries expressed in the preceding paragraph regarding the morally problematic nature of the relations that often obtain between aid givers and recipients. There is also much to be said for seeking political and economic methods of aiding the needy that do not involve such problematic relations. I shall return to these points, and largely endorse them, in Chapter 10. However, it is important not to oversell the virtues of the third approach, or to undersell the virtues of the first two approaches. All three approaches, and others as well, have their strengths and weaknesses. Our task is to carefully consider both the strengths and weaknesses of each approach to aiding the needy, and to give each its due weight in determining how to be good in a world of need.

Thus, the aim of my discussion of the virtues, and the importance, at least at times, of directly confronting others in need, one-on-one, and responding appropriately to their plight, has not been to advocate for any single approach to aiding the needy, but merely to stress that we need to consider the full range of factors that are relevant to leading the fully moral life. The "do the most good" approach of Effective Altruism reflects one very important factor that needs to be considered. However, it is not, in my judgment, the only one.

3.9 Personal versus Political Domains

The preceding suggests a further way of thinking about Singer's original Pond Example, and how much one can legitimately generalize from that example to other cases of need. As we have seen, in Singer's original Pond Example, a passerby found himself directly confronting the imminent death of an innocent child. I have suggested that the direct one-on-one nature of that confrontation, combined with the fact that the passerby was the only person in a position to effectively save the drowning child, gave rise to a host of relevant considerations that made it morally compelling for him to save the child, even if the cost of his doing so was to ruin a watch that had great monetary and personal value.

---

[41] This comment closely paraphrases some remarks Kieran Oberman made in correspondence, for which I am grateful.

One way of putting this point would be to claim that the circumstances of Singer's original example placed the plight of the drowning victim squarely within the passerby's *personal domain*, a domain over which he has responsibility, whether or not he wants it or has voluntarily undertaken it. Moreover, my arguments suggest that the moral demands relevant to helping someone that lies within one's personal domain reflect an assortment of virtue-based and deontological-based reasons that need not apply in the same way, or to the same degree, to needy people who lie outside of one's personal domain. By contrast, the outcome-based reason for doing as much good as one can may support in the exact same way, and to the same degree, helping anyone in need regardless of whether they lie within, or outside of, one's personal domain.

To help illustrate this, consider a variation of Singer's Pond Example.

Empty Pond: Nick isn't especially poor, but neither is he rich, at least not by U.S. standards. His only real luxury item is a valuable Rolex watch, worth $5,000 on the resale market, which was bequeathed to him by a favorite uncle. One day, Nick walks by an empty pond. Next to the pond is a sign which reads as follows: Each year, countless children drown in ponds, just like this one. If you send $5,000 to the *Drowning Prevention Fund*, your money will be used to encircle an open pond with a safety fence, to hire a lifeguard to watch over a pond like this, or to hire an instructor to teach swimming classes. The result is that you will prevent an innocent child from drowning.

Nick pauses to read the sign. He knows that he could sell his watch, and donate the proceeds to the Drowning Prevention Fund. However, his watch has great sentimental value, so he continues on his way, and doesn't give the matter much further thought.

As the sign predicted, an innocent child ends up drowning who would not have done so, if Nick had sold his watch and donated the proceeds to the Drowning Prevention Fund.

In Empty Pond, a child ends up dying because of Nick's response. Even so, I believe that most people would regard Nick very differently than they would regard someone who abandoned the drowning child in Singer's original Pond Example. Whereas most would regard someone who simply walked away from a drowning child as a terrible person who committed a heinous act, I believe that most would regard Nick, and his response, much less negatively.

There are, I believe, many important disanalogies between Singer's original Pond Example and Empty Pond that would not only explain but justify our reacting to them so differently. I shall detail many of those disanalogies in later chapters. Here, I simply want to suggest that whereas in Singer's example the drowning child seems to have landed squarely within the personal domain of the passerby, for whom he must assume responsibility whether or not he wants to, in Empty Pond, whoever would later die if Nick failed to contribute to the Drowning Prevention Fund seems, at least intuitively, to lie outside of Nick's personal domain.

Nick can, if he chooses to, take responsibility for some of those who will die if he doesn't contribute to the Fund, and in this way bring such people within his personal domain. However, unlike the passerby in Singer's original example, he isn't required, by basic human decency, to take the necessary steps to prevent someone from drowning. Thus, we see that in some cases someone may come to lie within our personal domain, and we may find ourselves responsible for them, whether or not we chose for that to be the case, or previously acted in some way so as to make ourselves responsible for the predicament that led to their being in our personal domain. That is the case, I believe, in Singer's original Pond Example. However, in other cases, someone may lie outside our personal domain, unless we choose to make them a part of our personal domain, or previously acted in some way so as to make ourselves responsible for the predicament they face. That is the case, I believe, in Empty Pond. Moreover, as these cases are intended to illustrate, whether or not someone lies inside or outside of one's personal domain does not merely depend on the consequences for the person in question of one's acting or failing to act.

If those who might be adversely affected by Nick's failing to contribute to the Drowning Prevention Fund lie outside of Nick's personal domain, one might wonder to what domain, if any, they belong. Several answers to this are possible. However, from Nick's perspective, one plausible answer might be the *political domain*. Nick might readily agree that it would be good for there to be fences around ponds, lifeguards attending unfenced ponds, and swimming lessons for those who can't swim. However, he might contend that it is the state, or local municipalities, that have a responsibility to provide such protections, not individual citizens, per se.

To be sure, individual citizens have reason to empower their representatives to act on their behalf to safeguard their community.[42] Hence, individual

---

[42] Tom Nagel offers an interesting argument in support of this position as a morally legitimate way of avoiding having to take personal responsibility for the world's ills. See his *Equality and Partiality*, New York: Oxford University Press, 1991.

citizens, working collectively, will have reason to want their representatives to take the most effective steps to prevent drownings. However, this will be only one desirable aim among many others that will compete for attention and resources, and whether or not the government will ultimately address the issue of unprotected ponds, or do so adequately, will ultimately depend on the relative importance of that issue, and the effectiveness and responsiveness of the government to its citizens' interests, needs, and rights. Still, the key point, here, is that while an individual is certainly permitted to voluntarily take on the issue of unnecessary drownings, it does not seem that any morally decent individual must contribute to the Drowning Prevention Fund, or pursue some other route to personally fund fences, lifeguards, or swimming lessons, even in the absence of adequate government policies regarding that issue.

Now nothing said here is intended to support the view that one can simply ignore the plight of someone who lies outside of one's personal domain. To the contrary, as I have long claimed, and still firmly believe, there are many powerful reasons to help such people, if one can. It is merely intended to suggest—contrary to the view of classical utilitarianism—that it is not the case that the entire world lies within one's personal domain. Accordingly, one cannot leap to any conclusions about how a good person must, or should, respond to the plight of someone who lies outside of one's personal domain, based on our intuitions about how someone must, or should, respond to the plight of someone who lies within one's personal domain. In essence, however, I believe that this is what Singer and many of his followers have done, in suggesting that we can infer a great deal about the nature and extent of our obligations to help the world's needy, based on our intuitive reactions to Singer's original Pond Example.[43]

3.10 Concluding Remarks

Let me conclude this chapter by returning to the upshot of Singer's original Pond Example, and considering whether that example, together with either of

---

[43] In his book, *Living High & Letting Die*, Unger goes to great length to debunk the view that there is a difference between directly helping a drowning child, and indirectly helping a dying child on the other side of the world. Though in many ways his book is quite brilliant and illuminating, ultimately, I believe, his efforts were doomed to fail. This is because, in my judgment, the normative realm has a place for rightly distinguishing between those matters that lie within one's personal domain, and those that lie beyond it. Classical utilitarianism denies this. However, most normative theories, including virtue ethics, deontological ethics, and care ethics, accept this. Ultimately, I believe that clear-thinking pluralists must recognize this important truth.

Singer's weak or strong principles, support Effective Altruism. Recall that Singer originally presented his Pond Example as simply an application of his weak principle:

> *Preventing Bad without Moral Loss*: if it is in our power to prevent something very bad from happening, without thereby sacrificing anything morally significant, we ought, morally, to do it.[44]

Surely, this position is compatible with everything that I have said in this chapter. If, for example, one believes that one should save the drowning child in cases like Sudden Epiphany and Well-Intentioned Donor, one can point to the child's life as having moral significance in support of the view that one need not act as Effective Altruism would seemingly urge in such cases. Moreover, as we saw, there are a host of other morally significant factors that would also need to be sacrificed were we to simply act so as to bring about the most good in our efforts to aid the needy. Similarly, for cases involving dramatic rescues, and the question of whether it can be enough to concentrate on donating to the most effective charities in lieu of more personal involvement in aiding the needy, and the issue of whether one's choice of jobs, and the actions one ought to undertake in performing one's jobs, should only be constrained by the goal of maximizing one's donations to effective charities. In all these cases, we have seen that Preventing Bad without Moral Loss would not entail that we act as certain Effective Altruists would say we should, since there are many factors of "moral significance" that one would have to sacrifice in order to do the most good on behalf of the needy.

As for the stronger principle that Singer himself actually favors, Preventing Bad without Comparable Moral Loss, the judgments of that principle regarding the cases I have been discussing will depend on how we interpret what counts as a "comparable moral loss," which, as we saw, Singer himself glossed as: "without causing anything else comparably bad to happen, or doing something that is wrong in itself, or failing to promote some moral good, comparable in significance to some bad thing that we can prevent."[45] It is arguable that we can have a particular agent-relative duty to aid someone we are in a special position to help, and that in some such cases, such as Sudden Epiphany, and Well-Intentioned Donor, our failure to save the drowning child would be wrong, even if saving the child wouldn't do the most good.

---

[44] "Famine, Affluence, and Morality," p. 231.   [45] "Famine, Affluence, and Morality," p. 231.

It is also arguable that it will often be the case that failing to act virtuously, failing to respond to the needs of another that one is confronting one-on-one, failing to act with integrity or uphold one's good name, failing to get directly involved in aiding the needy, and so on, are, taken individually or in combination, of comparable moral significance to doing more good rather than less. This simply reflects the pluralistic perspective that many factors have great moral significance other than promoting the good, and some of these, at least in combination, are even on a par with saving fewer lives rather than more.[46*]

Of course, some Effective Altruists will deny all this. Or they will argue that the cases where competing moral factors are comparable in moral significance with saving more lives are far fewer than this discussion suggests.[47] This, of course, is a substantive matter that my discussion has not settled. However, I hope to have said enough, already, to suggest that we need to be sensitive to a wide range of morally relevant factors in determining how to be good in a world of need. Maximizing expected welfare is *one* desirable goal that one might have in aiding the needy; but, I have argued, it is not *all* that matters.

[46*] Importantly, Peter Singer responds to this paragraph, in correspondence, as follows: "Yes, I agree with all this. FAM ["Famine, Affluence, and Morality"] doesn't entail EA [Effective Altruism], though it may suggest it to some people. It defends a broader range of views. EA is a further development of a position compatible with FAM."

[47] Nick Beckstead observes, in correspondence, that this is roughly his perspective of the matter, though he agrees with me, in opposition to Peter Unger's views, about cases where people would need to violate deontological constraints to most effectively aid the needy. This is, I believe, an important concession. Once one recognizes one important value category besides maximizing the good, as relevant to how we ought to respond to the plight of the needy, such as deontology, it makes it harder to argue against the possible relevance of other important moral categories, such as virtue.

4

Direct versus Indirect Aid

In Chapter 3, we saw that for all its well-deserved fame and influence, Singer's Pond Example doesn't actually take us very far in answering the question of what we should do, all things considered, to aid the world's needy. Nor does it offer much support for Effective Altruism, though it is compatible with it. This will not come as a shock to Singer himself, nor to sophisticated leaders of the Effective Altruism Movement. However, it will come as a bit of a shock to anyone whose thinking about our obligations to the needy has been largely shaped by Singer's example, or to those who have thought that Singer's Pond Example provides compelling reason to be an Effective Altruist. Unfortunately, after lecturing to countless audiences over the years on the topic of our obligations to the needy, I am convinced that there are many such people, perhaps far more than Singer himself, or the founders of the Effective Altruism Movement, realize.

In this chapter, and the following ones, I shall raise a number of further worries about the relevance and scope of Singer's Pond Example to the general lesson that that example is often thought to support; namely, that we should be donating money to support international development organizations that aid the world's needy.

In Section 4.1, I briefly discuss whether membership in one's own community or proximity is morally relevant to our obligations to the needy.

In Section 4.2, I note that Singer's Pond Example is disanalogous from the case of giving to international development organizations, in that in the latter case, but not the former, there are a host of agents who stand between me and the execution of my intentions. I suggest that this may be normatively significant, as the more people that stand between me and the execution of my will, the more possibilities there are for something to go awry.

In Section 4.3, I note another normatively significant disanalogy between saving a drowning child and giving to international development organizations, in that in the latter case, unlike the former, my contribution may, in fact, be helping to defray the cost of any number of perfectly legitimate business expenses and laudable goals that are distinct from, though they may (or may not) contribute to, the saving of a life. I suggest that the reasons supporting the

Being Good in a World of Need. Larry S. Temkin, Oxford University Press. © Larry S. Temkin 2022.
DOI: 10.1093/oso/9780192849977.003.0004

two activities are not the same, nor are they of equal strength. As such, one cannot derive an obligation to contribute to international relief organizations, from the obligation to save a drowning child.

In Section 4.4, I summarize this chapter's main claims.

4.1 Ground Clearing: Community Membership, Proximity, and Cultural Differences

Consider again Singer's original Pond Example. You are walking past a pond within which there is a drowning child, you can wade in and save the child at the cost of getting your clothes muddy, or you can let the child die. Surely, Singer is right that you ought, morally, to save the child, and that you would be acting deeply wrongly if you failed to do so. But can this example bear the weight that Singer, and others, have put on it? If we agree with Singer's judgment about this example, when, if at all, does it follow that we should be sending a check to international relief organizations who work to save needy people in distant lands?

I have already argued, in Section 3.5, that we may have special agent-relative positive duties to aid people with whom we come into direct contact. I shall set that line of reasoning aside, here. I shall also set aside two other lines of reasoning that may be pertinent, but only after first identifying, and then commenting upon them. Finally, I will briefly introduce a third line of reasoning which, I believe, is relevant here, but which I will later discuss at greater length in Chapter 10.

In Singer's example, you are able to directly save a drowning child who is right in front of you. Accordingly, it is natural to assume, from Singer's example, that you and the drowning child are members of the same community. By the same token, when you send money to international aid organizations, you are almost certain to be helping someone who is a member of a different community than you are. Given this, some would argue that Singer's example has little bearing on whether you have an obligation to help needy people in distant lands. The reason for this, they think, is that one has special obligations towards members of one's own community that one does not have towards members of other communities.

I, myself, am not particularly tempted towards this position. My own moral and philosophical leanings tend more towards cosmopolitanism, and I am inclined to think that though I am a citizen of the United States, other things equal, my duty to save a drowning child is no greater if the child is a compatriot of mine than if it is not. So, for example, if, just before I waded in to save the child, I realized that the child was from New Zealand, rather than the U.S., that wouldn't, to my mind, lessen the strength of my duty to save the child. Similarly, if I were traveling in New Zealand when I came across the drowning child, I would not think that I had less of a duty to save the child, on the assumption that the child was a New Zealander, than I would have had if the child were a U.S. citizen, or than I would have had had I come across a drowning child in the U.S. who was a U.S. citizen.

I also note that a similar sounding claim is morally repugnant when put in the mouth of the racist or religious bigot, who might only choose to save a child if they were, say, white or Christian.

However, having said that, I admit that there are contexts where giving preference to fellow citizens over non-citizens may be both morally and politically defensible, and perhaps even obligatory, in ways in which racism and religious prejudice are not. Membership in a community is often associated with such factors as sharing a common language, culture, ideals, interests, goals, and so on, as well as a host of social, political, economic, and personal interactions and entanglements. In some cases, such factors may involve normatively significant relations and obligations between members of a community that tend not to hold, or typically hold to a lesser extent, between members of different communities.[1] If this is so, and I'm willing to grant that it may be, then an argument can be given that Singer's example is importantly disanalogous from the typical cases of children dying in foreign lands, insofar as we implicitly assume that the drowning child in Singer's example would be a fellow citizen.

Still, even if we grant that in some contexts perhaps we are morally permitted, or even required, to give greater weight to saving the life of a fellow citizen over that of a foreigner, we can imagine variations of Singer's example that would support the judgment that there is compelling reason to save the life of a foreign child who is drowning if the cost of our doing so is merely that we end up with some muddy clothes. So, I shall set aside the issue of whether there is a disanalogy between Singer's example, as most naturally interpreted, and the typical case of supporting international relief organizations, in that the former implicitly directs aid to a fellow citizen and the latter directs aid to foreigners. While that distinction may have some moral significance,

---

[1] On this issue, see Section 3.4 of my "Thinking about the Needy, Justice, and International Organizations" (*The Journal of Ethics* 8 (2004): 376–83), including the recognition there that this may be less so in today's era than in previous eras.

ultimately, I believe there are other factors that play a much larger role in determining the nature and extent of our obligations to the world's needy.

Second, Singer considers, and quickly dismisses, the view that proximity or distance could have moral significance in a very important passage worth quoting in detail. He writes:

> I do not think I need to say much in defense of the refusal to take proximity and distance into account.... If we accept any principle of impartiality, universalizability, equality, or whatever, we cannot discriminate against someone merely because he is far away from us.... Admittedly, it is possible that we are in a better position to judge what needs to be done to help a person near to us than one far away, and perhaps also to provide the assistance we judge to be necessary.... This may have once been a justification for being more concerned with the poor in one's own town than with famine victims in India.... [However] instant communication and swift transportation have changed the situation.... Expert observers and supervisors sent out by famine relief organizations or permanently stationed in famine prone areas, can direct our aid to a refugee in Bengal almost as effectively as we could get it to someone on our own block. There would seem, therefore, to be no possible justification for discriminating on geographical grounds.[2]

In Appendix B, I suggest that the issue of whether proximity and distance are themselves irrelevant from the moral point of view is much less clear than Singer, and most people, have assumed. However, even if we grant, as most believe, and as I shall assume for the remainder of this book, that spatial or temporal relations such as "near to" or "far from" cannot *themselves* be morally relevant, it does *not* follow that differences in spatial or temporal relations lack *practical* significance. I shall elaborate on this with respect to differences in spatial location. Similar considerations could be adduced regarding differences in temporal location.[3]

Even if Singer were right that, in this modern era of globalization, "instant communication and swift transportation" have made it almost as easy to help someone in need on the other side of the world, as someone drowning in a pond right in front of one, that only speaks to *one* way—regarding the causal

---

[2] "Famine, Affluence, and Morality." *Philosophy and Public Affairs* 1 (1972): 232.
[3] The remainder of this section is deeply indebted to Brian Oosthuizen. Much of it paraphrases comments he provided on an earlier draft. As importantly, he urged that I include some discussion of this issue at this point in the text, and not wait until Chapters 9 and 10, as I previously had.

efficacy of our actions—in which the geographical differences between people no longer have the normative significance that they might have once had. That is a very important fact. However, we cannot allow that fact to obscure another important fact; namely, that in many *other* ways the differences between people often remain almost as large as ever, and in ways that can have great normative significance.

As noted previously, it is natural to assume that the drowning child in Singer's example is a member of one's own community, whereas the distant needy are typically members of different communities. Alas, talk of "instant communication and swift transportation" utterly ignores the normatively significant respects in which membership in different communities often involves possession of different histories, participation in different social, political, cultural, and economic institutions, and acceptance of different worldviews reflecting different interests, goals, ideals, and moral and religious values.

There is an old saying that "fools rush in where angels fear to tread."[4] Unfortunately, the ease with which we can now causally intervene in, and significantly impact, the course of events on the other side of the world, has led many well-intentioned people to intervene even when they don't fully understand the cultures and worldviews of the communities they are seeking to aid, or the full impact that their well-intended interventions will have on those communities.

So, for example, thanks to the very features that Singer praises—"instant communication and swift transportation"—it is now possible for well-meaning individuals or groups from, say, California, to head off at a moment's notice to attend to the victims of a natural disaster, whether those victims are in California, New Orleans, Haiti, Indonesia, India, or Somalia. Unfortunately, however, whenever a well-meaning volunteer or so-called "expert" enters a "foreign" space—which may be any community that is significantly different from their own—there is a risk of misjudgments based on a lack of understanding about the unique circumstances of the communities within which they are working. Moreover, the unforeseen effects of such misjudgments on the local community can range from being mildly inconvenient to devastating, and they may persist long after the international do-gooders have returned safely to the comforts of their own local communities.

---

[4] See Pope, Alexander, "An Essay on Criticism," *Poetry Foundation*, URL: https://web.archive.org/web/20200901022554/https://www.poetryfoundation.org/articles/69379/an-essay-on-criticism, accessed August 31, 2020.

The point is that it is extremely important, particularly in a post-colonial context, to be sensitive to the uniqueness of each individual case of need or underdevelopment, and this is not always easy to do. As such, there might be good reason to prioritize aiding those whose unique position of need one understands best—perhaps in virtue of being from the same or a closely similar community. Short of that, there is a heavy burden on well-intentioned outsiders to ensure, to the best of their ability, that whatever aid they administer to other communities is provided in close collaboration with those who have the relevant local expertise or, at the very least, on the basis of the most thorough understanding of, and respect for, the local community's history, culture, mores, and worldview of which an outsider is capable.

To be sure, virtually every major international aid organization has long recognized the importance of this point. However, too often there remains a large gap between an aid organization's stated policy on this matter—its aspirational goal, as it were—and its on-the-ground practice. Similarly, there is a growing consensus within the development literature that each situation of underdevelopment or poverty is unique, and that development models which have succeeded when applied in some locations and contexts, have failed when applied in other locations and contexts.[5] Unfortunately, however, the factors accounting for this reality, and their significance, are too often overlooked in the rush to aid people in need.

Interestingly, Adam Smith offers a similar argument to the effect that, before we can help someone in need, we have to truly understand what their needs are, and before we can truly understand what their needs are we have to know them well. Such a view, if true, would, other things equal, offer practical reason to favor aiding people we know well over aiding strangers, and members of our own community over members of other communities. Smith view does not suggest that those we know well are more important, or more deserving of our help—merely that, other things equal, we are more likely to be able to effectively address the needs of those we know well, or those people who are most like us in terms of their interests, desires, needs, and worldview.[6]

---

[5] See, for example, Rodrik, Dani, "Diagnostics Before Prescriptions." *The Journal of Economic Perspectives* 24 (2010): 33–44. See, also, Deaton, Angus and Nancy Cartwright, "Understanding and Misunderstanding Randomized Controlled Trials." *Social Science & Medicine* 210 (2018): 2–21. Deaton and Cartwright's article discusses the importance of this fact in the context of casting doubt on the appropriateness of using randomized control trials—which play an important role in certain scientific contexts—for predicting what aid efforts will work in the real world, where contexts vary significantly. I shall return to this important topic in Chapter 9.

[6] See, Adam Smith's *The Theory of Moral Sentiments*, edited by Knud Haakonssen, Cambridge: Cambridge University Press, 2012. I am grateful to Reilly Schladt for bringing Smith's view to my attention.

Against such views, one might argue that certain needs and interests are cross cultural, such as the needs for food, shelter, medical care, safety, and the interests in living to a ripe old age, or protecting one's child from death or mutilation. However, while there is much to be said for such claims, they, too, are controversial, as evidenced by the fact that some communities allow children to die, rather than have them receive a blood transfusion; other communities engage in female circumcision; still other communities practice female infanticide; and so on.

In sum, however true it may be that "instant communication and swift transportation" have largely obliterated the normative significance of geographical differences between people; they have *not* rendered normatively insignificant the vast array of social, political, historical, cultural, moral, and religious differences between people. This reflects a fundamentally important disanalogy between Singer's Pond Example and most cases of international aid. I will return to these important points in Chapters 9 and 10.

4.2 Expert Observers and Intervening Agents[7]

One obvious disanalogy between the Pond Example and the typical case of giving to an international relief agency is that in the former case I personally and directly save the life of a child. In the latter case, my intervention only has an effect, if at all, through the cooperation and intervention of other agents. Singer's discussion implies that this difference has virtually no normative significance. As noted, in support of his position, Singer writes: "Expert observers and supervisors, sent out by famine relief organizations or permanently stationed in famine-prone areas, can direct our aid to a refugee in Bengal almost as effectively as we could get it to someone on our own block."

In the many years that I have taught the topic of obligations to the needy, I have always assumed that surely Singer was right about this claim. I have always told my students that with just a few hours of research on the internet they could easily identify international relief and development agencies that could be counted on to save lives and efficiently use any funds that they were given to benefit the world's needy "almost as effectively as I could ... [aid] someone on ... [my] own block," say, by saving a drowning child. However,

---

[7] For an empirical analysis supporting some of the claims made in this section and the following one, see Nunnenkamp, P. and H. Öhler, "Funding, Competition and the Efficiency of NGOs: An Empirical Analysis of Non-charitable Expenditure of US NGOs Engaged in Foreign Aid," Kiel Institute for the World Economy Working Papers, Number 1640, 2010.

I now believe that this important claim warrants much more scrutiny than I have previously given it. To see why, let me first say a few words about the scope of the issue of intervening agents, and why it gives rise to certain reasonable worries.

When I send money to an international relief organization that operates on the other side of the world, it is not as if I am reaching across the ocean with super long arms, and personally plucking a drowning child out of the water.[8] Nor is it as if I am deputizing a single, trusted, agent to exercise my will. Rather, I am indirectly relying on a bevy of intermediaries to act on my behalf. How many? It is difficult to say.

Presumably, there will be someone who opens my envelope or handles my credit card transaction in an office somewhere, let's say in Boston.[9] There will presumably be others who decide how my contribution will be used. Of course, I am counting on them following any express wishes that I convey—for example, to use the money to do as much good as possible, or to use the money to save lives. But the reality is that they will typically make their decision based on their organization's aims and guidelines, which themselves will typically be based on the input of many others, including local employees of the organization, agents of the organization on the ground in other countries, members of the organization's Board of Governors, and so on. There may be yet another person tasked to deposit my contribution into another account, based on the guidance of the Boston decision-makers. If all goes well, the money will then presumably arrive in some foreign country, where a similar array of agents will be involved at a local office in, say, Somalia.[10] Someone, or more likely various people, at the Somalian office will have access to whatever funds arrive, and will presumably be given some guidance on how the funds are to be used. Still, it will be local people on the ground, in Somalia,

---

[8] I here borrow from an ingenious thought experiment of Frances Kamm's. See Chapter 11 "Does Distance Matter Morally to the Duty to Rescue," in *Intricate Ethics: Rights, Responsibilities, and Permissible Harms*, New York: Oxford University Press, 2007, 345–67.

[9] Boston is the headquarters of Oxfam America, and the location to which I have long addressed my own contributions to Oxfam.

[10] In correspondence, Peter Singer acknowledges that the case of Somalia is a particularly difficult one. He writes: "A very tough example. Tragic as the situation in that country has been, I would not donate to help people there, for reasons given here: https://www.givewell.org//donate-to-Somalia." ("Donating to the Somalia Famine." *GiveWell*, The Clear Fund, August 11, 2011.)

It is not a coincidence that I chose to use Somalia in my example, since many have come to believe that aid efforts in Somalia have probably, overall, done more harm than good. However, my worries also arise for aid given to the Democratic Republic of Congo, Indonesia, Bosnia, Haiti, etc. Of course, the extent to which the worries I raise lead to negative outcomes, if any, depends on the facts on the ground in each unique aid environment. I am merely illuminating the many ways in which the Pond Example is not analogous to real-world instances of aid giving and, ultimately, the different factors that influence the impact of aid efforts, depending on the unique on-the-ground facts of each aid environment.

who will ultimately withdraw the funds and decide what, actually, to do with the funds, perhaps based on input from numerous local sources both within, and outside of, the agency. Next, someone will direct one or more people to buy relevant aid supplies. One or more others may then be employed to transport those supplies to an area of need. And presumably one or more people on the other end of the route will actually take the delivery of the supplies. Those people, in turn, will need to decide in whose hands those supplies should be entrusted. And perhaps, at that point, the supplies will end up in the hands of the people who are supposed to actually use them to aid others! There may also be a host of local, state, or national leaders, government officials, or others with whom the members of the international organization must cooperate to work in the areas of greatest need.

In sum, when dealing with large international relief organizations very many intervening agents will be involved in executing my intentions. In Singer's Pond Example, I only need to count on *one* person to execute my intentions, and that person is *me*. Does this difference have normative significance? It might.

In the children's game of "telephone" some number of children sit in a circle, and one child whispers a sentence in the ear of the child sitting next to it, that child, in turn, is supposed to whisper the same sentence into the ear of the child sitting next to it on the other side, and so on, until the sentence goes all the way around the circle and is finally whispered into the ear of the child who first uttered it. Notoriously, whether by a series of cumulative minor or major mishearings or misspeakings, a series of cumulative intentional "sabotagings" of the effort, or a combination of the two, the sentence that returns to the original speaker often bears little, if any, resemblance to the sentence that that child first whispered. In addition, the more children there are who are sitting in the circle, the more likely this is to be true. What makes the game fun, of course, is to see the massive, and often hilarious, discrepancies that can arise between the first utterance of the sentence, and the last utterance of what is supposed to be the same sentence. Clearly, Robinson Crusoe (prior to his discovery of his man, Friday), would never have tried to play the game of telephone as a means of entertaining himself while stranded on his island; since no matter how many times he might play it, whatever sentence he might speak aloud to himself would be the very same sentence that he heard.[11]

---

[11] See Stevenson, Robert Louis and Hiram Albert Vance, *Treasure Island*, New York and London: The Macmillan Company, 1902.

The point is that the more agents who stand between me and the execution of my intention, the more possibilities there are for something to go awry, whether intentionally or not, and whether for nefarious reasons or not. This dovetails with our previously noted point that there are significant dangers of misunderstanding the historical, social, political, religious, moral, and cultural realities of communities different than our own; so that there is a much higher risk of misalignment between intentions and outcomes associated with international, multilateral approaches to aid. Together, these factors reflect important disanalogies between Singer's Pond Example and the typical case of giving to an international relief organization that are all-too-often blithely ignored.

4.3 Saving Lives versus Supporting Effective Aid Organizations

Singer and his followers want us to believe that since "Expert observers and supervisors, sent out by famine relief organizations or permanently stationed in famine-prone areas, *can* direct our aid to a refugee in Bengal almost as effectively as we could get it to someone on our own block [emphasis added]," then giving to an effective relief organization is morally equivalent to saving lives. Yet, however well-intentioned Singer's argument may be, and however plausible it may be "on average," or "in the aggregate," at the individual level such a claim is highly dubious. Perhaps, in giving to an effective relief organization, you will, in fact, be responsible for saving someone's life. But perhaps not.

When I wade into the pond, I know exactly what I am getting in return for my ruined clothes or my destroyed Rolex—by hypothesis, *I am saving a drowning child's life*. But money is fungible, and while international aid agencies may solicit funds from donors by telling them of the lives they will save if they send in a check, the stark reality is that a donor's money may be going to pay for any number of perfectly legitimate business expenses that the charity incurs.

When you write on your check: "spend it where it will do the most good," your check may well end up in the organization's general operating expenses fund. Indeed, directly or indirectly, your check may well end up supporting the organization's general operating expenses even if you explicitly write on it "to be used solely to save innocent lives." Thus, when you write your check to an effective international development organization, it may end up helping to pay for any of the following: salaries of the organization's members, rent of its

Boston office, utility bills, stamps or fundraising brochures, food and alcohol at dinners where key Members of Congress or local leaders are lobbied to support the organization's efforts, gas and repairs for the vehicles that transport the medicine or food in Somalia, etc. Likewise, perhaps the development organization is working to educate young people, or empower women through small business loans, or build wells, or aid farming. In that case, your check might help pay for a teacher's salary, books, or desks for an elementary school; it might provide the loan that enables a woman to buy dyes for fabrics, supplies for a store, or a restaurant appliance; it might pay for equipment to dig a well, bricks and mortar to build it, or a motor to pump water; or it might pay for a pair of oxen, a plow, or perhaps a tractor.

The preceding are but a small sample of the many perfectly legitimate expenses and goals that any reputable international relief organization may incur or pursue. There is nothing nefarious, vicious, or inappropriate about such expenditures—though there *is* something inappropriate about misleading potential donors as to how their contributions will be used, in an effort to maximize donations—and they may all be well worthy of support from affluent people. Even so, intuitively, the difference between saving a child's life and paying for most of these other expenses seems sufficiently great, that there is reason to question the purported analogy between our obligation to save an innocent child in the Pond Example and our obligation to give to effective development organizations.

Consider, for example, the following case.

Aid Worker and the CEO's Salary: Nick is a man of modest means who only has one luxury item of significant value. The item, a $5,000 Rolex watch, has great sentimental value to Nick, as it was bequeathed to him by his favorite uncle. One day, as Nick is out for a walk, he spots a drowning child in a pond on one side of the street and an international development worker on the other. The worker honestly claims that he works for an effective international relief organization, which has a very talented CEO who earns $200,000 a year and is worth every penny. With a less talented CEO, the worker points out, his relief organization would accomplish far less good in the world than it currently does. The worker then notes that if Nick saves the drowning child his watch will be ruined. If, on the other hand, Nick lets the child drown, he can give the aid worker the intact watch, which he will sell for $5,000, every penny of which will go towards helping to pay for the CEO's salary.

Suppose that Nick believes the worker. Suppose, further, that Nick knows that, on average, for every $5,000 the development organization receives in donations, it saves two innocent children. Even so, intuitively, it seems clear that Nick should save the drowning child.

Or consider the following variation of the above case.

Aid Worker and an Aid Organization's Rent: Nick is a man of modest means who only has one luxury item of significant value. The item, a $5,000 Rolex watch, has great sentimental value to Nick, as it was bequeathed to him by his favorite uncle. One day, as Nick is out for a walk, he spots a drowning child in a pond on one side of the street and an international development worker on the other. The worker honestly claims that he works for an effective international relief organization, which has an office in Boston that it rents for the very low rate of only $10,000 per month (they get a special deal, because the landlord supports the organization's goals, normally that space in Boston would cost at least $30,000 per month). The worker notes that if Nick saves the drowning child his watch will be ruined. If, on the other hand, Nick lets the child drown, he can give the aid worker the intact watch, which he will sell for $5000, every penny of which will go to help pay for the organization's rent.

Once again, even if Nick believes the worker, and knows that, on average, for every $5,000 the development organization receives in donations, it saves two innocent children, intuitively, it seems clear that Nick should save the drowning child.

A similar intuitive response would result, I believe, if the worker had honestly promised that every penny from the proceeds of Nick's watch would go towards any of the other worthwhile uses noted above on which his organization might appropriately and efficiently spend its money.

Consider one last example, which more realistically tracks what typically happens when someone sends an aid agency money.

Aid Worker and the General Operating Fund: Nick is a man of modest means who only has one luxury item of significant value. The item, a $5,000 Rolex watch, has great sentimental value to Nick, as it was bequeathed to him by his favorite uncle. One day, as Nick is out for a walk, he spots a drowning child in a pond on one side of the street and an international development worker on the other. The worker honestly claims that he works for an effective international relief organization. On average, for every $5,000 that is donated, his agency promotes a total amount of good that is equivalent to the good that would be produced by saving two innocent children from drowning. Of course, there are various worthwhile activities that his agency promotes that makes this true, and numerous different kinds of expenses that they incur to attain those results.

If Nick saves the drowning child his watch will be ruined. If, on the other hand, Nick lets the child drown, and gives the aid worker his watch, the aid worker will sell it for $5,000, and every penny of the proceeds will go into the aid agency's general operating fund. The agency will only draw on the funds to help defray their legitimate expenditures. Accordingly, Nick can think of his contribution as paying a small share of each of their expenditures, proportional to the amount that those expenditures are of the agency's total budget.

Thus, in essence, the money the agency gets from selling Nick's watch will be used, proportionally, to help pay for salaries, rent, utility bills, office supplies, transportation costs, medicines, food, educational supplies, small business loans for women, well materials, farming supplies, and so on.

The worker's pitch would earn high marks for honesty. But I am guessing it would be ineffective. Intuitively, it seems clear that Nick should save the drowning child, given the two options he would be facing.

Of course, our intuitions about these cases may be mistaken. I have not argued otherwise. However, for many, the conclusion of Singer's argument, that we have a moral obligation to help the needy by contributing to effective aid agencies, derives much of its force from our intuitive reaction to the Pond Example, and its purported analogy with giving to an effective international development organization and, prima facie, the analogy between the two seems strained at best.

Singer and his followers can *assert* that "Expert observers and supervisors, sent out by famine relief organizations or permanently stationed in famine-prone areas, can direct our aid to a refugee in Bengal almost as effectively as we could get it to someone on our own block." However, the reality is that what I actually do in the Pond Example—personally wading in and directly saving an innocent life—is very different from what I actually do when I contribute to an international relief organization—personally sending a check that helps to defray a large number of different and legitimate expenses that the organization must incur which, together with the contributions of countless others, indirectly leads to the promotion of any number of valuable goals, which may include the saving of innocent lives, but may also include the education of children, the empowerment of women, the improvement of living conditions, the provision of healthcare for debilitating but non-fatal illnesses, and so on.[12*]

In Singer's original Pond Example, most people have the powerful intuition that we ought to save the drowning child. I believe that most would have similar intuitions about the examples just considered. That is, I believe that most people would intuitively think that we ought not to let the child drown to preserve the value of our Rolex watch, so that it could be sold by an effective aid agency with the proceeds going to help pay for the CEO's salary, or the agency's rent, or the agency's general operating expenses. If this is right, it reveals that there are features of the drowning child option that are intuitively compelling, that are lacking in the option of giving one's watch to an effective development agency. Thus, it seems a mistake to argue that we have a compelling moral obligation to give to international development organizations based largely on our intuitive reaction to Singer's Pond Example.

4.4 Summary

The main takeaways of this chapter include the following. First, even if we can have greater obligations to help members of our own community rather than members of other communities, this hardly shows that there are not

---

[12*] Recognizing that people feel very differently about the two situations, for many years international aid agencies tried (or pretended!) to link particular donors to particular aid recipients, typically children. This was so, for example, of the charitable organization Save the Children, and the organization that my father contributed to, as described in Section 2.1. However, this system was prone to abuses. For example, people being told their aid was helping a young child who had long since grown up, or a child who had since died, or the same child being "saved" or having her school supplies provided by multiple donors, or people being told all of their money was going to aid a particular child, when in fact very little, if any of it, was reaching that particular child, and so on. (For a scathing attack on some of Save the Children's previous abuses in this regard, see Michael Maren's *The Road to Hell: The Ravaging Effects of Foreign Aid and International Charity* (New York: The Free Press, 1997).) Also, it was extremely inefficient and a bureaucratic nightmare to try to establish and keep accurate records of a direct link between individual donors and individual recipients.

As a result of this, large international aid agencies generally regard it as a form of malpractice to promise that a donor's funds will be dedicated to addressing the needs of any particular aid recipient. So, for example, claiming that all funds will be used to aid the victims of Hurricane Maria in Puerto Rico is permissible (though typically misleading), but claiming that some particular donor's funds will go to restore the power at Luis Miguel Hernadez's home is inappropriate. (I am grateful to Angus Deaton, for comments that prompted the writing of this note.)

Of course, on a local level, there are often school, church, or community groups that hold fundraisers to benefit a particular member of the community that needs help. Likewise, one of the great appeals of Habitat for Humanity is that workers often get to meet the particular family whose home they are helping to build. For this reason, certain local charities, and charities like Habitat for Humanity, effectively avoid some of the worries raised here.

compelling reasons to help people in need, whether or not they are members of our community. Second, while I grant, for this book's purposes, the view that proximity *itself* is not morally relevant to the strength of reasons for aiding someone, I argue in Appendix B that this view is not as indubitable as most have assumed. Third, even if, due to technological advances, geographical differences between people lack the normative significances they might have once had, there remain many other social, cultural, historical, and political differences between people that are crucial to bear in mind, and appropriately respect, when considering international aid efforts. Fourth, when one contributes to an international aid agency, countless people play a role in developing and executing the agency's aims. The more such people there are, the more opportunities there are for things to go awry, in terms of the realization of one's aims in contributing to that agency. Moreover, this can be so for a variety of accidental, benign, or pernicious reasons. Fifth, when one contributes to an aid agency, one is, in effect, supporting all of that agency's goals, and helping to defray all of the expenses incurred in the realization of those goals. Even where those goals are laudable, and the expenses legitimate, they may not be as morally compelling as literally saving a person's life.

Finally, in Chapters 2 and 3, I argued that there are a host of powerful moral reasons to help the world's needy, including outcome-based reasons, virtue-based reasons, and deontological-based reasons. Together, these reasons may often support contributing to certain effective international aid organizations. However, while there will be some overlap in the nature of the underlying reasons that support giving to international aid organizations and the underlying reasons that support saving a drowning child—reasons that we may become aware of by reflecting on cases like Singer's Pond Example—it is, I believe, a mistake to think that the reasons are (basically) all the same, or of (roughly) equal strength. Similarly, I believe it is a mistake to think that the obligation to support effective international relief organizations is (basically) the same as the obligation to save a drowning child, or that the former directly follows from the latter. Likewise, while our intuitive reactions to Singer's Pond Example are compatible with Effective Altruism, it is a mistake to think that the correctness of the former entails the truth of the latter.

5

The Dark Side of Humanity, Part I

Worries about Internal Corruption

In Chapter 4, I noted that there may be perfectly legitimate reasons why any money that a donor gives to an international aid organization may end up being spent in ways other than what the donor intended. However, many potential donors are less worried about that possibility, than they are about the possibility that their money may be diverted for more nefarious reasons. I shall call this the worry about *internal corruption* when it concerns the possibility that some or all of one's contribution to an international aid organization may be misappropriated by one or more of its agents for their own benefit or purposes.

Good-hearted people tend to ignore, or downplay, such worries; often assuming that the aid that they give will avoid these issues. However, I believe that this is counterproductive, and plays into the hands of the opponents of international aid who claim that its proponents are naïve Pollyannas.

Since this book aims to be as honest and clear-eyed as possible, I think we should take this worry seriously. In Section 5.1, I present considerations reminding us of the dark side of humanity. I note that evil is prevalent within human society, and that many people can be easily led to act badly, even horrendously. This raises the natural worry that international aid agencies may be subject to internal corruption. This is not a worry that arises in Singer's Pond Example, pointing to another important disanalogy between Singer's example, and the real-world issues related to supporting international aid agencies. In Section 5.2, I consider two responses to the worry about internal corruption and suggest that they are unsatisfactory.

In Section 5.3, I question whether we can trust the rosy picture that is generally painted by aid organizations. I point out that aid organizations often adopt a "see no evil, hear no evil, speak no evil" approach when it comes to public reports about the nature and impact of their work. This reflects the fact that there are strong incentives for aid agencies to emphasize any positive effects of their operation, and to deemphasize, ignore, or even cover up any

Being Good in a World of Need. Larry S. Temkin, Oxford University Press. © Larry S. Temkin 2022.
DOI: 10.1093/oso/9780192849977.003.0005

negative effects of their operation. In Section 5.4, I summarize the chapter, and conclude by acknowledging that worries about internal corruption are hardly unique to international aid organizations. They could be similarly raised about any large organization, whether charitable or not.

5.1 The Dark Side of Humanity

In this section, I address the dark side of humanity. In doing this, I will be pushing a line that many, including me, will find ugly, disturbing, and dispiriting. It concerns the corruptibility and potential baseness of human agents.

I begin with several observations. First, some years back, I needed to hire a caregiver to stay with my mom. In discussing this with a dear friend, my friend advised me to be sure to empty the home of any valuables and to remove my mom's checkbook, before bringing any stranger into her home. I confess, I was rather taken aback by this advice, and when I questioned if that was really necessary, my friend insisted that it was, since "everybody steals"!

I remember thinking that my friend had a very sad, jaded, and pessimistic view of human nature, and that I wouldn't want to go through life looking at people the way he did. I still think that. However, I confess that while I believed, and continue to believe, that my friend's claim was far too sweeping, on reflection, I thought that I should follow his advice, and remove the valuables from my mom's home. In fact, the more I thought about it, the more I recalled a surprisingly large number of family members and friends who had had items of value stolen from their homes by visiting work people, house-cleaners, friends, relatives, and so on. Indeed, as it happens, my mom, herself, had had a long-time trusted handyman forge three of her checks for many thousands of dollars in a desperate attempt to pay off massive gambling debts that he had accrued.

Second, there is an old saying that "a lock is for the honest person." This saying dovetails with a famous line from the Lord's Prayer, which is recited by hundreds of millions of Christians on a regular basis: "lead us not into temptation and deliver us from evil."[1] The idea is simple. Committed criminals will find a way to commit crimes, locks or no locks. But most normal people will remain decent, law-abiding citizens if they stay sufficiently clear from corrupting temptations. Unfortunately, however, for many people weakness of the will is a common phenomenon, and temptations can be hard to

---

[1] *King James Bible*, Matthew 6; see, also, Luke 11:1–4.

resist in the wrong circumstances. Hence, the necessity of locks to keep honest people honest, and the daily prayers of millions that they should not be led into temptation and should be delivered from evil (people and circumstances).

Third, one lesson that the Holocaust made painfully clear is how easy it is for normal, everyday, people to be swept up in the circumstances of their time and place, and to participate in unimaginable evils.[2] Lynchings of blacks throughout the American South, and similar mob actions throughout the world, teach the same lesson. Unfortunately, it is not only madmen and psychopaths who are capable of participating in rape, murder, enslavement, and so on, but ordinary people from all walks of life.

Jonathan Glover's powerful book *Humanity: A Moral History of the Twentieth Century*[3] contains a litany of man's inhumanity to man over the course of the 20th century, touching on countless examples of repression, rape, torture, murder, starvation, massacre, firebombing, chemical warfare, nuclear devastation, terrorism, enslavement, and so on perpetrated by, or in, countries or territories such as Abyssinia, Afghanistan, Albania, Argentina, Austria, Belgium, Bosnia-Herzegovina, Burma, Cambodia, China, Croatia, Cuba, Czech Republic, Dubai, England, Falklands, France, Gaza, Germany, Holland, Hungary, India, Iran, Iraq, Israel, Italy, Japan, Korea, Kuwait, Lebanon, Libya, Northern Ireland, Poland, Rwanda, Serbia, Slovenia, Soviet Union, South Africa, Spain, Syria, Thailand, Turkey, Uganda, the United States, Vietnam, the West Bank, and Yugoslavia, among others. And while it is easy and tempting to ascribe many of the great horrors of the 20th century to the machinations of a few evil men with great power—Hitler, Stalin, Mao, Pol Pot, Idi Amin, and so on—the reality is that the great horrors of the 20th century could never have happened without the complicity and active participation of legions of ordinary people.

The roughly 340,000 people who were killed at Hiroshima and Nagasaki, most of whom were innocent non-combatants, did not die solely because Harry Truman ordered the dropping of the atomic bomb. Their deaths resulted, in part, from the combined efforts of countless people just doing their jobs—including, among others, pilots, navigators, bombardiers, mechanics, soldiers, engineers, scientists, Members of Congress, cabinet members, drivers, factory workers, defense contractors, plant managers, and secretaries. And the up-close-and-personal atrocities of the Holocaust, Mai Lai Massacre, Killing Fields, Gulag Archipelago, and Rwandan genocide were typically

[2] On the "banality of evil" see Hannah Arendt's classic work, *Eichmann in Jerusalem: A Report on the Banality of Evil* (New York: Viking Press, 1963).
[3] Glover, Jonathan, *Humanity: A Moral History of the Twentieth Century*, New Haven: Yale University Press, 2001.

committed by young men who in other circumstances might just have been devoted family members, god-fearing church/temple/mosque/ashram goers, law-abiding citizens, and hard-working students, farmers, factory workers, or professionals.

Moreover, it is not just in the darkest times of famine, war, and political instability that humans can be led to treat each other terribly. The infamous Milgram experiments amply illustrate how easily humans can be led to treat each other inhumanely merely because of the insistent urging of an apparent authority figure.[4] Likewise, the phenomenon of two demographically similar groups demonizing or antagonizing one another for trivial reasons is a familiar one from sports rivalries around the globe. And, of course, it is deeply disturbing how often grown adults end up shouting at each other, intensely disliking each other, and/or (nearly) coming to blows at t-ball, youth soccer, or pee wee football games, where the athletes competing with one another are under the age of ten!

William Golding's classic story, *Lord of the Flies*, portrays how thin the veneer of civilization is over the primitive and savage animals that humans are capable of being, even in the most sophisticated and supposedly "advanced" societies.[5] And the reason Golding's book is so powerfully chilling is precisely because it rings true. After all, Hitler's Germany—the Germany of Kepler, Bach, Handel, Kant, Goethe, Schiller, Beethoven, Hegel, Wagner, Marx, Brahms, Nietzsche, Cantor, Planck, Hilbert, Mann, Hess, Brecht, and countless other intellectual and artistic giants—was arguably among the most "advanced" civilizations that the world had ever seen.

So where does all this leave us? I am acutely aware that the picture I have painted here conveys an appallingly negative and one-sided view of the human story, and it is one that is ugly, disturbing, and dispiriting. The *full* story of humanity includes love as well as hate, hope as well as desperation, kindness as well as cruelty, generosity as well as selfishness, and so on. Still, while I vehemently reject the view that human nature is fundamentally evil, along with my friend's contention that "everybody steals," it would be folly to fail to recognize that far too many "normal" humans are capable of the most abominable acts depending on their circumstances—including rape, murder, torture, and enslavement. And if this is so, then is it unduly pessimistic, or

---

[4] See Milgram, Stanley, "Behavioural Study of Obedience." *Journal of Abnormal and Social Psychology* 67 (1963): 371–8.

[5] Golding, William, *Lord of the Flies*, London: Faber and Faber, 1954.

merely realistic, to worry that more people than we might care to admit might well lie, cheat, or steal if a low-risk opportunity arose to benefit themselves, or their loved ones, by doing so?

The point, of course, is that when I see a drowning child in a pond, there is just me and the child. As the example is presented, whether the child is saved is solely up to *me*. When I send a check to an international aid organization, numerous intervening members of that organization stand between me and the effective use of my donation to benefit the needy. Any one of them might have the opportunity to divert my contributions for their own purposes. Any one of them might take advantage of that opportunity. The more such people there are in the chain between me and those in need, the greater the possibility that someone will take advantage of my largesse to feather his or her own nest.

Thus, one respect in which the Pond Example is disanalogous from the standard case of giving to international relief organizations is that the latter gives rise to worries about organizational corruption that the former does not. It is not enough, I think, to simply sweep such worries aside with the claim that "Expert observers and supervisors . . . can direct our aid to a refugee in Bengal almost as effectively as we could get it to someone on our own block."

5.2 Two Responses to the Worry about Internal Corruption and Why They Are Problematic

In this section, I will consider two responses to the worry about internal corruption and suggest that they are problematic. The first response might be put roughly as follows: the sort of people who are attracted to work for international relief organizations are not "typical" people. They genuinely want to make the world a better place. They are often willing to work long hours with low pay, often in difficult conditions that expose themselves to numerous risks. Surely, it might be thought, we do not have to worry that *such* people will be corrupt and steal the funds that we, or others, have sent to save innocent people from dying!

There are several problems with this response. First, while many of us know aid workers who fit the stereotypical profile just described, it is a romanticized picture that will not accurately reflect many of those who work for large international aid agencies in the U.S. and abroad, and who stand in the long chain between me, my donation, and a needy person on the other side of the world. People join honorable professions for all sorts of reasons and, sadly, their motivations are not always honorable. Moreover, some people may join an honorable profession with the noblest of intentions, but lose their bearings along the way.

Consider an analogous claim that might be made on behalf of policemen or priests: the types of people who are attracted to work for police departments or the church are not "typical." They genuinely want to make the world a better place or to serve God. They are often willing to work long hours with low pay, often in difficult conditions that expose themselves to numerous risks. Surely, it might be thought, we do not have to worry that *such* people will be corrupt.

Yet, sadly, while no doubt countless policemen and priests really do live to serve others or God, there is no shortage of scandalous stories about policemen and priests who have abused their positions for personal gratification, often preying on the most vulnerable members of their communities. Likewise, stories abound about trusted scout leaders, teachers, and coaches who have violated that trust and abused young children in their care; about health professionals whose actions have not always been guided by what is best for their patients; about scientists and researchers, including academics, whose research has been funded by, and often serves the interests of, the military, tobacco companies, the sugar industry, or pharmaceutical companies; about banks and investment advisors who have betrayed the trust of their customers, including, in some cases, elderly pensioners who lost their entire life savings, and so on. Indeed, returning to the topic of charities, countless stories surface on a regular basis of so-called charities that supposedly aid the poor, the sick, orphans, veterans, etc., but that turn out mainly to be scams, or of other so-called charities that turn out to be fronts for terrorist organizations.

In sum, while no doubt charitable organizations attract many people who are above reproach in their motivations and subsequent behavior, it is naïve to suppose that charitable organizations, by their very nature, are immune to the sort of worries that I have been raising. Indeed, unfortunately, the very fact that so many people will naturally be trusting of charities that purport to aid the needy is likely to serve as a beacon to some scoundrels seeking to take advantage of that fact.

There is a second response to the worry about internal corruption. Effective Altruists are decidedly not claiming that we should give our contributions to just any old charity that pulls at our heartstrings. To the contrary, they are insisting that one should only give to the most effective aid organizations, where presumably this is empirically ascertained by independent agencies whose reputations and assessments are themselves above reproach. I do believe that, in principle, this is a compelling response to the worry about institutional corruption so far raised. In practice, however, things look a little different.

Unfortunately, in the real world, there are countless aid organizations involved in massive numbers of aid projects and programs. According to Roger Riddell, a respected development economist, "The London School of Economics' *Global Society Yearbook* estimated... in the year 2003, that there were 59,000 international NGOs active in the world."[6] Riddell also observed that "Together, they [NGOs] are implementing what must now amount to many hundreds of thousands of substantial aid-funded projects and programmes in the development and humanitarian fields."[7] Riddell was writing in 2007. The number of international NGOs and aid funded projects and programs is almost certainly much larger now than it was then. Unsurprisingly, then, the vast majority of international aid organizations and their projects and programs are evaluated only in the most superficial ways, if at all. After all, no organization has the time, energy, staff, resources, and incentive to do a careful, thorough, detailed, and wholly independent vetting of even a significant proportion of the active aid agencies, projects, or programs, let alone all of them.

Consider, for example, GiveWell, which, for good reason, is generally regarded in the Effective Altruism community as the gold-standard for organizations that evaluate the effectiveness of aid agencies. GiveWell doesn't even attempt to evaluate the majority of aid agencies. Rather, GiveWell starts by identifying certain areas of giving that merit priority, based largely on academic studies of the effectiveness of such areas in terms of improving the lives of the world's neediest members. Then, GiveWell invites agencies which are working in those areas of priority, and who might be interested in being endorsed by GiveWell, to submit to GiveWell's evaluation process. As GiveWell describes their evaluative process, "Most of our investigation [of aid agencies] generally consists of conversations with charity representatives [typically by video-conferencing, but sometimes by in-person interviews or both] and review of their documents.... In addition, we often speak to other current and potential funders of the charity in question, and we typically conduct at least one site visit to see the charity's work in the field."[8]

[6] Riddell, Roger, *Does Foreign Aid Really Work?*, Oxford: Oxford University Press, 2007, p. 54.
[7] Riddell, *Does Foreign Aid Really Work?*, p. 54.
[8] The quoted passage, and a description of GiveWell's process for identifying and evaluating charities can be found at https://www.givewell.org/how-we-work/process#Introduction, accessed June 28, 2019.

Strikingly, and importantly, an organization like GiveWell not only has nothing to say about the overwhelming majority of aid agencies—many of which are akin to "mom and pop" operations in size and scope—it has little to say about the largest international "mega-charities"—those with budgets of $250 million or more per year, such as UNICEF, Oxfam, Mercy Corps, Catholic Relief Services, Save the Children, and CARE.[9] Largely, this is because the mega-charities—which are by far the most impactful international aid organizations—see no reason for, or are simply not interested in, being evaluated by organizations like GiveWell.

Hence, while an organization like GiveWell makes every effort to provide a careful, thoughtful, and detailed assessment of those charities that it assesses, it is a relatively small, self-selected group of charities that it evaluates. More importantly, for my present purposes, GiveWell's evaluation is necessarily limited in the extent to which it can be truly "independent." In particular, as GiveWell openly acknowledges, their evaluations depend heavily—and inevitably so—on the information that is provided to them by the organizations that they are assessing, via the interviews, documents, or onsite visits.

The upshot of these remarks is that if the people providing the relevant information are themselves corrupt, they will aim to cook the books to cover up their malfeasance, and outside evaluating organizations may well lack the resources or independent access to the information necessary to discover this.

5.3 See No Evil, Hear No Evil, Speak No Evil

In this section, I question how much we can trust any internal reports released by aid agencies. After all, even if the people providing the information are not themselves corrupt, in the sense of stealing from the organization's coffers or inappropriately taking advantage of their organizational position for personal gain, if their livelihoods depend on the organization's success or if, as importantly, they are deeply committed to the organization's goals, then they may well perceive it to be in their interests, and that of their organization, to provide and/or withhold any information so as to paint the rosiest possible picture of the organization's effectiveness.

---

[9] A GiveWell blog, "Mega-charities," which discusses this fact, some of the reasons for it, and what, if anything, this says about the desirability of giving to such charities can be found at https://blog. givewell.org/2011/12/28/mega-charities/, posted December 11, 2011, updated June 13, 2013, accessed June 28, 2019.

Consider, for a moment, the 2018 Oxfam sex scandal. In the wake of that scandal, the following facts emerged: the scandal didn't break until *The Times* published a front page article on February 9, 2018, detailing events that took place following the massive Haitian earthquake of 2010—this means that somehow the scurrilous events had been kept out of the public eye for roughly eight years, though officially, of course, Oxfam vehemently denied that any cover-up had occurred; Oxfam claimed to have first uncovered the accusations in 2011, but the report of its internal investigation only revealed that "serious misconduct" had been involved; subsequently, Oxfam admitted that several of its aid workers had used prostitutes in a villa rented by Oxfam; allegations emerged that at least some of the "prostitutes" were survivors of the earthquake who had been taken advantage of by the Oxfam aid workers; allegations also emerged that some of the "prostitutes" were below the age of legal consent—underage girls ranging from 14 to 16—allegations that Oxfam claimed were "unproven" (which is hardly the same as a ringing denial of the claims); in the wake of its 2011 investigation Oxfam dismissed four staff members, but three others, including the then-director of Oxford operations in Haiti, Roland Van Hauwermeiren were allowed to resign; it further emerged that Hauwermeiren went on to work elsewhere in the aid sector, and that Oxfam had not warned other aid agencies about problem staff caught using "prostitutes."[10]

While the naïve public was aghast by these revelations, long-time aid workers cautioned that this was only the tip of the iceberg—that it had long been an open, and dirty little secret in the aid world that some aid workers employed prostitutes in regions of need, that some of these prostitutes were underage girls and boys, that in some cases aid workers abused their positions to take advantage of the very people they were supposed to help, vulnerable victims of poverty, hunger, disease, natural disasters, sectarian violence, or oppression, and so on; and, most importantly for our present purposes, that higher ups in the organizational chart tended to adopt a "see no evil, hear no

---

[10] There has been a massive amount written about the Oxfam scandal. The interested reader can find out much more about it with a quick internet search. Most of the details noted here, and below, were taken from the BBC article "Oxfam Haiti allegations: How the scandal unfolded," February 21, 2018, URL: https://www.bbc.com/news/uk-43112200, accessed June 28, 2019. A version of *The Times* article that originally broke the story, "Top Oxfam staff paid Haiti survivors for sex" is online at https://www.wordandaction.org/single-post/2018/02/08/Top-Oxfam-staff-paid-Haiti-quake-survivors-for-sex, accessed June 28, 2019. See, also, Matthew Green's "Oxfam and the Dark Side of the Aid Industry," *The Financial Times*, February 15, 2018, URL: https://www.ft.com/content/8799725c-123c-11e8-8cb6-b9ccc4c4dbbb, accessed June 20, 2019.

evil, speak no evil" stance to any whispers or reports of such inappropriate, and in some cases deeply immoral, conduct.

Sure enough, within days of the Oxfam story breaking, allegations emerged that Oxfam staff had used prostitutes on a mission to Chad, also headed by Van Hauwermeiren, in 2006; that Van Hauwermeiren had been investigated for using prostitutes in Liberia in 2004 before working for Oxfam; that Médecins Sans Frontières had repatriated 17 of its staff members working in Haiti without explanation; that Save the Children investigated 53 allegations of misconduct in 2016; and that 120 workers from UK charities were accused of sexual abuse in the previous year.[11]

Furthermore, despite the uproar that arose following the Oxfam sex scandal, numerous resignations in the wake of it, vows to clean things up, and a massive ad by Oxfam telling the world "WE ARE SO SORRY...We are listening...We want you to know that we are working hard to rebuild [your trust],"[12] on the very day that I am typing these words, *The Times* has published another story in which it alleges that to this day Oxfam aid workers in African refugee camps "have been promising to pay teenage girls' school fees in return for sex and trading basic food and supplies for sexual favours. [And that m]en have lost...jobs in the camps and vital income because their wives 'refused to have sex with "the boss"'."[13]

The issue, here, is not the relatively small number of bad people, in any large organization, whose actions can give that organization a black eye. It is, rather, that time and again large organizations turn a *blind* eye to such actions, or deal with them internally to keep them out of the public eye. So, the harsh reality is that we rarely learn of such untoward events, except as a result of brave whistle blowers who have gone public, or the hard work of investigative reporters.

Indeed, one of the most striking lessons to be learned from some of the most high-profile scandals of recent years is how often organizational leaders who are above reproach in their own personal conduct have gone to great lengths to cover up of the wrongdoing of others in their organizations, so as to protect the image and reputation of their organizations, and not lose the trust of their supporters. Moreover, they have done so, even when such conduct continues to put other vulnerable people at risk of the predatory actions that they are

---

[11] Again, see the BBC article, "Oxfam Haiti allegations: How the scandal unfolded" cited in the previous note.

[12] "Oxfam Haiti allegations: How the scandal unfolded."

[13] "Oxfam scandal: staff still offering aid for sex, report claims," Sean O'Neill, Chief Reporter, *The Times*, June 28, 2019 available with a subscription at https://www.thetimes.co.uk/article/oxfam-scandal-staff-still-offering-aid-for-sex-report-claims-pbx32xctw, accessed June 28, 2019.

attempting to cover up. This has been so with the financial industry, the Catholic Church, the Boy Scouts, boarding schools, and universities, among others.

With regard to sex scandals alone, there has been extensive reporting establishing that:

- Catholic Church leaders around the globe covered up abuses of untold numbers of children, some as young as three, by thousands of priests spanning more than five decades. Those accused of participating in the cover-up include some of the most admired and highest ranking members of the Catholic hierarchy.
- Leaders in the Boy Scouts of America covered up abuses by scoutmasters for decades. Again, many of those leaders were highly respected members of their communities who would never, themselves, have engaged in such heinous activities.
- Top administrators at Penn State University, including the President and head football coach, covered up the abuse of more than 30 young children by Jerry Sandusky, a long-time assistant coach of the football team. The head football coach, Joe Paterno, had long been regarded as a paragon of virtue in his community.
- Leaders at Baylor University—a religious institution—covered up multiple cases of rape and sexual assault over many years by members of the football team and fraternity members. This ultimately led the President and Chancellor of the University, Kenneth Starr, to resign. Starr, a former Solicitor General of the United States, had previously been regarded as a man of impeccable integrity.
- U.S.A. gymnastics covered up the sexual molestation of hundreds of female athletes over several decades, most of them minors, perpetrated by gym owners, coaches, and staff across the United States. The most famous perpetrator, Larry Nassar, was a trusted team doctor for U.S.A. gymnastics, and his victims included numerous members of the Olympic and U.S. National Team.
- Larry Nassar was also a longtime professor and doctor at Michigan State University, where he sexually abused hundreds of young women over several decades. Nassar was allowed to remain in his position where he would continue to assault young women long after allegations of sexual abuse against him had been lodged with trusted and high-ranking university faculty and administrators. As a result, MSU has agreed to a settlement of half a billion dollars to be paid to 332 of the victims of Nassar's abuse.

- Countless underage girls in different cities, states, and countries complained to friends, family members, and/or authorities that they had been sexually assaulted by the rich, powerful, and well-connected American financier Jeffrey Epstein and his friends. However, for many years, strikingly little was done to prevent him from continuing to prey on vulnerable young girls.
- At least 12 former teachers had sexually molested students at the elite Connecticut boarding school Choate for decades. Yet administrators who were aware of such misconduct failed to report it to the police, allowed some of the perpetrators to resign, and in some cases wrote letters of recommendation for the teachers who were fired. And so on.

Often, priests, teachers, coaches, and others who were found to have abused their charges were quietly reassigned, or allowed to move on to similar positions in other locations without prosecution or even public censure, enabling them to victimize other innocent youth elsewhere.[14]

The preceding is but a small sample of high-profile cases where trusted figures ignored, covered up, and/or failed to appropriately respond to heinous actions of which they were well aware. No doubt for every recognizable high-profile case, there are untold numbers of similar cases that never see the light of day. I have little doubt that this pattern of behavior holds true in communities around the world, and for every manner of blameworthy action. Surely, all this must give one serious pause about how much confidence one can place in the accuracy of any reasonably large organization's reports as to that organization's integrity and accountability, including, as I have been arguing, within the aid world.

Unfortunately, if the officers of an international aid organization hope to generate revenue to support the organization's worthy goals based on how effective their organization is, there will be strong pressures to oversell the organization's successes, and to undersell its failures. Moreover, as with any other organization that depends for its viability on the trust of its customers, shareholders, or followers, there will be powerful incentives for the officers of an international aid organization to not look for, or even to cover up, any evidence of substantial malfeasance, lest current and potential donors take

---

[14] The sad, sordid, and often tragic details about these cases, and countless others, are easily accessed via the internet. Simply type the relevant keywords into one's web browser—for example, "Catholic Church sex scandal," "Baylor University sex scandal," or "Jeffrey Epstein"—and a flood of pertinent news stories, articles, and videos will pop up.

their donations elsewhere.[15] Moreover, the point here is generalizable, and goes well beyond merely failing to look for, or report, any malfeasance on the part of an agency's workers. The reality is that aid agencies have little incentive to report any negative impacts that their organizations may have in the short or long term, either directly or indirectly. And, as already noted, they have every reason to paint the rosiest possible picture of the positive impact that they have, even if that picture is misleading. Thus, in an industry that is increasingly judged by the efficacy of its results, there is increasing reason to worry whether self-reported results are themselves trustworthy and, as noted, it is not clear that independent evaluating agencies are really able to accurately make such judgments for themselves.

Moreover, if the lessons of the oversight of big businesses by the big-five accounting firms are anything to go by, the more an independent firm works with, and gets to know, the principals of an international aid organization, the more difficult it becomes for that firm to retain its independence and to preserve its impartiality. Plus, whenever large sums are involved, the worry about corruption can be re-raised, as independent evaluators can be provided with a variety of incentives to generate a favorable report.

In sum, the worry about organizational corruption can be alleviated to some extent, by appealing to the evaluation of the effectiveness of aid organizations by supposedly trustworthy, independent evaluating agencies. But the worries will not disappear entirely, for the reasons suggested.

5.4 Partners in Crime, a Concluding Remark

In this chapter, I have argued that we need to take seriously the possibility that any large international aid organization may be subject to internal corruption. I have also suggested that international aid organizations often take a "see no evil, hear no evil, speak no evil" approach when it comes to the issue of internal corruption, or, for that matter, any other negative aspects of their organizations. Of course, I have not claimed that every international organization does, in fact, suffer from such corruption, much less that every international aid

---

[15] This is no mere academic worry. After the Oxfam scandal broke, donations to Oxfam dropped precipitously. Of course, it may well be the case that, in the long run, Oxfam and other organizations would do better to get out in front of such scandals, on their own, and not wait until the story breaks from other sources. However, it is all too common for people to avoid the immediate short-term losses, which might well be significant, in hopes that the losses will never occur, or that if they do, they will come in the distant future.

organization suffers from internal corruption to a significant or unacceptable degree. Nor have I claimed, much less shown, that every international aid organization has substantial negative impacts that they are failing to recognize or report. (I shall say more about this possibility in later chapters.) Still, one is unlikely to see what one isn't looking for, and even more unlikely to see what one is averting one's eyes from. This should give us pause about the reliability of any self-reports published by international aid organizations, regarding the conduct of their members and the overall impact of those organizations.

None of this chapter's worries arise in Singer's Pond Example. But they are real, and they need to be duly considered when thinking about how best to respond to the plight of the world's needy.

Let me conclude this chapter, by acknowledging that while the worry about internal corruption within international aid agencies is legitimate, that worry also arises for organizations like the Sierra Club, Nature Conservancy, PETA, the ASPCA, Big Brothers and Big Sisters, the United Way, Planned Parenthood, the World Wide Fund for Nature, Shriner's Hospitals, the Dana Farber Foundation, the March of Dimes, the American Heart Association, the Salvation Army, the Girl Scouts, the Harvard University Foundation, and so on. That is, worries about general human weakness and corruptibility can be raised about any large-scale charitable organization for which it is true that many intervening agents may stand between a donor and the final distribution of the donor's contribution. Accordingly, unless one is prepared to restrict one's charitable contributions to very small organizations—preferably, ones where one personally knows the members of the organization that will be acting on one's behalf—or to organizations where one is personally involved in the charity's activities or the distribution of one's donation—so that one can directly see for oneself the benefits that one's efforts or contributions produce—the possibility of institutional corruption is something with which, regrettably, one may simply have to come to terms.

The thought that we may just have to "come to terms" with the possibility of corruption is one that I take seriously. I shall say more about that thought in the next chapter, in the context of discussing another, deeper, worry about corruption that often arises in some of the poorest, and most troubled, regions of the world.

6

The Dark Side of Humanity, Part II

Worries about External Corruption

In Chapter 5, I discussed the worry of internal corruption within an international aid organization. In this chapter, I discuss another, deeper, worry about corruption. This is a worry about corrupt individuals or institutions external to aid agencies themselves, with whom, or with which, aid agencies might become enmeshed. I call this the problem of *external corruption*.

In Section 6.1, I present the problem of external corruption. I suggest that the problem of external corruption may be especially prevalent in some of the world's most desperate regions where the need is greatest, and so where international aid agencies often operate and focus much of their energy and resources. In Section 6.2, I briefly consider two responses to the problem of external corruption and suggest that they are inadequate. In Section 6.3, I develop the suggestion floated at the end of Chapter 5, that perhaps we must simply learn to live with corruption. In this section, I focus on the issue of external corruption, but what I say would apply, mutatis mutandis, to the problem of internal corruption as well. Section 6.4 provides a brief chapter summary and concluding remark.

6.1 The Worry about External Corruption

Many people worried about corruption in the aid world are much less concerned about internal corruption than they are about external corruption. That is, they are much less concerned about the possibility that a donor's funds may be diverted from aiding the needy into the pockets of some people *within* the aid organization, than they are about the possibility that a donor's funds may be diverted from aiding the needy into the pockets of some people *outside* of the aid organization. More particularly, they fear that, often, to provide aid to those most in need, perfectly honest officials within an international aid organization will require the cooperation of corrupt officials outside of the

Being Good in a World of Need. Larry S. Temkin, Oxford University Press. © Larry S. Temkin 2022.
DOI: 10.1093/oso/9780192849977.003.0006

organization, cooperation for which they will have to pay, in some coin or other.

Angus Deaton provided one example of the on-the-ground realities underlying this concern when he observed that "the government of Meles Zenawi Asres in Ethiopia received more than \$3 billion of aid in 2010, from the United States, Britain, and the World Bank, among others. Meles, who died in 2012, was one of the most repressive and autocratic dictators in Africa."[1] The worry, of course, is that too often, in some of the regions where the need is greatest, aid that is intended to help the needy ends up in the hands of corrupt government officials, business leaders, or other powerful individuals, rather than in the hands of those who desperately need that aid.

Some people are uncomfortable with people in the West talking about corruption in the developing world. I understand this sentiment, as such talk often reflects a smug attitude of moral superiority reminiscent of the worst days of imperialism and can often amount to a form of so-called "third-world" bashing. It also ignores the many respects in which Western countries have their own forms of corruption, for example, politician buying. Or the ways in which previous Western interventions, and ongoing international law and economic practices have helped give rise to, and continue to provide support for, corrupt regimes in the developing world.

I trust that Chapter 5 makes it clear that I do not believe that corruption is solely a problem in the developing world. Nor am I denying the West's role in fostering the conditions that enable corruption to often flourish in many of the world's poorest regions. However, with that said, I believe that we must confront worries about all forms of corruption head on, and not sweep them under the rug, if we hope to have anything remotely approaching an honest appraisal of the possible drawbacks, as well as benefits, of foreign aid. I proceed accordingly.

The fact is that in many countries, what *we* regard as corruption, bribery, and graft is deeply woven into the fabric of society, stretching back for centuries. Often, it is just accepted as an everyday fact of life—part of the natural order of things. Accordingly, to do any kind of business in those places, one must be prepared to "pay off" any number of local, state, or national authority figures to secure their cooperation. Moreover, this situation tends to be particularly prevalent in the world's poorest countries where the need is greatest, often including war-torn countries, poverty-stricken

---

[1] Deaton, Angus, *The Great Escape: Health, Wealth, and the Origins of Inequality*, Princeton: Princeton University Press, 2015, p. 286.

countries, countries dominated by dictators or political instability, or regions controlled by warlords or gangs. Accordingly, there is the very real possibility that funds that are given to aid the needy will end up lining the pockets of corrupt authority figures in many of the countries where international aid organizations operate.

It is worth noting, here, that corrupt officials have various direct and indirect methods of getting their hands on a piece of the international aid pie. They may demand payment upfront from aid organizations, perhaps in the form of out-and-out bribes, but perhaps in more subtle forms such as "permit" fees to work in the region. However, they may equally allow food, medicine, supplies, and money to flow directly from aid workers to needy individuals, and then effectively demand kickbacks from the recipients of such aid of which the aid agency may be blissfully unaware.[2] Or, indeed, they might simply pass "above board" legislation that effectively imposes a tax on the recipients of foreign aid, filling their coffers with income that was originally intended by generous donors to be used solely for the benefit of those in need.

This is the worry about corruption that vexes many people the most when they contemplate contributing to international relief organizations. It is a worry that most people believe either doesn't apply or applies to a much smaller extent, regarding large-scale charitable organizations that operate largely in Western democracies, such as those listed earlier in Section 5.4.[3]

6.2 Two Responses to the Worry about External Corruption

In this section, I will briefly present two responses to the worry about external corruption and note that I do not find them compelling. I shall discuss a third, more plausible, response, in the following section.

---

[2] This is similar to how "protection" rackets work with many criminal organizations. Criminal organizations don't "tax" each customer who frequents a given business. Instead, they demand a fixed amount, or percentage of the company's revenue in exchange for the businesses being "allowed" to "safely" operate within the criminal organization's domain. Similarly, during the Vietnam War, U.S. military forces would sometimes provide food, medicine, and other supplies to Vietnamese villages during the day, only to have their enemies, the Viet Cong, enter those same villages at night and confiscate some or all of those provisions for themselves. (See *The Vietnam War: A Film by Ken Burns & Lynn Novick*, directed by Ken Burns and Lynn Novick, Florentine Films and WETA, 2017.)

[3] This belief may or may not be as well-founded as many people assume. Certainly, there are areas in the U.S. where graft, bribery, and corruption obtain to a much larger extent than most people realize. Still, according to one frequently cited measure of corruption, the *Corruption Perceptions Index*, in 2017 the United States was ranked as the 22nd least corrupt country in the world of the 180 countries ranked. (See "Most Corrupt Countries," *World Population Review*, August 20, 2019, available at http://worldpopulationreview.com/countries/most-corrupt-countries/, accessed August 30, 2019.)

The first response is just to deny that the facts on the ground are as the worry portrays them to be. This would require adducing empirical evidence in support of the view that corruption is much less prevalent, or problematic, in the areas where international aid organizations operate than this worry presupposes, so that, for practical purposes, we can safely ignore the worry. The problem is that here, as elsewhere, most of the available evidence is inconclusive, and the same evidence may be appealed to by those on opposite ends of the question.[4]

Still, of the 20 least corrupt countries of the 180 ranked by the 2017 *Corruption Perception Index*—Denmark, New Zealand, Finland, Singapore, Sweden, Gabon, Norway, the Netherlands, Canada, Luxembourg, Germany, United Kingdom, Australia, Hong Kong, Iceland, Austria, Belgium, Estonia, Ireland, and Japan[5]—one would expect to find few international aid agencies operating extensively in those countries to help the needy. On the other hand, of the 20 most corrupt countries of the 180 ranked by the 2017 *Corruption Perception Index*—Somalia, Syria, South Sudan, Yemen, North Korea, Sudan, Afghanistan, Libya, Burundi, Venezuela, Iraq, Angola, Republic of the Congo, Chad, Turkmenistan, Haiti, Cambodia, Zimbabwe, Uzbekistan, and Mozambique[6]—one would expect to find a large presence of international aid agencies operating in many of those countries to aid the needy. This suggests (though I grant it is not conclusive) that in many contexts where aid organizations are operating the worry about external corruption needs to be taken seriously.[7*]

The second response to the worry about external corruption is to admit that there may be many layers of corrupt officials within the countries where the need is greatest, but to contend that this is why it is important to support the aid efforts of non-governmental organizations (NGOs), rather than government-to-government aid efforts. The idea is that NGOs supposedly

---

[4] See Chapter 2 note 2. Also, Riddell, Roger, *Does Foreign Aid Really Work?*, Oxford: Oxford University Press, 2007.

[5] Again, see "Most Corrupt Countries," *World Population Review*, August 20, 2019.

[6] "Most Corrupt Countries," *World Population Review*, August 20, 2019.

[7*] Some people look at the impact of aid in some of the world's poorest regions and conclude that on-the-ground aid efforts contribute to the problem of corruption. (See Deaton's *The Great Escape*.) Others claim that the evidence suggests that aid decreases corruption. (See Jose Tavares's influential paper "Does Foreign Aid Corrupt?" *Economics Letters* 79 (2003): 99–106.) Notice, however, that even if, on average, foreign aid decreased corruption, that would not establish that it was desirable. Suppose, for example that foreign aid had the effect of changing a country from being *extremely* corrupt, to "merely" being *seriously* corrupt. It could still be that having benefited from an influx of foreign aid, a wealthier and stronger government that was seriously corrupt might do more harm in the long run, and perhaps even in the short run, than a government that was extremely corrupt but, having not benefited from foreign aid, was considerably poorer and weaker.

operate *directly* with the people who need their help, thereby bypassing government officials and agencies who might otherwise siphon off a significant portion of the aid, and ensuring that all of the aid ends up in the hands of those it is intended to benefit. Singer's optimistic claim that "Expert observers and supervisors, sent out by famine relief organizations or permanently stationed in famine-prone areas, can direct our aid to a refugee in Bengal almost as effectively as we could get it to someone on our own block" may be implicitly reflecting this view.

I would like nothing more than for this second response to be adequate, but for reasons given above I find it less than convincing. NGO or non-NGO, any organization that hopes to operate effectively in a foreign land will ultimately need the approval and support of the relevant local power brokers. Accordingly, I find it hard to believe that in those areas that are controlled by some combination of powerful and corrupt dictators, generals, warlords, chiefs, gang leaders, policemen, politicians, or local leaders, such people will not find a way, directly or indirectly, to get a piece of whatever funding or supplies are intended to help the needy.

Angus Deaton shares this worry. He writes that corrupt officials "can (and do) levy taxes on goods and equipment imported by the NGOs, or require expensive operating licenses. The same thing happens in humanitarian emergencies, especially in time of war, when warlords have to be bought off in order to allow humanitarian access to their own people."[8] Unfortunately, the aid literature is rife with examples where NGO aid has been siphoned away by local warlords or corrupt local or national leaders.[9]

Moreover, even if vicious and corrupt officials allow NGO aid funds to go, untouched, to those in need, or for some other reason do not manage to get their hands directly on the aid money, their positions may still be substantially strengthened due to the fungibility of money and other resources. Specifically, money and effort that the government might otherwise have had to spend on

---

[8] *The Great Escape*, p. 264.
[9] See Easterly, William, *The White Man's Burden: Why the West's Efforts to Aid the Rest Have Done So Much Ill and So Little Good*, New York: Oxford University Press, 2006; de Waal, Alex, *Famine Crimes: Politics & the Disaster Relief Industry in Africa*, Oxford: James Currey and Bloomington: Indiana University Press, 1997; Rieff, David, *The Reproach of Hunger: Food, Justice, and Money in the Twenty-First Century*, New York: Simon & Schuster, 2015; Maren, Michael, *The Road to Hell: The Ravaging Effects of Foreign Aid and International Charity*, New York: The Free Press, 1997; Epstein, Helen, *Another Fine Mess: America, Uganda, and the War on Terror*, New York: Columbia Global Reports, 2017; Moyo, Dambisa, *Dead Aid: Why Aid Is NOT Working and How There Is a Better Way for Africa*, New York: Farrar, Straus and Giroux, 2009; Polman, Linda, *The Crisis Caravan: What's Wrong with Humanitarian Aid?*, New York: Metropolitan Books, 2010; Dichter, Thomas W., *Despite Good Intentions: Why Development Assistance to the Third World has Failed*, Amherst: University of Massachusetts Press, 2003; and Deaton, *The Great Escape*.

the most pressing needs of their citizens, to avoid political unrest, would now be available for the government to use to advance its own agenda. This might include vicious acts of repression and suppression, as well as more venal ends, such filling the pockets of its leaders and providing benefits for their followers and supporters. I shall discuss this point further in Chapter 7.

6.3 Learning to Live with Corruption?

There is a third response to the problem of external corruption, which parallels the response already noted, at the end of Chapter 5, regarding the possibility that there may be some level of internal corruption within any large-scale organization, charitable or otherwise. This response acknowledges that some contributions to international aid organizations may end up lining the pockets of corrupt individuals outside of those organizations, but suggests that we must simply learn to live with that unfortunate fact. I believe that there is much to be said for this response, at least in certain contexts and for certain kinds of corruption. Let us explore this issue further.

Consider first, the Old Testament story of the destruction of the cities of Sodom and Gomorrah. As the story goes, God informs Abraham that He intends to destroy the two cities, because they are teeming with irredeemable sinners. Abraham begins to argue with God, asking if He would be willing to spare the cities if 50 righteous people could be found within them. God agrees. Abraham continues to argue with God, asking if He would spare the cities if 45 righteous people lived within them. Once again, God agrees. Abraham then continues to argue with God, lowering the threshold for sparing the cities down to 40, then to 30, then to 20, and, finally, to 10. At each step, God agrees. Unfortunately, in the end, there are not even ten righteous people found within the cities. However, Abraham's cousin, Lot, is shown to be righteous, and he and his family are transported by two angels out of Sodom. Afterwards, the two cities, presumably consisting of many hundreds or thousands of inhabitants, are destroyed in a hail of fire and brimstone.

There are many fascinating elements of this story—including the awe-inspiring example of Abraham, a puny human, having the effrontery to stand up to Almighty God Himself, challenging His wisdom and moral judgment in order to preserve innocent human lives. More importantly, for our present purposes, the story explicitly teaches us that it is better to allow many hundreds or perhaps thousands of unrepentant sinners to escape punishment and continue to thrive, than to unjustly take even ten innocent lives.

One need not be religious to believe that there is something deeply important about this lesson from the story of Sodom and Gomorrah. Accordingly, one might similarly believe that if the cost of saving some number of innocent people from death by starvation, disease, disaster, or war is to add some resources to the coffers of corrupt officials, then that is a cost worth bearing.[10] One doesn't have to *like* contributing to the high-flying lifestyle of a corrupt official, but one can learn to live with it. Indeed, it may sicken one's stomach when one thinks about how many other lives might be saved with the money that corrupt officials spend on palatial mansions, fancy cars, and other luxury items. Still, on this view, if the alternative is to do nothing, and let innocent people die, or to save innocent people, but at the cost of helping to enrich corrupt individuals, one should hold one's nose and do the latter.

Next, consider a more mundane example.

Jane's Starbucks Fix: Jane goes into her local Starbucks. She orders her daily Cinnamon Dolce Latte, to which, let's face it, she is more or less addicted. She is always tempted by the 31 oz. Trenta, or the 20 oz. Venti, but she resists, limiting herself to the 16 oz. Grande. She pays $5 for her coffee. Jane never really stops to ask herself exactly what her $5 is paying for. All that really matters, to her, is that she loves her morning joe, and she is happy to pay the $5 that it costs to satisfy her daily craving for coffee.

Jane's Starbucks Fix represents a daily ritual engaged in by countless people around the globe. The reality underlying that ritual is something like this. When Jane pays her $5 for coffee, some of that $5 goes to pay for the rent of the building in which her Starbucks is located. Some goes to pay for the utilities and insurance on that building. Some goes to pay for the salary of the student serving her. Some goes into the pocket of the manager of the local franchise, and even more goes into the pocket of the local franchise owner, who may or may not be a nice person. Some goes to defray the cost of the franchise fee. Some goes for advertising. Some goes for packaging and napkins,

---

[10] Strictly speaking, this does not automatically follow from the lesson to be learned from the story of Sodom and Gomorrah. In that case, the thought was that to avoid some innocent people being *killed*, one might have to *allow* some evil people to flourish. In this case, the thought is that to *save* some innocent people from dying, one might have to *contribute* to some evil people flourishing. Deontologists often treat cases of *not killing* differently than cases of *saving*, and they also often treat cases of *allowing* evil people to flourish differently than cases of *contributing* to the flourishing of evil people. Even so, while I believe there are many contexts where the distinctions deontologist appeal to are morally relevant, I also believe that for many contexts if one accepts the former position one should also accept the latter position.

which will soon end up in the trash. Some goes for the packing of the coffee from its original destination to the distribution center in the U.S. Some goes for the unpacking and repacking of the coffee at the U.S. distribution center, the salaries of the people at the distribution center doing the unpacking and repacking, the rent and utilities of the distribution center, the salaries of the manager and owner of the distribution center, and so on. Some goes for the multiple layers of transportation from the coffee's place of origin to its final destination. Since Starbucks is a publicly owned company, some goes into the pockets of those who own stock in the company, who may or may not be nice people. And so on. Moreover, while Starbucks advertises its commitment to offering "high quality, ethically purchased, and responsibly produced products," they also receive some of their coffee from places like Mexico, Guatemala, Ethiopia, and Rwanda,[11] countries for which worries about corruption often arise. So, *some* of the money that Jane spends on her coffee may be supporting the lavish lifestyles of corrupt officials in the countries where her coffee beans were originally produced. The upshot of all this is that of the $5 that Jane spends on her coffee, only a small fraction goes to the workers who produced the main food ingredients that ended up in her cup: the coffee beans, the cinnamon, the milk, the sugar, and the salt.

A similar story can be told about many of the products that consumers buy in today's global economy. Consumers pay a given price for a pair of sneakers, a dress, or a TV that is made on the other side of the world, and only a small fraction of the price actually goes to pay for the raw materials and the salaries of the workers who produce the products that they end up with. The rest pays for the countless intervening agents and actions that play some role in the pipeline between the original creation of the materials that go into the production of the item, and the customer who finally takes possession of it. In the modern global economy, most people have learned to live with this. And we have done so even though, at some level, we understand that often the production of the goods that we covet and pay so dearly for involves the employment or exploitation of underprivileged workers in other countries in poor working conditions at low pay, and often lines the pockets of owners, business people, stockholders, government officials, and others at least some of whom engage in questionable business practices or corrupt behavior.

---

[11] See the *Starbucks Social Impact* page, URL: https://www.starbucks.com/responsibility, accessed August 30, 2019. See also the list of Starbucks Farmer Support Center Locations, available at https://www.starbucks.com/responsibility/community/farmer-support/farmer-support-centers, accessed August 30, 2019.

In sum, in the modern global economy, most affluent consumers have learned to live with the reality that many of their purchases may ultimately help line the pockets of an array of corrupt or unsavory individuals. As long as they get the products they want, they don't peer too closely or ask too many questions about where the profits from their purchases are ending up. But then, if we are willing to condone such a view, as most of us implicitly do, for the sake of trivial consumer products like a cup of coffee, a pair of sneakers, a dress, or a TV, shouldn't we be able to accept similar consequences for the sake of saving innocent lives? How come people are so worried about the problem of corruption and where their money is ending up, when the discussion turns to contributions to international relief organizations, when they basically ignore such questions when it comes to the purchase of consumer goods?[12*]

As noted, when Jane buys her $5 Cinnamon Dolce Latte, she doesn't really care what percentage of her cost went to salaries, advertising, packaging, transportation costs, food ingredients, and so on. What matters to her is that she gets her morning fix, and she thinks it is worth spending $5 to get that fix, wherever her money ends up. Similarly, it might be argued, if I am willing to dive into a pond to save a drowning child, even if doing so would utterly ruin my $5,000 Rolex watch, I'm indicating that I think it is worth losing $5,000 of mine to save an innocent life. But if that is so, then why should I object if, rather than totally ruining my watch, which I was prepared to do, I sell the watch instead, with the proceeds going to pay for a whole lot of costs associated with running an effective international relief organization, such as rent, salaries, transportation, procurement of lifesaving supplies, and so on?[13]

[12*] There is an excellent discussion of this question in Leif Wenar's *Blood Oil: Tyrants, Violence, and the Rules that Run the World* (New York: Oxford University Press, 2017); see, especially, the Introduction, and Chapters 5 and 14. However, Wenar turns this question on its head. The upshot of Wenar's discussion is to be highly critical, and rightly so, of the complacency with which we typically view our purchases of consumer goods, choosing to ignore the impact that our purchases have on others elsewhere in the world due to the workings of the global economic system.

Blood Oil provides a powerful and eye-opening discussion of the many ways in which Western-style consumerism often benefits and encourages the rise of ruthless dictators in countries whose rich natural resources fuel such consumerism, resources such as oil (which, besides its obvious role in supplying fuel for transportation, plays a crucial role in agricultural production, as well as the production of countless everyday items such as "asphalt, aspirin, balloons, blenders, candles, car bumpers, carpets, contact lenses, crayons, credit cards, dentures, deodorants, diapers, digital clocks, dinnerware, dyes, eyeglass frames, furniture fabrics, garbage bags, glue, golf balls, hair dryers, infant seats, lipstick, lubricants, luggage paint, patio screens, pillows, shampoo, shaving cream, slippers, syringes, tents, tires, toothpaste, toys, umbrellas, vinyl, vitamins, and wall paper" (*Blood Oil*, p. xxxvi)) and coltan which is used in almost every kind of electronic device, including cell phones.

[13] But note, in the one case, I am required to save the drowning person, and ruining the watch is a mere side-effect of an action that I am required to do. In the other case, I am being required to use something that is very important to me, namely my watch, as a means to saving someone's life. For non-consequentialists, at least, one cannot infer that the latter is permissible, or required, just because

Moreover, if some of the money that I donate unavoidably ends up lining the pockets of a local official whose cooperation the international agency needs, and the official uses that to help pay for a new Mercedes, why shouldn't I regard that as regrettable, but worth it, for the sake of saving an innocent person who would otherwise have died?

Consider next the following example.

> *Three Charities*: Indira is considering selling her $5,000 watch and giving it to charity. She learns that if she gives it to charity A, it will use the money to provide costly medical care to someone in a highly remote region on the other side of the world, thereby saving a single life. If she gives it to charity B, it will use the money to provide moderately costly medical care to people in a moderately remote village, thereby saving three lives. If she gives it to charity C, it will use the money to provide inexpensive medical care in an easily accessible city on the other side of the world, thereby saving six lives. By hypothesis, each of the people that Indira's money will save are equally deserving and wholly innocent, and each will die without the medical care that her money might provide.

Three Charities is the sort of example where Effective Altruists, and many others, would say that it would be best if Indira gave her money to charity C, and worst if she gave her money to charity A. Moreover, other things equal, this seems right.

Suppose next, however, that Indira learns the following. Charity A is a corruption-free charity. None of the money that Indira gives to charity A will be siphoned off into the pockets of a corrupt individual. Charity B, however, must deal with a mildly corrupt local chief. The chief insists on receiving 10 percent of the medical supplies, which he sells on the black market and then uses the proceeds to buy Xboxes for his friends. Charity C, on the other hand, must deal with a very corrupt, and greedy, local gang leader. He insists on

---

the former is. Often, on non-consequentialism, it can be permissible or required to bring about an undesirable outcome, B, as a side-effect of producing some other desirable outcome, A, in a morally permissible way, where it wouldn't be permissible or required to bring about undesirable outcome B, as a means to producing desirable outcome A. So, unless one is a consequentialist, one cannot assume that just because one might be required to save someone from drowning, even if that led to the loss of one's expensive watch, that it must also be the case that you are required to give up your watch for the sake of saving someone.

I am grateful to Shelly Kagan for stressing that non-consequentialists have reason to be wary of the general pattern of reasoning in question. However, I should also add that non-consequentialists typically balk at the reasoning in question when it is applied to the treatment of persons or agents. It is not clear at all that their concerns apply to mere things or inanimate objects, such as watches.

receiving 50 percent of the value of the charity's expenditures in his city, in cash, which he then spends on fancy cars and other luxury items.

As described, I believe there is still reason to think that Indira should give her money to charity C. Of course, it burns her up to think that some of her money will be going to line the pockets of a selfish gang leader, when so many needy people are dying of readily preventable causes. She would much prefer to find a fourth charity, D, that would use her money the way that charity C does, but without having to lose half of it to a gangster. If she could save twelve lives with the money she donates, by avoiding a corruption-tainted charity, rather than six, that would be her clear first choice. Still, if there is no charity D, and her options are charities A, B, or C, she may well reason that it is better to save six lives, and help pay for a corrupt gang leader's Mercedes, than to only save three lives, and help pay for some Xboxes for a corrupt chief, or only save one life, even though in the latter case none of her contribution will be lost to corruption.

The preceding argument is intended to suggest that in giving to charities one should not lose sight of the main goal that prompts us to give in the first place. Arguably, if our concern is to save innocent lives, then there should be a strong presumption in favor of giving to whatever international relief organizations will save the most lives with the money we donate. If doing that necessarily involves dealing with corrupt individuals who will line their own pockets with the money that they extort from us, then so be it. To be sure, this is something to be avoided, if possible; but, if not, then we must simply swallow hard and learn to live with it. As the lesson from Sodom and Gomorrah teaches us, we ought not to allow our distaste for the flourishing of evil people to prevent us from saving as many innocent lives as we can.

6.4 Brief Summary and Concluding Remark

In this chapter, I first argued that there is reason to be concerned about external corruption. I suggested that there are numerous ways in which corrupt individuals and institutions can divert money intended to aid the needy to line their own pockets and further their own goals. I also suggested that for a variety of reasons this may be a particularly pressing problem in some of the world's poorest regions where international aid organizations often operate.

I next briefly presented two possible responses to the worry about external corruption. The first is that external corruption is not prevalent enough, or substantial enough, to be a serious worry. The second is that the problem of external corruption only arises for government-to-government aid efforts— where governmental aid organizations funnel money directly to foreign governments with the aim of helping those governments to fund programs and projects that will provide for their neediest citizens. On this view, the problem of external corruption does not arise for NGOs which work directly with the neediest people in the world's poorest regions to improve their lot. I expressed skepticism about the adequacy of each of those responses.

I next considered a third response to the problem of external corruption. In essence, this response is that perhaps we must learn to live with external corruption, as a regrettable but necessary aspect of aiding needy people in some of the world's most desperate regions. I offered various considerations in support of that perspective. Correspondingly, I believe that that perspective should be borne in mind whenever worries are raised about internal or external corruption in connection with international aid efforts. Minimally, it is not clear to me that there is strong justification for holding international aid organizations to a much higher standard than we do coffee chains, fast-food chains, clothing chains, sneaker chains, and so on.[14]

Still, in this chapter, I have only discussed one element of the problem of external corruption: the worry that funds may be diverted from aiding the needy to feather the nest of corrupt individuals. As we will see next, there are problems of perverse incentives, and other direct, indirect, and long-term effects of dealing with corrupt individuals, that make the issue of corruption much more complicated, and troubling, than it has appeared to be in our discussion so far.

[14] To be sure, aid organizations portray themselves as doing a great deal of good, and rely on donations from good-hearted individuals to promote their ends, whereas most purveyors of consumer goods make no such claims, and do not rely on the generosity of good-hearted people to produce their profits. So, there are some reasons for holding aid organizations to a higher standard than for-profit corporations. (I am grateful to Brian Oosterhuizen for this point.)

Still, when one considers their actual impact on the world, it is by no means evident that we should be so much more concerned about the negative impact of aid organizations than the negative impact of corporations selling consumer products. Though, as we saw in note 12 of this chapter, one obvious response to this claim, to which I am very sympathetic, would be to insist that we should hold for-profit corporations to a much higher standard than we typically do, rather than that we should hold aid organizations to a laxer standard than we now do.

7

The Dark Side of Humanity, Part III

Where Evil Walks

In previous chapters, I have presented numerous disanalogies between jumping into a pond to save a drowning child and contributing to an international aid organization in order to benefit the needy. In this chapter, I present further disanalogies between those cases, and discuss their normative significance.

In Section 7.1, I point out that in Singer's original Pond Example, we naturally assume that the child is innocent, that the child is drowning due to some terrible accident, and that no one stands to gain from the child's being saved other than the child herself. I note that *all* of these factors may be missing in real-world aid cases. In particular, I argue that in some cases those in need may not be "innocent," or they may be responsible for their plight. In many cases, those in need may be the victims of social injustices or atrocities. And, most importantly, in some cases, bad people stand to gain from the efforts of aid organizations, including, at times, the very people responsible for the desperate conditions of those in need.

In Section 7.2, I discuss the normative significance of some of the disanalogies noted in Section 7.1. Of particular importance, I note that aid to the victims of social injustices and atrocities can end up in the hands of local or national warlords and tyrants via several different routes. This can bolster the wealth, status, and power of the warlords and tyrants, who may, in fact, have been the perpetrators of the very social injustices or atrocities that the international aid efforts were seeking to redress. This, in turn, can incentivize those warlords and tyrants to commit further injustices or atrocities against the very same people the aid organizations were intending to benefit, as well as other innocent people in the region. It can also incentivize other evil or corrupt leaders to perpetrate similar injustices or atrocities against other innocent people, as a means of attracting aid dollars that they can divert, thereby bolstering their own wealth, status, and power.

In Section 7.3, I reflect on the implications of Section 7.2, and some responses it might provoke. I note that while my claims are fully compatible with Singer's official position, they show how real-world issues of aid are much

Being Good in a World of Need. Larry S. Temkin, Oxford University Press. © Larry S. Temkin 2022.
DOI: 10.1093/oso/9780192849977.003.0007

more complex, and murkier, than those that arise in Singer's Pond Example. Thus, our intuitive reactions to the latter provide little guidance as to how we should respond to the former. I briefly consider, and dismiss, the views that we only have to aid people with whom we stand in special relations, or those whose plight we are responsible for. I also reject the claim that if another agent is responsible for someone's being in need, then this lets everyone else off the moral hook of having to help the person in need. I further argue that we can bear some responsibility for the evil actions of another, if we could have reasonably predicted that our dealings with them would contribute to the success of their actions. If deontologists are correct, this puts significant limits on the manner and extent to which we can "deal with the devil" for the sake of the greater good, limits that non-consequentialist Effective Altruists should respect.

I note that consequentialists, including consequentialist Effective Altruists, will fully endorse the importance of determining *all* of the effects of aid interventions. However, echoing a point made in Section 5.3, I note that it will often be difficult to properly account for all of the effects of aid interventions. In part, this is because aid agencies have a strong incentive to look for all of the direct and indirect, short- and long-term, *positive* effects of their aid efforts, but much less incentive to look for, or report, all of the direct and indirect, short- and long-term, *negative* effects of their aid efforts. And, of course, as noted previously, external evaluating agencies rely heavily on the self-reporting of aid agencies in evaluating their overall effectiveness. Finally, I note that aid interventions to benefit the victims of disease or natural disasters can have a similar impact as aid efforts to benefit the victims of social injustices or atrocities, in terms of indirectly buttressing the wealth, status, and power of warlords and tyrants, thereby inadvertently supporting their nefarious agendas.

In Section 7.4, I return to the suggestion raised in Section 6.3, that perhaps we must simply "learn to live" with certain types of corruption. I argue that there is no clean distinction between illnesses or natural disasters on the one hand, and social injustices on the other. To the contrary, many disasters are hybrid in nature, owing to both man-made policies and natural events. Unfortunately, efforts to ameliorate the effects of man-made/natural disasters can incentivize corrupt leaders to continue the practices that lead to such disasters, and incentivize other corrupt leaders to follow their example. As the consequences of this can be terrible, this has a bearing on the appropriateness of learning to live with corruption, even in those cases where the aim of the corruption is "merely" to line the pockets of the corrupt individuals and their followers.

In Section 7.5, I discuss Goma, a case study in how international aid efforts can have tragic consequences. Goma serves as a stark reminder that the issues raised in this chapter, and the book more generally, are not mere intellectual exercises. Reflecting on Goma, I argue that we cannot ignore the worries raised by aid skeptics. I also urge that we resist the temptation to dismiss cases like Goma as rare "one-off" instances perpetrated by a "few bad apples." Instead, we must take seriously the possibility that such cases are merely the tip of the iceberg when it comes to aid efforts going awry.

In Section 7.5, I summarize the chapter's main claims.

7.1 Social Injustice, Unjust "Victims," and the Beneficiaries of Suffering

In Singer's original Pond Example, we are told nothing about how the child came to be in the pond. And, frankly, such information *seems* irrelevant. We don't care how the child came to be drowning; all that matters, or so it seems, is that the child *is* drowning, and that we could save it at no significant cost to ourselves. However, reflection suggests that this attitude of indifference as to *how* the child came to be in need may not be appropriate when our attention turns to the plight of the world's needy.

Let me begin by suggesting that for most people, at least, when they first confront Singer's example, they implicitly assume that the child is drowning as a result of some terrible accident. Since the person in need is a child, we assume that she is not responsible for her plight. We also assume that no parent, guardian, or other responsible agent was purposely trying to drown the child. Notice, also, that so far as Singer's story is concerned, no one stands to benefit from the child's being saved—other than the child herself, whose only gain is continued life. That is, in Singer's example, neither the child herself, nor anyone else, would be better off as a result of the child's being saved, than they would have been had the child never been drowning in the first place.

We might add that if Singer's readers had paused to consider the terrible possibility that the child's predicament might not be an accident, but the result of a responsible agent *intentionally* trying to drown the child, they might still have been confident that they ought to save the child, since, as the example was given, the evil agent was nowhere in sight, and presumably didn't stand to gain from the child's being saved. Moreover, most of Singer's readers have probably implicitly assumed that the child was drowning in a developed country with effective social services and an effective judicial system. Given this, if they had contemplated this darker version of Singer's example, they might have reasonably hoped that, in time, the appropriate authorities would eventually catch the evil agent and stop him or her from doing further harm to that child or any other child, and would also prevent the agent from profiting from his or her nefarious action (though there would, of course, be no guarantees about this).

The "terrible accident" feature of the Pond Example is replicated in cases of diseases or natural disasters that no one could have predicted or prevented and for which human agents are not responsible, in the sense of voluntarily and intentionally producing them. When people are struck down by diseases like malaria, AIDS, Ebola, tuberculosis, avian flu, Zika, Covid-19, etc., or by natural disasters such as earthquakes, floods, tsunamis, typhoons, hurricanes, tornadoes, fires, or droughts, it is ordinarily assumed that such people are the innocent victims of natural misfortunes for which they are not responsible. Accordingly, there will be a host of powerful moral reasons to help the victims of such natural misfortunes, akin to the reasons to help an innocent child who, due to some terrible accident, is drowning in a pond.

Unfortunately, however, the "terrible accident" feature of the Pond Example is lacking in many cases where people are needy.[1] This is because many of the world's neediest people are so as the result of grave social injustices—massive inequality, discrimination and persecution, neglectful governments, unjust wars, enslavement, torture, attempted genocides, and so on. Of course, the victims of such circumstances may be every bit as innocent and deserving of our aid as the drowning child in the pond. However, the fact that other agents are responsible for their plight introduces a complicating element not present in the Pond Example as it is typically understood.[2*] Moreover, often the

---

[1] This is a point independently noted by Frances Kamm. See her "Does Distance Matter Morally to the Duty to Rescue," in *Intricate Ethics: Rights, Responsibilities, and Permissible Harms* (New York: Oxford University Press, 2007, especially, 161–2).

[2*] To be sure, if *we* are the agents responsible for the grave social injustices, or our ancestors are and we have been the beneficiaries of them, then we may have a special responsibility for rectifying them, perhaps even greater than our responsibility to save a child who is accidentally drowning. I return to this important point in Section 14.1, where I discuss the view of Thomas Pogge, who rightly emphasized it. (See Pogge's *Realizing Rawls* (Ithaca: Cornell University Press, 1989).) Similarly, if we are responsible for allowing, or not preventing, someone from perpetrating grave injustices when we could have done so, then we may have a special responsibility for rectifying those injustices. It is possible that this responsibility could be greater than our responsibility to save someone who is accidentally drowning, and even as great as that of those who directly perpetrated the injustices. There are a host of difficult and important issues related to positive versus negative responsibility that I cannot take on in this book. However, my point, here, is simply that *how* someone came to be in need may have some bearing on the nature and extent to which we have a moral obligation to respond to their predicament. I am not claiming that it *always* has a bearing; nor have I yet discussed how much of a bearing it might have.

perpetrators of the worst social injustices are local or national despots, tyrants, warlords, politicians, army officers, secret police, or gangs who are largely beyond the reach of the law. This introduces a further complication not present in the Pond Example, where, as noted previously, one might plausibly assume that even if a responsible agent had intentionally tried to drown the child, that agent would typically be subject to criminal proceedings and punishment for his or her deeds.

Furthermore, notwithstanding Section 1.6's working assumption of innocence, which I have adopted throughout most of this book, it needs to be acknowledged that *some* responsible adults may face dire circumstances that they could have avoided had they been more prudent. Moreover, and more importantly, some of the world's neediest people may be perpetrators of heinous acts, or the victims of retaliation for such acts—perhaps they supported terrorist actions, or participated in unjust wars, atrocities, acts of aggression, or sectarian violence against others who are now being avenged.[3] Such cases, where those who are badly off are not innocent, or are largely or wholly responsible for their plight, are importantly disanalogous from the innocent child in the Pond Example. While there may still be important moral reasons to aid such people if we can, for example, humanitarian reasons, there may also be countervailing reasons not to, or, as importantly from a practical perspective, such people might appropriately receive lower priority than more innocent victims in deciding whom we should aid when our resources are limited.[4]

I shall return to this issue in Section 7.5, where its importance will become clearer. However, other than in that section, I shall largely set it aside going forward. This is because, in debating about the nature and extent of our

---

[3] An excellent discussion of cycles of violence that give rise to this sort of suffering can be found in Jonathan Glover's *Humanity: A Moral History of the Twentieth Century* (New Haven: Yale University Press, 2001). See, especially, Part Three, "Tribalism," pp. 117–52, where Glover notes the deep-rooted conflicts between the Israelis and the Palestinians, the Greeks and the Turks in Cyprus, and the Armenians and the Azerbaijanis, and explores, in more depth, the conflicts between the Tutsis and the Hutus in Rwanda, the Serbs, Croats, and Muslims in Serbia, Croatia, and Bosnia-Herzegovina, and the Protestants and the Catholics in Northern Ireland. For a discussion of the cycle of violence between the Israelis and the Palestinians, see, for example, Jaeger, David A. and M. D. Paserman, "Israel, the Palestinian Factions, and the Cycle of Violence," *AEA Papers and Proceedings: The Economics of National Security* 96 (2006): 45–9. For a discussion of the cycles of violence among different factions in Lebanon, see Miller, R., *From Lebanon to Intifada* (Lanham: University Press of America, 1991, p. 104).

[4] There are different types of imprudence. For example, some imprudent actions are also immoral for putting other people needlessly at risk. Others imprudent actions may recklessly put oneself at risk for short-term pleasures. Still other imprudent actions may put oneself at risk, but for the sake of significant benefits to others. Clearly, the reasons, if any, for aiding, or giving less priority to someone who is needy due to imprudence may vary depending on the nature of their imprudence.

obligations to aid the needy, there are millions of needy people—often women, children, and the elderly—for whom such considerations do not apply. Such people are often sufficiently like the child drowning in the pond, in being innocent and not being responsible for their plight, that it makes sense to wonder to what extent we ought to help them, if we can, just as we ought to help the drowning child. So, having recognized that some needy people may not be innocent, or may be largely responsible for their plight, and hence may have no claim on our assistance, or less of a claim than others, we should not, I believe, let that fact unduly distract us. There remains a large and pressing question about what, if anything, we ought to do on behalf of the countless needy people who *are* innocent, and are not, in any significant way, responsible for their predicament.

The "no one stands to gain" aspect of the Pond Example—in the sense of being better off due to our intervention than they would have been had there not been anyone in dire straits in the first place—is also lacking in most cases where international development aid is involved. As we will see, this disanalogy introduces further complications that we must attend to, in considering the overall desirability of contributing to international aid efforts.

7.2 Dealing with the Devil

Having noted several respects in which the Pond Example may be disanalogous from many situations involving the global needy, let us explore some of the ways in which these disanalogies may have normative significance. I shall start that exploration here, and continue it in the remainder of this chapter.

First, let's just focus on the many cases where the needy are innocent, but where their dire predicament is the result of social injustices or atrocities, rather than disease or natural injustice. By hypothesis, these are cases where human agents have intentionally acted in ways that have caused people to be very badly off. How, if at all, might this have a bearing on the moral desirability of our intervening to aid the needy?

Consider, first, the following example.

Peter's Simple Extortion Attempt: Peter is a very bad man. He tells us that unless we give him a $5,000 Rolex, he will kill an innocent person. He assures us that the innocent person is in no danger now, and that he will remain that way if we cooperate. However, if we don't give him what he wants, then the person will die.

Even if Peter's extortionist threat is credible, we might think it would be a bad idea to give in to it. Of course, if we could be confident that giving Peter the $5,000 Rolex would prevent him from killing the innocent person, and that that would be the end of the story, then we might feel compelled to do so. The problem, though, is that giving in to such threats is rarely the end of the story. To the contrary, giving in to such threats is likely to embolden Peter to make similar threats against us, and others, in the future. Moreover, if it becomes common knowledge that we, and others, will give in to such threats, then this will provide incentive for others to act in similarly nefarious ways. Ultimately, this may produce far more people who are threatened with death, and perhaps far more people who are ultimately killed, than if we refused to cooperate in the first place.

If someone threatens another with dire harm unless we cooperate with him, and we refuse to do so, then it will generally be the case that the dreadful outcome that results will be on the threatener's head, not ours. We may regret terribly the outcome that results, and we might do everything in our power to prevent that from happening compatible with our refusing to cooperate with such a heinous person. Still, if our efforts are unsuccessful, the responsibility for the terrible outcome will typically lie with the evil agent, not with us.[5]

Suppose, however, that we cooperate, and true to his word the evil agent spares the person he was intending to kill. We might feel good about that result, and relieved that we intervened. But if our cooperation emboldens that agent, and perhaps others, to subsequently issue many similar extortionate threats, occasionally following through on them when people refuse to pay to prove that their threats are credible, then we will rightly feel terrible about the results, and we are likely to feel at least partially responsible for the many resulting horrible deeds.

The global proliferation of kidnapping for ransom in many parts of the world reveals the long-term dangers of giving in to such demands.[6] Of course,

---

[5] This discussion is, perforce, oversimplified. Important distinctions need to be made between someone forcing, manipulating, encouraging, enabling, failing to intervene, failing to prevent, fostering conditions, and so on, when it comes to assessing the extent to which one person or group can be wholly or partially complicit in, or responsible for, another person or group's actions or the consequences of those actions. These issues are extremely interesting, and they have great significance across a wide array of practical domains, including just war theory. However, they are also extremely complex, and an adequate treatment of them would carry us too far afield for this book's purposes. I believe that the oversimplified discussions I offer here, and later, of the scope and limits of one person's being complicit in, or responsible for, the actions of others suffice for the points I am trying to make. Undoubtedly, however, a satisfactory treatment of these issues would require much more attention.

[6] A useful starting point for understanding the scale of this issue is "Kidnap for Ransom, Global Trends 2017," *AIG*, NYA24, 2018, URL: https://www.aig.dk/content/dam/aig/emea/denmark/documents/k-r-trends2017-nya.pdf, accessed August 31, 2019. A similar problem has now arisen with the global proliferation of ransomware.

where one's loved one is involved it may be psychologically difficult, unwise, and perhaps even immoral not to cooperate with such rogues. But this is a classic example where if each person does what is best for herself, or her family, it increases the risks for most people and produces greater overall harm. Thus, however difficult it may be, there are powerful reasons, at least where our loved ones are not involved, to not give in to such demands.

Next, suppose we change the example slightly.

Peter's in Progress Extortion Attempt: Peter doesn't just threaten to kill someone unless we give him a $5,000 Rolex, he first sets in motion a chain of events that will inevitably result in someone dying, unless someone intervenes. Peter then tells us that he will save that person, or allow someone else to save him, or allow us to save him, but only if we give him a $5,000 Rolex.

I believe that in this case, too, there are powerful reasons to resist giving in to such demands. Of course, if we could temporarily cooperate, and then bring Peter to justice, so that neither he, nor others, had incentive to continue such activities, then that would be another matter. However, if there is a strong chance that Peter will get away with it, or that our cooperation will provide others with the perverse incentive to act as he did, then there would be strong reasons to resist.

The sad worry is that in some instances where the need is greatest because of grave social injustices or atrocities, those responsible for perpetrating the injustices or atrocities may be in positions of power that effectively place them outside the reach of the law. They may be local or national tyrants, despots, warlords or gang leaders. Moreover, as the effective power and authority in the region where the need is greatest, these people may benefit in a host of ways, both directly and indirectly, from international efforts to relieve the burdens of the victims of the social injustices or atrocities.

Accordingly, our efforts, however effective at aiding those who are presently in need, may directly or indirectly buttress the position of the very people who have caused the great need in the first place. This may allow such people to continue perpetrating great injustices or atrocities against the very people we aim to help, or against other innocent victims. Moreover, if, in fact, our intervention does buttress the wealth, status, and power of local or national tyrants, this will not be lost on other despots elsewhere, who may learn the unfortunate lesson that certain crimes do pay, and will be motivated to perpetrate similar injustices and atrocities within their own domains as a way of increasing their own wealth, status, and power.

To be sure, to a certain extent I am engaging in worst-case speculation. Ultimately, more needs to be said about the various mechanisms I am alluding to, and their prevalence, or not, globally. But the point is that in Singer's original Pond Example there is an innocent victim whose plight is presumably the result of a terrible accident, where no one stands to gain from my intervention beyond the position they would have been in had the accident never occurred in the first place. Whereas, tragically, many of the world's neediest members are so due to social injustices or atrocities perpetrated by evil despots, where, potentially at least, the evil despots may be able to gain in various ways through international efforts to help their victims.[7] The latter situation is fraught with moral complexities that the former lacks. Accordingly, the clear intuition that *of course* we ought to wade in and save the drowning child, does not automatically entail that *of course* we ought to contribute to effective international relief organizations to save the world's neediest members. Attention must be paid to the many possible negative indirect effects of our doing the latter—including any perverse incentives that our actions may give rise to—whereas, by hypothesis, there are no negative indirect effects from our doing the former.

Consider the following series of examples.

Mukantagara's Series of Demands: Imagine that Mukantagara is a Hutu chief and commandant who has destroyed the cattle and other belongings of a Tutsi village, and is starving the villagers to death with a total blockade. An effective international relief organization tries to bargain with Mukantagara to allow it to bring needed food and medicine to the villagers. Mukantagara agrees on one condition: the head of the organization must kill each of the first-born males of the Tutsi village. Or, the organization must supply Mukantagara with ten Uzis, which Mukantagara will (or may) then use to gun down innocent Tutsis. Or, the organization must supply Mukantagara with 100 bullets, which Mukantagara will (or may) then use to gun down innocent Tutsis. Or, the organization must supply Mukantagara with food and medicine for his villagers, half of which will then be sold on the black market to buy Uzis and bullets to (possibly) kill Tutsis. Or, the organization must supply Mukantagara with food and medicine for his villagers, or must pay a daily "permit" fee of $100 to work in the region, or the organization

---

[7] I am not saying this is so of most of the world's neediest people, but it is certainly so of many of them.

must buy all its supplies from Mukantagara's village, and must employ Mukantagara's villagers for any local tasks that need to be performed— none of which is directly used to kill Tutsis, but all of which bolsters Mukantagara's wealth, status, and power within his village, enabling him to commit similar atrocities in the future, and incentivizing other warlords in Rwanda and elsewhere to perpetrate similar atrocities and drive similar bargains as a means of increasing their wealth, status, and power.

I presume that no international relief organization has been asked to fulfill something like the first demand—themselves participating in the killing of innocents—as a condition of the cooperation of a local warlord so that they can provide aid to the desperately needy. However, I suspect that most international relief organizations who have tried operated in war-torn countries, where genocide or brutal sectarian violence are part of the background conditions, have faced versions of the other demands.[8*]

One pertinent example where the delivery of development aid involved propping-up a bloody regime and played a significant role in exploitation and death on a massive scale took place during the great Ethiopian famine of 1984, when more than $104 million was raised by Live Aid concerts to help feed the famine victims. According to the journalist Linda Polman, who reported from war zones for more than 15 years:

> The money, coming from private donors, was spent by private INGOs [International Non-Governmental Organizations]...in compliance with conditions laid down by the Ethiopian Regime. Thousands of Western aid workers and journalists flew in along with the money. They were forced to change their dollars for local currency at rates favourable to the regime, and this alone helped to keep the Ethiopian war machine running. Food aid from INGOs was used as bait to lure starving villagers into camps.... A life of forced labor lay ahead. The government army that guarded the camps took a share of the food aid, and even requisitioned trucks from aid organizations to move people out.... About six hundred

---

[8*] I recall a lecture at Princeton some years back, organized by Peter Singer, where the President of Oxfam America discussed this very issue. He noted that to work effectively where aid is needed most, Oxfam often must "deal with the devil." Normally they hold their nose and do so, to help people desperately in need. However, he noted that in some cases the people they have to work with are so bad, and commit such heinous acts, that they have to back out of the region to avoid being accomplices in unconscionable actions. He spoke powerfully of one case where this was so. (I believe it was in Somalia, but it might have been in some other region dominated by a warlord.)

thousand people were moved, and an estimated one hundred thousand of them perished on the way.[9]

Unfortunately, Polman's account is hardly a one-off. In many regions where urgent humanitarian disasters occur, aid agencies need the approval and cooperation of local forces, which may themselves be largely or partly responsible for the disasters in question, or for other, terrible, social injustices. In a host of direct and indirect ways, the efforts of the aid agencies may bolster the wealth, status, and power of the forces in question, and incentivize their behavior, and that of others who would mimic them. Suffice it to say, these are real-world moral problems that many international relief organizations must come to terms with that do not arise in Singer's Pond Example.

7.3 The Problem of Dirty Hands

In this section, I offer several comments prompted by the preceding considerations. Some of these relate to what is often called *the problem of dirty hands*. Roughly, this is the deep, and complicated, moral issue of under what conditions, if any, it is morally permissible or required to "deal with the devil" for the sake of the good that one might produce. To address this question adequately, would require a book of its own. Though I can't do that here, I can point to a few of the relevant avenues requiring further thought.

To a large extent, this section consists of a series of important clarifications, qualifications, and observations. However, much of this material addresses issues, and relies on terminology and distinctions, that will be unfamiliar to non-philosophers. Accordingly, some readers may want to skip the first three points below, and just skim the rest of this section.

First, it must be noted, once again, that nothing that I have said in this chapter is incompatible with anything that Singer argues for in "Famine, Affluence, and Morality." Recall, that Singer's central conclusion is merely that we have an obligation to aid those in need, if, in doing so, we are not sacrificing anything of moral significance, or of "comparable" moral significance to the good we would be accomplishing. It is open to Singer, or any of his followers, to readily acknowledge that if the cost of aiding the needy is our acting in immoral ways, or our cooperating with warlords, in ways that would

---

[9] Polman, Linda, *The Crisis Caravan: What's Wrong with Humanitarian Aid?* (New York: Metropolitan Books, 2010, 123–6).

enable them, or incentivize others, to act in immoral ways, then, depending on the nature or effects of the immoral actions in question, such a cost *would* involve sacrificing something of moral significance or of comparable moral significance and we ought not to do it. Still, many international relief organizations *do* face moral quandaries of the sort I describe in certain cases where the need is particularly urgent, and a lot of hard moral questions need to be addressed to determine whether providing aid, in such circumstances, *is* morally obligated or even permitted.[10] Unfortunately, Singer's Pond Example offers no guidance to answering those pressing questions.

Second, some may hold that I only have a duty to aid those in need if they stand in a special relation with me—for example, I am their father—or I am personally responsible for their predicament—for example, they are starving because I stole, or burned, their crops. On this view, if I am not responsible for the plight of the needy then acting on their behalf is supererogatory, and while, in some circumstances, at least, it may be permissible for me to help them, if I choose, I am never required to do so.[11] As indicated in Chapter 2, I believe this is a bad mistake.[12]

Third, another possible line is that while I may have a duty to aid those in need whose predicament I am responsible for, or a duty to aid those in need who are innocent victims of accidents or natural disasters, I have no duty to aid anyone in a dire predicament for which another rational agent is responsible. On this view, only the rational agent who is responsible for the predicament has a duty to rectify it, not I, or any other "non-involved" person. This, too, is a mistake. I wholeheartedly agree that if an agent is responsible for an innocent person being in great need, then he may have the *primary* responsibility to aid that person. However, that doesn't mean that I have *no* responsibility to help, if I can.

Indeed, I am inclined to believe that if the person responsible for the individual's plight could not, or did not, take steps to alleviate it, then my

---

[10] Nick Beckstead has suggested, in correspondence, that "GiveWell's top charities may be substantially exempt from this critique. GiveWell is in a lot of contact with these charities, and I haven't heard of cases where they had to make hard calls like the scenarios above." Beckstead's reaction is a fairly common one. Many people who work in the aid field readily acknowledge that the worries I have been raising are genuine, and no doubt arise for *some* charities, but they tend to be fairly confident that they don't apply to *their* favorite charity. I respond to this objection in Chapter 12.

[11] This is the view of Robert Nozick and Jan Narveson. See, Nozick, Robert, *Anarchy, State, and Utopia*, New York: Basic Books, 1974, and Narveson, Jan, "Welfare and Wealth, Poverty and Justice in Today's World" and "Is World Poverty a Moral Problem for the Wealthy?" *The Journal of Ethics* 8 (2004): 305–48 and 397–408.

[12] See, also, my articles "Thinking about the Needy, Justice, and International Organizations," and "Thinking about the Needy: A Reprise," *Journal of Ethics* 8 (2004): 349–95 and 409–458, and "Justice and Equality: Some Questions about Scope," *Social Philosophy & Policy* 12 (1995): 72–104.

duty to aid would be just as great as if the person's plight were a result of an accident or natural disaster, though not as great as if I were responsible for the person's plight. I believe the same is true where we think some other agent— such as a parent—or collective group—such as a government or community— may have a greater obligation than I to help someone in need, even if they are not responsible for the plight of the person in need.

No doubt, there is an ordering among different individuals or groups relating to who has the greatest obligations or would have to make the greatest sacrifice to help someone in need, between, for example, an evil agent responsible for someone's plight, a non-evil agent responsible for someone's plight, someone bearing a special relation to the person in need, members of the person's community or nation, a complete stranger, and so on. However, my own sense is that the strength of my obligation to help a stranger in need isn't diminished by the fact that others may have an even greater obligation to step in. Rather, others may have even stronger obligations to step up, and to step up before I have to; however, if, for some reason, they are unable or unwilling to fulfill their duties, then, to the extent the stranger still needs my help, I will have an obligation to help him in accordance with the strength of any duty that someone in my situation has to help someone in his situation. To my mind, the fact that lots of others have even stronger duties to aid someone in need than I have, and that the person wouldn't require any aid from me at all if others had fulfilled their duties, doesn't lesson my duty to help, to the extent that I have such a duty, in those cases where the other agents don't, in fact, fulfill their duties.[13*] (Note, here, and elsewhere, I put my claims in terms of "duties" and "obligations." Some philosophers prefer to talk of "reasons" and "oughts." I don't believe that anything substantive turns on this. Thus, for example, I might equally well have written the following rather than the previous sentence: To my mind, the fact that lots of others have even stronger

---

[13*] Here I am agreeing with a point Singer makes in "Famine, Affluence, and Morality," *Philosophy and Public Affairs* 1 (1972): 229–43. Singer points out that if there are many people standing around a pond where a child is drowning, and none of them jump in to save the drowning child, that doesn't lessen my responsibility to save the child. Presumably, Singer would believe this even if he thought that some of the others standing around had an even greater duty to save the drowning child than I.

My point here is orthogonal to, but fully compatible with, Liam Murphy's claim that I only have an obligation to do my "fair share" to address the plight of the needy. Roughly, on Murphy's view, each person has a duty to shoulder their "fair share" of the burden of global poverty, but no one has a burden to shoulder more than their fair share. So, for example, if it were the case that if everyone did their fair share to alleviate global poverty it would be totally eliminated, and it were also the case that my fair share of that burden would be $2,000, then I would have a duty to contribute $2,000 towards alleviating global poverty—my fair share, but no more than that. This is so, according to Murphy, whether or not others have contributed *their* fair shares to eradicating poverty. So, for Murphy, my duty to help, if I have one, doesn't lessen just because others don't do their duty, but neither does it increase. See Murphy, Liam B., *Moral Demands in Nonideal Theory*, New York: Oxford University Press, 2000.

reasons to aid someone in need than I have, and that the person wouldn't require any aid from me at all if others had done what they ought to given the reasons that they have, doesn't weaken my reasons to help, to the extent that I have such reasons, in those cases where the other agents don't, in fact, act as they ought to given the reasons that they have.)[14]

Fourth, there is a strand of deontological thinking according to which I am responsible for what *I* do, but I am not, except under exceptional circumstances, responsible for what *other* rational agents choose to do.[15] On the extreme version of this view, it would be wrong for me to kill several innocent people as a condition of my being able to save a large number of innocent lives, but it wouldn't be wrong for me to provide other rational agents with resources as a condition of my being able to save a large number of innocent lives, even if I can predict with reasonable certainty that they will use those resources to kill other innocent people. On this view, if I provide a warlord with cash, food, or medicine, which they then turn around and convert to weapons to kill innocent people, the deaths of the innocent people lie on the heads of the warlord, not on my head. Indeed, on this view, even if the warlord insists that I provide him with guns or bullets as the price of operating effectively in his territory, I can be morally comfortable in doing so. The lives I save go on *my* moral ledger, while any lives that the warlord takes goes on *his* moral ledger.

Presumably, when I gave the warlord the guns or bullets, I didn't want him to kill innocent people, I didn't intend for him to kill innocent people, and I didn't in any way coerce, encourage, or wish that he would use the guns or bullets to kill innocent people. To the contrary, I may have fervently hoped that he would "beat the guns into plowshares," and I may have even told him, in giving him the weaponry, that it was to be used solely for self-defense, and in no circumstances was to be used to kill innocent people. Thus, it might be said that the deaths of the innocents were merely a foreseen but unintended side-effect of the actions I took to save innocent lives and that, as such, as long as the deaths caused by the warlord were not disproportional to the number of lives that I saved, I was justified in my actions.[16]

---

[14] I am grateful to Ingmar Persson for calling my attention to the fact that some people, including him, would prefer that I frame my discussion in terms of "reasons" and "oughts," rather than "duties" and "obligations" (in correspondence).

[15] Exceptional circumstances might include where I have coerced, hypnotized, drugged, or tricked another agent into doing my bidding.

[16] There are many important issues and distinctions that deontologists see as relevant here. See, for example, Philippa Foot's seminal article, "The Problem of Abortion and the Doctrine of Double Effect."

There are a host of deep and difficult issues connected with the question of when, if at all, it is permissible for a rational agent or group of rational agents to act in ways that will directly or indirectly contribute to negative consequences, via the actions of intervening rational agents. I cannot pursue these issues here.[17] My own view is that in some cases, at least, it can be impermissible to fail to intervene to prevent the actions of an evil agent, whether out of cowardice or willful ignorance (burying one's head in the sand, as it were, to avoid seeing what one would otherwise see and be compelled to do something about), and that this is certainly the case if one can easily and safely do so. Even more, in my judgment, it can be impermissible for one to knowingly provide an evil agent with the means of carrying out his evil intentions, or to deal with an evil agent when one has good reason to believe or suspect that one's dealings will enable him to carry out an evil agenda. In such cases, I believe, one will be acting wrongly, even if one is not acting as wrongly as the evil agent himself. Moreover, I believe that the extent of one's wrongdoing will be in part determined by the extent of the harm that the evil agent produces, and the extent to which one could have reasonably foreseen or expected the harms in question.[18]

Of course, even if I am right, this does not settle the question of whether or not one should abet an evil person all things considered. Perhaps, if one could accomplish sufficient good by doing so, one ought to. Still, the greater the evil to which one's actions might contribute, the more powerful the objections to one's doing so and, on my view, these objections can be deontological in nature and not merely consequentialist. That is, on my view, the objection to one's aiding an evil person in accomplishing their designs does not merely lie in the bad consequences that may result, but in one's knowingly or predictably participating in the victimization of other people. There are, I believe, strong deontological prohibitions against engaging in such behavior, even if one only does so to for the sake of accomplishing some greater good.

If I frequent an excellent restaurant and, unbeknownst to me, the profits of that restaurant go to support terrorist activities, then unless I ought to have known about the connection in question, which is always a possibility, I am

Oxford Review 5 (1967): 5–15; Judith Thomson's classic article, "Killing, Letting Die, and the Trolley Problem." The Monist 59 (1976): 204–17; Jeff McMahan's important book, The Ethics of Killing: Problems at the Margin of Life, New York: Oxford University Press, 2002; and Frances Kamm's significant contributions, Morality, Mortality: Volume I, Death and Whom to Save from It and Morality, Mortality: Volume II, Rights, Duties, and Status. New York: Oxford University Press, 1993 and 1996, and Intricate Ethics.

[17] For more on the complexity of these issues, see Section 14.1.

[18] I am grateful to Ingmar Persson, who suggested a more perspicuous wording of this paragraph than I had originally written (in correspondence).

blameless as to the consequences that result from my actions. However, if I know, or have good reason to believe, or think it likely that proceeds from the restaurant support terrorism, then I cannot simply wash my hands of the consequences of my actions by appealing to the intervening intentional actions of the rational agents who actually carry out the terrorist acts.

In this domain, much depends on what I could be reasonably expected to know or believe about the agents with whom I am dealing. When I am dealing with tyrants, warlords, or gangs, I have a special responsibility to be concerned with how my dealings with them may advance their agendas, both directly and indirectly. Unfortunately, we need to be aware of the possibility that our efforts to aid the *victims* of social injustice may directly or indirectly benefit the *perpetrators* of the social injustice, enabling them to commit similar crimes in the future against the same, or other, groups. Unfortunately, I believe, this is the predicament that many international relief organizations must contend with in some of the most desperate places on earth where the needs of innocent victims are extremely high.

Reflecting on the preceding, I believe that even if, overall, I might be producing more benefits than harms by contributing to an effective aid agency, it may be impermissible for me to do so for deontological reasons, if my contribution ultimately involves my participating in the victimization of people. Relevant issues here include whether the people my aid helps are the same as the people my aid helps victimize, in which case if the benefits outweigh the harms we might be able to reasonably assume hypothetical consent on the part of the relevant people to my contributing to the aid agency. If, on the other hand, the people my aid helps victimize are distinct from the people my aid benefits, then even if the overall benefit produced by my aid exceeds the overall harms produced by my aid, it may not be permissible for me to contribute to the aid agency. This might turn on such factors as whether the people victimized by my aid would be morally required to sacrifice themselves to the extent that I would be harming them, for the sake of the benefits that would accrue to the others from to my aid. If they would be, then it might well be permissible for me to contribute to the aid agency. However, if they wouldn't be, then it might be impermissible for me to contribute to the aid agency, for deontological reasons, because my contribution would, in essence, be unjustifiably harming or sacrificing some, for the sake of a greater good to others.[19]

---

[19] I am grateful to Frances Kamm for comments that led to the writing of this paragraph. For a much more thorough discussion of the issues raised in this paragraph, and a greater understanding of their bases and significance, see Kamm's *Morality Mortality*, 2 vols., and her *Intricate Ethics*.

Fifth, the preceding considerations are relevant, and must be taken account of, by any non-consequentialist Effective Altruists. That is, if one believes that the goal of "doing the most good" is constrained by what is impermissible, and that this is in part determined by deontological considerations, then one may often be prohibited from "dealing with the devil" for the sake of the victims one would be aiding via such dealings, even if one could produce more overall good by dealing with the devil than not. In general, deontological consider-ations tell against harming some for the sake of benefiting others. Accordingly, if one's dealing with the devil involves playing a responsible and significant role in the harm of others, via the predictable intermediary actions of the agent one is dealing with, then one may be prohibited from engaging in such dealings even for the sake of producing the greater overall good.

Sixth, I have been suggesting that even from a deontological perspective there are reasons to be concerned about the actions of evil agents with whom we might have to deal for the sake of aiding the needy. Clearly, a consequen-tialist perspective will also require us to pay attention to any bad consequences that may result from our efforts to aid the needy, whether directly or indir-ectly. Of course, consequentialists will only be concerned about the total balance of good or bad effects that result from our action. Fundamentally, they won't be concerned about the assignment of responsibility for such effects and, in principle, they would even require us to kill some innocent people if that were the only way to promote the greatest amount of good. But even if we think this position is mistaken, as I do, on the pluralistic approach to morality that I favor, we certainly must give some weight—and, in fact, I believe substantial weight—to consequentialist considerations in determining what we ought to do, all things considered. This is no less true when considering our obligations to the needy than it is when considering other moral issues.

Accordingly, in contemplating providing support for international relief organizations, we must pay attention not only to the good that we will do through our efforts, but to any comparable bad that may result, directly or indirectly, from our efforts. Considering cases where to effectively deal with the needy we may have to deal with, and benefit, the very people who were responsible for the people being needy in the first place—evil agents respon-sible for perpetrating grave social injustices—reminds us that however clear our obligation to aid the needy is in an artificially pure case like the Pond Example, in the real world the situation is often much murkier and fraught with moral complexities.

Seventh, these considerations return us to a previous point. International relief organizations have every reason to want to appear to be as effective as possible for the purposes of raising further funds to help the needy. So, as already noted in Section 5.3, they have every incentive to tot up each bit of good that they accomplish, and not to turn over too many rocks looking for negative side-effects of their interventions. If they want to provide aid in a foreign country, and a condition of their working in the country is that they buy a daily permit, or provide some food and medicine, or hire their workers from the local leader, they have strong incentive to assume or hope for the best, and to just list such costs as among the necessary and reasonable expenses for aiding the needy.

Likewise, an external evaluating agency may be unaware of any specific reasons to question the veracity of such a report or the legitimacy of such expenses. However, as our discussion suggests, if the international agency is providing desperately needed help in Rwanda, but the local leader that they have to work with happens to be a Hutu who is perpetrating genocide against his Tutsi neighbors, then there may be much more to put in the negative column regarding the agency's effects than they themselves have noted, and our overall assessment of the desirability of supporting such activities may change dramatically.

Once again, the point I am making here is fully compatible with Singer's official position, that we have an obligation to aid the needy if our doing so does not involve sacrificing anything of moral significance or comparable moral significance. It is also fully compatible with the goals of Effective Altruism. Effective Altruists who seek to produce as much overall benefit for the needy as possible, will want to take account of the atrocities perpetrated by a zealous Hutu commander (to the extent that they do, indeed, result from the interactions between the commander and an international relief organization) every bit as much as the good produced by the relief organization in aiding the victims of previous atrocities. So, what I am offering, here, is no criticism of Singer or Effective Altruism. It is just a reminder of how far real-world cases are from the Pond Example, and of how difficult it may often be to determine to what extent, if any, our interventions are doing more good than harm.

If our assessments of international relief organizations are to be accurate, we need to be every bit as attuned to the possible negative consequences of our interactions as we are to the possible positive consequences of our interactions. The latter may be more easily identified and quantified, but the former are every bit as important for the evaluation of an international relief organization's overall effectiveness.

Eighth, while the worries I have been raising may be especially easy to spot in cases where the needy have been victims of grave social injustices, many of these same worries arise in cases where the victims are so as the result of illness or natural misfortunes. Suppose a terrible disease or famine afflicts the poorest members of a desperately poor country. The natural and powerful temptation, motivated by the noblest of moral considerations, will be to provide aid to the innocent victims who are suffering so. Moreover, while, as noted previously, in Singer's Pond Example, no one is better off as a result of my saving the child, than they would have been had the child not been drowning in the first place, in cases involving international development agencies the *goal* is to leave people considerably better off than they were before they found themselves in their current dire predicament, in part, to prevent similar occurrences in the future. This might involve effecting improvements in infrastructure, water, energy, hospitals, schooling, etc.

As noted previously, however, in many of the world's regions where the need is greatest, there are local and national leaders who are corrupt. Moreover, unfortunately, some of these leaders are not merely greedy self-interested agents who will find a way to line their own pockets with any influx of resources into their regions. Rather, some of these are people who perpetrate unjust acts of aggression against some of their citizens or the citizens of neighboring regions. Given this, one must recognize that even if the leaders in question are not themselves responsible for causing the illness or famine which prompted the interventions of international relief agencies, they may nevertheless stand to benefit from such interventions. That is, as we have noted, there are a host of direct and indirect pathways in which such interventions may boost the wealth, status, and power of the relevant local and national leaders, enabling them to take advantage of the plight of their citizens to further their own political agendas. When those agendas are morally problematic, that is a crucially important consideration that must be entered on the negative side of the ledger when considering the otherwise laudable goal of aiding the world's needy.

7.4 Blurry Lines

In Section 6.3, I offered considerations in support of the view that, for the sake of aiding people in great need, perhaps we must simply "learn to live" with certain types of corruption. In this section, I note that the distinction between illnesses or natural disasters on the one hand, and social injustices on the other, is not always a clean one. This has, I believe, a bearing on whether, and to what extent, it really is appropriate to "learn to live" with the behavior of corrupt people who are mainly concerned to line their own pockets.

When a moderate earthquake causes catastrophic damage that could have been prevented if basic building codes had been enforced, or flooding causes massive losses that could easily have been prevented with a better upkeep of dams that were known to be in disrepair, or waterborne diseases such as cholera, diarrhea, malaria, typhoid, and dengue fever wreak havoc due to pollution, contamination, and lack of basic sanitation of the water supplies, the resultant suffering is as much a man-made disaster as a natural one. And the 2000-year-old biblical lesson of Joseph and the Pharaoh is that even famines brought on by severe drought can often be prevented with advance planning and careful husbanding of food supplies during times of plenty.

It is a truism among certain development economists that in those countries with good governance aid isn't needed, and in those countries with poor governance aid is often needed, but it won't help. We might call this truism the *Paradox of Aid*. The thought is that good governments will find a way to effectively provide for their citizens' basic needs, while aid to poor governments will be squandered and/or pilfered by incompetent or corrupt agencies and officials.[20] Surely, this picture is too simplistic. However, there is an important kernel of truth to the position being expressed. No doubt, an influx of aid during desperate times will help save or significantly improve the lives of countless innocent people. And, in principle, ongoing development aid will make a long-term difference, as well as a short-term difference, in the lives of those impacted. Unfortunately, however, when human calamities arise, they often reflect the choices and priorities of a region's ruling class. In many cases, the disasters that arise are hybrid disasters—both man-made and natural.

Too often, corrupt leaders choose policies that line their own pockets, and those of their followers, at the foreseeable expense of the suffering of fellow citizens. Perhaps they choose to accept bribes from contractors, which allow substandard buildings to be erected in an earthquake-prone area. Or perhaps they sell their country's excess food products to rich countries, pocketing a significant portion of the profits, rather than using the country's resources to pay for the purchase and storage of food that might later be distributed during a severe drought to peasants lacking the means to pay for it.

The worry is that if the cost of such corrupt practices is ultimately borne by a country's poor and disenfranchised, and by international development

---

[20] Angus Deaton presents the Paradox of Aid, though not by that name, in *The Great Escape: Health, Wealth, and the Origins of Inequality* (Princeton: Princeton University Press, 2013). He traces the original insight to Peter Bauer. See Bauer's "Dissent on Development," *Scottish Journal of Political Economy* 16 (1969): 75–94, and Bauer's classic book *Dissent on Development* (London: Weidenfeld and Nicolson, 1971).

organizations and their supporters, then such leaders will have little incentive to change their ways. Worse, assuming that the corrupt figures who are partly responsible for any man-made/natural disasters will find a way to profit from the misery around them by diverting for their own ends, or those of their supporters, some portion of whatever resources pour into their region to help the needy—a key assumption, here, but not, I think, an unrealistic one in many regions where the need is greatest—such individuals will have every incentive *not* to alter the behaviors that contributed to such dire predicaments in the first place. After all, doing so would adversely affect their personal finances and welfare and those of their followers on two fronts—first, by curtailing the income they receive from the activities that helped lead to the disaster originally, and second, by curtailing the income they receive from taking a cut of the disaster relief resources.

Indeed, such leaders will have selfish reasons to seek ways of undermining the long-term developments goals of the aid agencies and/or to continue to foster conditions that will promote similar man-made/natural disasters in the future. In regions that are desperately poor, and a global environment where there is a concern to alleviate such conditions, this will provide a steady stream of revenue for their coffers.

Here, we see a real danger about simply "learning to live" with corrupt leaders who "merely" take advantage of their positions of power and influence to greedily feather their own nests. The problem is that if we allow them to do so, for the sake of saving the innocent, this may incentivize them, and other greedy people in positions of power, to pursue comparable policies in the future. If that happens, that will place other innocent people at risk, and ultimately lead to large-scale losses and human misery. This is a possibility that we must face squarely and take into consideration in determining which aid organizations to support. This is so, I believe, whether or not we are Effective Altruists.

7.5 Goma

In April 1994, extremist Hutus in Rwanda began a campaign of genocide against their Tutsi fellow citizens.[21] In the span of three weeks, some 800,000 Tutsis and moderate Hutus were slaughtered. By the time journalists were

---

[21] This section is heavily indebted to Linda Polman's powerful and important book, *The Crisis Caravan*. In particular, all the factual claims made in this section are taken from Chapter 1, "Goma: 'A

telling the story of the Rwandan genocide on the nightly news, they were also filming a mass exodus of some 2,000,000 Rwandan refugees, flooding into the neighboring countries of Tanzania, Burundi, and the Democratic Republic of the Congo (DRC) (which was still Zaire at that point). The largest of the groups of refugees, some 750,000 people, ended up in refugee camps near the city of Goma in the DRC. As Goma was the only refugee area that had a landing strip, it was the only area where the refugees' plight could be captured live on the nightly news. When cholera broke out, taking the lives of an estimated three thousand people a day at one point, journalists referred to it as a "second genocide," and the world watched graphic scenes on the nightly news of dead bodies being bulldozed into mass graves.

The result was a massive, and record setting, global fundraising campaign to aid the Rwandan victims of genocide in the Goma camps. More than 1.5 billion dollars was raised for immediate relief, and "Donor governments gave the UN refugee organization UNHCR and the humanitarian organizations affiliated with it $1 million a day to spend, while another $1 million a day, according to the best estimates, poured in through private channels. The rescue operation...became the best-funded humanitarian operation in the world."[22]

Every major international aid organization flew into Goma. They saw it as imperative that they be seen, by their donors, and the public, as responsive to the largest genocide the world had seen since the 1970's Cambodian genocide, perpetrated by the Khmer Rouge. They also recognized the fact that the refugee camps offered them an extraordinary opportunity to establish their "brand," and to secure contracts from governments, foundations, and individual donors that would enable them to continue doing their work for years to come. In Goma, "No fewer than 250 [international aid organizations] threw themselves into the aid operation...along with eight UN departments, more than 20 donor governments and institutions, and an untold number of local aid organizations financed by foreign donors.... Never before had so many aid workers been gathered together in a single 'humanitarian territory.'"[23] Daily press conferences were held, hosted by the UNHCR, and each major NGO would be introduced, in turn, to give an account of what was happening in the refugee camps. According to one journalist who was there at the time, "Each one would give a higher death toll [than the last], because each

Total Ethical Disaster,'" pp. 13–35. At the time her book was published, Polman had been a journalist reporting from war zones for more than fifteen years for a range of European radio stations and newspapers.
[22] *The Crisis Caravan*, p. 20.   [23] *The Crisis Caravan*, pp. 20–21.

one would know that the man with the highest death toll would get on the nine o'clock news that night. And being on the nine o'clock news meant you got money and that is how the NGOs were trying to manipulate the media in Goma."[24]

By the end of 1995, an inventory of Goma's four main refugee camps "rendered up 2,324 bars, 450 restaurants, 590 shops, more than 60 hair salons, 50 pharmacies, 30 tailors, 25 butcher's shops, 5 blacksmiths, 4 photo studios, 3 cinemas, 2 hotels, and a slaughterhouse."[25]

So far, the picture that emerges is one of international aid organizations using the background of the tragic Rwandan genocide to burnish their own credentials, fill up their coffers, and attract donors and contracts, by providing aid to refugees long past the point at which aid was required. However, if one peels back the convenient surface story that the world willingly bought into, the picture becomes far darker.

Countless donors thought that they were providing much needed, even if belated, aid to the survivors of the Rwandan genocide, who were then suffering from a *second* "genocide" due to the cholera outbreak. What they didn't know, and what the international aid organizations were either willfully ignorant of or purposely declined to make plain, is that the refugees in Goma were not, in fact, Tutsi, but Hutu. And, as noted above, it was the Tutsi who were the victims of the Rwandan genocide, and extremist Hutus who were the perpetrators of that genocide. "The exodus from Rwanda, had ... [been] a tactical withdrawal ... to avoid defeat"[26] at the hands of a Tutsi army that had invaded from Uganda to put an end to the genocide of their fellow Tutsis. So, in fact, the stream of "refugees" fleeing Rwanda—which the world watched in horror on the nightly news—"included the entire Rwandan Hutu army ... and tens of thousands of members of extremist citizens' militias that had helped carry out the killings in Rwanda."[27] In addition, "the entire extremist Hutu government had relocated to Goma. The prime minister and his cabinet took up residence in the tourist hotels just outside the town.... [Thus] the old, extremist Rwanda ... had settled undisturbed in Goma, and was reborn as a state within a state."[28]

---

[24] *The Crisis Caravan*, pp. 18–19. According to Polman, the quote is from a talk given by Richard Dowden, at the London School of Economics, on January 17, 2007; at the time of his talk, Dowden was Director of the Royal African Society in London, after having previously served in Goma as a reporter for the British newspaper, *The Independent*.

[25] *The Crisis Caravan*, p. 33.   [26] *The Crisis Caravan*, p. 25.

[27] *The Crisis Caravan*, p. 17.   [28] *The Crisis Caravan*, pp. 25–7.

The consequences of all this were described by Linda Polman in chilling detail. It is, I believe, so important as to merit quoting at length:

> [S]ome of the dead [in Goma] had not succumbed to cholera but had been murdered by Hutu militias, on suspicion of disloyalty.... [I]n the first month of the crisis alone, four thousand people were beaten or stabbed to death.
>
> [T]he Hutus in the camps were kept under extremely tight control by the [extremist Hutu] regime. On all food rations distributed by aid organizations, the Hutu government, from its tourist hotels, levied a "war tax" to pay its army, which enabled it to continue its campaign of extermination against the Tutsi enemy back in Rwanda. The inhabitants of the camp, now rested, well nourished, and inoculated, were a source of new recruits. Inflammatory radio stations based in the camps ... ensured they were properly motivated.
>
> "Crushing a cockroach [a Tutsi] isn't murder. It's a hygiene measure!" ... crackle[d] from transistor radios.
>
> Almost every night, militias crept back over the border into Rwanda to go "hunting Tutsi." They struck mercilessly at Zairean Tutsis born in Goma as well. Hundreds of local Tutsis went missing or were found dead with bullets through their hearts or with their throats slit.
>
> The violence perpetrated by the Hutus went unpunished. "Everyone knows what has to be done, but who will bell the cat?" asked Shahryar Kahn, special representative of the UN secretary general....
>
> A year after the arrival of the Hutus, "traitors" to the Hutu cause were still being carried into camp clinics with arms or legs hacked off by [Hutu] militias, and dead [rape] babies were still being pulled out of camp latrines....
>
> In their evaluations, some INGOs [international non-governmental organizations] estimated that on average militias stole 60 per cent of all aid supplies being distributed, partly for their own use, partly to sell back to civilians in the camps.... The World Food Program once found a boat on the lake at the entrance to its food camp. The crew was calmly loading it with sacks of rice to take to the hotels where members of the government were staying. Fearful of bad publicity and a consequent decline in financial support, the INGOs kept quiet about the thefts. Instead they inflated the number of people living in the camps in reports to their donors, so that the losses would be made up. By contrast, press releases were issued every time the package of humanitarian provision was expanded....
>
> Several thousand extremists insisted that they be given jobs as drivers, maintenance technicians, administrative staff, cooks, cleaners, and managers

in the many food and nonfood distribution centers run by INGOs, and in their water supply and building projects, social programs for orphans and disabled people, and family reunion and educational services. Hutu leaders in the camps creamed off a percentage of every salary. At one point, MSF [Médecins Sans Frontières/Doctors Without Borders] Belgium was employing 550 Hutu personnel in one of the camps, at an average monthly salary of $100. According to some estimates, the Hutu leaders were collecting "taxes" of $11,000 a month from the staff of that one organization alone.

Charities providing medical treatment hired Hutu nurses for night duty, since it was too dangerous after dark for Western staff.... Fiona Terry [project manager of MSF France in the region at the time, later] admitted that doctors suspected the night-shift nurses of murdering patients who were insufficiently loyal to the Hutu cause. In the mornings, when the international staff would return to work, they would find family members or more distant relatives of Hutu leaders in the beds that had become free....

[One] day a planeload of munitions landed [at Goma]. It wasn't the first weapons delivery the Hutus had received, UN inspectors said. Arms dealers were routinely paid in cash by Hutu leaders, although sometimes weapons were bartered for stolen aid supplies.[29]

Eventually, some 600,000 Hutu returned to Rwanda from the camps in Goma. But another 200,000 militia and their families fled deeper into the bush. Those militia and their families—protected, cared for, nourished, and rearmed thanks, in part, to the massive international aid effort in Goma—continued to play a significant role in the decades-long bloodletting that engulfed Central Africa; a bloodletting which, by 2010, had already claimed an estimated five million lives.

Fiona Terry, the former project manager in the region for MSF France, once described Goma as a "total ethical disaster."[30] I have gone into detail about that disaster, because Goma is a stark reminder that the worries raised in this book are not merely abstract philosophical possibilities. They arise in real-world contexts, sometimes in unimaginably horrifying ways.

Goma concretely illustrates virtually all of the worries raised in this chapter, and more. In Goma, charitable organizations provided aid to people who were largely responsible for their plight. Beyond that, many of the recipients of aid were the opposite of "innocent victims"; they were mutilators and murderers who had committed crimes against humanity on a grand scale. Oddly, aid

---

[29] *The Crisis Caravan*, pp. 19–33.   [30] *The Crisis Caravan*, p. 33.

organizations either failed to notice or conveniently declined to explain to their donors that the recipients of their aid were *not* the victims of the Rwandan genocide, but rather, in many cases, the perpetrators of that genocide.

Relatedly, in Goma, many aid organizations seemed more concerned about being seen as delivering aid during a widely perceived global emergency, and raising funds for their organization, than about whether the aid was actually needed, who was receiving it, and what was happening as a result of their efforts. Aid organizations also made sure to loudly trumpet their aid distributions, but they weren't looking for, much less reporting, the many ways in which their aid was being diverted or misused. Nor did they report the terrible consequence of all that. Indeed, even where they knew that aid was being stolen, organizations often covered up that fact, in some cases even falsifying their reports, so as to keep the aid funds flowing. And, of course, no one was looking at the possible long-term consequences for the region of healing, protecting, nourishing, and enabling the rearming of a Hutu government and extremist militias that had already proved their willingness to commit genocide.

In Goma, we also see concrete examples of many of the ways that corrupt powers can profit from international aid efforts. Extremist Hutu militias and the Hutu government received aid provisions directly, stole aid provisions, forced aid organizations to employ their members, and "taxed" those who were employed by the aid organizations. Together, the massive aid effort in Goma increased the wealth, status, and power of the Hutu government and the extremist Hutu militias. Unfortunately, they didn't use their improved situation merely to heal, or to feather their own nests. They used it to regroup, consolidate their power, recruit new members, and continue their campaign of murder, rape, and mutilation against the Tutsi, and anyone who was "insufficiently loyal to the Hutu cause."

In sum, the worries raised in this chapter, and throughout this book, are not merely academic. They are very real. When realized, they can be deadly, even catastrophic, as they were in Goma.

Goma was not the canary in the coal mine. Goma was the disaster that ensued when the canary's death was ignored. Moreover, unfortunately, there have been many dead canaries, and many aid disasters. That is, while Goma is a classic case of how international aid efforts can go terribly awry, it is hardly the only such case. Horror stories abound concerning aid in virtually every region dominated by armed conflict and, more generally, wherever aid is needed in regions controlled by thugs, warlords, tyrants, or corrupt officials. Sadly, this includes many of the regions where the need has been greatest, and aid efforts, correspondingly, have been extensive: for example, Afghanistan, Algeria, Angola, Biafra, Bosnia, Congo, Croatia, East Timor, Ethiopia, Haiti, Indonesia, Kenya, Liberia, Libya, Monrovia, Pakistan, Serbia, Sierra Leone, Somalia, Sri Lanka, Sudan, Uganda, and, of course, as we've already seen, Rwanda and the Democratic Republic of the Congo (formerly, Zaire).[31]

There have always been aid skeptics.[32] People who have warned of the misuse, ineffectiveness, and counterproductiveness of foreign aid. They have come from the ranks of journalists, aid workers, government officials, and academics. Their warnings have often been met with three types of responses.

The first type of response has been to dismiss the warnings of the aid critics by impugning their characters, motives, or judgment: the aid skeptics are "disgruntled" former employees; they are "disillusioned idealists"; they are "greedy" or "attention-seeking"—trying to increase the sales or readership of their articles or books by making them as scandalous as possible; they are "left-wing radicals" or "right-wing libertarians" trying to advance their social or political agendas; or, perhaps, they are simply "outliers" whose "fringe" views are so out of step with that of the majority of the members of their field that they don't need to be taken seriously.

The second type of response to the aid critic is to push back, by claiming that even if their character and motives are above reproach: their claims are exaggerated, misleading, taken out of context, or simply false; the cases they describe are the exceptions, not the rule; or, the picture they portray is only one side of the story, as their scathing criticisms have left out all the good that international aid efforts have achieved—for example, even in Goma, there were presumably untold numbers of moderate Hutu refugees who did not participate in, or even courageously opposed, the Tutsi genocide, many of whom, as displaced persons in the middle of a cholera epidemic, were no doubt in desperate need of, and greatly benefited from, the food, shelter, and medical supplies that the international aid community provided them.

---

[31] For accounts of the misuse, and ill effects of aid in these countries, see de Waal, Alex, *Famine Crimes: Politics & the Disaster Relief Industry in Africa*, Oxford: James Currey and Bloomington: Indiana University Press, 1997; Deaton, *The Great Escape*; Easterly, William, *The White Man's Burden: Why the West's Efforts to Aid the Rest have Done So Much Ill and So Little Good*, New York: Oxford University Press, 2006; Epstein, Helen, *Another Fine Mess: America, Uganda, and the War on Terror*, New York: Columbia Global Reports, 2017; Maren, Michael, *The Road to Hell: The Ravaging Effects of Foreign Aid and International Charity*, New York: The Free Press, 1997; Moyo, Dambisa, *Dead Aid: Why Aid Is Not Working and How There Is a Better Way*, New York: Farrar, Straus and Giroux, 2009; Polman, *The Crisis Caravan*; and Rieff, David, *The Reproach of Hunger: Food, Justice, and Money in the Twenty-First Century*, New York: Simon & Schuster, 2015.

[32] One of the earliest, and best known, aid skeptics in the "modern" era of foreign aid (from the 1950s on) is Garrett Hardin. See Hardin's classic article "Lifeboat Ethics: The Case Against Helping the Poor," *Psychology Today Magazine*, Ziff-Davis Publishing Company, 1974.

The third type of response is simply to ignore the warnings of the aid skeptics. Typically, this reflects sheer ignorance of the warnings in question. The ignorance comes in different forms. There is *blissful ignorance*. This is the ignorance of those who have never even heard of Goma, or of other purported instances where aid efforts have been deeply problematic.

There is also *willful ignorance*, which itself comes in at least two forms. First, there is the ignorance of those who have vaguely heard of certain scathing accounts of the aid industry and its impact, but who have declined to look more deeply into the matter, in part, because they suspect there may be something to those accounts. These people may have always thought that they had a duty to aid the needy, and that they were fulfilling that duty, and therefore acting rightly, when they contributed to international aid agencies. Moreover, they may have felt rather good about themselves for doing so. Unsurprisingly, such people may not be particularly keen to find out that they may have been mistaken about all this.

Second, there may be those who suspect that the scathing accounts of the aid skeptics are likely to be true, so far as they go. However, they don't bother looking into them, because they are convinced that any untoward events that the aid skeptics describe *must* be the exception rather than the rule. More particularly, they may be convinced that the international aid agencies that *they* support avoid the shortcomings described by the aid skeptics, or that even if their favorite aid agencies have made some mistakes along the way, *surely* they must be doing much more good than harm, on the whole. On this view, there isn't much point in learning about a few one-off horror stories where aid has, inadvertently and unfortunately, gone awry.

Of the three types of responses to the accounts of aid skeptics the first is, as all ad hominem arguments are, irrelevant, inadequate, and reprehensible. It is no answer to a substantive worry to question the character, motives, or judgment of the person who raised the worry.

The second type of response is wholly appropriate. But it requires seriously engaging with the skeptics' views, and showing where they are mistaken or misleading, and why they fail to establish the skeptics' conclusions. This is hard work, and to do it properly requires a lot of information that that most opponents of the aid skeptics lack, and that is difficult, if not (practically) impossible to come by.

The third type of response is, perhaps, the most common. Indeed, I am embarrassed to admit that despite having lectured, published, and read a fair amount of important philosophical work on the topic of global aid, I had never even heard of Goma until quite recently. Indeed, it was only after I'd already completed my Uehiro Lectures, and the first draft of this book, that Angus Deaton called my attention to Goma, and suggested that I might want to take a look at Polman's chilling account of it. Prior to that, I had been blissfully ignorant of the tragedy that was Goma.

With that said, not all my ignorance of the aid skeptic's position was blissful. Some was willful, and for both of the reasons noted above. I had long heard about Michael Maren's classic book *The Road to Hell: The Ravaging Effects of Foreign Aid and International Charity*, and of William Easterly's equally classic *The White Man's Burden: Why the West's Efforts to Aid the Rest Have Done So Much Ill and So Little Good*. However, despite my life-long conviction as to the importance of aiding the needy, or perhaps because of it, until embarking on this work, I couldn't quite bring myself to read either of those books. I told myself that I was too busy, and that I didn't have time to read books by non-philosophers. But the reality is that when it came to global aid, I didn't really want to risk learning that everything that I had believed, actively supported, and urged countless students to do for many decades might have been badly mistaken and misguided. That was willful ignorance of the first kind.

However, I was also convinced, in my mind, that Maren or Easterly *must* be mistaken, though I had no evidence to support that conviction. More particularly, I assumed that even if what they were saying was true, so far as it went, it *couldn't* generalize sufficiently to support *overall* skepticism about contributing to international aid organizations. Indeed, without even reading what Maren, Easterly, or other aid skeptics had to say, I was convinced that any negative consequences they might accurately point to regarding aid efforts must be "one-offs"—the exceptions to the vast amounts of overall good that international aid organizations were doing in the world's poorest regions. Even more, I was confident that must be especially true for the particular aid agencies that I had supported throughout my life. That was willful ignorance of the second kind.

Suffice it to say, I now believe that simply ignoring the worries of the aid skeptics is a serious intellectual mistake. Even worse, it may be a serious moral mistake.

As for the claim that Goma can be safely ignored as a "one-off"—a tragic exception to the overwhelming good that international aid agencies do—I continue to want that to be true, but I am increasingly leery of such claims.

When rumors first started about pedophiles within the Catholic Church, nobody really wanted to take those claims seriously or investigate them. Most people's attitudes were that even if there were a few bad priests, guilty of a few instances of terrible "misjudgment," surely they were the exceptions. Surely, there was no reason to think there was a major, pervasive, problem throughout the Church! Similar responses arose, at least initially, when concerns bubbled up regarding sexual predation within the Boy Scouts, within the gymnastics community, and within various Olympic sports beyond gymnastics. Likewise, when the allegations regarding Bill Cosby, Harvey Weinstein, and Jeffrey Epstein first emerged, they were initially dismissed, and only later, grudgingly, regarded as the "inappropriate" actions of a few "bad apples." And, of course, each time an African-American is brutally beaten or killed by the police or white Americans—from Rodney King, to Trayvon Martin, to Eric Garner, to Michael Brown, to Breonna Taylor, to Ahmaud Arbery, to George Floyd, and countless others—one always hears the same refrain. These are all tragic incidents, to be sure. But they are "one-offs"; heinous acts perpetrated by a few bad apples.

It is, of course, obviously a bad logical mistake to make inferences about what is true of all, or most, based on what is true of one, or some. Not all priests, scout leaders, coaches, or wealthy businessmen are sexual predators. Not all men are rapists, or even sexist. Not all police officers and whites are murderers, or even racist. And so on. However, it is also a bad mistake to too quickly dismiss bad events as isolated "one-off" examples of misdeeds perpetrated by a "few bad apples."

Agents and their actions do not exist in a vacuum. Unfortunately, there are often widespread, systematic attitudes and behaviors that give rise to the "few bad apples" and their misdeeds. Moreover, the attitudes and events that are so egregious that they cannot be ignored once they become public, are often only the tip of the iceberg in terms of attitudes and events of that kind that persist throughout society. And, of course, like the bulk of an iceberg, what lies unobserved, beneath the surface of society, can be even more extensive and destructive than what lies out in the open for all to see. (This is why some African-Americans claim that they would rather be surrounded by virulent racists who are open about their beliefs, than by less virulent racists who mask their beliefs, including, perhaps, from themselves. This is because in the former case, but not the latter, they at least know where they stand, and can respond accordingly.)

Thus, my worry is that Goma is not a "one-off." It may be only the tip of the iceberg; a particularly hellacious example, but far from the only one, of the many ways that aid efforts can go seriously awry. If we really care about aiding the needy, and not merely feeling good that we have tried to do so, then we cannot afford to be either blissfully or willfully ignorant about cases like Goma, or the wider questions that they raise.

7.6 Summary

In this chapter, I have presented some new disanalogies between Singer's original Pond Example, and real-world instances of people in need. I have noted that in some cases people in need may not be "innocent" or they may be responsible for their plight. I have also noted that often people in need are the victims of social injustice or human atrocities. Most importantly, I have shown that often efforts to aid the needy can, via various different paths, increase the wealth, status, and power of the very people who may be responsible for the human suffering that the aid is intended to alleviate. This can incentivize such people to continue their heinous practices against their original victims, or against other people in the region. This can also incentivize other malevolent people in positions of power to perpetrate similar social injustices or atrocities.

My discussion raised a host of complex issues related to the problem of dirty hands; that is, the problem of under what conditions, if any, one can cooperate with, or help promote the actions or ends of evil agents, for the sake of the greater good. I suggested that there may be strong deontological restrictions on aiding people in need—even innocent people in great need—if we have good reason to believe that our efforts will help promote the agendas of warlords or tyrants in ways that will, predictably, significantly harm other innocent people. I also noted that many disasters are hybrid in nature, part man-made and part natural. When this is so, I argued, efforts to aid the victims of such hybrid disasters can incentivize corrupt leaders to continue the very practices that lead to such disasters. It can also incentivize other corrupt leaders to engage in such practices.

Finally, I discussed Goma, a real-world case where virtually all of the worries raised in this chapter, and others, were realized, with devastating consequences. Goma starkly reminds us that this book's worries are not merely abstract, philosophical possibilities. I suggested that ignoring the worries of aid skeptics is not an option. Neither is dismissing cases like Goma as "one-off" exceptions perpetrated by a "few bad apples." We must take seriously the possibility that cases like Goma are merely the tip of the iceberg, when it comes to instances of aid efforts going awry.

In sum, corrupt individuals in positions of power have several ways of diverting funds intended to benefit people in need. This can bolster their wealth, status, and power, and that of their followers, and make it easier for them to advance their personal and political agendas. This incentivizes such individuals to persist in their nefarious ways, and it incentivizes others to follow their example. This can have horrendous effects on the victims one's aid was intended to help, and also on other innocent people who stand to be victimized by emboldened, and empowered, warlords and tyrants. Together, the normative significance of these factors makes the case for contributing to international aid agencies much more complex, and murkier, than the case for saving the drowning child in Singer's famous example.

8

Marketplace Distortions
and Human Capital

In Chapters 6 and 7, I discussed many ways in which expenditures by international relief organizations might give rise to a host of negative indirect effects by benefiting evil agents, and providing perverse incentives for such agents to continue their evil ways, and for other agents to follow in their footsteps. Unfortunately, expenditures by international relief organizations can also give rise to negative indirect effects in cases where everyone's motives are benign, and there are no issues of corruption or evil actions involved. Moreover, often these negative indirect effects are easily overlooked and difficult to quantify.

Development economists have discussed numerous ways in which an influx of outside workers and money can give rise to local marketplace distortions in ways that can be problematic for local communities.[1] For example, outsiders may pay handsomely for food, lodging, services, and transportation, driving up the price of such items and making it harder for poor locals to acquire them. Likewise, an influx of outside cash can put upward pressure on the exchange rate of local currency, and this can make it harder for poorer countries to effectively compete in the international marketplace.[2] This can adversely harm anyone whose livelihood depends on the export of local goods, and has the potential to slow economic growth.

In this chapter, I discuss marketplace distortions in the realm of human capital. Many people believe that the most valuable natural resource is human capital—which is to say, all those moral and intellectual abilities and virtues that have enabled humans to flourish as a species; to wit: trustworthiness, cooperativeness, sociability, determination, skills, problem solving, ingenuity, creativity, strategic reasoning, goal setting, expertise, and so on. It is difficult to over-emphasize the importance of human capital for human development and, more

---

[1] For an extensive and balanced discussion of these issues, see Roger Riddell's *Does Foreign Aid Really Work?* (Oxford: Oxford University Press, 2007, especially Part III).

[2] "This is the so-called Dutch disease effect, so named because the upward movement of the exchange rate was first detected in the Dutch economy following the rise of foreign-exchange earnings from the sale of natural gas in the early 1980s" (Riddell, *Does Foreign Aid Really Work?*, p. 227).

Being Good in a World of Need. Larry S. Temkin, Oxford University Press. © Larry S. Temkin 2022.
DOI: 10.1093/oso/9780192849977.003.0008

particularly, the efficient use of human capital. Unfortunately, there is a worry that international aid efforts can set up incentives that distort the market in human capital in ways that make it less efficient, and perhaps significantly so.

This is often associated with what has been called the problem of *brain drain*, but I shall describe it as a problem of both *brain drain* and *character drain*, to explicitly acknowledge the importance of both intellectual and moral virtues for development. I have not seen the topic of brain and character drain discussed in the context of foreign aid, per se. This is unfortunate, since I believe that the misallocation of human capital through marketplace distortions, prompted by international aid efforts, can potentially have far-reaching negative implications for the moral, political, and economic progress of poor nations.

In Section 8.1, I note how the problem of brain drain has been recognized in the field of global health.

In Section 8.2, I note that global aid efforts can lead to a problem of *internal* brain and character drain well beyond the field of global health. I suggest that internal brain and character drain can have significantly deleterious effects on a local community. Unfortunately, these effects are difficult to identify and quantify. Correspondingly, they have typically been overlooked in discussions of aid effectiveness.

In Section 8.3, I note that global aid efforts can also lead to *external* brain and character drain. This, too, can have significantly deleterious effects on the local community. Again, these effects have typically been overlooked in discussions of aid effectiveness. However, I also acknowledge that external brain and character drain often have positive effects not associated with internal brain and character drain.

Section 8.4 concludes the chapter.

8.1 Global Health and the Problem of Brain Drain

I start with a point familiar to those working in global health.[3] Suppose there is a Western aid organization seeking to address the healthcare of people who have been ravaged by AIDS in remote African villages. Since its donors demand proven results and outstanding effectiveness, the organization will

---

[3] A canonical source for the line of argument presented here is the World Health Organization's *The World Health Report 2006: Working Together for Health*, Geneva: WHO, 2006. I am grateful to Nir Eyal for this cite.

seek to hire the very best doctors and nurses that it can, to work in its clinics. Often, for a variety of political, cultural, and medical reasons, they will also want to hire local doctors and nurses to advance their agendas. Ideally, they will seek to hire highly skilled practitioners, who are outstanding leaders with strong managerial skills, who are personable, who communicate and work well with others, and who are dedicated, trustworthy, hardworking, conscientious, reliable, and so on. Of course, the pool of people with such characteristics who are willing to toil away in remote African villages will be small, and there will be a host of rival aid organizations with their own agendas who will be seeking to hire the same sort of people to work for their organizations. Still, thanks to the largesse of its donors, the aid organization will be able to offer much higher pay, fewer hours, and outstanding working conditions in comparison with the local standards. Accordingly, the positions in question will be plum jobs and, predictably, many of the region's very best doctors and nurses will seek to work for the aid agency.

As described, so far, this sounds like a win/win/win situation. Hiring such talented people will be great for the victims of AIDS in the remote villages, it will be wonderful for the doctors and nurses and their families, and it will significantly advance the organization's ends, enabling it to truthfully show its donors how it has effectively addressed the pressing needs of AIDS patients in Africa's remote villages. Unfortunately, however, this rosy picture only focuses on the positive side of the story. Left out of this account is what happens *elsewhere* in the healthcare system because of the successful, well-intentioned, efforts of the relief organization.

The doctors and nurses who come to work for the aid agency were almost all working elsewhere before moving to their new place of employment. In some cases, they may have been the only person providing Western medicine to a number of villages in their region. If the local healer's traditional medicines failed, they may have been the only person the villagers could turn to if they were suffering from AIDS, but also if they were suffering from malaria, dysentery, malnutrition, river blindness, and so on. Likewise, they might have been the only source for Western-style medical information and care regarding pregnancy, pre- and post-natal healthcare, maternal healthcare, and so on. Alternatively, the doctor or nurse may have eagerly moved to his or her position from one of the terribly overworked and drastically underfunded national clinics in Kibera, Africa's largest urban slum. But in so doing, they might be serving only 1/100th of the population base and addressing only a small fraction of the many different types of pressing medical needs than they were previously.

Unfortunately, in cash-strapped countries there is no guarantee that when a healthcare professional leaves a local region or clinic that there will be the funds to replace them. But even if they are replaced, there may well be a fairly significant gap in coverage until that occurs. Moreover, even if they are replaced in a timely fashion, by hypothesis, the departing healthcare provider was amongst the best of the best—that is why the effective aid organization was so eager, for its purposes, to hire the person—accordingly, the replacement health provider is highly unlikely to be as good as the person who left, subjecting all of the provider's patients to comparatively inferior healthcare. And, of course, if the provider was an outstanding leader with strong managerial and communication skills, then his or her departure would presumably have a significant impact on any team or clinic of which he or she was a part, negatively affecting far more than just his or her own individual patients.

The upshot of these remarks is that often the positive reduction in poor health that an international relief organization genuinely produces, which are often readily identified and quantified, may in fact be offset by indirect increases in poor health elsewhere in the system, but in ways that are easily overlooked and extremely difficult to quantify. This can result in a distorted picture of the overall good that is being done by international relief organizations.

I am not claiming that the overall net effect of such trade-offs will always be negative, though I am fairly confident that there are some cases where this is so. However, here, as elsewhere, an overall assessment of the desirability of supporting an aid agency must take *full* account of the opportunity costs of doing so. In the cases that I have been considering, opportunity costs involve much more than just a consideration of where else I might spend my money. They also involve a consideration of what else an agency's workers would be doing if they were not working for the agency.

8.2 Global Aid and the Problem of Internal Brain and Character Drain

The point noted above extends well beyond the field of global health. It applies to international aid efforts generally. Unfortunately, this is a point which, to my knowledge, has been overlooked in discussions about the overall impact of global aid efforts.

When an international development organization moves into an area, it may have many worthy projects it wants to support. It might want to improve the water supply, build a new school, bring electricity to a village, and so on. As a result, it may seek to hire many people to work locally, on the ground, for the aid agency. It may want to hire a manager, some engineers, a principal, some teachers, and so on. It may need administrative staff, drivers, well diggers, electricity or telephone line stringers, road pavers, and so on. These are all valuable steps that donors to international development agencies might well want to support. But note, for each hire they make the agency will have every incentive to hire the best people they can for the jobs in question. If you want to be an especially effective agency, you will want the very best people working for you. Ideally, as before, this will involve hiring people with outstanding job-related and personal skills. Other things equal, one will want to hire people with good leadership, managerial, and communication skills, and one will want to hire people who are personable, who work well with others, and who are dedicated, trustworthy, hardworking, conscientious, reliable, and so on.

Again, one will be in competition with other international relief organizations to hire such people. However, thanks to the largesse of one's donors, one will be able to offer higher pay, fewer hours, and better working conditions than the local standard, often significantly so. Accordingly, highly qualified people from across the region will be more than eager to apply for such plum jobs.

Once again, one needs to be worried about the indirect effects of hiring such people away from whatever jobs they might otherwise occupy. Governments, especially governments in poor countries, need a host of high-quality engineers, accountants, lawyers, teachers, and civil servants working on behalf of the general public. And they really do need such people to be willing to be acting on behalf of the public, rather than corruptly lining their own pockets with government funds. That is, not only do poor countries need technically skilled experts filling important positions in civil government, but they also need people with integrity filling such positions; that is, people who are honest, hardworking, trustworthy, reliable, and so on.

Unfortunately, many poor governments will not be able to match the pay scale or working conditions that Western international development organizations can offer, and this may result in an internal brain drain and character drain away from public sector jobs. This, in turn, can have a significantly deleterious effect on the efficiency and success of the government, the economy, and public projects, at least in the short run, and perhaps even in the long run.

Moreover, depending on the disparities between salaries, hours, and working conditions, one might not merely see competent engineers or teachers leaving one important job for another job of the same sort. One could also see highly trained professionals leaving a job that demands all of their talents and abilities, for a job for which they are highly overqualified. Thus, due to distortions in the marketplace that well-funded relief organizations may inadvertently create, some outstanding teachers, engineers, accountants, lawyers, and civil servants may happily give up their positions to assume positions as administrators, translators, clerks, drivers, or manual laborers digging wells, paving roads, or pouring concrete for a new school. If that happens, the overall opportunity costs that their society incurs, due to the people in question no longer performing jobs befitting their considerable talents and abilities, may substantially outweigh, at least in the short run, the relative gains that their society gets as a result of their successfully fulfilling their new jobs—jobs that much less qualified people than they could perform almost equally as well.

8.3 Global Aid and the Problem of External Brain and Character Drain

Here is a related problem. Highly talented, hardworking people of great character will always be in demand. Such people may well get used to the pay scale and relatively high-quality working conditions that come with working for a well-funded international relief organization. Moreover, such people may receive special training and/or make connections with well-placed agency officials, which place them in a good position to compete for comparable positions outside of their home countries. Accordingly, what happens when the international aid agency shuts down its local operations, or moves on to other regions of great need when the local emergency-of-the-moment abates?

At that point, the talented, hardworking people of great character might return to the low pay and poor working conditions of their previous places of employment, where their skills might be desperately needed. On the other hand, if the opportunity arises, they might follow the aid agency to other locations, or seek better prospects in the developed world where the need for their talents and skills is much less great, but the personal rewards are far greater.

There is an old question: "how do you keep people down on the farm once they have seen the lights of the big city?" There is a kernel of truth embedded in that question which underlies my worry here. One can certainly understand why an international aid organization would seek to hire the most talented people it can, to promote its important goals as efficiently as possible. And one can certainly understand why people of great skill and character would want to better themselves and their families as much as they can. On the face of it, such aims are perfectly rational and morally commendable. Yet, together, these independently laudable goals raise the prospect that, over time, international aid organizations may inadvertently contribute to both internal and external brain and character drains. Given the thousands of aid organizations that operate in the world's poorest regions, the cumulative negative effects of such developments may be substantial.

Need I add that *none* of these negative effects are counted in a typical project evaluation report written up by aid organizations for their donors and funding sources? Nor are they counted in the sort of randomized control trials that Effective Altruist organizations such as GiveWell advocate, as much as possible, in evaluating aid agencies. Nor is this surprising. As with so many of the other negative effects that this book presents, effects of this sort may be difficult to spot and tally, especially in comparison with the readily identified successes that international aid organizations can often point to as due to their activities.

To be fair, a certain amount of brain drain from poor countries to rich countries is inevitable. Nor is it clear that external brain drains are, on balance, bad for poor regions.[4] Remittances from talented people who have met with success in wealthy countries, sent back to family members in poor countries, are often crucial components of the economies of poor countries and the welfare of their citizens. Moreover, it is not uncommon for those who have trained and become successful elsewhere to eventually return with valuable technical knowledge and substantially enhanced skill sets that are a boon to their homelands. However, the important point, here, is that one cannot simply ignore the extent to which aid efforts may contribute to both internal and external brain and character drains, and both the positive and negative effects of such movements, if one is serious about determining whether aid efforts are, on the whole, more beneficial than detrimental for the world's needy.

8.4 Summary and Final Remark

In this chapter, I have called attention to a problem that has been recognized in the field of global health, but which has been overlooked in the field of global aid generally. This concerns certain marketplace distortions that may arise due

---

[4] I am grateful to Angus Deaton for reminding me, in correspondence, that external "brain drain" often has positive, as well as negative, benefits for the world's poorest regions.

to local aid efforts in desperately poor countries. More particularly, I have suggested that the hiring practices of international aid organizations may lead to both brain and character drains from extremely important, but lower paying jobs, in civil government or public service, to less important, but higher paying jobs, inside or outside of the region. Thus, aid efforts may be unwittingly leading to an inefficient use of valuable human capital, from the standpoint of local social, political, and economic development.

I have not taken a stand on what the net effect may be of marketplace distortions in human capital. However, I believe that the issue raised in this chapter is important and needs to be taken seriously. If one really wants to consider the effectiveness of international aid efforts, one must take account of the overall impact of those efforts, both direct and indirect, and both short-term and long-term. This means that one cannot simply tally up the benefits that aid efforts provide. One must also look for, and tally up, the losses that occur elsewhere in the system as result of those aid efforts. If, in fact, part of the success that international aid organizations achieve stems from the highly talented and principled locals that those aid organizations hire to help advance their goals, then one must consider what else those workers would be doing if they were not working for the aid organizations. More specifically, one must consider any losses to society that might arise if the talented and principled workers are not replaced at their old jobs, or if their replacements are not as skilled, or principled, as they.

Finally, I note that in addition to the problems of brain drain and character drain, other problems may also arise as a result of local salary increases due to on-the-ground aid efforts in low-income countries. The natural thought is that increasing wages should always be a good thing for desperately poor people in desperately poor regions. And there is an important kernel of truth to that thought for those who are lucky enough to be the beneficiaries of such wage increases. However, as development economists have recognized, one must be attuned to the larger macro-economic impact of such increases. An interesting case study is that of Afghanistan, where NGO wage premiums, when compared against civil service wages, massively distorted labor markets, and threatened fiscal stability.[5] This is the sort of indirect impact of aid interventions that are all too common, and yet all too often overlooked, when aid organizations and those evaluating their effectiveness are assessing the impact of aid interventions.

---

[5] See Dost, A. N. and H. A. Khan, "Explaining NGO-State Wage Differentials in Afghanistan: Empirical Findings and New Theoretical Models with Policy Implications in General Equilibrium," *MPRA Paper*, Number 66639, 2015, URL: https://mpra.ub.uni-muenchen.de/66639/1/MPRA_paper_66639.pdf, accessed September 10, 2018.

9

Model Projects and the Difficulty of Predicting Future Success

Effective Altruists, and others, want to be sure that they are supporting the most effective international relief organizations. This requires gathering data on the relative successes, and failures, of different relief organizations. More particularly, this requires a determination of which organizations can be counted on to deliver aid successfully and effectively in current and future projects. This chapter explores some of the difficulties of ascertaining such information. It also illustrates how even the most carefully planned projects can go significantly, and unexpectedly, awry.

In Section 9.1, I argue that it is difficult to establish the "proven effectiveness" of any approach to aid for two reasons. First, each circumstance of need is, in its own way, unique. Thus, an approach which is successful in one village or region may not be successful in another village or region. Second, projects which appear to be successful in the short term may prove to be unsuccessful in the long run, for unexpected reasons.

In Section 9.2, I discuss the problem of *scaling up*. I show that for a variety of reasons it may be difficult to replicate the success of a model aid program that worked well on a small scale, when that program is attempted on a large scale.

In Section 9.3, I discuss a model project that failed from another field, the field of education. The discussion illustrates the general point that even the best laid plans of people with good will and nearly unlimited resources can fail badly in ways that nobody involved with the project foresaw. Further, reflection suggests that even if, contrary to fact, the project had succeeded, there is reason to wonder whether it could have been replicated elsewhere as the visionaries behind the project had hoped. The discussion also reminds us of the importance of looking elsewhere in the system for possible costs associated with the project's success. Thus, the discussion dovetails with, and buttresses, the arguments of Sections 8.2, 9.1, and 9.2.

In Section 9.4, I consider a response to this chapter's arguments offered by some Effective Altruists. In essence, this response accepts that the worries I raise may apply to many, and perhaps even most, international aid

Being Good in a World of Need. Larry S. Temkin, Oxford University Press. © Larry S. Temkin 2022.
DOI: 10.1093/oso/9780192849977.003.0009

organizations. However, it denies that they apply to the most effective aid organizations, such as the ones endorsed by Effective Altruist organizations like GiveWell. I grant that there is much to be said for this response. However, I suggest that there is some reason to take it with a grain of salt, as even those organizations deemed most effective may be less effective than one might have thought.

In Section 9.5, I summarize the chapter's main claims.

9.1 The Uniqueness of Each Circumstance and Unforeseen Developments

Often, an aid agency will come up with an idea for improving the lot of some particularly needy people in some poor region, will pour a lot of time, effort, and resources into addressing the problems that prompt their intervention, will point to great successes as a result of their efforts, and then will seek funds from donors to enable them to replicate their approach on a much larger scale throughout the region, on the grounds of the proven effectiveness of their approach. However, there are at least three worries that might be raised about this line of argument. This section discusses two of these worries, and the following discusses the third.

The first worry relates to the fact that in many respects each aid context is unique. Each has its own blend of social, political, cultural, religious, ethnic, economic, genetic, and historical factors that impact why the condition of need obtains, and what must be done to address it. Because of this, an aid approach that has proven to be effective in one village or region may not be equally effective when introduced into another village or region.[1]

There are many reasons why a model project may succeed, yet be atypical. Perhaps the project needs the close cooperation and support of the local leaders, and the model project was located in a village where the chief, or

---

[1] Many development economists have noted this problem. See, for example, Angus Deaton's *The Great Escape: Health, Wealth, and the Origins of Inequality* (Princeton: Princeton University Press, 2013), and Roger Riddell's *Does Foreign Aid Really Work?* (Oxford: Oxford University Press, 2007). Effective Altruist organizations like GiveWell have also been aware of, and deeply concerned about, this problem. GiveWell seeks, as much as possible, to support interventions whose efficacy has been tested in multiple contexts, and in their cost-effectiveness analysis they explicitly adjust for the likelihood of failures in trying to scale up an aid intervention or extend an intervention that was successful in one context into another, distinct, context. Of course, as GiveWell is aware, any attempts to anticipate, in advance, whether any particular aid intervention may or may not successfully transfer from one environment to another will, perforce, be highly speculative. Where possible, they have to rely on a combination of intuitive judgment and best-guess estimates in extrapolating on the basis of past efforts that were as similar as possible to the aid intervention and contexts currently under consideration.

one of his family members, was educated abroad, or had been the great beneficiary of Western medicine. In that case, the chief might have willingly provided support that was crucial to the success of the agency's efforts, which might be lacking in other villages where the background circumstances might be markedly different. Perhaps, for example, in a neighboring village the local leaders had been previously taken advantage of by unscrupulous outsiders, or had had loved ones die while under the care of Western medicine. In such a case, the local leaders might fail to support, or even oppose, the efforts of the development agency, with the result that those efforts might be much less effective or doomed to failure.

Similarly, perhaps one village is Christian, and so fully cooperative with a Christian charitable organization, while another village is Muslim, and so deeply suspicious of the very same organization and the very same prescriptions for how best to improve its wretched conditions.[2] For example, the original 12 step approach of Alcoholics Anonymous emphasized putting one's faith in Jesus Christ as the way to deal with addiction. This might work very effectively in a small Christian village that is wracked by addiction problems. However, it might provoke resentment and suspicion in a non-religious village, or a religious village that wasn't Christian. Likewise, one village might have deep-seated cultural mores which run counter to the prescriptions of an AIDS prevention organization, which another village lacks. In this case, the hugely successful efforts to combat AIDS in one village—say, via the willingness of tribal males to be circumcised or to use condoms—may be utterly ineffective in the other village. More generally, the reasons why a model project may succeed in one context but fail in another are as various, and boundless, as the ways in which the social, political, cultural, religious, ethnic, economic, genetic, and/or historical makeup of one group may vary from another.

The second worry about any organization's claims to the "proven effectiveness" of their aid projects is that such claims are always time bounded. Even if an approach has been shown to be "effective" for a certain period, there is no guarantee that this effectiveness will persist.

A relatively short-term example of this worry was given by Michael Maren, in his classic book *The Road to Hell*.[3] Maren reports a discussion that he had with an American, Andrew Clarke, who "had drilled some wells in his day and

---

[2] This case isn't just hypothetical, it occurs regularly. See, for instance, Obadare, E., "Religious NGOs, Civil Society and the Quest for a Public Sphere in Nigeria." *African Identities* 5 (2007): 135–53.

[3] Maren, Michael, *The Road to Hell: The Ravaging Effects of Foreign Aid and International Charity*, New York: The Free Press, 1997.

knew lots about Kenya's dry frontier areas" concerning the desirability of drilling wells to provide water for the nomads in Kenya's desert regions:

[Clark] drew a small circle in the center of a sheet of paper. 'This is the desert,' he said . . . [indicating] the whole sheet of paper. Then he pointed to the circle: 'Here is your well. During the rainy season this well will provide extra water for the nomads. It will allow them to have bigger herds. When the dry season comes, the nomads will begin to migrate toward your well . . . . They will arrive with larger herds and begin to denude the land closest to the well. Soon, they'll have to wander farther and farther from the well to find food . . . . Cows must eat and drink water every day. As soon as it is more than a day's walk from the water to the grass, the cows will die . . . . Goats and sheep can go several days without water, but as soon as the food is consumed for a two-day radius from the water, the goats and sheep will die . . . . The camels can go days without drinking water, but soon the walk will be too great for them. And when the camels die, the people die.'

This was not a hypothetical scenario, Clarke explained. It had happened, and it was still happening. Aid organizations were coming in and giving water to nomads, the gift of life, and it was killing them.[4]

A second case where an aid intervention appeared highly effective for a period, but proved disastrous in the long term, is noted by Maggie Black, who writes:

A classic example is the adoption of handpump tubewells as the main device for supplying village drinking water in Bangladesh, supported by UNICEF and other donors. When the water table dropped because sources were over-pumped for irrigation, arsenic contaminated the groundwater. A program heralded as a success for 20 years was roundly condemned . . . no judgment about 'success' or 'failure' can be guaranteed over time, especially given constant contextual changes.[5]

Other famous examples of this include the widespread use of thalidomide in the late 1950s and early 1960s to treat nausea in pregnant women, which later, in the 1960s, was determined to have caused severe birth defects in thousands

---

[4] Maren, *The Road to Hell*, pp. 9–10.
[5] See, Maggie Black's *International Development: Illusions and Realities* (Oxford: New Internationalist Publications, 2015, p. 50).

of children;[6] and the global use of DDT to increase food production and to combat malaria and typhoid, which persisted for many decades before it was discovered that DDT had significant long-term deleterious effects on humans, wildlife, and the environment—so much so that in 1972 the United States banned DDT for agricultural use, and in 1991 the Stockholm Convention on Persistent Organic Pollutants instituted a worldwide ban on DDT for agricultural use.[7]

We see, then, that claims to an aid project's "proven effectiveness" must be taken with a grain of salt. What works in one context may not work in another. And what appears to be a success for any given period, may, for unexpected reasons, prove to be a failure over a longer time span.

9.2 The Problem of Scaling Up

In this section, I discuss a third problem about supporting aid projects that have supposedly been proven to be successful. It might be called the problem of *scaling up*. Unfortunately, for a variety of reasons, it is often difficult to replicate small-scale successes on a large scale. Let me explain.

Often, when a model program is launched, it is the result of many weeks, months, or even years of careful planning and preparation. It has the personal backing and involvement of the organization's leaders. The testing site is carefully selected. There is close oversight from the highest levels of the organization to ensure that the plans for the program are being followed to a T. The model is given ample resources for its purposes. In addition, those recruited to carry out the program's mission are the very best people that the organization can find for the roles that need to be filled. In short, a model program is often the closest thing to a scientific experiment performed in a high-quality laboratory that can be found in the world of international relief, as every effort is made to achieve "ideal" conditions where any factors that might threaten the success of the project are removed or minimized as much as possible.

---

[6] There is a massive literature on the thalidomide tragedy. For an interesting review, fifty years on, see Kim, James H. and Anthony R. Scialli, "Thalidomide: The Tragedy of Birth Defects and the Effective Treatment of Disease." *Toxicological Sciences* 122 (2011): 1–6, available at https://academic.oup.com/toxsci/article/122/1/1/1672454, accessed July 1, 2019.

[7] DDT continues to be used, mostly in sub-Saharan Africa, to control malaria carrying mosquitoes. The turning point for the use of DDT in agriculture was Rachel Carson's classic book *Silent Spring* (New York: Houghton Mifflin, 1962), which carefully detailed the disastrous environmental and human consequences of the overuse of pesticides, in general, and DDT, in particular.

Unsurprisingly, the more one tries to scale up a model project, the harder it will be to replicate the conditions that may have accounted for the project's initial success. Weeks and months of careful planning, that took account of the details of the local context, might be replaced by days or hours of last-minute preparations as an organization moves into a new village or region. "Cookie cutter" blueprints might be developed offering onsite representatives a basic set of limited options to follow depending on what they find on the ground when they arrive. The highly qualified executives that were personally involved with the original planning and oversight might now have turned their attention to other concerns, delegating responsibility for the success of the programs to other, less qualified, managers. In attempting to bring the program to more and more locations, the locations may be decreasingly suitable for the program's success. There may be fewer resources available per site. Moreover, having already hired the very best workers that they could find for the initial program, the talent pool to draw from will inevitably shrink with each iteration of the program. So, while the first group of workers may be exceptionally skilled, hardworking, and have great character, the second group are likely to be a bit less so, the third group even less so, and by the thirtieth group, who knows what the talent pool will look like? Perhaps, at that point, the potential workers will be barely competent, lazy, and only minimally decent, if not downright incompetent, derelict, and corrupt!

To be sure, the world of international franchises—McDonald's, Kentucky Fried Chicken, Starbucks, etc.—has proven that certain types of enterprises can be successfully scaled up in many areas without significant loss in quality. And I have no doubt that, similarly, certain types of international relief projects can be replicated with similar success on a large scale in different regions and contexts. Nevertheless, there are plenty of examples where a local enterprise has been an enormous success, yet where attempts to franchise those enterprises have been colossal failures. Often, this is because much of the success of the initial enterprise was due to the vision, energy, commitment, special talents, and personal involvement of the people who launched the original enterprise, as well as the fabric of the local environment in which their enterprise flourished. Likewise, even if there is firm evidence that some international development organization's project achieved great success in one, or even a few, contexts, there are, alas, no guarantees that a large scale-up of such efforts would meet with similar success.[8]

---

[8] Effective Altruists sometimes write as if aid interventions should, at least where possible, be evaluated using the methodology of randomized control trials (RCTs) used with such success in the

9.3 The Rice School—A Cautionary Tale

In this section, I present an example taken from a different domain that helps illustrate several concerns relevant to our topic, including the main concerns that I raised in the previous two sections, as well as in Section 8.2.[9]

Many years ago, when I taught at Rice University, Rice became involved in a joint project with the Houston Independent School District (HISD) to create a K-8 elementary/middle school. The school was expected to be a huge success along many important dimensions, and the hope was that it would serve as a model school for other schools to emulate throughout the city, state, and even country.

The Rice School, as it was called, was to have a dual specialization in Technology and Spanish, and it was to serve children from both affluent and underprivileged populations. The school had many influential backers who were deeply committed to its success. This included the Superintendent of the School Board, powerful members of the School Board, important local politicians, influential business leaders, high level Rice University Administrators, and key members of Rice University's Department of Education.

The initial planning for the school began in 1989, and it continued for several years before construction finally began. The building itself was an architectural marvel, reflecting the substantial resources that were poured into its design and construction. The school was to be cutting edge in every respect, including in its application of the very latest in educational theories. Compaq, a leading local business, contributed two million dollars' worth of computers. The original principal was a rising star in HISD, as were her assistants. Teachers from all over the school district clamored to be transferred to the school, and only the best of them were selected. Unsurprisingly, there were many doctors, lawyers, college professors, and other professionals who

sciences. Often, they suggest that if an aid intervention has been shown to be a success by the lights of RCTs, it can be counted on to be a success when scaled up, or repeated elsewhere. However, Angus Deaton and Nancy Cartwright have argued that RCTs don't scale up, as a matter of logic, and hence that RCT results can serve science, but are weak grounds for inferring "what works" in the field of aid. See Deaton and Cartwright's "Understanding and Misunderstanding Randomized Controlled Trials." *Social Science & Medicine* 210 (2018): 2–21.

[9] Most of the claims I make regarding the Rice School are based on personal recollection. I knew some of the people involved with planning the Rice School, followed its proposal and development closely at the time, considered sending my own children to the school, and spoke with a number of people who did send their children to the school about their experiences with it. The example I am giving was a major topic of conversation in Houston, and at Rice University in particular, during its planning and rollout. For further background and details, see https://en.wikipedia.org/wiki/The_Rice_School, accessed August 30, 2017, and Tim Fleck's "What Went Wrong at the Rice School?" *Houston Press*, August 21, 1997, available at http://www.houstonpress.com/news/what-went-wrong-at-the-rice-school-6570776, accessed August 30, 2017.

tried to find backdoor ways to ensure that their children would be admitted to this state-of-the-art model of education.

When the Rice School finally opened its doors, in 1994, it did so with great fanfare. Unfortunately, by the beginning of the 1997–8 school year, the Rice School was in disarray. After only three years, it was already on its fourth principal, few of the original teachers remained, affluent parents had pulled their children in droves, and the Texas Education Agency had ranked the Rice School as the *only* "low performing" elementary school in the entire Houston Independent School District.[10]

I relay the story of the Rice School for several reasons. First, it is a cautionary tale that reminds us that even the best of intentions, the direct and committed involvement of a host of high level and extremely talented people, seemingly unlimited resources, and the enthusiasm and cooperation of all relevant stakeholders are not always enough to ensure the success of a project, no matter how important and feasible it may look on paper. Unfortunately, even our best laid plans can go terribly awry, and often for a host of subtle, indirect, and interrelated reasons that are so complex that they are difficult to identify and disentangle even after the fact. Certainly, during its planning stage, nobody deeply involved with and invested in the success of the Rice School would have, or could have, predicted its disastrous future.[11*] Similarly, few people deeply committed to the importance and success of international development are open to "seeing," and really taking seriously, the many intricate ways in which their efforts might cause problems.

Of course, by itself, the mere possibility of failure is not good reason to refrain from pursuing a morally desirable goal via a project that we honestly believe is going to succeed. And I am not suggesting otherwise. However, it is important that we not let the desirability of our immediate goal, and our personal investment in the success of a project designed to achieve that goal, blind us to the possible negative effects that our project may produce. Ultimately, whatever the domain, one needs a clear-eyed assessment of the likely success of any project, all things considered, and not merely in

[10] The information in this sentence is taken, almost verbatim, from the eighth paragraph of Fleck's "What Went Wrong at the Rice School?"

[11*] However, some "outsiders" had worries to which "insiders" were blind. Tim Fleck reveals a poignant story relayed by Marvan Hoffman, who was a professor of clinical education at Rice University, and an enthusiastic representative of Rice University on the Rice School's planning team. During the planning stages of the school Hoffman was warned by David Cohen, an outside expert on experimental schools from the University of Michigan, that "ventures like this seldom succeed." Three years after the Rice School opened its doors, Hoffman reported, with the resignation of hindsight, "I was so devastated and really angry with him [Cohen], at that point. I didn't want to hear that. But God, he was right." See Fleck's "What Went Wrong at the Rice School?"

terms of the immediate aims that might motivate one to pursue a project in the first place.

As it happens, the Rice School ran into serious problems from the start. However, suppose that had not been the case. Suppose it had met, and even exceeded, the wildest expectations of its most ardent supporters. Would that have been enough to brand it a success, all things considered? I think not. To assess that, one would need to carefully explore the indirect effects of all the effort that went into making the Rice School a success.

The Rice School consumed a great deal of time and effort from a host of high-level officials—members of the School Board, local politicians, Rice University Administrators, and others. There are opportunity costs to such expenditures of time and energy by such high-level officials. What might have they accomplished if they had devoted their time and effort to other pressing problems facing HISD, Houston, and Rice University?

The construction cost alone of the Rice School was 11 million dollars. How might that money have been spent elsewhere within HISD? If each of 11 already existing schools had received $1,000,000 grants, or each of 22 schools had received $500,000 grants, how many students might have benefited, and by how much, from the resulting upgrades to their schools? Similarly, it was wonderful that Compaq donated $2,000,000 worth of computers to help create a state-of-the-art technology school. However, think of how many underprivileged students in some of Houston's most desperately underfunded schools might have benefited, if only their schools had received an influx of, say, $200,000 worth of new computer equipment. It might well have been that virtually every child at ten different schools could have benefited significantly if Compaq's generous bequest had been distributed that way, rather than having only one group of students at a single school benefit from Compaq's largesse.

Similarly, the exceptionally talented principal and her two highly qualified assistants came from elsewhere in the system. So, presumably, the new school's gains were their old schools' losses. Likewise, for every child in the Rice School who benefited from the presence of one of its superstar teachers, there was a student at his or her previous school who didn't get the benefit of learning from such an inspiring teacher. Furthermore, it is arguable that the net benefit of having *one* classroom of 30 students being taught by, say, six inspiring teachers each day, is much less than the net benefit of *six* classrooms of 30 students at six different schools being taught by one inspiring teacher each day. Yet that is precisely the kind of trade-off that is made if one gathers many of the very best teachers from across a school district into a single school where there is a single student population that stands to benefit from the excitement and knowledge that such talented teachers bring to their classrooms.

Here, the Rice School serves as an example of the sorts of considerations I presented in Section 8.2. Those who are invested in the success of a project like the Rice School will tend to focus on the easily identifiable and perhaps quantifiable positive results of such a project. Had they achieved such results, within the Rice School's student population, no doubt the school would have been regarded as a resounding success, and no doubt there would have been a groundswell of support for creating other schools like the Rice School throughout HISD, and elsewhere. However, there remains the distinct possibility that even if, contrary to fact, the Rice School *had* produced genuinely significant success for its student population, it would, in essence, only have achieved that success by robbing Peter to pay Paul.[12*] That is, its successes may have come at the cost, including opportunity costs, of much less readily identifiable and quantifiable losses elsewhere in the system; losses that, though easily overlooked, may have actually outweighed the very real gains that the Rice School might have shown.

I believe that this might have been a real possibility *even if* the Rice School had proven to be a great success by most of the standard measures by which one measures the success of a school. Similarly, I believe that an analogous worry arises in some cases where an international development organization's efforts are (rightly) judged as successful by the "local" criteria that many people focus on when making such judgments.

The issues being raised here are akin to those raised by well-known debates in the field of global health about the trade-offs between so-called "vertical" healthcare interventions—which involve focused approaches to a single major health problem, or a small group of health problems—and so-called "horizontal" interventions—which seek a systematic and fully integrated approach for delivering comprehensive primary healthcare services. Although certain past vertical interventions have been spectacularly successful, such as those aimed at eradicating smallpox and polio, more recent vertical approaches have

---

[12*] One is reminded here, for instance, of Mao's steel campaign, during which there were strict quotas for certain amounts of steel to be produced in communities across China. To meet those quotas, villages often took "all sorts of household implements made of steel—pots, pans, doorknobs and shovels" and melted them down in furnaces to produce steel, "whether the steel was any good . . . [one might wonder] about using furnaces to 'melt steel to produce steel, to destroy knives to make knives'" (Glover, Jonathan, *Humanity: A Moral History of the Twentieth Century* (New Haven: Yale University Press, 2001, p. 284).)

been more controversial, such as PEPFAR (the President's Emergency Plan for AIDS Relief), and the Global Fund to Fight AIDS, Tuberculosis, and Malaria.

Although there is general agreement that there are certain contexts where focused vertical health interventions may be desirable, there is also general agreement that vertical programs "often have limited chance of sustainability and have negative spillover effects on health systems and non-targeted populations" as valuable and limited resources and personnel are focused on a limited population with a particular disease, rather than the general population and the wide array of diseases that afflict people, especially among the needy in the world's poorest countries.[13] So, for example, "in several countries in the eastern part of the WHO [the World Health Organization] European Region... vertical [health] programmes appear to have impaired the effective management of HIV, tuberculosis, substance abuse and mental health."[14] The focused approach of vertical programmes is at odds with the "WHO's emphasis on strengthening health systems and primary care," and its recent push for universal healthcare throughout the world, including in the world's poorest regions, at least at the level of primary care.[15]

The Rice School also raises worries of the sort noted in Sections 9.1 and 9.2. Even if the Rice School had been deemed a great success, based, say, on the test scores of its students, it does not follow that similar successes would be achieved if one tried to replicate the Rice School elsewhere, or on a large scale. For one, for any number of local reasons, residents in other districts might have been less enthusiastic about transferring their students from their current neighborhood schools to a new experimental school. Yet support of the local residents might have played a significant role in any achievements that the Rice School obtained.

Similarly, while the Superintendent of HISD, members of the School Board, local politicians, and Rice University Administrators might have been eager and able to expend significant amounts of time, energy, and resources towards ensuring that the first model school was a great success, presumably, they

[13] See Rifta Atun, Sara Bennett, and Antonio Duran's 2008 Health Systems and Policy Analysis policy brief for the World Health Organization, the European Observatory on Health Systems and Policies, and HEN (Health Evidence Network, Evidence for Decision Makers), "When Do Vertical (Stand-Alone) Programmes Have a Place in Health Systems?" URL: https://www.who.int/manage ment/district/services/WhenDoVerticalProgrammesPlaceHealthSystems.pdf, accessed July 19, 2019. I am grateful to Nir Eyal for directing me to this article.

[14] "When Do Vertical (Stand-Alone) Programmes Have a Place in Health Systems?"

[15] "When Do Vertical (Stand-Alone) Programmes Have a Place in Health Systems?" For further discussion of the push by the UN and others for universal healthcare, and some worries about that push in the world's poorest countries, see my article "Universal Health Coverage: Solution or Siren? Some Preliminary Thoughts." *The Journal of Applied Philosophy* 31 (2014): 1–22; doi: 10.1111/japp.12050.

would have had much less time, energy, and resources to spend to ensure the success of subsequent schools. Indeed, it is reasonable to assume that soon after the first school or first few schools were completed, the key executives would delegate their roles to subordinates, who may or may not subsequently delegate their roles to *their* subordinates, and at some point the crucial managerial and oversight roles would be filled by staffers, bureaucrats, and civil servants who were just doing their jobs.

Furthermore, if, contrary to fact, the Rice School had met with great success, originally, it is likely that much of that success would have stemmed from the exceptional talents, power, and prestige of the top officials whose personal involvement "ensured" that failure was not an option. And there is no guarantee that a similar constellation of high-powered movers and shakers would have gotten behind such a project in other municipalities, even if the Rice School had been a success. Moreover, there tends to be a significant difference in the level of commitment between those who originally formulate and champion an idea—throwing their heart and soul into making it a success—and those who merely try to follow the blueprint of someone else's idea because of its original success.

Relatedly, the Rice School was fortunate to have a local business which was willing and able to contribute $2,000,000 worth of computers to support the school's goals. And presumably, that gift would have played a significant role in any successes that the Rice School had as a state-of-the-art technology school. However, one could hardly expect Compaq to make a similar gift even a second time, let alone ten, or a hundred, or a thousand times. Moreover, there is no guarantee that other communities would have had local businesses with the wherewithal or willingness to make comparable contributions to the success of a local kindergarten/elementary school—especially in many of the poorest school districts which could most benefit from a state-of-the-art school like the Rice School.

Finally, to ensure success, the Rice School tapped the very best administrators and teachers that it could find to fill the school's positions. Following this model, each subsequent school would, at least for some period, have had a smaller and less exceptional talent pool to draw on, than the previous one.[16]

---

[16] Jake Nebel suggests that the shortage of talented people to draw on might only be a short-term problem. If lots of school districts began pouring more resources into creating model schools, the greater salary and prestige of teaching at such schools might eventually lead to more talented people going into the teaching profession. This is, in principle, correct. However, it would likely take a number of years for the sort of shift that Nebel is imagining to eventuate. So, for some years, at least, the

But, of course, insofar as one believes that truly outstanding administrators and teachers play a substantial role in the academic success of a school's student population, this means that one should expect poorer and poorer results the more one scales up the original model.

In sum, the Rice School was a well-intentioned non-profit endeavor in the important field of education, which failed to deliver on its initial promise, and which may not have been replicable elsewhere, or on a large scale, even if it had been a success.[17] Though the analogy may not be perfect, I believe that it serves as a cautionary tale for many well-intentioned endeavors in the important field of international development, whether those endeavors are government sponsored, or supported by NGOs. Unfortunately, the best laid plans can go terribly awry, for a host of complex, indirect, and unforeseen reasons. And if this can happen when one's plan concerns a local project that is literally in one's neighborhood, as it did with the Rice School, imagine how easily it can happen when the plan concerns a project in a distant land, where the possibilities of misunderstandings and missteps are almost boundless, due to significant differences in histories, politics, economics, cultures, religions, worldviews, and forms of communication. Moreover, even if a model project is a great success in one context, for the reasons given in Sections 9.1 and 9.2, that is no guarantee that the project's approach would meet with similar success in other contexts, or if it was substantially scaled up.[18]

---

problem of scaling up that I am describing here is likely to obtain. Moreover, the history of public education in the United States doesn't inspire confidence that enough school districts would, in fact, be prepared to raise taxes and increase teachers' salaries sufficiently so as to induce significantly greater numbers of highly talented people to pursue elementary, middle, and high school teaching, rather than the alternative careers that such people often pursue now, in light of their substantially greater salaries, benefits, working conditions, and prestige.

[17] Interestingly, the Rice School eventually gained its footing. While it never succeeded in becoming the model school that its early advocates hoped for, it did eventually become an above average public school in the city of Houston. (See, https://www.niche.com/k12/the-rice-school—la-escuela-rice-houston-tx/, accessed July 1, 2019.) However, this was only after it abandoned many of its early "revolutionary" methods and returned to many of the "tried and true" approaches for running a public school in a large metropolitan area in the United States.

[18] The fact that each case of need has its own unique local conditions and context, which often make it difficult to scale up projects, or to simply transfer a successful aid intervention from one situation to another, is widely recognized among development economists. Deaton puts this point succinctly, claiming "there is no reason to suppose that what works well in one place will work somewhere else" (*The Great Escape*, p. 291). See also, Nancy Cartwright and Jeremy Hardie's *Evidence-Based Policy: A Practical Guide to Doing It Better* (New York: Oxford University Press, 2012); Riddell's *Does Foreign Aid Really Work?*; and Obadare's "Religious NGOs, Civil Society and the Quest for a Public Sphere in Nigeria."

9.4 An Effective Altruist's Response and Some Reasons to Take It with a Grain of Salt

In this section, I would like to consider, and briefly respond, to a view that is common within the Effective Altruist community. In essence, the view accepts this chapter's arguments as relevant to many international aid organizations and their projects, but it denies that they apply to the most effective international aid organizations and their projects. This view is put nicely by Nick Beckstead, who writes:

> I agree with this [the arguments of Chapter 9] as stated, but I have different thoughts about most international aid versus GiveWell's top charities. Consider especially the *Against Malaria Foundation*:
>
> 1. 22 RCTs [random control trials], presumably in many different countries, showing the efficacy of the program.
> 2. Specific, highly-validated mechanism of action.
> 3. Limited scope for variation in how instructions for implementation of the program are understood by those implementing the program.
> 4. Inspections collecting data on delivery and proper installation of bed nets, with linkup to well-validated mechanism of action.
> 5. Country-wide rollouts of bed nets; bed nets generally associated in mainstream history of malaria with global decline in disease burden.
> 6. Not implemented by governments.
> 7. Single-purpose charitable organization—all funds go to bed net rollout.
>
> My guess is that you'll see a fair amount of this with GiveWell's top charities, and that makes it important to not paint them with the same brush as [most] non-profit endeavors in international development.[19]

I have nothing bad to say about the Against Malaria Foundation, and have, myself, contributed to that organization for a number of years. Moreover, there is much to be said for Beckstead's position. One does have to be careful not to fault all international aid organizations or projects, because of the failings of some, or even most. Furthermore, Beckstead's remarks are on target for how, in principle, the kind of aid offered by the Against Malaria Foundation can be scaled up in a variety of countries and contexts.

---

[19] I am grateful to Beckstead for sending me these comments in replying to an earlier draft of this book. I have added periods at the end of each numbered clause, and corrected two typos, but otherwise have quoted Beckstead verbatim here.

Unfortunately, however, there are cautionary remarks to be applied even to the case of bed nets, which are widely regarded as among the lowest hanging fruit for those seeking proven, cost-effective ways of helping the needy.

I once spoke with a high-level government official working with the National Institutes of Health, who reported the great zeal with which certain U.S. aid programs pursued the low-hanging fruit of malaria reduction through the distribution of bed nets. This official noted that while distributing bed nets was easy and cheap, getting people to properly use them was another matter. This official reported that in some villages the bed nets had been set up improperly, so that there were gaps between the nets and the beds. In other villages, the mosquito nets remained unopened on the floor of the huts to which they had been distributed, still in their original boxes (marked as having come from the U.S. of course). This could be for any number of reasons— because the mosquito nets had never been a part of their culture, because the villagers didn't really believe that the mosquito nets would help (after all, they spent most of their waking hours outside in the fields, exposed to the elements), or simply because the villagers "couldn't be bothered" with the inconvenience of using the mosquito nets properly on a daily basis. So, for example, after completing a five-year impact evaluation of the Millennium Villages Project in Ghana, Chris Barnett noted that "people were not always using bed nets, finding [it] hard at certain times of the year to reconcile the use of bed nets with the night heat."[20] (There are parallels here with the difficulty of getting some men in villages ravaged by AIDS to regularly use condoms. Despite the overwhelming dangers of AIDS, of which they are acutely aware, and the free distribution of condoms and their ease of use, there are many people who simply refuse to use condoms for a wide variety of reasons.)

In his classic work, *The White Man's Burden*, William Easterly speaks with compassion and poignancy about the fact that malaria remains a terrible global scourge, despite the widespread recognition among politicians, economic leaders, and celebrities of its devastating effects; concerted global efforts to raise money for its eradication; how easy, in principle, it is to prevent or cure it; and the proven effectiveness of anti-malarial programs in countries like Vietnam and Tanzania. Easterly speaks of "the tragedy in which the West spent 2.3 trillion dollars over the last five decades and still had not

---

[20] Chris Barnett, "Thumbs up or thumbs down? Did the Millennium Villages Project work?" *From Poverty to Power*, Oxfam Blog, September 20, 2018, URL: https://oxfamblogs.org/fp2p/thumbs-up-or-thumbs-down-did-the-millennium-villages-project-work/, accessed March 30, 2021. Barnett is Director of Technical Excellence for Itad, and his impact evaluation was funded by the United Kingdom's Department for International Development.

managed to get twelve-cent medicines to children to prevent half of all malaria deaths... [or] four-dollar bed nets to families."[21]

Easterly asks "if bed nets are such an effective cure, why hadn't... [the West] already gotten them to the poor?"[22] In partial response, he sadly points out that "Unfortunately, neither celebrities nor aid administrators have many ideas for how to get bed nets to the poor. Such nets are often diverted to the black market, become out of stock in health clinics, or wind up being used as fishing nets or wedding veils."[23] Or, as Chris Barnett, gently and wryly put it, it is "surprising how many creative uses for bet nets there were, whether as screens for toilets or bathing areas, to protect young fruit trees, to cover store rooms, as pillows or bedding to lie on, as fishing nets, door curtains and sun blinds."[24] And, of course, if the bed nets have other uses of value, and are being distributed in regions controlled by dictators, warlords, gang leaders or thugs, then the concerns of Chapter 7 come into play, as some of the value of the bed nets can be siphoned off to support evil doers and their actions.

In sum, the Against Malaria Foundation is in a better position than many international aid organizations to avoid some of this chapter's worries. I readily grant that. And the same may be true for some of the other top-rated international aid organizations endorsed by Effective Altruist organizations like GiveWell. But no matter how effective an aid project may be in theory, in practice, the success of that aid project will always depend on the cooperation and support of local officials, a clear understanding of what needs to be done, a willingness to follow through, and so on. Unfortunately, for a host of reasons that aid donors often don't anticipate or fully understand, the local compliance necessary to make an aid intervention effective may not be reliably forthcoming. This is so for even a "no-brainer" "low fruit" aid intervention like bed net distributions.

As I am writing these words in the middle of a global pandemic, I cannot help adding the following. Covid-19 is a highly contagious disease that, as I type these words, has infected more than 4,000,000 U.S. citizens and claimed more than 145,000 U.S. lives in less than five months. U.S. citizens have been clearly informed that social distancing and wearing masks are effective means to counter the spread of the disease. But tens of millions of U.S. citizens can't be bothered to follow those simple guidelines, even as the infection and death

---

[21] The quote is from p. 4 of Easterly's *The White Man's Burden: Why the West's Efforts to Aid the Rest Have Done So Much Ill and So Little Good* (New York: Penguin Press, 2006), but see also pp. 13 and 252.

[22] Easterly, *The White Man's Burden*, p. 13.   [23] Easterly, *The White Man's Burden*, p. 13.

[24] Barnett, "Thumbs up or thumbs down? Did the Millennium Villages Project work?"

rates are increasing in 39 of the 50 U.S. states. Moreover, even if every U.S. citizen were given a free supply of masks, there is every reason to believe that tens of millions of U.S. citizens wouldn't bother using them. So, it is not enough to have a "proven effective" solution to a problem if, for whatever reason, people will not avail themselves of that solution.

Does this mean that we shouldn't distribute bed nets or masks? Of course not. Even if not everyone will use them properly, many will, and this may, predictably, save lives. It is just a reminder that the rosy picture that is often portrayed about the proven effectiveness of certain aid operations should be taken with a grain of salt.

9.5 Summary

In this chapter, I have offered three reasons why one can't confidently assume the future success of a project based on the supposed success of similar projects in the past. The first reason is that each aid circumstance is unique. So, a project that may succeed in one context may fail in another. The second is that evaluations of project success are always time bound and, in fact, they are often fairly short-term. However, there are many cases where projects that appeared to be a great success in the short term, proved to be failures in the long term, for unanticipated reasons. Third, there are often a host of factors present that contribute to the success of the initial trials of a project, which may be attenuated or missing in successive trials. This can make it difficult to replicate the success of a model project when that project is scaled up.

I also considered an example of a model project from the field of education, the Rice School. The Rice School vividly illustrates how even the best laid plans of well-intentioned and well-funded individuals can unexpectedly fail. I suggested that reflection on the case of the Rice School buttresses many of this chapter's claims, as well as some of the central claims of Chapter 8.

Finally, I considered a response that some Effective Altruists offer to this chapter's claims. I granted that there was much to be said for this response, but that, even so, there was reason to take it with a grain of salt. Unfortunately, even the most effective aid organizations may not be *as* effective as their "proven approaches" to aid might lead one to expect.

10

Ethical Imperialism

Some Worries about Paternalism,
Autonomy, and Respect

In this chapter, I would like to develop several worries, touched on briefly in
Section 3.8. The worries concern the way in which efforts of international
development agencies to improve conditions in the developing world often
involve paternalistic attitudes and actions that may be problematic from the
standpoint of autonomy and respect. In doing this, I shall focus my attention
on the efforts of international development agencies based in developed
Western countries.

In Section 10.1, I comment on the long and ugly history of Western
interventions in the developing world. I note that colonialists and imperialists
generally lacked respect for the people and autonomy of the natives whose
lands they colonized. Often, they regarded natives as "inferiors" who needed to
be "civilized" in order to "save" them from their "backward" ways.

In Section 10.2, I argue that while aid workers generally lack the reprehensible attitude that those they are helping are inferior, many of the other
unsavory aspects of colonialism may accompany the attitudes and actions of
international aid organizations. I point out that, in the name of *progress* and
benefiting those in need, aid organizations frequently act so as to undermine
longstanding social, cultural, and economic practices—practices often viewed
as backward, ignorant, primitive, stunting, immoral, and, in some cases,
barbaric. I suggest that such actions often have consequences that are both
morally and practically problematic. Moreover, this is so, I argue, even if the
aid organizations' views about the practices they are undermining are correct.

In Section 10.3, I discuss the outsized influence that financial considerations
can have on people's choices. I suggest that international aid agencies may
induce locals to shift their priorities, and divert them, or alienate them, from
important aspects of their social, cultural, historical, and religious traditions.
Moreover, this can happen in the absence of any of the offensive and objectionable attitudes discussed in Section 10.2. I suggest that this can be unsettling

Being Good in a World of Need. Larry S. Temkin, Oxford University Press. © Larry S. Temkin 2022.
DOI: 10.1093/oso/9780192849977.003.0010

when it occurs at the individual level, and worrisome when it occurs at the collective level.

Section 10.4 concludes the chapter with a final remark.

10.1   Remembering Colonialism

The history of Western intervention in the developing world is a long and sordid one. That history, which involves colonialism, imperialism, and exploitation on a massive scale, naturally gives rise to suspicions regarding any Western interventions in the developing world. Sadly, those suspicions are often well-founded, even in the domain of so-called foreign aid.

Often, government-to-government aid has been unrelated, or only loosely related, to humanitarian concerns, and instead is offered to prop up the political, economic, and strategic interests of the donor nations.[1*] So, for example, a significant portion of U.S. government foreign aid has always been given in the form of military aid, and much of U.S. foreign aid has been given to strengthen strategic alliances against Russia and China, as well as, more recently, North Korea, Iran, and terrorism.[2*] The rhetoric of foreign aid tends to be high minded, but the reality is often something rather different.

[1*] Riddell makes the point that "The primary purpose of United States' aid has always been to further and promote its own interests, with foreign aid seen as an essential arm of foreign policy, playing 'a vital role in supporting US geostrategic interests' (USAID 2004: 3). As a result, foreign aid allocations have always been critically influenced by national security priorities, with massive amounts of aid channeled to America's allies" (Riddell, Roger, *Does Foreign Aid Really Work?* (Oxford: Oxford University Press, 2007, p. 94)). Similarly, Deaton observes that "in most cases, aid is guided less by the needs of the recipients than by the donor country's domestic and international interests" and "Aid is not given person to person; most of it is government to government, and much of it is not designed to lift people out of poverty" (Deaton, Angus, *The Great Escape: Health, Wealth, and the Origins of Inequality* (Princeton: Princeton University Press, 2013, pp. 274, 281)).

[2*] Some people are surprised to learn that military aid and assistance counts as foreign aid. However, in the United States, this has always been the case, at least for most official government purposes, since the current foreign aid system was created by the *1961 Foreign Assistance Act*. "The statute defines aid as 'the unilateral transfers of U.S. resources by the U.S. Government to or for the benefits of foreign entities.' These resources include not just goods and funding, but also technical assistance, educational programming, health care, and other services. Recipients include foreign governments, including foreign militaries and security forces, as well as local businesses and charitable groups, international organizations such as the United Nations, and other nongovernmental organizations." According to the nonpartisan Congressional Research Service, in 2016, 42% of all U.S. aid went to long-term development aid, 33% went to military and security aid, 14% went to humanitarian aid, and 11% went to political aid. (The information and quoted material in this note is from the Council on Foreign Relations article "How Does the U.S. Spend Its Foreign Aid?" backgrounded by James McBride, updated October 1, 2018, URL: https://www.cfr.org/backgrounder/how-does-us-spend-its-foreign-aid, accessed June 3, 2019.)

The percentage of U.S. foreign aid that is spent on military aid has fluctuated over the years. For example, from 1970 to 1996, it ranged from a low of 15% in 1993, to a high of 47% in 1979, with an average of 31% during that 26-year period. (See *Table No. 1313. U.S. Foreign Economic and Military*

During the height of the colonial and imperialistic eras, Western governments didn't talk about exploiting the people and resources of the countries they were controlling. Rather, they spoke about the benefits which their involvement would bring to the local populations. Of course, many colonialists were hypocrites or scoundrels, who knew exactly what they were doing when they took over another country—in some cases, enslaving or otherwise subjugating the native population for their personal benefit; in other cases, confining local populations to reservations or detention camps; and in other cases, pursuing policies of ethnic cleansing through genocide, or by driving native populations out of their own territories.

However, there are few limits to the scope of false-consciousness or self-deception, and no doubt many of the Westerners involved in colonialism actually believed what they were telling themselves and the rest of the world. Some of them were well-intentioned, if often benighted, religious missionaries. Many others acted with the zeal of missionaries whose "calling" was to bring civilization to the barbaric natives! After all, colonialism was to bring, and in some cases did bring, roads, Western-style education, Western religion, Western-style government, Western-style farming, and Western culture to countries that, by Western lights, were "backward."

It is not my point, here, to debate the pluses and minuses of colonialism. However, I do want to say a word about the *attitude* of those who participated in colonialism. Colonialism was an example, par excellence, of hegemony—the political and cultural domination of one group, or nation, over another. It was motivated, for some, at least, by the spirit of *noblesse oblige*, which held that it was the duty of those members of the "higher" classes, birth, or social rank, to act with kindness, honor, and generosity towards those of the "lower" classes, birth, or social rank. Correspondingly, during the colonial era, many Westerners believed that they were superior to those in the "uncivilized" world. Often, they believed that they knew better than the indigenous peoples themselves what the indigenous people needed and what was good for them. Further, many colonialists believed that they had a moral obligation to help improve the lives of their unfortunate inferiors, by doing for them what they would be incapable of doing for themselves; namely, bringing them Western civilization with its many "undeniable" benefits.

Aid Programs: 1970–1996, U.S. Census Bureau, the Official Statistics, *Statistical Abstract of the United States: 1998*, September 25, 1998, URL: https://www2.census.gov/library/publications/1998/compendia/statab/118ed/tables/sasec28.pdf#, accessed July 3, 2019.)

This depiction of colonialism is an ugly one, and intentionally so. But it is important to bear in mind that the colonialists did not see themselves the way we now see them. Many of them saw themselves, and their actions, as noble. Many of them saw themselves as taking great personal risks and making great personal sacrifices to improve the quality of lives of people who were needy. No doubt, for some colonialists, this self-conception was an accurate one, so far as it goes. Still, however much good the colonialists may or may not have done—and that is a large topic—it is hard to deny that their hegemonic and paternalistic practices revealed a fundamental lack of respect for both the people that they were (supposedly) aiming to help, and for their autonomy. That is, they believed that the native populations were inferior to Westerners, and that they were incapable of formulating and successfully pursuing meaningful life plans of their own choosing.

10.2 Some Worries about Thinking We Know Better—Even If We Are Right

I raise these points about colonialism, because I believe that some of the unseemly aspects of colonialism also accompany certain international development efforts; not inevitably, but more often than is typically acknowledged.

I believe that most people involved in international development efforts lack the racist attitudes of many colonialists, and don't think of themselves as superior in virtue of their nature, race, religion, nationality, or birth to those people needing their help. This is important. Still, there are psychological barriers that may be difficult to overcome whenever people from significantly different social and cultural backgrounds confront one another. When these barriers are combined with the fact that those involved in international development efforts *do* regard themselves as significantly better off, and much more fortunate, than the needy, it will often be difficult for those who are better off from one culture, to genuinely relate to those who are much less well off from another culture—the "unfortunate others"—as equals, and to truly treat them as equals during interactions.[3]

---

[3] I am grateful to Roger Crisp for suggesting the role that significant cultural differences can play in contributing to this problem. However, it is worth noting that significant problems of being treated as equals often arise between those needing help and those administering it, even in settings where there are not substantial cultural differences; for example, the aged and disabled frequently face this problem in their interactions with doctors, psychologists, and other caregivers who are members of their same cultural community. (I am grateful to Jeff McMahan for this observation.) But one can understand how such problems may be easily exacerbated where there are also significant cultural differences in play.

To be sure, there has been a growing sense within the development community that there is no need for "white saviors"; and at one level many people have come to recognize that simply being materially better off than another person doesn't provide one with privileged insights as to how best to remedy their poverty or need. Yet, while many working in development are aware of these facts, and seek to collaborate with rather than prescribe to those in need, it is all too easy to lose one's grip on this insight when genuine differences in goals or approaches arise between those aiming to help, and those they are seeking to help.

Moreover, if a Western development organization sees local customs or ways of life as serious impediments to the goals it wishes to achieve, it will often paternalistically work, both directly and indirectly, to weaken or undermine the people's customs or ways of life "for their own sake." This is true, for example, of aid efforts which aim to improve the quality of people's lives by: ending female circumcision; promoting male circumcision in areas where AIDS is rampant; educating members of the lowest castes or better yet ending the caste system entirely; ending rights of primogeniture; ending child marriages; ending female infanticide; keeping girls in school beyond child-bearing age; introducing modern birth-control methods; ending the way Sharia Law is practiced in certain countries, such as the stoning of adulterers; combating bribery, kickbacks, and "quid pro quo" business practices; encouraging the adoption of Western medicine over the reliance on tribal healers for certain medical conditions; introducing new crops and Western farming methods; changing the way people use rivers for washing, bathing, dumping garbage, and human waste disposal; ending or altering the dowry system; fighting human trafficking in its many forms, where this might include selling people as slaves, selling people as sex-slaves, forcing people into lives of servitude, or even such practices as arranged marriages or polygamy in those cases where such practices leave women or girls in vulnerable situations akin to slavery or indentured servitude; empowering women and girls through education, loans, business training, and birth control; and so on.

As already noted, in seeking to produce such changes, Western development agencies operating in foreign societies will often be at odds with longstanding social, cultural, and economic norms of those societies. Correspondingly, they may well be acting in direct opposition to the desires and values of many of the people that they are aiming to help. Still, they will justify their actions, to themselves and others, on the grounds of the benefits that they are providing to people in need, benefits that those people are not able to secure for themselves, and that hopefully they will one day come to recognize and value even if they do not fully do so now. They are not intervening to benefit themselves, the development workers will claim, but to improve the societies in which they are working and to make their members better off.

To be clear, I fully approve of the various projects that I noted above—that is the reason I chose to enumerate those projects here—and I believe that development agencies *should* pursue them where they effectively can. However, if we are being honest, we must recognize that, in proceeding as they do, international aid agencies are acting in the name of *progress*, and in the belief that *their* values and practices are *better* than the ones that they are seeking to overturn. Indeed, if we are brutally honest with ourselves, we will admit that we regard many of the practices in the societies that we are seeking to change as backward, ignorant, primitive, stunting, immoral, and, in some cases, barbaric.

We may (or may not) understand the social, cultural, religious, and historical forces that gave rise to the values and practices that we are seeking to undermine, but we should not pretend that we *respect* those values and practices. To the contrary, our actions indicate that we condemn the values and practices in question, as we seek to replace them with more progressive ones that are *better* and more *enlightened*. Finally, having admitted this much, shouldn't we also admit that all this has a whiff of many of the attitudes that we associate with colonialism, and that we rightly condemn?

We know better than they what is best for them. *Our* values, practices, and way of life are better than theirs. They, or their descendants, will appreciate *later* what we are doing for them now, even if they are don't understand it or appreciate it now. We, who are better off, have a *moral duty* to help those who are less fortunate, since they are incapable of helping themselves. And so on.

Many people find it shocking that the Taliban, Al Qaeda, ISIS, and similar groups find it so easy to find recruits to fight the evil West. But is this really so surprising? Among other things, they tell their followers that the West disrespects their values, their social, cultural, and religious heritage, their customs, and their way of life. More than that, they portray themselves as in an existential fight against the West which, if it had its way, would undermine, permanently alter, or destroy their way of life. Are they really that far wrong in making such claims?

I am not an ethical relativist. I believe that some customs, values, and ways of life are worse than others.[4] I also believe that certain actions are both

---

[4] Martha Nussbaum is one of many who holds a similar view. She writes that it cannot be maintained "as some relativists in literary theory and in anthropology tend to assume, that all world

reprehensible and morally impermissible, even if done to preserve one's way of life. Thus, nothing in my remarks is intended to serve as an apology for, much less a justification of, the values and practices of the Taliban, Al Qaeda, ISIS, or other similar groups, or of the actions that they perpetrate in defense of their ways of life. However, having said that, we must be honest with ourselves, and others, when our actions implicitly or explicitly condemn or undermine the values, practices, and lifestyles of others. And we must be prepared to truly listen to those whose values we reject, and try to genuinely understand their positions, and the pervasive impact that our words and actions may have on them psychologically (for example, in terms of their self-respect and their worldview) as well as materially.

Many actions that international relief organizations undertake to aid the needy will be uncontroversial, and wholeheartedly welcomed by the societies in which they are operating. However, as is implied by the preceding list of prevalent cultural practices that we, in the West, decry, this will not always be the case. Whenever members of one culture go into another with the aim of making things go *better*, the possibility arises for deep misunderstandings and fundamental clashes of values and worldviews. Local citizens may be excused if they perceive attempts to undermine their traditions, values, and ways of life—however well-intentioned and morally justified on "objective" grounds (at least according to the value systems of those "outsiders" making those attempts)—as disrespectful, demeaning, condescending, paternalistic, and a threat to their autonomy. They may also be excused if they think that we should be focusing on taking care of the many deep and pervasive problems in our own backyards—for example, in the United States, the plight of Native Americans, the inequities that continue to persist between African-Americans and whites, the mistreatment of immigrant populations, the lack of adequate healthcare for millions, the barriers that women and members of the LGBTQ community continue to face, the massive inequalities between the rich and the poor, and so on—before interfering in other people's affairs. Such perceptions and thoughts, which may in turn give rise to anger, resentment, distrust, and resistance, may be provoked by many well-intentioned outside interventions by international aid and development organizations. Together, these considerations suggest very real costs, both practical and moral, that must be taken into account when considering such interventions.

---

interpretations are equally valid and altogether non-comparable, that there are no good standards of assessment and 'anything goes'" ("Non-Relative Virtues: An Aristotelian Approach," in *The Quality of Life*, edited by Martha C. Nussbaum and Amartya Sen (Oxford: Oxford University Press, 1993, p. 260)).

Let me conclude this section with a final, sobering, thought. For those of us who are confident that our intentions and actions in intervening on behalf of the less fortunate are above reproach, utterly devoid of the disrespectful attitudes associated with colonialism and imperialism, and not liable to be misinterpreted or resented by those we aim to help, it is worth pausing, for a moment, to consider the example of John Stuart Mill. The author of *Utilitarianism*[5] and co-author of *On Liberty*,[6] Mill was a leading liberal and one of the most progressive figures of his day. He was a defender of female rights, an opponent of slavery, and an organizer of the *Jamaica Committee*—a group of British luminaries which demanded that the British Colonial Governor of Jamaica, Edward John Eyre, stand trial and be brought to justice for brutal excesses in the suppression of the Morant Bay rebellion of 1865.[7] Yet, despite that, Mill worked full time for the British East India Company for thirty-five years, from 1823, when he was 17, until 1858, when, at the age of 52, the East India Company was disbanded. A loyal servant of the British East India Company, rising from the ranks of a lowly clerk to the prominent and powerful position of Examiner,[8] Mill argued in support of a "benevolent despotism" regarding the colonies.[9] Indeed, Mill contended that "To suppose that the same international customs, and the same rules of international morality, can obtain between one civilized nation and another, and between civilized nations and barbarians, is a grave error.... To characterize any conduct whatever towards a barbarous people as a violation of the law of nations, only shows that he who so speaks has never considered the subject."[10]

Looking back, we shudder at Mill's language, and his loyalty to, and defense of, a company that has long since come to be seen as one of the great symbols of colonialism and imperialism and their many evils. At the same time, we

[5] Mill, John Stuart, *Utilitarianism* (Indianapolis: Hackett Publishing Company, 1979).

[6] Mill, John Stuart, *On Liberty* (London: Longman, Roberts & Green, 1869).

[7] Other notable members of the Jamaica Committee included Charles Darwin, Thomas Henry Huxley, and Herbert Spencer. For more information on Governor Eyre, the Morant Bay rebellion, and Mill's role in organizing the Jamaica Committee, see the Wikipedia articles on Edward John Eyre and the Jamaica Committee, available at https://en.wikipedia.org/wiki/Edward_John_Eyre and https://en.wikipedia.org/wiki/Jamaica_Committee, respectively, accessed August 8, 2019.

[8] See Chew Yong Jack's "J.S. Mill's Career at the East India Company," *The Victorian Web: literature, history, & culture in the age of Victoria*, URL: http://www.victorianweb.org/philosophy/mill/career.html, accessed August 8, 2019. Also, Al Harris's "John Stuart Mill: Servant of the East India Company," *The Canadian Journal of Economics and Political Science* 30 (1964): 185–202; doi:10.2307/139555.

[9] See, David Theo Goldberg's "Liberalism's Limits: Carlyle and Mill on 'the negro question'," *Nineteenth-Century Contexts: An Interdisciplinary Journal* 22 (2000): 203–16; doi:10.1080/08905490008583508.

[10] See John Stuart Mill's *Dissertations and Discussions: Political, Philosophical, and Historical*, Vol. 3 (New York: H. Holt & Co., 1874, pp. 252–3).

have to wonder about how Mill, of all people, could have been guilty of so much self-deception or false consciousness, as he must have been, when it came to colonialism and imperialism. The point, here, is not to engage in Mill bashing with the hindsight of 150 years. It is, rather, to remind ourselves to be cautious, and perhaps a bit more modest, when self-appraising our intentions and attitudes, and the impact of our interventions in the world's poorest regions. If someone as brilliant, liberal, and (comparatively) progressive as Mill could be so far off when it came to such matters, might not something similar be true of us?[11]

10.3 Money Talks

There are a series of related issues that some find worrisome. To help illustrate them, let me begin with a few commonplace observations unrelated to the field of international development.

It is often said that "money talks," and similarly that "he who pays the piper calls the tune." Such well-known expressions give voice to the substantial role that money, and valuable resources more generally, play in people's lives. Of course, people are motivated by more than money, and there are some who are seemingly oblivious to the lure of money and the material possessions, security, and influence that it often offers. Still, it is difficult to exaggerate the role that money often plays in people's choices, and thus their lives.

The tale of the company town is well known. A major company comes into a small town. It ends up directly, or indirectly, employing a significant percentage of the town's population. Before long, the town is shaped by the company's ethos and ends, as the town re-orientates its politics, priorities, and perhaps even its educational and vocational training to serve the company's purposes, which have now become inextricably linked with the town's. As the company goes, so goes the town. If it flourishes, the town flourishes as well. If it falls on hard times, the town falls on hard times. In some cases, several generations end up working for the company and, as they owe their livelihoods to the company, they may become intensely loyal to it. When the company

---

[11] Jeff McMahan called my attention to the tension between the side of Mill reflected in his lengthy employment with the British East India Company, and the side of Mill that led him to spearhead the Jamaica Committee in response to Governor Eyre's abhorrent actions (in discussion). McMahan shares my worries about the denigrating attitudes that often accompany efforts on behalf of others who are less well-off.

arrived the interests and goals of many of the citizens may not have aligned with the company's; but, over time, that changed. Some people manage to avoid the company's gravitational pull, but it isn't easy. Most either move away or "fall into line." Importantly, most who fall into line do so of their own volition. It is easiest, and typically most profitable, to work for or support the company, either directly or indirectly.

Something similar often happens in academia. A promising graduate student goes off to graduate school enamored with subfield X. She plans to write her dissertation on subfield X, and to devote her life to studying it. Once she attends graduate school, she learns that no "serious" person in her field studies subfield X. No courses are taught in that subfield. No one wants to advise a dissertation in that subfield. Most importantly, she learns that there are few, if any, postdocs, or jobs, in subfield X. Thus, in countless ways, she is discouraged from pursuing the area about which she most cares. At this point, she can try to find another school that would support her interests, and try to transfer to that school; or, she can become disillusioned with the field and drop out of graduate school; or, she can find other interests in her field that *will* be supported and pursue those. If the first alternative is not really feasible, her life path will dramatically alter, of her own free will, because of the practical, largely financial, options that she finds herself facing.

The example of the graduate student applies to research more generally. Potential scientists may go off to school enamored with all sorts of questions in basic science. However, they may find their path "diverted" in countless ways by the financial realities and opportunities that scientists face. Unsurprisingly, scientists end up doing research in the areas for which there is financial support—support in the form of graduate fellowships, postdocs, academic posts, and positions in industry. If one has an antecedent interest in doing research on a topic that NASA, the National Science Foundation, the National Institutes of Health, the military, or some major business wants funded, one is in luck. One can do what one wants to do. Otherwise, one must find some way to rustle up support for the research one wants to do—typically, no easy task—or change one's research interests. For most scientists, whose initial research interests don't line up with those of the major funding sources, the latter option is the most practical, and in some cases the only financially feasible option.

An unfortunate corollary of all this, of course, is that it is striking, but ultimately not all that surprising, how many "independent" and "reputable" scientists end up doing research that just happens to further the interests of those who provide them with their funding! This is so whether their funding source is the U.S. military, pharmaceutical companies, major oil companies, tobacco companies, the sugar industry, or something else.[12*]

The point of these banal observations is to remind one of the power that financial incentives can have to seduce, or divert one from a chosen path merely by offering one an easier, or more profitable, path in life. Bearing this point in mind, let us return to the case of international development aid.

An international development organization arrives in a desperately poor village with the aim of promoting X, and an outsized budget for doing so by local standards. X may be a genuinely important goal, and one of which many local inhabitants approve. Still, antecedently, promoting X may not have been among the goals that the village prioritized. As importantly, joining up with the international agency to promote X may require the locals to abandon their chosen paths. It may require them to divert their time, effort, and energy towards a new project, one which, so far as the project itself is concerned, is not as important to them as the projects that they were previously focusing on. The aid agency will want to alter the conditions which gave rise to the importance of promoting X in the first place. And they will also want to promote X as effectively as possible. This may require alterations in the villagers' lifestyles. It may require them to deviate from longstanding cultural norms and practices. Indeed, pursuing X effectively may even require the villagers to abandon, or at least act contrary to, some of their most deep-seated social or religious beliefs.

In the scenario I am imagining, the members of the aid agency do not believe that they are superior to the villagers. They fully respect the villagers and their autonomy. Indeed, they may even deny any suggestion that their ways are better than those of the villagers (though whether they actually believe this may be questionable). Still, the members of the international development organization see something that they, and their donors, would like to address. And they would like to do so with the support and cooperation of the villagers. To accomplish this, they offer substantial resources to

---

[12*] One example of this, that only came to light some fifty years after it occurred, involved the research of Harvard scientists, funded by the sugar industry, which effectively (and conveniently!) shifted the blame for coronary heart disease from sugar to fats. See Kearns, C.E., L.A. Schmidt, and S.A. Glantz, "Sugar Industry and Coronary Heart Disease Research: A Historical Analysis of Internal Industry Documents," *JAMA Internal Medicine* 176 (2016): 1680–5; doi:10.1001/jamain-ternmed.2016.5394; Domonoske, C., "50 Years Ago, Sugar Industry Quietly Paid Scientists To Point Blame At Fat," The Two Way, NPR, September 13, 2016, available at: https://www.npr.org/sections/thetwo-way/2016/09/13/493739074/50-years-ago-sugar-industry-quietly-paid-scientists-to-point-blame-at-fat, accessed September 1, 2019; and O'Connor, A., "How the Sugar Industry Shifted Blame to Fat," *The New York Times*, September 12, 2016, available at https://www.nytimes.com/2016/09/13/well/eat/how-the-sugar-industry-shifted-blame-to-fat.html, accessed September 1, 2019.

promote X. The villagers are perfectly free to continue living in according with their traditional ways, and to remain on their current path. However, if they do so, the international agency will take its resources to another village to promote X.

As described, this version of the activities of an international aid organization is free of the objectionable attitudes that I delineated previously. Even so, one can see how the offer of assistance and opportunities to aid a village by promoting X, combined with the financial incentives to accept the offer, may make the offer too attractive, overall, to turn down. Nevertheless, the effect of the international agency may be to divert or alienate the local villagers from their previous projects and priorities, and from important aspects of their social, cultural, and religious traditions. When this happens on an individual level it can be unsettling. When it happens on the scale of an entire village, or region, it raises familiar worries about the many ways in which the modern world can impact indigenous peoples, and the competing costs and benefits of such impacts.

One way to put this point is as follows. Although the central aim of aid organizations may simply be to improve the lot of the world's neediest people, the path to doing so often involves providing "advanced" Western-style solutions to local problems. Where development aid is concerned, this often involves advancing the ends of globalization, or what some might derisively call the hegemonic domination of Western values and a Western lifestyle.

Having already expressed my cosmopolitan leanings in Section 4.1, it perhaps will not surprise the reader to learn that I am not an opponent of globalization, per se. More particularly, I believe that there is much to be said in favor of globalization when it helps those in need, by reducing suffering and death due to hunger, disease, and poverty. Nevertheless, it must be admitted that progress is often a two-edged sword, and that there can be significant social, cultural, and spiritual costs when "traditional" ways of life are cast, or pushed, aside. I believe that Western aid interventions often, inadvertently, contribute to such costs. This is not always so; however, when they do, one has to reckon with them when considering the overall benefits and harms of global aid.

10.4 Final Remark

In the television show, *Star Trek*, the *Prime Directive* was supposed to be the guiding principle for those members of the United Federation of Planets engaging in space exploration. It prohibited members of the Federation from interfering with the internal development of alien civilizations. As it happens, the show's plot requirements required the Prime Directive to be violated on a regular basis. However, I believe there is a certain wisdom to the Prime Directive. In essence, it cautions against the hubris of so-called advanced civilizations assuming that they know what is best for other civilizations. Relatedly, it insists on a healthy measure of respect for different life forms and alternative ways of life.

To be sure, the obligation to show respect for alternative ways of life is a defeasible one. Standing by in the face of avoidable evils, pain, and death may not only be difficult, it may be morally impermissible. Even so, I believe that one must be wary of the impact that any outside interference may have on local ways of life, and the overall desirability of that impact.[13]

In the West, many people have become attuned to the possible negative impact on indigenous populations and local customs of economic globalization and commercialization. However, my own sense is that most people are much less attuned to the possible negative effects of actions motivated by compassion rather than greed. The worry expressed in this chapter is that some of the same problems for indigenous populations and local customs may arise from altruistic interventions as arise from self-interested interventions. Perhaps they are less widespread, or severe, in the former case than in the latter. However, even if that is so, and it may not be, the negative impacts on indigenous people and their customs from the interventions of international aid agencies may still be significant. We must bear this in mind when assessing the overall desirability of supporting such agencies.

---

[13] For an example where this point is also made in the development literature, see Charusheela, S., "Social Analysis and the Capabilities Approach: A Limit to Martha Nussbaum's Universalist Ethics," *Cambridge Journal of Economics* 33 (2008): 1135–52.

11

On the Relation between Aid, Governance, and Human Flourishing

Deaton's Worry

In this chapter, I present a controversial worry raised by Angus Deaton, one of the world's leading development economists.[1] In essence, the worry is that international aid efforts tend to undermine good governance on the local level, and that good governance is crucial for social and economic development, and the long-term wellbeing of a country's citizens. If this is right, then, however successful international aid organizations may be in achieving their immediate ends, they may ultimately do more overall harm than good for the citizens in the countries in which they operate.

In Section 11.1, I note that that there is surprisingly little hard evidence regarding the long-term effectiveness of international aid efforts in promoting social and economic development, and long-term wellbeing. I also note that Angus Deaton holds a view that most people find almost impossible to believe; namely, that Peter Singer, and his followers, have actually done more harm than good, by promoting the efforts of international aid organizations.

In Section 11.2, I present Deaton's view regarding the crucial importance of good governance for social and economic development, and long-term wellbeing.

In Section 11.3, I discuss ways in which international aid efforts may undermine good governance.

In Section 11.4, I discuss Jeffrey Sachs's approach to international aid, and the Millennium Villages Project. I argue that there were numerous ways in which the Millennium Villages Project was problematic, that it met with mixed success, and that Sachs and his followers have good reason to be concerned about Deaton's view.

Section 11.5 sums up Deaton's controversial view.

---

[1] See Chapter 7 of Angus Deaton's *The Great Escape: Health, Wealth, and the Origins of Inequality* (Princeton: Princeton University Press, 2013, especially, 294–307).

Being Good in a World of Need. Larry S. Temkin, Oxford University Press. © Larry S. Temkin 2022.
DOI: 10.1093/oso/9780192849977.003.0011

11.1 Has Singer Done More Harm than Good?

As noted previously, Angus Deaton is one of the world's leading international development experts and the 2015 Nobel Prize Winner in Economics. He is also deeply concerned about the plight of the needy. However, Deaton believes that there is little hard evidence supporting a positive, long-term correlation between the amount of international aid that a poor country receives and the amount of social and economic development that it experiences.[2*] Moreover, he believes that there are significant reasons to worry about the overall effects of economic aid spent in many of the world's poorest countries. Indeed, after decades of studying global poverty and the impact of global aid on the developing world, Deaton has arrived at the view that people like Peter Singer are actually doing more harm than good.[3] If we genuinely want to aid the world's neediest people, Deaton believes, we need to find some routes to do so other than by contributing to international relief and development organizations that work directly in the world's poorest regions to ameliorate the desperate conditions in those regions.

This is a striking conclusion. It is not one with which Deaton is particularly happy. However, as indicated, it is the one that Deaton has come to after many decades of considering relevant empirical evidence (which he, like many others, agrees is not super clear), and thinking hard about the logic of how political and economic systems work. Deaton readily recognizes that his conclusion is at odds with what we think should be the case. It is, after all, deeply counterintuitive to believe that if there are areas of great need, and external funding pours into a region explicitly earmarked to address those needs, that somehow the result of such efforts should prove fruitless, at best, or harmful, at worst. Deaton also recognizes that providing a wholly satisfactory explanation of why his view might be true is no easy task. Nevertheless,

---

[2*] Deaton, *The Great Escape*. Other development economists have come to a similar conclusion. See, for example, Riddell, Roger, *Does Foreign Aid Really Work?* (Oxford: Oxford University Press, 2007). Deaton and Riddell don't deny that there have been many individual aid programs that have been effective in achieving their immediate short-term aims, and some that may even have produced positive results in the long run. Their point concerns whether the *overall* impact of foreign aid has been, in the long term, a net positive.

I hasten to add that Riddell does not believe that there is firm evidence showing that the overall long-term effect of foreign aid has been negative, either. He is agnostic on the matter, suggesting that the evidence is insufficient to establish the matter one way or the other. My reading of Riddell is that he believes that that, overall, there probably *has* been a net positive impact of foreign aid, although probably not a substantially large one, whereas Deaton suspects the reverse is true.

[3] Deaton has made this claim, in conversations with me, on several occasions. Although he stops short of explicitly saying this in print, much of Part III of *The Great Escape* supports this conclusion.

Deaton offers several factors that might help support his counterintuitive conclusion. I turn to those, in the following two sections.

11.2 On the Importance of Good Governance

Return to the so-called Paradox of Aid, previously introduced in Section 7.4: in countries where the need is greatest, aid won't help, and in countries where it would help most, aid isn't needed. Presumably, if there is a kernel of truth to this Paradox, as Deaton and many other development economists believe, it is related to the crucial role that national and local governments play in their countries' social and economic progress.

The basic thought is that in countries with good governance, the governments find a way to take care of their people's basic needs. In countries with poor governance, on the other hand, the governments are unable or unwilling to take care of their people's basic needs, and so there are many people in great need. In that case, it is thought, the dysfunctional governments will ultimately obstruct the efforts of outside aid organizations, and any gains that outside efforts make will be temporary, at best. To have genuinely substantial and long-lasting social and economic gains a nation needs a well-functioning government which can effectively formulate and pursue plans to develop infrastructure, energy, food production, schools, the health system, etc. This is not something that outside development organizations, no matter how well-intentioned or well-funded, can accomplish, or impose, on their own. (To which Angus Deaton added, "Nor should they. Why should Bill Gates run CAR [the Central African Republic]? We tried colonialism."[4*])

[4*] Angus Deaton appended the quoted remark to the preceding sentence in correspondence. The attitude expressed by Deaton here is shared by William Easterly, among others. It reflects a concern about the grand design approach to solving poverty in other countries by "planners" from the world's wealthiest countries, such as Bill Gates (principal founder of the Microsoft Corporation, for many years the world's richest man, and, along with his wife, Melinda, head of the philanthropic Bill and Melinda Gates Foundation), and Jeffrey Sachs (University Professor at Columbia University, and longtime special advisor to the UN for both the Millennium Development Goals and the Sustainable Development Goals, Sachs is one of the world's most influential development economists in the fight against global poverty). Deaton and Easterly share the worry that the approaches for solving global poverty of people like Gates and Sachs are uncomfortably reminiscent of the failed and morally problematic policies of colonialism. (See Deaton's, *The Great Escape*, and Easterly's *The White Man's Burden: Why the West's Efforts to Aid the Rest Have Done So Much Ill and So Little Good* (New York: Penguin Press, 2006).) Though my own views about the approach to global poverty of people like Gates and Sachs are considerably more favorable than those of Deaton and Easterly, I share some of their worries about how efforts to aid the needy often involve unseemly attitudes and elements associated with colonialism and imperialism. For more on this, see Chapter 10. Also, see Section 11.4 for a discussion of Sachs's approach.

What makes a government well-functioning? Deaton believes that a key—and perhaps *the* key—component of a well-functioning government is that it be responsive to the needs, interests, and wills of its citizens. We think of democracy as a good form of government. However, what makes democracy a good form of government, when it is, is its responsiveness to its citizens. So-called democratic governments that are not, in fact, responsive to their people are not good governments; while non-democratic governments that are responsive to their people can, in principle, be perfectly good, well-functioning governments.

With that in mind, Deaton's contention is that international aid efforts in the world's poorest regions tend to be counterproductive, because they tend to undermine the responsiveness of the national governments to their peoples. But, to repeat, on Deaton's view, it is precisely such responsiveness that is *necessary* for any poor country's long-term social and economic development.

11.3 Ways in which Aid Efforts May Undermine Good Governance

The mechanisms by which international aid may undermine a government's responsiveness to its people are many. They include the following. First, if a government is corrupt, then, as discussed in Chapters 6 and 7, it may find many ways of capturing resources from outside agencies to further its own purposes. It may impose licensing fees on outside agencies that fill its coffers. It may demand kickbacks from beneficiaries of outside aid. It may require bribes from the agencies for the government's cooperation. It may insist that the aid agencies hire government officials, or the government's supporters, to perform all or most of the local work that the agencies require. It may require the aid agencies to supply it with arms, or other supplies that it desires, or it may find ways of diverting food, medicine, and other resources intended for the needy into government hands, which may then be sold or otherwise used to advance the government's purposes. Or it may simply use resources that would otherwise have been used to address the needs of its citizens to advance its own agenda.

In sum, there are many ways, both direct and indirect, that a corrupt government can take advantage of outside resources to strengthen its own internal position and further its own agenda. Such resources can enable corrupt governments to remain indifferent and unresponsive to the needs and wills of their citizens, and to continue to put their own interests, and those of their crucial supporters, ahead of the general population's interests.

Second, thanks to modern communication, affluent people around the globe can learn about, and even "experience," the plight of the needy in distant lands in real time. One can see and hear people suffering "live," not only on television but on YouTube, or many other forms of social media. Modern technology also makes it possible, in ways never before seen, for people scattered across the globe to band together to address the suffering of others, by supporting any of the many well-known international development organizations, but also by forming non-profits of their own, to address the specific needs that have come to their attention and that concern them the most. Correspondingly, as one essayist optimistically put it, "the number of not-for-profit organizations is now virtually uncountable, meaning more people doing more positive things for those in need. The advances made in mobile and computing technologies are enriching the lives of those who really need it."[5]

One result of all this is that in many of the world's poorest regions there are numerous international aid organizations operating, and perhaps even competing, to address the plight of the needy. Some aid agencies will address the plight of the hungry; others will aid victims of rape or sectarian violence; others will help victims of illnesses, such as malaria, tuberculosis, diarrhea, or AIDS; others will address pre-natal, post-natal, and maternal healthcare; others will seek to improve healthcare more generally; others will aim to improve education; others will work to improve infrastructure; and so on. Of course, some agencies will address multiple concerns.

This all sounds very desirable. Yet, if so many agencies are seeking to help in so many ways, how come the problems of the needy continue to persist in the world's poorest regions year after year and decade after decade? Is it merely because not *enough* agencies have come to the aid of the downtrodden, or not *enough* resources have been *effectively* provided to totally eradicate the problems?

That is the view of most proponents of aid.[6] However, Deaton has another hypothesis. One of the downsides of so many international agencies rushing in to meet the needs of the downtrodden is that local governments can abdicate their responsibilities to provide for the basic needs of their citizens and leave that task to the international development agencies. If basic needs remain

[5] Alcos, Carlos, "50 Nonprofits Making a Difference in the World," November 2, 2011, *Matador Network*, URL: https://matadornetwork.com/change/50-nonprofits-making-a-world-of-difference/, accessed September 14, 2017.

[6] For representative texts, see MacAskill, William, *Doing Good Better: How Effective Altruism Can Help You Help Others, Do Work that Matters, and Make Smarter Choices about Giving Back* (New York: Avery, 2016); Singer, Peter, *The Life You Can Save* (New York: Random House, 2009); Singer, Peter, *The Most Good You Can Do* (New Haven: Yale University Press, 2015); and Sachs, Jeffrey, *The End of Poverty* (New York: Penguin Books, 2015 edition).

unmet, the local governments can shift the blame and attention to the international development agencies, who have failed to fully deliver on their promises to help the needy. In other words, the well-intentioned interventions by international aid agencies can undermine the responsiveness of the local governments to the needs, interests, and wills of their citizens. Moreover, this is so whether or not the governments are corrupt. But, of course, if Deaton is correct, such responsiveness is a key characteristic of good governance, and without good governance there can be no hope of a lasting solution to the social and economic woes of the world's poorest nations.

The preceding two points are intimately related to a third. Generally, effective governments depend on taxing their citizens to generate revenue to provide for the needs of their citizens, to pay for basic government functions, and to advance their political agendas. However, the relation between a government and its taxpaying citizens is a special one. In return for providing the government with their "hard earned dollars," taxpaying citizens expect a return on their investments. They want a say in how their money is spent, and they want their government to provide for their basic needs, to promote their interests, and to reflect their wills. In other words, there will always be great pressure for a government that taxes its citizens to be responsive to those citizens. If it is not, there is always a risk of the citizens bucking the government, avoiding their taxes, and, if the situation is dire enough, supporting efforts to undermine and replace the current government, in favor of one that will be responsive to their wills.

However, in countries where there is a substantial influx of resources from foreign aid organizations, which one way or another finds its way into the government's coffers, governments can function and pursue their agendas without having to tax their citizens, at least not to the same degree that they otherwise would. Unfortunately, this is the case in much of Africa, where "thirty-six (out of forty-nine) countries have received at least 10 percent of their national income as ODA [Overseas Development Assistance] for three decades or more . . . . [T]he ratio of aid to government expenditure is larger still. Benin, Burkina Faso, the DRC [Democratic Republic of Congo], Ethiopia, Madagascar, Niger, Sierra Leone, Togo, and Uganda are among the countries where aid has exceeded 75 percent of government expenditure for a run of recent years. In Kenya and Zambia, ODA is a quarter and a half of government expenditure, respectively."[7]

---

[7] *The Great Escape*, p. 296.

Development economists have long recognized what has come to be known as the *Resource Curse*. Ironically, many of the countries richest in natural resources are among the worst-off in terms of sectarian violence, poverty, illness, need, and general social, political, and economic development. In large part, this is because whoever controls the resources can become enormously wealthy, provide for their supporters (typically, members of their religion, sect, or tribe), and pay off the army and police. Since the ultimate source of the government's power lies in the country's rich natural resources, they can successfully advance their political and economic agendas without the political support of the general population or substantial tax revenue from the people.

Unsurprisingly, then, many resource-rich countries have authoritarian or military governments that are largely unresponsive to the needs and interests of their general populations. This helps to explain why large pockets of poverty, poor health, great need, and underdevelopment are often the hall-marks of resource-rich countries.[8] The point, of course, is that substantial infusions of external aid can create a resource curse of its own, with analogous (which is not to say identical) effects to those of internal natural resources.

Naturally, if, thanks to external funding, a government can get by with less financial support from its citizens, in the way of taxes, its citizens may feel less entitled to demand more from their government. They cannot insist on having more of a say in how "their" money is spent, if the government isn't actually spending *their* money, or money derived from *their* natural resources. Moreover, with a government that is receiving little or no tax money from some or all of its citizens, and where many of the most pressing needs of its citizens are being addressed by international aid agencies, the government can always claim, whether truthfully or not, that it lacks the resources to do more to help its citizens and that it has, in essence, established relations with external agencies to provide for its citizens' needs. Therefore, if the citizens' basic needs are not being met, the government can claim that the fault lies with the external agencies from the world's richest countries, not with any inad-equacies of its own.

In this way, too, the efforts and resources of international aid agencies can undermine the responsiveness of governments in poor countries to their citizens' interests, needs, and wills. It does this, in part, by shifting the responsibility for the countries' needy from the local governments to outside

---

[8] For the long list of the resource-rich countries that fit this description, and an extremely illuminating discussion of this problem, see Wenar, Leif, *Blood Oil: Tyrants, Violence, and the Rules that Run the World* (New York: Oxford University Press, 2017).

agencies. As importantly, it does this, in part, by upsetting the relationship that normally exists between a nation's government and its taxpayers; the relationship by which taxpaying citizens can reasonably expect to have a say in their government's direction and priorities, in virtue of the fact that *they* are the ones who are funding their government's activities.[9*]

Next, recall the old adage, noted in Section 10.3, that "he who pays the piper, calls the tune." Combined with the first and third points, this adage suggests that in poor countries where much of a government's income is derived from external agencies, rather than internal taxes, the governments of those countries will have strong reason to be responsive to the external agencies, and much less reason to be responsive to their own citizens. One might think that this shouldn't be a problem. After all, aren't the interests of the outside agencies just whatever is best for the countries' neediest peoples?

This returns us to an earlier line of discussion, introduced in Chapter 10. No doubt most international aid organizations and their donors are genuinely concerned to help the needy of the world's poorest countries. That is why they are there in the first place. However, each international aid agency will have its own agenda. Each will have its own particular problem, or set of problems, to which it will give priority, and each will have its own often paternalistic view about the best way of fostering its agenda "on behalf of the needy." Unsurprisingly, there is often likely to be a gap between what the *outsiders* would like to accomplish, and how they plan to accomplish it, and what the *needy themselves* would like done, and how they would like it done.

Of course, beggars cannot be choosers. And the needy are not in any position to dictate what the outside agencies should be providing them, and how they should go about providing it. Still, however much good the international agencies may accomplish via their intervention, there is reason to believe that being responsive to the benevolent and paternalistic aims of international development organizations is *not* the same as being directly responsive to the interests, needs, and wills of a government's citizens. It is the latter that is the mark of good governance, not the former.

[9*] The view that aid disrupts the relationship between a government and its taxpaying citizens was famously argued by Dambis Moyo in her book *Dead Aid: Why Aid Is Not Working and How There Is a Better Way for Africa* (New York: Farrar, Straus and Giroux, 2009). It is also held by Hyeon-Jae Seo, who claimed that "Even in non-democratic societies, the need to raise funds results in a degree of accountability towards the population providing the resources, since they are the ones who will ultimately be affected by any policies instituted or projects undertaken by the governing body. Disrupting the relationship between the government and taxpayers removes that degree of accountability" ("Politics of Aid: A Closer Look at the Motives Behind Foreign Assistance," *Harvard International Review* 38 (2017): 42–7).

Finally, it is worth bearing in mind a national government's purview. The government sets fundamental policies affecting international relations, national defense, fire, police, and other emergency services, economic development, education, infrastructure, energy, housing, healthcare, climate, human rights, and so on. Individually, each one of these domains is extraordinarily important for a nation's wellbeing; jointly, it is almost impossible to exaggerate their significance. Given this, is it not evident that even small reductions in good governance along one or more of these dimensions can have massively negative implications for a country's population and its prospects? Correspondingly, is it not also evident that even a small chance that one's actions might reduce the level of good governance is something to be extremely concerned about? Deaton rather matter-of-factly contends that good governance is essential for long-term social and economic progress. In doing this, I believe that, if anything, he underemphasizes just how crucial good governance is for a country's population and its future generations.

11.4 Jeffrey Sachs and the Millennium Villages Project

In this section, I discuss the *Millennium Villages Project*, which seemingly embodied an approach to global aid that is diametrically opposed to Deaton's.[10]

In 2000, the United Nations hosted the *Millennium Summit*. The Summit led to the establishment of eight *Millennium Development Goals* (MDGs). All 191 United Nations member states, and at least 22 international organizations, committed to helping achieve the MDGs by the year 2015. These goals were:

1. To eradicate extreme poverty and hunger.
2. To achieve universal primary education.
3. To promote gender equality and empower women.
4. To reduce child mortality.
5. To improve maternal health.
6. To combat HIV/AIDS, malaria, and other diseases.
7. To ensure environmental sustainability.
8. To develop a global partnership for development.[11]

---

[10] I am grateful to Leif Wenar for comments that prompted the writing of this section.

[11] "Millennium Development Goals," *United Nations Development Programme*, URL: https://www.undp.org/content/undp/en/home/sdgoverview/mdg_goals.html, accessed April 1, 2021.

Jeffrey Sachs, Founder and Director of Columbia University's Earth Institute, and a longtime Special Advisor to the UN Secretary General, played an instrumental role in the formulation of the UN's Millennium Development Goals. In 2002, the United Nations created the Millennium Project, whose aim was to determine the best way of meeting the MDGs. Sachs was named Director of the Millennium Project, and he and the other members of the Project determined that creating the Millennium Development Villages would be the best way of achieving those goals.

Sachs believed that most earlier aid efforts had failed because they spent too little and were too focused on a single area of improvement. Efforts to improve education as a way of eliminating poverty were doomed to fail, in the absence of a developed economy that could take advantage of an educated workforce; efforts to improve crop yields were ineffective, in the absence of improvements in storage facilities, infrastructure, and appropriate trade agreements; efforts to improve infrastructure were of little use if there were insufficient products to transport, or energy to transport them; and so on. For Sachs, then, just as there is little point in repairing a single hole in a bucket full of holes, there is also little point in addressing any one of the many roots of poverty, unless one addresses them all, simultaneously. At least this is so insofar as one's concern is with ending global poverty. (There may be *other* reasons for addressing some of the roots of global poverty, unrelated to poverty itself.) Thus, Sachs believed that the key to ending global poverty was holism. In particular, he claimed that one must simultaneously address "economic development, social inclusion, and environmental sustainability in an integrated and holistic manner. This holistic approach is Africa's best bet. Success in ending Africa's extreme poverty can be summarized in four broad categories: infrastructure, social services, industrialization, and environmental sustainability."[12] So, the conceit behind the Millennium Development Villages was that the UN, together with wealthy countries and organizations, would attack global poverty one village at a time, with a massive infusion of funds that would simultaneously address, and eliminate, *all* of the factors that contribute to endemic poverty in that village.[13]

Sachs's approach had the strong backing of the United Nations, substantial funding from both international organizations like the Word Bank and the Islamic Development Bank, and individual countries like Japan, South Korea, Mali, Senegal, Uganda, and Rwanda, private donors (including $50 million from George Soros's *The Open Society Foundation*), and the enthusiastic

---

[12] Sachs, *The End of Poverty*, p. xl.   [13] See, Sachs's *The End of Poverty*.

endorsement of a host of celebrities, including Bono and Angelina Jolie. The first Millennium Village was launched with great fanfare in 2005, in Sauri, Kenya. With his characteristic bravado, Sachs triumphantly asserted that "This is a village that is going to make history. It's a village that is going to end extreme poverty and show other villages not only in its area but around the world how this can be accomplished."[14]

The original plan was for there to be ten Millennium Villages, each of which would achieve a lasting eradication of extreme poverty within five years. Soon afterwards, the ten villages were expanded to fourteen. The original project was intended to run from 2005 to 2010. However, additional funding was secured, and the length of the project extended another five years, to 2015. The additional funding enabled the Villages to expand the scope of their activities to include surrounding populations, and gave the Villages more time to achieve the Millennium Development Goals. However, four of the fourteen sites were not scaled up, or had their funding discontinued, due to funding constraints or regional conflicts.

The Millennium Villages Project had its critics from the start. Foremost among them, William Easterly famously castigated it as yet another ill-conceived and doomed-to-fail "Big Plan" developed and imposed by well-meaning Western "Planners" who failed to recognize the facts on the ground and the futility of trying to end poverty through large-scale outside interventions.[15] Many people initially dismissed Easterly's concerns as that of a disillusioned and overly pessimistic aid critic. However, eight years into the project, some were claiming that Easterly's worries had proven to be on target. Thus, one critic observed that "The MVPs follow the arc of previous 'big push' efforts, such as Integrated Rural Development—new crops rot in the absence of roads or markets; stuff gets stolen; governments fail to allocate cash to fill new schools and hospitals with staff and equipment. Technical fixes founder because there is no understanding of (or interest in) power, politics, or how stuff happens (or doesn't)."[16*]

A larger-than-life figure, Sachs's personality has evoked strong reactions, both positive and negative. *The New York Times* once described Sachs as

[14] "The Diary of Angelina Jolie and Dr. Jeffrey Sachs in Africa," *MTV*, 2005, URL: https://www. youtube.com/watch?v=_kv0VdBkkno, accessed April 5, 2021.

[15] Easterly, *The White Man's Burden*. See, especially, Chapters 1 through 4, pp. 3–162.

[16*] Duncan Green, "*The Idealist*: a brilliant, gripping, disturbing portrait of Jeffrey Sachs," *From Poverty to Power*, October 31, 2013, URL: https://oxfamblogs.org/fp2p/the-idealist-a-brilliant-gripping-disturbing-portrait-of-jeffrey-sachs/, accessed March 28, 2021. Green is a strategic advisor for Oxfam Great Britain, and Professor in Practice at the London School of Economics. He is also a lead educator for the online course *Make Change Happen* developed by Oxfam with the Open University.

"probably the most important economist in the world,"[17] and his fans regard him as a brilliant, idealistic, messianic figure, whose ideas, charisma, energy, and conviction have galvanized the world to tackle global poverty.[18] His detractors regard him as a brilliant and charismatic idealist with a messiah complex—one who is convinced that he has all the answers, who doesn't listen to others, who is blinded to his own shortcomings and mistakes, and who doesn't take criticism well.[19]

Arguably, the two descriptions of Sachs reflect two sides of the same coin, and they might both be accurate. If so, this should not be surprising. After all, it is often the case that one's greatest strengths are also one's greatest weaknesses. For what it is worth, my own field is full of thin-skinned professors who have outsized egos, most of whom have not accomplished anywhere near as much as Sachs has. So, by themselves, the criticisms of Sachs's personality don't strike my ears as particularly damning. However, in most fields, the negative personality traits that some have attributed to Sachs are utterly irrelevant to the importance or success of someone's contributions. In the milieu that Sachs dominates, such traits are more worrying.

In a review of Nina Munk's The Idealist, Duncan Green relays the following vignette from the book, reflecting "a horrendous confrontation with aid donors in a posh Tanzanian hotel":

> Sachs asks to 'speak briefly' and launches into a lecture on how to end Tanzania's poverty and the case for distributing bednets. Any questions? Silence for a full minute, then this from USAID head Pamela White: 'I don't want to argue with you Jeff, because I don't want to be called ignorant or unprofessional. I have worked in Africa for 30 years. My colleagues combined have worked in the field for one hundred plus years. We don't like your tone. We don't like you preaching to us. We are not your students. We do not work for you.'
>
> Completely undeterred, Sachs goes off to his next meeting and persuades Tanzania's president of the case (against donor opposition) for free bednets.[20]

---

[17] Peter Passell, "Dr. Jeffrey Sachs, Shock Therapist," New York Times, June 27, 1993. URL: https://www.nytimes.com/1993/06/27/magazine/dr-jeffrey-sachs-shock-therapist.html?pagewanted=all&src=pm, accessed April 7, 2021.

[18] See, for example, Angelina Jolie's description of him in "The Diary of Angelina Jolie and Dr. Jeffrey Sachs in Africa," and Bono's characterization of him in his foreword to the 2015 edition of Sachs's The End of Poverty.

[19] See, for example, Nina Munk's The Idealist: Jeffrey Sachs and the Quest to End Poverty (New York: Doubleday, 2013), and Paul Starobin's "Does It Take a Village?" FP [Foreign Policy], June 24, 2013, URL: https://foreignpolicy.com/2013/06/24/does-it-take-a-village/, accessed March 30, 2021.

[20] Green, "The Idealist: a brilliant, gripping, disturbing portrait of Jeffrey Sachs."

One must wonder: if Sachs provokes such a response when dealing with his peers, how does he deal with locals who do not share his status, class, wealth, power, education, language, culture, history, and so on? Sachs *says* all the right things about having to treat locals as full partners in the quest to end poverty, and about the importance of understanding the local facts on the ground if one's efforts are to be successful. However, if, as seems to be the case, he has the crusader's unwavering conviction in the fundamental importance of his goal, and he is convinced that he knows what *really* needs to be done to achieve that goal, then it shouldn't be surprising if his actions belie his words. This, in turn, raises many of the worries about paternalism, autonomy, and respect discussed in Chapter 10.

Echoing these worries, Green asks "what if Sachs is wrong? Where does he get his cosmically forceful opinions and recommendations from? It certainly doesn't seem to be from listening to poor people (listening clearly isn't his thing)."[21] Another author, who offered a more balanced overall assessment of the Millennium Villages Project, expressed a related worry about the Project, noting that "The centrally planned approach that included provision of a streamlined basket of goods to each village was said to promote solutions derived from aloof economic models insensitive to local customs and constraints."[22] And yet another author, generally sympathetic to Sachs and the Millennium Villages Project, expressed a similar worry about the top-down one-size-fits-all approach of the Millennium Villages Project. Recognizing the problems that can arise when outsiders impose solutions on a local environment that they do not fully understand, he gently observed that "the project seemed to underestimate the need for considerable experimentation in each context—working with [as opposed to against or independently of] the grain of local government and communities, as well as working with [as opposed to ignoring] how people respond differently to interventions and adapt solutions."[23]

The Millennium Villages Project came to an end in 2015. Like many aid projects, it continues to have both supporters and detractors. Still, even its

---

[21] Green, "*The Idealist*: a brilliant, gripping, disturbing portrait of Jeffrey Sachs."

[22] Eran Bendavid, "The fog of development: evaluating the Millennium Villages Project," *The Lancet*, May, 2018. doi: https://doi.org/10.1016/S2214-109X(18)30196-7. URL: https://www.thelancet.com/journals/langlo/article/PIIS2214-109X(18)30196-7/fulltext#back-bib1, accessed March 29, 2021.

[23] Chris Barnett, "Thumbs up or thumbs down? Did the Millennium Villages Project work?" *From Poverty to Power*, Oxfam Blog, September 20, 2018, URL: https://oxfamblogs.org/fp2p/thumbs-up-or-thumbs-down-did-the-millennium-villages-project-work/, accessed March 30, 2021.

most ardent supporters must admit, as one writer put it, that "The Results are in. And boy are they mixed."[24]

In one important retrospective evaluation of the project, the authors—which included Sachs himself—concluded that when assessing the project in terms of outcomes that bore on whether the Millennium Development Goals were achieved, "we found that impact estimates for 30 of 40 outcomes were significant . . . and favoured the project villages."[25] The authors contended that the project had "a significant favourable impact on an index of asset owner-ship," and they noted that if one averaged across the outcomes within cat-egories then "the project had significant favourable impacts on agriculture, nutrition, education, child health, maternal health, HIV and Malaria, and water and sanitation."[26] Overall, the authors claimed that by the end of the project, one third of the Millennium Development Goals had been met at the project sites. However, importantly, the authors' analysis implied that two thirds of the MDGs had not been met, even after ten years. Additionally, they admitted that "the project was estimated to have no significant impact on the consumption-based measures of poverty" and that "[i]mpacts on nutrition and education outcomes were often inconclusive."[27] Furthermore, they acknowledged that "generalizability and sustainability are difficult to assess, so extrapolating the results to different scales, locations, and time periods should be done with caution. In particular, . . . local political buy-in and community ownership . . . could affect the generalizability of the results."[28]

A more focused six-year evaluation of the Millennium Village Project in northern Ghana yielded a similar "yes and no" conclusion as to whether the project had a positive impact. On the plus side, the evaluation "found statis-tically significant impact against 7 of the 28 MDG [Millennium Development Goals] indicators. For example, primary school attendance improved by 7.7 percent, intermediate health indicators improved for births attended by skilled professionals, children sleeping under bednets, and so on."[29] It also

---

[24] Beth Duff-Brown, "A Look at the Millennium Project," *Scope*, Stanford Medicine, April 24, 2018, URL: https://scopeblog.stanford.edu/2018/04/24/a-look-at-the-millennium-villages-project/#:~:text=The %20authors%20concluded%20that%20the,the%20project%20sites%2C%20they%20wrote, accessed March 29, 2021.

[25] Mitchell, S., Gelman, A., Ross, R., Chen, J., Bari, Sehrish, Huynh, U.K., et al., "The Millennium Villages Project: a retrospective, observational, endline evaluation," *The Lancet* 6, Issue 5, E500–E513, May 1, 2018; doi: https://doi.org/10.1016/S2214-109X(18)30065-2; URL: https://www.thelancet.com/ journals/langlo/article/PIIS2214-109X(18)30065-2/fulltext, accessed March 28, 2021. See the *Findings* section.

[26] Mitchell et al., "The Millennium Villages Project."

[27] Mitchell et al., "The Millennium Villages Project."

[28] Mitchell et al., "The Millennium Villages Project."

[29] Barnett, "Thumbs up or thumbs down?"

noted that "there were some good ideas, and things that worked well (for example, the tractor hire services, vaccinations, investments in health centres and school infrastructure."[30] On the minus side, despite the intense time, effort, and resources that were poured into achieving the Millennium Development Goals by the year 2015, and in particular, into eliminating poverty, there was no statistically significant impact in terms of "achieving the MDGs at a local level" for 21 of the 28 MDG indicators.[31] In particular, it was observed that "for the key indicators for poverty (MDG 1) there does not seem to have been a reduction. There were income improvements that could be attributed to the Millennium Villages project, but there was no accompanying increase in consumption, and the improvements in income were insufficient to break the poverty trap. The population remains poor."[32] Further, as with the previously discussed retrospective assessment, the evaluation recognized that "sustainability is a huge challenge. . . . Approaches like top-up allowances for education and health workers, new 'super' health facilities, and free ambulance services, etc., all had a measure of success, but were beyond what could be sustained locally. Spending by the project tended to focus on building infrastructure, providing supplies and extra staffing ('things') with insufficient attention to the behaviour change needed to create long-lasting impact. For example, statistical analysis shows a sharp increase in the access to toilets (part of MDG 7), with toilets rapidly built during the last two years of the project—yet the qualitative research highlights how people still preferred to go 'free range', under a 'nice baobab tree' or among rocks away from the village."[33*]

Yet another mixed assessment of the Millennium Villages Projected noted that "The one area in which unequivocal and substantial benefits are observed is maternal health, including contraception use, antenatal care, and use of skilled birth attendants. [However t]he effect sizes for other key outcomes, including child malnutrition and mortality, are small, heterogeneous, and unstable . . . . Moreover, . . . the end of poverty—arguably the raison d'etre

---

[30] Barnett, "Thumbs up or thumbs down?"   [31] Barnett, "Thumbs up or thumbs down?"
[32] Barnett, "Thumbs up or thumbs down?"
[33*] Barnett, "Thumbs up or thumbs down?" For a fascinating book detailing a similar experience in India, see Diane Coffey and Dean Spears's *Where India Goes* (Noida: HarperCollins, 2017). In their book, Coffey and Spears show how attempts to address the many serious problems associated with open defecation in India, by providing toilets throughout the countryside, have floundered in large part because of a failure to understand and address the deep-rooted customs, mores, and caste system of rural India.

of the entire project—was no closer in the MVP villages than in the comparison villages."[34]

Even where the Millennium Villages showed positive results, questions have been raised about their cost-effectiveness. Chris Barnett, who led a six-year evaluation of the Millennium Villages Project in northern Ghana, funded by the United Kingdom's Department for International Development, claimed that their analysis showed "that the returns to investment in education appear to be the highest, although both the returns in education and health could be achieved at a much lower cost."[35] Likewise, Michael Clemens, Director of Migration, Displacement, and Humanitarian Policy, and Senior Fellow of the Center for Global Development, has claimed that the Millennium Villages Project's own documents, made public by the UK government, reveal that "the project costs at least US$12,000 per household that it lifts from poverty— about 34 times the annual incomes of those households."[36] Clemens argued that "much more could have been done for poverty with other uses of the same money . . . . [For example, t]he same $12,000 in a bank account at 5 percent interest would yield $600, every year, year after year, forever. That interest, given to the households as cash, would cause their incomes to nearly triple, permanently and certainly. I stress: this effect on income would be *permanent*."[37] As for the positive "non-income effects of the project, like effects on health and education," Clemens notes that "[c]ash transfers have those effects too," adding that "[t]ransfers large enough to triple household income would have huge effects on health and education."[38]

The charge that the Millennium Villages Project wasn't cost-effective is serious and important. However, it is also somewhat misleading. It tells us that for any given amount of money, there were more cost-effective ways to aid the needy than the Millennium Villages. That may be so. However, it ignores the fact that without the soaring rhetoric and overblown promises that were made

---

[34] Bendavid, "The fog of development: evaluating the Millennium Villages Project."

[35] Barnett, "Thumbs up or thumbs down?"

[36] Michael Clemens, "New Documents Reveal the Cost of 'Ending Poverty' in a Millennium Village: At Least $12,000 Per Household," *Center for Global Development*, March 30, 2012, URL: https://www. cgdev.org/blog/new-documents-reveal-cost-%E2%80%9Cending-poverty%E2%80%9D-millennium-village-least-12,000-household#:~:text=%E2%80%9CThe%20Millennium%20Village%20aims%20to,up %20to%E2%80%9D%202%2C250%20households, accessed March 28, 2021.

[37] Clemens, "New Documents Reveal the Cost of 'Ending Poverty' in a Millennium Village." This quote was written in 2012, when it was easy to get a 5% return from a bank account. That is not so today, and it is an important reminder of the hubris that is usually involved when economists or others make bold predictions about the future in terms of "permanence" or "certainty." Still, Clemens's point is well-taken. For the vast sums that were involved with the Millennium Villages Project, there are numerous financial instruments that one could invest in that could reasonably be expected to generate 5% annual interest, on average, for the long term.

[38] Clemens, "New Documents Reveal the Cost of 'Ending Poverty' in a Millennium Village."

in launching the Millennium Villages, there may have been much smaller sums available to aid the needy.

Whatever else one thinks about Sachs, it is undeniable that he has been an extraordinarily powerful voice on behalf of the world's poor. His passion, vision, and total conviction that we can end poverty in our time by following his approach has inspired world leaders in politics, business, and philanthropy, as well as millions of ordinary people, to follow his lead. It enabled him to raise millions that might not otherwise have been available to aid the needy.

This is important to bear in mind, in assessing claims about cost-effectiveness. To be sure, if the money spent on the Millennium Villages would otherwise have been spent on more effective approaches to aiding the needy, then it would have been better had that been done. However, if, in fact, much of the money that was spent on the Millennium Villages would otherwise have been spent on behalf of well-to-do people in the world's wealthiest countries, then the charge of not being cost-effective largely misses the mark.

It isn't clear that Sachs could have been equally effective at inspiring people to aid the needy had he been advocating for more attainable goals and more effective approaches to achieving those goals. It was the heady mix of the audacious goal of ending poverty in our time, combined with the bold holistic approach of simultaneously addressing *all* of the underlying roots of poverty, that inspired so many to support his project. Ultimately, then, the force of the charge of not being cost-effective comes down to the complicated questions of how much the Millennium Villages diverted scarce resources away from other, more effective, approaches to aiding the needy; to what extent, if any, they benefited the needy, even if inefficiently, from funds that would otherwise have not been available for the needy; and whether Sachs or others could have raised similar amounts on behalf of other, more realistic goals, and other, more effective approaches to aiding the needy. It is not clear, to me anyway, what the answers to those complicated questions are.

There is another worry about the Millennium Villages Project, a methodological worry, that has been powerfully raised by numerous authors.[39] It is that Sachs was so convinced of the correctness of his approach to eradicating poverty, that he didn't take the steps necessary to assess whether or not he

---

[39] See for example, Nina Munk's *The Idealist*; Paul Starobin's "Does It Take a Village?"; and Eran Bendavid's "The fog of development: evaluating the Millennium Villages Project." Starobin notes how Edward Miguel, a development economist at the University of California at Berkeley, Nancy Birdsall and Michael Clemons of the Center for Global Development, and Angus Deaton have all raised the methodological worry that I'll be discussing.

was right. That is, he failed to run the Millennium Villages as a scientific experiment, so that one could meaningfully assess the impact that the Millennium Villages had in achieving the Millennium Development Goals relative to other villages that did not benefit from the interventions associated with the Millennium Development Project.

Arguably, this is the most troubling worry about the Millennium Villages Project. Eran Bendavid observed that "the absence of upfront plans for evaluating the project hinted at overconfidence in the righteousness of the approach, which was inconsistent with the prevailing equipoise about the effectiveness of approaches to improving the health and wealth of the world's poorest."[40] Paul Starobin put the point more strongly: "As his critics see it, Sachs botched his project by not putting in place a system by which progress (or a lack thereof) could be objectively measured, evaluated, and compared with trends in surrounding rural communities."[41] Worse, according to Starobin, "At the project's outset, Sachs resisted the idea of ongoing monitoring and assessment of MVP by independent experts unaffiliated with the project, as urged by Berkeley's [Edward] Miguel and Nancy Birdsall at the Center for Global Development . . . . [Because, according to Birdsall] 'Jeff felt it wasn't necessary.'"[42]

Furthermore, in choosing where to implement the Millennium Villages Project, "Countries were selected on the basis of political stability and government commitment to the MDGs [Millennium Development Goals]. Millennium Village (MV) sites were selected from rural areas . . . with local political buy in and community ownership."[43] Unfortunately, "the non-random selection" of MVP villages undermined the possibility of determining to what extent, if any, observed advances in terms of the Millennium Development Goals were due to the Millennium Village interventions, rather than the confounding elements of being in a country with political stability and government commitment to the MDGs and/or the villages having an "engaged and responsive local government."[44]

There is one other methodological concern worth noting. The most positive analyses of the Millennium Villages have been based on gains that were noted in the ten sites that received funding from 2005 through 2015.[45] However, as noted previously, there were four sites that were part of the project in the years

---

[40] Bendavid, "The fog of development: evaluating the Millennium Villages Project."
[41] Starobin, "Does It Take a Village?"   [42] Starobin, "Does It Take a Village?"
[43] See Mitchell et al., "The Millennium Villages Project."
[44] Bendavid, "The fog of development: evaluating the Millennium Villages Project."
[45] See, for example, Mitchell et al., "The Millennium Villages Project."

between 2005 and 2010, that were not were not scaled up, or that had their funding discontinued, due to funding constraints or regional conflicts.[46] Given how the test villages were carefully selected for their likelihood of success, it stands to reason that the four villages that were not scaled up, or discontinued, were those that were performing worst in terms of achieving the Millennium Development Goals. If this is so, it casts further doubt on the meaningfulness and generalizability of any positive results that were found in the ten sites that received funding for the full ten years.

To see this, consider the following analogy. Suppose some psychologists come up with a treatment method that they believe could effectively alleviate adolescent anxiety over the course of ten sessions. They set up a study to determine the effectiveness of their treatment method, and originally enroll fourteen carefully selected adolescents whom they believe could most benefit from their treatment method. As the ten sessions begin to wind up, the study has not yet achieved the level of success originally projected. However, it is thought that perhaps that success could be reached after another ten sessions. Unfortunately, several of the adolescents have begun to develop other symptoms (perhaps partly in reaction to the treatment method itself, but perhaps not) that make it unlikely they would benefit from further sessions. Furthermore, there is not enough funding to continue the sessions for more than ten adolescents. So, the ten adolescents who are showing the most promising results are reenrolled for another ten sessions, and the others are dropped from the study. Surely, any successes claimed for the treatment method based on that study would have to be taken with a large grain of salt, if they were only based on positive results in anxiety reduction among the ten adolescents who completed twenty sessions. Such "cherry-picked" results would be dubious, since they totally ignored the impact of the treatment method on four of the study's original participants—some 28 percent.

In sum, one would have good reason to wonder about the efficacy of the treatment method as a general solution to childhood anxiety, if those enrolled in the study were handpicked in the first place for the likelihood that they would benefit from the treatment method, and if, halfway through the study, over a quarter of the participants were weeded out because they were deemed the least likely to show benefits from twenty sessions of the treatment method. Yet something very similar to this seems to be going on, among those pointing to the benefits of the Millennium Villages Project at the ten sites that received funding for the full duration of the project.

---

[46] Mitchell et al., "The Millennium Villages Project."

Considering the methodological errors built into the Millennium Villages Project, some critics believe that "it is worthless as a showcase for what can lift the poorest of the poor out of their misery."[47] Of course, even if this were true, it wouldn't mean that the Millennium Villages weren't a success, only that there is no scientific way to tell whether or not they were. Yet, while there were undoubtedly some individuals, and villages, who benefited significantly from the interventions brought by the Millennium Development Project, it seems that, overall, the Millennium Villages were not a success. If they were, one would have expected countless Millennium Villages to spring up in poverty-stricken areas around the globe, after the initial project had come to an end, in 2015. But that has not been the case.[48]

Of course, proponents of Millennium Villages might claim that their failure to be duplicated on a grand scale is mainly due to lack of interest and funding from the world's wealthy. However, arguably, this would get things backwards. It ignores the possibility that interest and funding in the Millennium Villages have waned because the MVs failed to deliver on their promise.

I am acutely aware of the great apathy that most of the better-off have for the needy. However, there are plenty of well-off individuals, foundations, and international organizations that remain deeply committed to aiding the needy. Had the Millennium Villages proven to be cost-effective, and had they actually attained their goal of eradicating severe poverty one village at a time, I believe that there would have been many wealthy countries and donors who would have eagerly funded many more such villages. (Though, admittedly, probably not in the numbers, at the rate, or to the full extent that those of us concerned about the needy might want.)

Nothing in this discussion is intended to suggest that the Millennium Villages Project was not worth trying. To the contrary, as Eran Bendavid rightly observed, "Their [the Millennium Villages'] failure to become islands of progress is, nevertheless, a valuable lesson."[49] However, it is a valuable lesson only if those who were convinced that they were going to succeed— and I count myself among them—are prepared to admit that they were mistaken, and are open to an honest exploration of where things went wrong.

---

[47] Starobin, "Does It Take a Village?"

[48] I am certainly not claiming that the Millennium Villages Project has had no influence on poverty interventions since 2015. Nor even that there have been no interventions since 2015 modeled on the Millennium Villages. Only that there has not been a turn to the Millennium Villages model for poverty reduction on the scale that one would expect had the Millennium Villages Project been widely deemed a success.

[49] Bendavid, "The fog of development: evaluating the Millennium Villages Project."

In an interesting essay in the *Lancet*, Jeff Sachs offered his own perspective on the Millennium Villages Project, three years after it concluded.[50] For the most part, Sachs continued to express confidence in the basic idea of the Millennium Development Project, trumpeting numerous respects in which he judged it a success, and important lessons to be learned from it in attacking poverty going forward. It is notable, however, that he devotes a full quarter of his essay to explaining where things went wrong, and why the project failed to fully deliver on its lofty promises. In some cases, Sachs's explanations read like thinly-veiled blame shifting, as when he seems to imply that if the international community had followed through on its commitments to raise Overseas Development Aid to 0.7 percent of Gross National Income, the Millennium Villages Project might have succeeded.[51]

In other cases, Sachs's explanations are somewhat puzzling. He notes, for example, that the Millennium Villages Project was only able to raise half of the per capita amount for the second half of the project, running from 2011 to 2015, than for the first half of the project, running from 2005 to 2010, as if this helps to explain why the MVP failed to fully achieve its goals even after ten years.[52] However, the MVPs were originally supposed to take desperately poor villages, and provide them with massive upgrades across every relevant poverty-related dimension, so as to eradicate extreme poverty in a way that was sustainable after only five years. So, in the first five years, most of the major steps necessary to achieve sustainable progress should have already been implemented: new roads, new farming equipment and methods, new wells and methods of providing clean water, new clinics or hospitals, new energy grids, new skills training, provision of livestock, provision of needed healthcare, etc. If much of that was already accomplished during the first five-year period, and the villages were already substantially on their way to sustainable growth, one would expect that far fewer funds would be necessary during the second five-year period to maintain the gains that had already been made, and to finish off the massive improvements that had presumably already been well undertaken.

In other cases, however, Sachs's explanations are more revealing. He notes, for example, that "the MVP could build a local road, or a local micro-grid, but without the benefit of a national road network and power grid, the impact was restricted. The MVP could control a local disease outbreak, but not prevent its

[50] Jeffrey Sachs, "Lessons from the Millennium Villages Project: a personal perspective," *The Lancet* 6, E472-E474, May 1, 2018; doi: https://doi.org/10.1016/S2214-109X(18)30199-2; URL: https://www.thelancet.com/journals/langlo/article/PIIS2214-109X(18)30199-2/fulltext, accessed March 28, 2021.

[51] Sachs, "Lessons from the Millennium Villages Project."

[52] Sachs, "Lessons from the Millennium Villages Project."

reintroduction from a neighboring community."[53] Similarly, he notes that "the MVP focused on rural development, not on urban development nor on national infrastructure (roads, rail, power, fibre) connecting rural and urban areas. Most important, the MVs did not benefit from complementary donor spending to boost urban jobs and incomes. Given the tiny sizes of many rural farms . . . and the still rapidly growing rural populations, rural poverty will not end without the rapid growth of urban job opportunities alongside the higher productivity and incomes of farm households."[54] In addition, Sachs noted that "as an island of relative prosperity in the midst of poverty, the MVP's resources inevitably were shared beyond the MVs to the neighbouring areas, thus diminishing the spending per person and impact with the MVs. Partly, this sharing occurred as individuals from neighbouring communities came to the MVs to use the clinics, schools, and other expanded facilities. Partly, it resulted from . . . local authorities . . . direct[ing] . . . resources towards non-MVP areas. This dilution of the MVP investments was natural, unpreventable, and inevitable."[55]

In these passages, Sachs is recognizing the complexity of addressing global poverty, the incredible interconnectedness of what goes on throughout a state or region and, without explicitly saying so, the futility of trying to permanently end extreme poverty one village at a time. Easterly might claim that we already knew these truths; or should have. Still, for many who still needed convincing, the Millennium Villages Project verified these important truths. There is, I believe, significant value in confirming such lessons, once and for all; even if the cost of doing so was rather steep in terms of time, effort, and resources.

As helpful and reflective as Sachs's personal assessment of the Millennium Development Project was, in some respects, it contains one notable omission. At no point does he pause to consider, even for a moment, the possibility that Deaton might be right that large-scale outside interventions might help undermine the responsiveness of local governments to their citizens. This is, to my mind, striking. After all, as seen previously, Sachs's selection criteria for Millennium Village sites clearly recognized the importance of political stability, government commitment to the Millennium Development goals, local political buy in, and community ownership for long-term development.[56] Given this, shouldn't Sachs and his followers at least be concerned about the

[53] Sachs, "Lessons from the Millennium Villages Project."
[54] Sachs, "Lessons from the Millennium Villages Project."
[55] Sachs, "Lessons from the Millennium Villages Project."
[56] Mitchell et al., "The Millennium Villages Project."

possibility that significant outside interventions might negatively impact such factors? Might that help explain why the MVs didn't meet with as much success as they were expected to? Might it also help to partly explain why regional conflict arose in some of the sites, where such conflict was previously lacking? And if that were the case, is it possible that the Millennium Villages Project increased the risk of political instability in the other sites, even if that risk didn't materialize in the form of outright regional conflict? Surely, anyone attracted to Sachs's position has reason to worry about such possibilities.

Regarding Sachs's approach to global poverty, Deaton once wrote the following: "There is no evidence that the Millennium Development Villages—put in place to implement Sachs's ideas—are doing any better than other villages in the same countries . . . . [Sachs's] approach to aid ignores what I have argued is the central issue, that such amounts of aid corrupt local politics in a way that makes development more difficult. You cannot develop other people's countries from the outside with a shopping list from Home Depot, no matter how much you spend."[57] Whether or not Deaton is ultimately right about this, we owe it to the needy to take his position seriously.

In sum, given Sachs's own recognition of the importance of stable and responsive governments for long-term growth and development, and given the mixed results of the Millennium Development Project, it seems clear that Deaton's view about the relation between outside interventions and government responsiveness needs to be given a full and fair hearing. I try to provide that hearing in this and the following two chapters.

11.5 Summary and Some Suggestive Data

Let me sum up this chapter's claims. Deaton believes that good governance is a prerequisite for substantial and lasting social and economic progress in the world's poorest countries, and that good governance requires a government's being responsive to the interests, needs, and wills of its people. Unfortunately, however, there are several mechanisms by which international relief efforts in many of the world's poorest nations can serve to undermine the responsiveness of those nations' governments to their citizens. This helps to explain how, despite its counterintuitiveness, the best-intentioned efforts of the world's international relief and development agencies may be doing more harm than good. Correspondingly, this may help to account, at least in some part, for the

---

[57] Deaton, *The Great Escape*, p. 314.

empirical evidence, which appears to show that there has been little, if any, positive correlation between the amount of international development aid that a poor country has received, and the extent to which that country has experienced substantial and lasting social and economic progress.[58]

Indeed, it is worth recalling that in 1960, the world's poorest countries, as measured by per capita GDP (Gross Domestic Product), included China, Hong Kong, Malaysia, Singapore, South Korea, Taiwan, and Thailand, along with countries like the Central African Republic, the Democratic Republic of the Congo, Guinea, Haiti, Madagascar, Nicaragua, and Niger. But while the former seven countries saw their economies grow "at more than 4 percent a year from 1960–2010—a more than *sevenfold* increase in average income over five decades," the latter seven countries saw economic growth that was so meager that their purchasing power relative to other countries with more robust economies left them "actually poorer in 2010 than they were a half a century ago."[59] And while there are a multitude of complex factors in play that make it extremely difficult, if not impossible, to precisely identify the root causes of the enormous differences in economic growth between the two sets of countries, it certainly appears that the amount of per capita foreign aid received was not among those causes,[60] while, arguably, at least, the extent to which the governments of the countries were or were not effective and responsive to the needs of their citizens were among those causes.

Deaton himself sums up his position as follows:

> Aid and aid-funded projects have undoubtedly done much good; the roads, dams, and clinics exist and would not have existed otherwise. But the negative forces are always present; even in good environments aid compromises institutions, it contaminates local politics, and it undermines democracy. If poverty and underdevelopment are primarily consequences of poor institutions, then by weakening those institutions or stunting their

---

[58] See Deaton's *The Great Escape*, Riddell's *Does Foreign Aid Really Work?*, and The World Bank data on GDP per capita from 1960 to 2015, available at https://data.worldbank.org/indicator/NY.GDP.PCAP.CD?end=2015&locations=HK-GW&most_recent_year_desc=true&start=1960, accessed July 5, 2019.

[59] Deaton, *The Great Escape*, pp. 234–5. Also, The World Bank data on GDP per capita from 1960–2015 (see the previous note).

[60] See The World Bank data on "Net official development assistance and official aid received (current US$) from 1960–2017," available at https://data.worldbank.org/indicator/DT.ODA.ALLD.CD?locations=CN-HK-CF-CG-SG-NE-MG-MY-GQ-GW-KR-HT-NI-TH, accessed July 5, 2019. If one graphs the available data for the countries in question, it is apparent that the massive disparity in economic growth between the countries in question is not due to differences in economic aid, and this is especially so if one bears in mind the differences in aid on a per capita basis.

development, large aid flows do exactly the opposite of what they are intended to do. It is hardly surprising then that, in spite of the direct effects of aid that are often positive, the record of aid shows no evidence of any overall beneficial effect.[61,62*]

[61] *The Great Escape*, pp. 305–6.

[62*] Of course, not everyone will be convinced by the considerations offered here. For example, in correspondence, Ingmar Persson expresses skepticism about the view that international aid efforts actually *undermine* the responsiveness of a government to its citizens, suggesting, instead, that in countries that lack good governance, international aid efforts have been unable to *facilitate* such governance, because of powerful counteracting forces at play in those countries. Whether or not Persson is right about this, he accepts Deaton's fundamental point, that responsiveness of a government to the needs of its people is a necessary condition for long-term social and economic development.

So, although Persson's view stops well short of Deaton's claim that international aid efforts often do more harm than good, it comes close to granting that in countries that lack good governance such efforts may be largely wasted, and so not worth engaging in, at least insofar as the intent of such efforts is to bring about long-term social and economic progress. (Of course, there may be other important goals of international aid efforts—such as saving the lives of people who are desperately in need *now*— that are orthogonal to the goal of long-term social and economic progress. It is important not to lose sight of this, when confronted by arguments such as Deaton's. I return to this important point later.)

Many development economists accept the view that good governance is important for aid to "work." For considerations in support of this view, see the following articles coauthored by Dollar: Burnside, C. and D. Dollar, "Aid, Policies, and Growth," *American Economic Review* 90 (2000): 847–68; Burnside, C. and D. Dollar, "Aid, Policies, and Growth: Revisiting the Evidence," *World Bank Policy Research Paper*, Number 0–2834, Washington, DC: World Bank, 2004; and Collier, P. and D. Dollar, "Aid Allocation and Poverty Reduction," *European Economic Review* 45 (2002): 1–26.

On the other hand, as with the question of whether aid is generally effective, the question of whether aid promotes or hinders political stability and good governance is extremely complex, and one about which there is much disagreement among development economists. While some, like Deaton, think that, overall, aid hinders political stability and good governance, others believe that, overall, it promotes political stability and good governance. For example, Jones and Tarp believe that, overall, aid has a small, yet notably positive effect on political institutions, and that there isn't a systematic negative relationship as many have feared (see Jones, S. and F. Tarp. "Does Foreign Aid Harm Political Institutions?" *Journal of Development Economics* 118 (2016): 266–81).

Here, as elsewhere in the domain of aid research, it is plausible to believe that the evidence is insufficient to establish any general conclusions one way or the other. Rather, in some contexts aid has probably had a positive effect on political institutions, while in others aid has probably had a negative effect on political institutions. (I am grateful to Brian Oosterhuizen for much of the material in this note.)

12

Individual versus Collective Rationality and Morality

A Troubling Possibility

In Chapter 11, I presented Angus Deaton's worry that international aid efforts may do more harm than good, by undermining the responsiveness of governments to their citizens. There are many possible responses to Deaton's worry, some of which I consider in Chapter 13. In this chapter, I consider a particularly natural response to Deaton's worry which raises an especially important, and troubling, issue. This concerns the possibility that what each of us, *individually*, ought to do on behalf of the needy, might conflict with what we, *collectively*, ought to do on behalf of the needy. Unfortunately, the argument for this is complex, and requires quite a bit of background to be fully understood.

This chapter, and the following one, contain some of this book's most important contributions, and they are especially relevant to the views of many Effective Altruists. Unfortunately, however, some readers, without adequate background in philosophy or game theory, may find this material especially hard going. Such readers may want to skim these two chapters, to glean my main points without getting bogged down in the philosophical weeds. Alternatively, if necessary, they might just skip ahead to Chapter 14.

In Section 12.1, I present the natural response to Deaton's worry with which this chapter deals. Roughly, the response maintains that even if some aid organizations do more harm than good, surely it is deeply implausible to believe that all do. Accordingly, Deaton's worry just illuminates the importance of the Effective Altruism Movement. If we really want to aid the needy, we need to make sure that we identify and support the most effective aid organizations; ones that can be counted on to be doing more good than harm.

In Section 12.2, I present the famous *Prisoner's Dilemma*, and some examples of so-called *Many-Person Prisoner's Dilemmas*. These are examples of *Each/We Dilemmas*, and they illustrate how there can be conflicts between individual and collective rationality. That is, they show how it can be the case

Being Good in a World of Need. Larry S. Temkin, Oxford University Press. © Larry S. Temkin 2022.
DOI: 10.1093/oso/9780192849977.003.0012

that, by the lights of the standard theory of individual rationality, what it would be rational for *each* of us to do, *individually*, can conflict with what it would be rational for *us* to do, *collectively*. This is the first of several sections that provide the background needed to properly understand the significance of Deaton's worry.

In Section 12.3, I note that Parfit has shown that there can be Each/We Dilemmas for deontological moralities. In particular, he has shown that analogs of the Standard Prisoner's Dilemmas can arise for deontological moralities, where if each person in some group, individually, does what he ought to do by the lights of a deontological theory, they (the members of that group) together, will be doing what they ought not to do by the lights of that theory.

I claim that similar worries can arise for consequentialist theories. That is, I claim that there can be some cases where if each person in some group, individually, does what he ought to do according to according to consequentialism, they (the members of that group) together, will be doing what they ought not to do according to consequentialism.

In Section 12.4, I present and defend the plausibility of certain anti-additive-aggregationist principles.[1*] One such principle is the *Disperse Additional Burdens and Consolidate Additional Benefits View* (which I refer to as the *Disperse Additional Burdens View*, for short). I present several examples about which, I claim, most people's views reflect a principle like the Disperse Additional Burdens View. I also show that anti-additive-aggregationist

---

[1*] I realize that this is a bit of philosophical jargon that will make some people's eyes glaze over. But it reflects a position that is not too difficult to understand. Roughly, a *principle of aggregation* tells one how to assess the goodness of something, based on, or as a function of, various components of that thing. So, for example, one might determine the best bowling team, for different purposes, by "aggregating" the abilities of the various members of that team in different ways; say, by combining the average game scores of each team member, or by combining the total bowling scores of each member, or by focusing on the top score of the best bowler of each team, or by focusing on the lowest score of the worst bowler on each team, and so on. An *additive-aggregationist principle* adopts an *additive* approach to assessing the goodness of something; say, it adds up the scores of each team member to arrive at a judgment as to which bowling team is best. An *anti-additive-aggregationist principle* uses a non-additive approach to assessing the goodness of something. Utilitarianism is an example of an additive-aggregationist approach to outcome goodness—it says that the best outcome is the one with the greatest sum total of individual wellbeing. The principle of equality is an anti-additive-aggregationist principle for outcome goodness, as is John Rawls's maximin principle (see Rawls's *A Theory of Justice* (Cambridge, MA: Harvard University Press, 1971)); both principles reject the view that the best outcome is the one with the greatest sum total of individual wellbeing, with the former holding that the best outcome is the one in which wellbeing is most equally distributed, and the latter holding, roughly, that the best outcome is the one in which the worst-off individuals fare best. I hope that this chapter's jargon will be sufficiently clear from the discussion. However, for more on these distinctions see my *Rethinking the Good: Moral Ideals and the Nature of Practical Reasoning* (New York: Oxford University Press, 2012), where I first introduced these distinctions and discussed their significance for moral theory in detail.

reasoning is plausible in Derek Parfit's famous *Repugnant Conclusion*, and in a case of my own, which I call *Lollipops for Life*.

In Section 12.5, I present two examples that demonstrate how anti-additive-aggregationist principles, like the Disperse Additional Burdens View, can give rise to consequentialist Each/We Dilemmas. That is, I show how it can be the case that if each of us, as individuals, acts rightly, in consequentialist terms, we, together, may be acting wrongly in consequentialist terms. Specifically, I show that, if, as I have argued, certain anti-additive-aggregationist principles are correct, then the collective outcome that results when each person, individually, acts rightly in consequentialist terms, can be worse, in consequentialist terms, than the collective outcome that results when each person, individually, acts wrongly in consequentialist terms. This is a surprising result. Also, as will soon become clear, a very important one.

In Section 12.6, I consider the suggestion that good communication and enforceable agreements could provide practical solutions to Each/We Dilemmas. I offer two responses to this suggestion. First, I point out that in the real world, there are so many different aid organizations, each with their own distinct contexts, constituencies, and concerns, that the likelihood of having good communication and arriving at a mutually acceptable and enforceable agreement among all of them is remote. Second, I argue that while communication and enforceable agreements *could* provide practical solutions to rational Each/We Dilemmas—the dilemmas illustrated by the standard Prisoner's Dilemmas; and also to the deontological Each/We Dilemmas discussed by Parfit—they could *not* provide practical solutions to consequentialist Each/We Dilemmas. I conclude that consequentialist Each/We Dilemmas are the most troubling of the different types of Each/We Dilemmas, and that they remain practically important, as well as theoretically interesting.

In Section 12.7, I reconsider Deaton's worry that people may be doing more harm than good by contributing to on-the-ground international aid organizations. I argue that this chapter's results illuminate Deaton's worry, as well as most people's reactions to it. In short, I argue that even if people are right to believe that their *individual* contributions to international aid organizations are morally desirable, it could still be the case, as Deaton believes, that the *collective* impacts of such contributions are morally undesirable. That is, contributions to international aid organizations may manifest a consequentialist Each/We Dilemma. If they do, this makes Deaton's worry far more plausible than many people have thought.

In Section 12.8, I revisit two assumptions that I made in Section 12.2. These assumptions are favorable to the response to Deaton's worry presented in

Section 12.1. I argue that both assumptions are dubious, and that rejecting them only strengthens Deaton's position.

Section 12.9 concludes the chapter with a summary of its main claims.

12.1 One Natural Response to Deaton's Worry: The Importance of Effective Altruism

Many people who learn of Deaton's worry are unconvinced. They grant that there may be some international development efforts that inadvertently promote undesirable outcomes, and perhaps even more than we would normally assume. Even so, they contend, it is deeply implausible to believe that *every* international development organization is bringing about an undesirable outcome. Accordingly, these people insist that Deaton's critique just underscores the importance of the Effective Altruism Movement. Given that there are many people in great need throughout the world, and that many of us are able to do something about it at very little cost to ourselves, it is incumbent upon us to identify and support the most effective international development agencies. Obviously, we shouldn't be supporting aid organizations that ultimately promote worse outcomes, this reasoning goes, but equally obviously, there must be *some* international aid organizations that are promoting better outcomes, and we *should* be supporting *those* organizations, and, ideally, the most effective ones.

Deaton himself seems to offer some support for this position. He grants that there may have been some successful health initiatives whose costs may have been worth bearing. He suggests that this may have been true of "some of the early vaccination programs, as well as . . . [some] programs to eliminate pests—for example, mosquito control for malaria—or a disease such as small pox or polio."[2] Given this, doesn't it make sense to try to identify other programs that might be similarly successful—programs that, even with costs of the sort Deaton worries about, are worth bearing given the amount of good to be achieved? Why can't Deaton simply side with the Effective Altruists?[3*] Instead of claiming that we shouldn't be supporting international

---

[2] Deaton, Angus, *The Great Escape: Health, Wealth, and the Origins of Inequality* (Princeton: Princeton University Press, 2015, 308–9).

[3*] In correspondence, Deaton notes that he *would* side with Effective Altruism "if it could do its calculations correctly, including counting the loss of governance, of democracy, spillovers, etc. But Effective Altruism is instead focused on finding out what works using narrowly focused and non-generalizable RCTs [randomized control trials]." Here, we see that there is no deep theoretical difference between the approach Deaton favors, and the one that Effective Altruists favor. Deaton

development agencies operating directly in some of the world's poorest regions, why shouldn't Deaton simply contend, much more modestly, that we must be extremely careful about *which* international aid agencies we support, and must make sure that whatever agencies we support are, indeed, promoting morally desirable outcomes?

12.2 Each/We Dilemmas: The Possibility of Conflict between Individual and Collective Rationality

I believe there are reasons to worry about the preceding response to Deaton, even if one makes two assumptions that are particularly favorable for the response. The first favorable assumption is that when one donates to an effective aid agency, your donation *itself* has a major positive impact on the quality of some people's lives. The second favorable assumption is that no individual donation to an effective aid agency will have anything more than a negligible negative effect on the quality of any particular individual person's life, due to its reducing the responsiveness of a government to its citizens. In this chapter, I shall, for the sake of argument, initially grant these assumptions. However, in Section 12.8, I note that there are reasons to worry about each assumption, and note that this only strengthens Deaton's position.[4]

The key to understanding the shortcomings of the preceding response to Deaton's position—even given the two favorable assumptions—lies in an important, and troubling, fact about practical reasoning. The fact concerns possible conflicts that can arise between individual and collective rationality and morality; conflicts that Derek Parfit has referred to as *Each/We Dilemmas*.[5] The issues here are complicated, and tricky, but they are important to understand if we hope to do full justice to Deaton's concerns. Because of

---

simply believes that Effective Altruists have not correctly identified all of the factors that are relevant for assessing the overall effects of aid interventions. In theory, Effective Altruists could readily accept this criticism, and widen their criterion for assessing aid agencies accordingly.

I share Deaton's worries about the practical limitations of Effective Altruism's actual approach to assessing aid agencies. However, as should be clear by now, my own favored pluralistic approach to thinking about the needy implies that both Deaton's approach and Effective Altruism's approach are too narrow. In thinking about the needy, it is not enough, I believe, to focus on the single consequentialist question of what promotes the best overall outcome giving due weight to both the benefits and harms produced by any individual aid intervention or collective set of aid interventions.

[4] I am grateful to Jeff McMahan and Shelly Kagan for pushing me to acknowledge that the rosiest of assumptions typically won't obtain.

[5] On conflicts between individual and collective rationality or morality in the development literature see, for example, Kharas, H., "Trends and Issues in Development Aid," Wolfensohn Center for Development, Working Paper 1, Washington, DC: Brookings Institution, 2007. Also, Fengler, W.

their complexity, I need to provide a fair amount of background and argument beginning in this section and continuing through Section 12.6. Only in Section 12.7, will we finally be able to fully appreciate Deaton's position, and the inadequacy of the preceding response to it.

Each/We Dilemmas arise when, if each of a number of individuals does what is best, *individually*, by the lights of a given theory, they, *collectively*, end up doing worse by the lights of that theory. The most famous examples of Each/We Dilemmas are *Prisoner's Dilemmas*. In the classic Prisoner's Dilemma, each of two prisoners is being interrogated in a separate room. The prisoners, who jointly committed a crime, have no opportunity to communicate with each other. Nor will there be any opportunity, after the fact, for one of the prisoners to affect the other (say, by seeking reprisal for what the other prisoner did). Each prisoner is unconcerned about what happens to the other; or rather, more accurately, each prisoner ultimately wants to do whatever is best for himself, in purely self-interested terms.

Each prisoner is given two options. He can confess to their crime, and provide all the details of what they did, or he can keep silent. Each prisoner is then truthfully told the following:

1. If each prisoner confesses, there will be lots of evidence against them, and the jury will send each of them to jail for ten years.
2. If each prisoner keeps silent, there will only be circumstantial evidence against them, and while it will be enough to get them convicted, each will only serve two years of jail time.
3. If one of them confesses, and the other keeps silent, the one who confesses will be rewarded for his cooperation and will only be put on probation, so, in that case, he will serve zero years in jail. The other prisoner, on the other hand, will be convicted, based on the detailed evidence provided by the prisoner who confessed, and he will then be sent to jail for twelve years, to punish him for failing to cooperate.

Bearing in mind that each prisoner wants to do what is best for himself; that neither can communicate with the other in advance of his decision; and that there will be no subsequent repercussions for whatever decision a prisoner ultimately makes; what should the prisoners do?

and H. Kharas, "Overview: Delivering Aid Differently," Brookings Institution, 2016, p. 6, URL: https://www.brookings.edu/wp-content/uploads/2016/07/deliveringaiddifferently_chapter.pdf, accessed September 6, 2018.

As game theorists, decision theorists, and others have demonstrated, under such conditions it would be *individually* rational for each prisoner to *confess*. At least this is so according to the standard Self-Interest Theory of Individual Rationality, which holds, roughly, that an individual acts rationally when she acts so as to maximize the overall quality of her life (often understood in terms of the satisfaction of her interests and desires), treating each of the moments of her life equally. This is because, by confessing, each person will save himself two years in jail, *whatever the other prisoner decides to do*.

If the other person confesses, and he confesses, he will get ten years in prison, instead of the twelve years in prison that he would have gotten had he kept silent when the other person confessed. If, on the other hand, the other person keeps silent, and he confesses, then he will get zero years in prison, instead of the two years in prison that he would have gotten had he kept silent when the other person kept silent. In this case, confessing is the *dominant* strategy for *each* person. Each person knows that the other person will either confess or keep silent. He also knows that *whichever* choice the other person makes, he will save himself two years in jail by confessing, rather than keeping silent. Accordingly, for each person, the individually rational thing to do, according to the Self-Interest Theory of Individual Rationality, is to confess.

The problem, of course, is that if each of them does what is genuinely best for himself in self-interested terms, they, together, will end up serving twenty years in prison—ten years each—rather than four years in prison—only two years each. What makes the Prisoner's Dilemma particularly paradoxical is that each of them is fully aware that ten years in prison is obviously much worse than two years in prison, in purely self-interested terms. The problem is that, in the circumstances described, there is no *individually* rational way of arriving at the outcome in which each spends only two years in jail.

Here, we have a conflict between the individually rational choice and the collectively rational choice. From the standpoint of what would be *individually* best for *each* of them, each should clearly confess. However, from the standpoint of what would be *collectively* best for the two of them, *together*, they should clearly keep silent.

Two-person Prisoner's Dilemmas are rare in the real world. However, *Many-Person Prisoner's Dilemmas* frequently arise.[6] As the vast literature on Prisoner's Dilemmas has revealed, it is *often* the case that if each member of a large group of people does what is best for him or herself in self-interested

---

[6] Parfit, Derek, *Reasons and Persons* (Oxford: Clarendon Press, 1984; see, especially, Chapter 2).

terms, they, together, will be much worse off than they would have been if they had instead done what was best for the group as a whole. So, for example, in a rural society, it may be better, in self-interested terms, for *each* parent to have as many children as possible to help in the fields, however many children everyone *else* has—but, *together*, everyone would be better off if they had only a few children rather than many children, due to the strains that a large population makes on the environment and government services; *each* farmer is better off, in self-interested terms, bringing as many crops to market as possible, no matter what the other farmers decide to do—but, *together*, all the farmers may be better off if they bring fewer crops rather than more crops to market, since too many crops in the marketplace will collapse the price of the crop and be disastrous for all the farmers; *each* fisherman is better off, in self-interested terms, harvesting as many fish as possible, no matter what the other fishermen decide to do—but, *together*, all the fishermen may be better off if they harvest fewer fish rather than more, since harvesting too many fish may collapse the stocks and undermine their livelihoods for years to come; in a large city, it may be more convenient for each person to take his or her own car to work than to take public transportation, no matter what everyone else does—but, *together*, they might all be better off if they all took public transportation, than if they all took their cars, since the former leaves the roads open, while the latter leads to massive delays due to traffic congestion; from a purely self-interested perspective, it may be better for each individual to pollute rather than to incur the costs of pollution reduction, whatever other individuals decide to do—but, *together*, it may be much worse for all if everyone pollutes than if everyone refrains from polluting; each person has self-interested reason to avoid paying taxes, whatever everyone else decides to do—but, *together*, they may all be worse off if they don't pay their taxes than if they do, since a large tax base is necessary for the provision of crucial government services and public goods; and so on.[7]

The standard Prisoner's Dilemmas discussed by game theorists, decision theorists, and economists, illustrate the possibility of conflict between individual and collective *rationality*. However, as we will see next, there can also be conflicts between individual and collective *morality*; that is, between what each

---

[7] Some of the problems illuminated by Prisoner's Dilemmas are related to what economists call *general equilibrium effects*. This is especially so, for example, of the farmer example. I am grateful to Angus Deaton for bringing this to my attention. This is connected to the arguments referred to previously for the conclusion that randomized control trials don't scale up, as a matter of logic, and hence are of little use for inferring "what works" when evaluating the efforts of aid agencies (see Chapter 9, Note 8).

member of a group, individually, ought to do morally, and what they, the members of the group together, ought to do morally.

12.3 Each/We Dilemmas: The Possibility of Conflict between Individual and Collective Morality

In *Reasons and Persons*, Derek Parfit showed that the well-known conflict between individual and collective rationality illustrated by Prisoner's Dilemmas can also arise for morality. In particular, Parfit showed how analogs of the Prisoner's Dilemmas can arise for deontological moralities. Indeed, Parfit showed that for most plausible Each/We Dilemmas that arise for the domain of individual rationality, corresponding Each/We Dilemmas can arise for the domain of deontological morality, with the latter "piggybacking" on the former.[8*]

For example, since, on deontological morality, parents have special obligations to do what is best for their children (as long as, in doing so, they are not violating anyone else's rights), it could be that each parent ought, morally, to have as many children, raise as many crops, catch as many fish, and so on, as possible, since that will be best for each of the parent's children; and yet, if each parent does what is individually best for his or her children, collectively, they will do what is worse for their children.

Thus, Parfit showed that there can be cases in which, if each person does what is individually right, by the lights of some deontological theory, they, together, may be doing something which would be collectively wrong according to the deontological theory in question.[9] So, according to Parfit, on deontological theories, a group of people can find themselves in the troubling position where each person knows that if each of them does what he or she, individually, ought to do, they, together, will be bringing about an outcome which, collectively, they ought not to bring about.

[8*] *Reasons and Persons*, Chapter 4. Roughly, this is because the self-interest theory allows me to give special priority to myself, in deciding how to act, while deontological theories allow me to give special priority to my family members, or others with whom I stand in special relations. So, typically, if an Each/We Dilemma can arise for individual rationality because it would be better for each of us if each did X, but worse for all of us if all did X, then an Each/We Dilemma could also arise for deontological morality, because it would typically be better for each of those depending on each of us, if each of us did X, but worse for all of those depending on us if we all did X.

[9] *Reasons and Persons*, Chapter 4.

Parfit's result was fascinating and worrisome. In *Rethinking the Good*, I argued that similar worries can arise for consequentialist theories.[10] In particular, I argued that given certain kinds of widely-accepted principles, which I called *anti-additive-aggregationist principles*,[11*] even consequentialist theories can face the troubling possibility that if each person in some group does what she, individually, ought to do in consequentialist terms, then they, together, will be bringing about an outcome which, collectively, they ought *not* to bring about in consequentialist terms.

In Section 12.5, I show how anti-additive-aggregationist principles can give rise to consequentialist Each/We Dilemmas. But first, I must illustrate the plausibility of such principles. I do that next.

12.4 The Plausibility of Anti-Additive-Aggregationist Principles

In this section, I present and defend the plausibility of anti-additive-aggregationist principles. One such principle, which plays an important role in my subsequent arguments, is the following one.

Disperse Additional Burdens and Consolidate Additional Benefits View: In general, if additional burdens are dispersed among different people, it is better for a given total burden to be dispersed among a vastly larger number of people, so that the additional burden any single person must bear within her life is "relatively small," than for a smaller total burden to fall on just a few, so that their additional burden is substantial. And likewise, in general, if additional benefits are dispersed among different people, it is better for a given total benefit to be consolidated among a few people, so that each person's additional benefit is substantial, than for a large total benefit to be dispersed among a vastly larger number of people, so that the additional benefit any single person receives within her life is "relatively small."[12]

I believe that most people implicitly accept some version of the Disperse Additional Burdens and Consolidate Additional Benefits View, and that they employ it in their thinking about certain moral contexts. (Henceforth, I shall

---

[10] Temkin, *Rethinking the Good*, see Chapter 3, especially pp. 80–95.
[11*] See Note 1* in this chapter, for an explication of this terminology.
[12] For ease of presentation, I here present as a single principle what I have previously presented as two separate principles. See, *Rethinking the Good*, pp. 67–8.

use "Disperse Additional Burdens View" as shorthand for the longer, and more cumbersome, "Disperse Additional Burdens and Consolidate Additional Benefits View".)

To see this, consider the following example. Suppose that in one outcome, A, 10 million hours of great pain would be distributed across 10 million lives, so that each person suffered *one* additional hour of great pain during her 80-year life. An hour of great pain is never pleasant or desirable. Still, it is plausible to assume that, however well-off or poorly-off someone is, *one* additional hour of great pain during an 80-year life will not make a significant difference to the overall quality of her life. Alternatively, suppose that in a second outcome, B, 8 million hours of great pain would be distributed across 17 lives, so that each person suffered approximately 16 hours of great pain *every single day* during her 80-year life. In that case, the burdens that would be borne by the 17 people would be substantial; indeed, they would be extraordinarily horrible. In accordance with the Disperse Additional Burdens View, most people believe that the first outcome, A, in which each of 10 million people suffers *one* additional hour of great pain during her life, would be *better* than the second outcome, B, in which each of 17 people suffers 16 hours of great pain *every day* for 80 years.

Here are two other examples.[13] Suppose the World Health Organization could spend its resources so as to effectively prolong 1,000 people's lives for *fifty* years, or it could spend its resources to prolong 2,000,000 people's lives by *one month* each. Or suppose an international relief organization could relieve hunger for 1,000 people for *fifty years*, or it could relieve hunger for 4,000,000 people for a *week*. In accordance with the Disperse Additional Burdens View, I think most people believe that, ceteris paribus, the outcome in which 1,000 people had their lives extended for *fifty years* would be *better* than the outcome in which 2,000,000 people had their lives extended for one month, even though in the former case the World Health Organization would "only" be keeping people alive a total of 600,000 extra months, while in the latter case the World Health Organization would be keeping people alive for a total of 2,000,000 extra months. Likewise, I think most people believe that the outcome in which 1,000 people had their hunger relieved for *fifty years* would be *better* than the outcome in which 4,000,000 people had their hunger relieved for a week, even though in the former case there would "only" be 2.6 million weeks of hunger relief.

---

[13] See *Rethinking the Good*, pp. 79–80.

Not everyone accepts the preceding judgments. Among others, they would be rejected by many total utilitarians (at least classical utilitarians, like Bentham and Sidgwick, who reject discontinuities in value; henceforth, I omit this qualification). But, of course, total utilitarians would also accept Parfit's *Repugnant Conclusion*—that if only *enough* people existed with lives that were *barely* worth living, that outcome, Z, would be better than an outcome, A, in which billions of people lived lives of extraordinarily high quality.[14]

To make Parfit's example vivid, we can imagine that in Z there are people— or oysters for that matter—who are unconscious for their entire lives, except that they rise to consciousness for one moment. During that moment, they feel an ever-so-slight positive experience of warmth, before lapsing back into total unconsciousness and eventually death. In A, on the other hand, we can imagine that 10 billion people live lives of great length *filled* with everything that makes a life worth living—much love, great respect, extraordinary creativity, high achievements, deep friendships, perfect health, incredible food, enormously satisfying sex, and so on.

Likewise, consider my *Lollipops for Life* case, involving two alternatives, B and C.[15] In B, countless people all have enormously satisfying lives, which includes—in addition to all the incredibly valuable factors just noted (much love, great respect, extraordinary creativity, etc.)—lots of licks of many different lollipops over the course of their very long lives. However, B also involves one innocent person suffering unbearable agony for eighty straight years, before eventually dying a slow, lonely, torturous death. By contrast, in C, the same countless people live the same enormously satisfying lives, except that they each receive *one* less lick of a lollipop over the course of their very long lives. However, in C, the innocent person would be spared the agony and painful death, and would, instead, live a full rich life just like the others. Total utilitarians are committed to the view that if only there were *enough* people each enjoying a *tiny* amount of pleasure from the one extra lick of a lollipop, then B would be better than C.

Most people, including many consequentialists, are not total utilitarians. They side with Parfit in rejecting the Repugnant Conclusion, and they similarly reject the total utilitarian's judgment about my Lollipops for Life case. For certain comparisons, at least, they reject the simple additive-aggregationist

---

[14] See Chapter 17 of *Reasons and Persons*, especially pp. 387–90.
[15] See *Rethinking the Good*, pp. 34–5.

approach of total utilitarianism, in favor of an anti-additive-aggregationist approach embodied in principles like the Disperse Additional Burdens View.

12.5 How Anti-Additive-Aggregationist Principles Give Rise to Consequentialist Each/We Dilemmas

In Section 12.4, I claimed that for certain cases, at least, most people find anti-additive-aggregationist principles like the Disperse Additional Burdens View deeply compelling. In this section, I demonstrate that such principles can give rise to consequentialist versions of Each/We Dilemmas. To see this, consider the following example.

> *Red or Blue Button*: Suppose there are three different groups of innocent people, *A*, *B*, and *C*. *A* and *C* each have 500,000 members, while *B* has 1,000,000 members. Through no fault of anyone's, each member of *A* and *B* is facing periods of great pain, unless *C*'s members intervene. Each of *C*'s members is able to help only *one* unique member of *A*, though she can help that person immensely. Alternatively, each of *C*'s members can help *every* member of *B*, but only a small amount. Specifically, each of *C*'s members can intervene in only one of two ways. She can push a red button, in which case a unique member of *A* will suffer great pain for 16 hours a day every day of her 80-year life, but each member of *B* will be spared one hour of great pain over the course of her 80-year life. Alternatively, she can push a blue button, in which case each member of *B* will suffer one extra hour of great pain sometime during her life (assume, for this example, that any pains they experience will be spread evenly throughout their lives), but the unique member of *A*, whose fortunes lie in her hands, will be spared 16 hours a day of great pain for every day of her 80 year life and, as a result, will lead a very high quality life.

Each of *C*'s members is acutely aware of the fact that every other member of *C* faces an analogous choice. The only difference involves which member of *A* one is in a position to help. Each of *C*'s members is also acutely aware of the fact that no one is responsible for the predicaments that *A* and *B*'s members face, and that pushing neither button will produce the worst of the three possible outcomes that it is her power to produce, since in that case *everyone* will receive the pains that they are currently only facing. So, let us hope that each of *C*'s members will resolve, reasonably, to push one of the two buttons. Which one should each push?

I believe that if I were in such a position, I should push the blue button. Moreover, I think this is the case *whatever* the other members of C choose to do. This is because whether or not everyone else chooses to push the red button, or everyone else chooses to push the blue button, or some push the red button and the others push the blue button, having ruled out the option of doing nothing, *my* choice comes down to one of two remaining options. I can spare one person 80 *years* of unremitting misery, or I can spare each of 1,000,000 people one *hour* of great pain. The former will have a substantial impact on the overall quality of one person's life. It will literally make the difference between whether the person has a very high quality of life, or a life that is so utterly miserable that she would have been far better off dead. The latter will have a relatively trivial impact on the overall quality of many people's lives—surely, one *hour* of great pain, more or less, over the course of an 80-year life is basically insignificant in terms of the *overall* quality of that life.[16]

Bearing all this in mind, I believe, in accordance with the anti-additive-aggregationist reasoning of the Disperse Additional Burdens View, that I should push the blue button. Moreover, I believe that the reason I should do this is that of the three outcomes that are in my power to produce, the blue-button option is the best outcome, the red-button option is the second-best outcome, and the no-button option is the worst outcome. If this reasoning is correct, it follows that insofar as I want to act rightly, in consequentialist terms, I ought, morally, to push the blue button. Only by pushing the blue button do I bring about the best outcome, given the alternatives that I face.

There is, of course, nothing special about me when I consider myself facing such a predicament. My reasoning is generalizable, and perfectly applicable to *every* member of C facing the analogous choice. It follows that insofar as each of them wants to bring about the best outcome, given the alternatives each faces, each should push the blue button. Correspondingly, if each of them pushes the blue button, each, individually, will be acting rightly in consequentialist terms.

Still, reflection reveals that if each of them pushes the blue button, there will be one million people each of whom is suffering 500,000 hours of great pain spread evenly throughout his or her life. This comes out to just over 17 hours of great pain, every day, for each of their 80-year lives. Clearly, however, from a consequentialist standpoint, it is worse if one million people each suffer great

---

[16] For the sake of this argument, I am assuming that the one hour of great pain has no other impact on the person's life than the way it feels while it lasts.

pain for 17 hours a day for 80 years, than if 500,000 people suffer great pain for 16 hours a day for 80 years. So, here we have an example of a consequentialist Each/We Dilemma. If each individual does what is right, in consequentialist terms, they, collectively, will bring about an outcome which is clearly worse, and thus wrong, according to consequentialism.

Consider, next, the following example.

> *The Toxic Watch Battery*: Uhuru is walking by a reservoir in which an innocent child has just slipped under the surface of the water. If she dives in immediately, she can save the child from any major damage. If she pauses to remove her watch, which has a very difficult clasp system, the delay will cause the child to suffer significant brain damage from being under water too long. If Uhuru does not remove her watch, its battery will leach toxic chemicals into the reservoir, increasing its pollution level by a very small amount. The reservoir is the main source of water for the 1,000,000 inhabitants of the region's largest city. Ultimately, let us suppose, the effect of the increased level of toxic pollution would be for each inhabitant of the city to have one extra day of flu-like symptoms during their lifetime than they would otherwise have (chills, fever, headache, cough, fatigue, weakness, sore throat, and aching muscles).

What should Uhuru do? Uhuru might reason as follows. If she removes her watch before diving in to save the child, this will have a significant negative impact on the overall quality of the child's life. If she dives in with the watch, this will have a relatively small negative effect—one day of flu-like symptoms—on each of the million people who depend on the reservoir for their water supply.

Since there are so many people using the water supply, the *total* amount of negative effects that she produces might be *larger* if she fails to remove her watch than if she doesn't. For example, if the average life expectancy in the area is sixty years, and the child is ten, removing the watch will result in 18,250 days of significantly brain-damaged life which, let us assume, is far from flourishing, but not painful, while not removing the watch will result in 1,000,000 days of aches, chills, fatigue, headache, fever, and so on.

Nevertheless, the *distribution* of those effects is *very* different. If she removes her watch, *all* of the negative effects that she produces will be borne by one individual, the innocent child. If she leaves her watch on, the negative effects that she produces will be dispersed across a vast number of people in such a way that it would only have a negligible impact on the overall quality of each of their lives. Given this, Uhuru might plausibly conclude, in accordance with the Disperse Additional Burdens View, that if she wants to produce the best possible outcome, she should dive in immediately and spare the child significant brain damage.

Uhuru may be right about this. Suppose she is. She would then be acting rightly in consequentialist terms. Notice, however, that Uhuru might not be the only person facing such a decision. Suppose, say, that 30,000 other people found themselves in a similar predicament as Uhuru did. Each might reason and act as she did. In so doing, each might be producing the best outcome of those available to him or her, and so be acting rightly, as individuals, in consequentialist terms.

Still, the *cumulative* effects of 30,000 toxic batteries on the pollution level of the reservoir might be very bad indeed. In particular, while the *individual* negative impact on each person from the increased pollution level of a single watch battery might be very small—one *day* of flu-like symptoms—the *collective* negative effects of 30,000 batteries might be quite significant—flu-like symptoms every day for *eighty-two years*! Given the average sixty-year life expectancy of the population, this would involve the overwhelming majority of the city's one million inhabitants having flu-like symptoms every day for the rest of their lives. Correspondingly, we might well believe that, together, the significant negative impact on the city's million inhabitants of having flu-like symptoms every day for eighty-two years, if they managed to live that long, might be *worse* than the significant negative effects on 30,000 innocent children of having to live out the remainder of their lives with severe brain damage. If this is so, this would be another example of a consequentialist Each/We Dilemma. In accordance with the anti-additive-aggregationist reasoning of the Disperse Additional Burdens View, if each individual does what is best in consequentialist terms, they, together, end up producing an outcome which is worse in consequentialist terms.

The results in this section are very surprising. Most people have not realized that consequentialism could face Each/We Dilemmas. In fact, Derek Parfit once argued that one advantage of consequentialism, over deontological moral theories, was that the former *couldn't* face Each/We Dilemmas, while the latter could.[17] However, as we have seen, Parfit was mistaken about this. At least this is so if, as Parfit and most people believe, the anti-additive-aggregationist reasoning that supports Parfit's view of the Repugnant Conclusion is correct.

---

[17] See Part One of *Reasons and Persons*.

In Section 12.7, we will see that this section's results are not merely surprising. They are important for fully appreciating Deaton's views, and may have deeply troubling implications for the topic of global aid. But first, I will consider the suggestion that consequentialist Each/We Dilemmas are of little practical significance.

12.6 Is Good Communication a Solution for Consequentialist Each/We Dilemmas?

Some people have suggested that if, in the real world, we were able to communicate with each other, when we found ourselves facing a consequentialist Each/We Dilemma, we would be able to agree on a collective strategy to bring about the best outcome. If this were right, then in those circumstances where enforceable agreements between agents were possible, there would be no real dilemma. On this suggestion, however interesting consequentialist Each/We dilemmas may be *theoretically*, they are of limited significance *practically*.[18]

There are two responses to this suggestion. The first is a practical response that can be stated briefly. The second is a theoretical response that requires much more discussion.

The practical response is simply that, as noted previously, there are multiple international aid donors, and literally countless NGOs, each with their own political agendas, priorities, constituencies, and so on. Hence, it is by no means evident that these many different groups could effectively communicate with each other, or that, even if they could, they would, in fact, come to a shared and mutually enforceable agreement as to what should be done to aid the needy.

This is especially problematic, practically, when one bears in mind that for a host of complicated social, cultural, historical, and bureaucratic reasons, to a large extent donor organizations have come to exist in order to donate—that is their raison d'être, so-to-speak. Given this, it will likely be very hard, practically speaking, to get donor organizations to agree to stop giving, even when they can see that their giving is part of a set of activities that is collectively doing more harm than good. Furthermore, the practical difficulty of coming to

---

[18] Both Ingmar Persson and Angus Deaton suggested this view in correspondence. Arthur Applbaum also suggested this view following my lecture "Being Good in a World of Need" (delivered, via Zoom, as the *Inaugural Mala and Solomon Kamm Lecture in Ethics* for Harvard's Edmund J. Safra Center for Ethics, February 11, 2021; available online at https://www.youtube.com/watch?v=CMHgZP4PwP8).

an enforceable agreement to limit or end aid efforts is exacerbated by the fact that recipient governments have learned how to effectively play different donors off against one another, to maximize the donations that they receive in order to promote their political agendas and promote the interests of their leaders and supporters.[19]

The theoretical response is to argue that the suggestion in question turns on the assumption that there must be an ascertainable "best" outcome, which an enforceable strategic decision procedure could bring about. However, as I argue in Rethinking the Good, this natural and intuitively plausible assumption may fail to recognize the true nature and structure of the good. As a result, both the assumption, and the suggestion, may be deeply mistaken.

The argument for this is lengthy and complex, spanning many hundreds of pages, and I cannot repeat that argument here. But the gist of the argument is that if, indeed, a principle like the Disperse Additional Burdens View is correct, as many believe, then in the cases I am describing there will be no best alternative for us to collectively settle on. Moreover, and more importantly, this is not for the familiar reason that there may be several alternatives that are equally best, or several alternatives that are all on a par. Rather, it is for the far more striking, and radical, reason that for *any* alternative that we might consider settling on, there will be another alternative available that we might settle on instead, that is clearly *better* than the one we were considering. Thus, even if we could communicate, and arrive at an enforceable strategic decision procedure for our collective action, there would be no satisfactory, non-arbitrary, solution to our predicament.

In Rethinking the Good, I argued that this is a feature of consequentialist Each/We Dilemmas that make them much more problematic, and intractable, than classical Prisoner's Dilemmas or Parfit's deontological Each/We Dilemmas. In fact, in *those* dilemmas the suggestion in question is plausible, as it will always be patently clear what strategy we should, and could, collectively agree

---

[19] The aid literature is filled with examples of the difficulty involved in getting aid organizations to stop giving, and of foreign governments playing different donors off against each other. See, for example, Deaton, The Great Escape; de Waal, Alex, Famine Crimes: Politics & the Disaster Relief Industry in Africa (Oxford: James Currey and Bloomington: Indiana University Press, 1997); Rieff, David, The Reproach of Hunger: Food, Justice, and Money in the Twenty-First Century (New York: Simon & Schuster, 2015); Maren, Michael, The Road to Hell: The Ravaging Effects of Foreign Aid and International Charity (New York: The Free Press, 1997); Moyo, Dambisa, Dead Aid: Why Aid Is Not Working and How There Is a Better Way for Africa (New York: Farrar, Straus and Giroux, 2009); Polman, Linda, The Crisis Caravan: What's Wrong with Humanitarian Aid? (New York: Metropolitan Books, 2010); and Dichter, Thomas W., Despite Good Intentions: Why Development Assistance to the Third World has Failed (Amherst: University of Massachusetts Press, 2003). (I am grateful to Angus Deaton for both raising the suggestion under discussion, and then offering this practical response to it, in correspondence.)

to, if we could communicate and effectively bind ourselves to an agreed course of action. However, as I argued in *Rethinking the Good*, that is decidedly not the case where consequentialist Each/We Dilemmas are involved.[20]

Let me briefly illustrate this point. Recall the classic Prisoner's Dilemma for individual rationality, where each prisoner is in a separate cell, and each can either confess or keep silent. If they each confess, they will each end up with ten years in prison; while if they each keep silent, they will each end up with two years in prison. That Prisoner's Dilemma *depends* on the inability of the two prisoners to communicate and to settle on an enforceable collective strategy. If the prisoners *could* communicate, and settle on an enforceable collective strategy, the dilemma would evaporate, and they would immediately agree on the obvious, stable, strategy of each keeping silent.

Similarly, consider one of the deontological Each/We Dilemmas mentioned earlier. Take, for example, the farmer's dilemma. Each farmer wants to raise as many crops as possible, to provide for his children as best he can. However, each farmer knows full well that if each farmer does what is individually best for his children, too many crops will be brought to market. If that happens, the price of the crops will crash and, collectively, the farmers will be doing what is worse for their children. Since no individual farmer could reasonably or morally compel the other farmers to limit their crop production, while he raised as many crops as possible, if communication and enforceable agreements between the farmers were possible, the farmers would all immediately agree that they should limit their production to keep the crop price high. Such an agreement would enable them, together, to do the best they could for their children, both rationally and morally, given their mutual predicament. Thus, here, too, we see that the sting of the deontological Each/We Dilemma is removed as soon as communication and an enforceable collective strategy becomes available.[21]

By contrast, consider again one of my previous examples of a consequentialist Each/We Dilemma. Each of 500,000 members of a group, C, must choose between pushing a red button or a blue button. If one pushes the blue button, each of 1,000,000 members of another group, B, will suffer *one*

---

[20] For the arguments supporting these claims, see *Rethinking the Good*, pp. 67–95.

[21] For deontologists, it might be enough for the strategy to be "enforceable" in the relevant sense, if the farmers made a conditional promise of the form "I promise to limit my crop production if each of the other farmers likewise promise to limit their crop production," since each would then have a deontological duty to keep their promise, based on *both* their duty to keep their promises and their duty to do whatever they can to benefit their children most. Rational self-interested agents who were not deontologists might require more for a strategy to be "enforceable" before they would have sufficient reason to act in accordance with it.

extra hour of great pain over the course of an 80-year life. If one pushes the red button, one unique member of yet another group, *A*, will suffer *sixteen* hours of great pain *every day* over the course of an 80-year life. Here, I believe, that even if the members of the *C* group could all communicate, and enforce any strategic course of action that they agreed upon, there would be no stable, non-arbitrary strategy that they should adopt. To the contrary, for any strategy that someone might propose, another would be available that would clearly be better.

Specifically, in accordance with the Disperse Additional Burdens View, it would be better if they collectively agreed to have one blue button pushed rather than none; better if they collectively agreed to have two blue buttons pushed rather than one; better if they collectively agreed to have three blue buttons pushed rather than two; and so on. That is, for *any n* between 0 and 499,999 the outcome would be *better* if, between the 500,000 members of *C*, $n + 1$ members pushed the blue button, and the rest pushed the red button, than if only *n* members pushed the blue button, and the rest pushed the red button. However, as we saw earlier, if *everyone* pushes the blue button, the outcome will be clearly and undeniably worse than if *no one* pushes the blue button, and they all push the red button.

Thus, we see that if, as many believe, the Disperse Additional Burdens View (or something like it) is correct, then it will be possible to face consequentialist Each/We Dilemmas that will not evaporate or lose their sting *even if* communication is available, along with the possibility of enforcing any strategic set of actions that might be mutually agreed upon. In this way, as indicated, consequentialist Each/We Dilemmas are more deeply troubling and intractable than standard Prisoner's Dilemmas or deontological Each/We Dilemmas, and this is so practically, as well as theoretically.

12.7 Reconsidering Deaton's View— A Troubling Possibility

Bearing the results of Sections 12.2–12.6 in mind, we are now, finally, in a better position to assess Deaton's view. This is because we can now carefully distinguish between two questions that Deaton, himself, perhaps conflates:

1. When is an individual, or collective group of individuals, doing *more* good than harm?
2. When is an individual, or collective, doing what they *should* or *ought* to do, by bringing about a morally desirable outcome?

Sometimes the answer to the latter question depends on the answer to the first. However, as our earlier discussion of the Disperse Additional Burdens View reveals, for most people those two questions can come apart. This is because, for most people, in determining whether an outcome is desirable, or preferable to another available alternative, we must pay attention not merely to the *sum total* of goods and harms which obtain in those outcomes, but also to the *distribution* of those goods and harms and the impact which that distribution has on the lives of the people in those outcomes.

Deaton believes that, collectively, we may be doing more harm than good in contributing to on-the-ground relief efforts in many of the world's poorest countries. But in saying this, he needn't deny that each of us, *individually*, could be promoting a desirable outcome by supporting such organizations, and hence that each of us, individually, has compelling moral reason to do so. However, as we have seen, even if that is so, that doesn't settle the question of whether we, collectively, should be contributing to such organizations. It is the latter question, I believe, on which Deaton is pushing us to focus.

To be clear, there are multiple groups of "we" that anyone will be a member of when they contribute to any given individual relief organization. One is the "we" that represents all, and only, the individuals who contribute to any *particular aid organization*. Let us call any such group of individuals, a bit awkwardly, a "*PAO we*." Another is the "we" that represents all, and only, the individuals who contribute to *any aid organization*. Let us call the group that includes all those individuals, also a bit awkwardly, the "*AAO we*." What I have argued is that it is possible that even if each person, individually, helps bring about the best outcome by contributing to the individual aid agencies that he or she does, and even if each PAO we, individually, brings about the best outcome available to it, it is still possible that, collectively, AAO we will be bringing about an outcome that we have compelling moral reason to avoid.[22]

I believe these considerations help illuminate Deaton's position, as well as most people's intuitive reactions to it. Deaton urges us to refrain from supporting international relief organizations that operate in many of the world's poorest countries. He does this largely on the grounds of the respect in which such organizations weaken the responsiveness of the local governments to

---

[22] I am grateful to Roger Crisp for suggesting that I provide this clarification. Note, given the logic of my argument, it is also possible that each individual contribution to a given aid organization does more good than harm, but that, collectively, *all* of the contributions to the organization produce a bad outcome; and also that each individual aid organization of a particular kind does more good than harm, but that, collectively, all of the aid organizations of that kind, together, produce a bad outcome. There are various ways in which this sort of consequentialist Each/We Dilemma might obtain.

their citizens. But most people find this line of reasoning very hard to believe. As individuals, each person thinks of the good that she could do with a contribution of a given amount. Given the claims that relief agencies often make about how little it costs to feed a child, vaccinate against TB, provide bednets for malaria prevention, and so on, it is natural for a contributor to think that her individual contribution would have a major positive impact on someone's life—it might even save a life, or several lives. (As we saw previously, in Chapter 4, and will return to shortly, this natural thought is often mistaken. However, given how relief agencies tend to advertise, it is common to think of one's contributions in this way.)

On the other hand, an individual contributor to an effective aid agency will quite plausibly think that the extent to which her individual contribution will weaken the responsiveness of the poor nation's government to its citizens will be ludicrously small. Correspondingly, she might naturally think that the actual negative effect that *her* contribution will have on each of the country's many citizens will be so small as to not even be measurable. Therefore, in accordance with the reasoning of the Disperse Additional Burdens View, it may seem clear that each individual is, in fact, likely to be promoting a morally desirable outcome, and hence that she has compelling moral reason to do so. Thus, it may seem clear that individuals should, in fact, contribute to effective aid agencies, precisely as Peter Singer and other Effective Altruists have urged.

This reasoning is cogent, so far as it goes. However, it misses Deaton's point. Deaton is not taking the ground-level perspective of what each individual, or even each individual aid organization, is or is not accomplishing via its individual actions. Deaton is taking the 30,000-foot view of things. He is looking at the net, collective, effect of vast numbers of individual acts by individual actors or aid organizations acting on their behalf. And what he sees, from that perspective, is that the *collective* negative effect of a vast number of individual actions is often quite substantial.

Moreover, as we have seen, this could be so even if, when considered alone, each individual action had only a tiny, insignificant negative impact on each of many people. Thus, while I, individually, may have virtually no impact on the responsiveness of a government to its citizens, we, together, can have a substantial negative impact on its responsiveness. And, of course, it is part of Deaton's contention that, ultimately, the responsiveness of a government to its citizens is a crucial component for substantial and lasting social and economic progress.

This is why Deaton urges us not to support international development agencies. His contention isn't, or at any rate needn't be, that each of us, individually, is bringing about a morally undesirable outcome. It is, rather, that we, collectively, are bringing about a morally undesirable outcome. As we have seen, if anti-additive-aggregationist principles like the Disperse Additional Burdens View are correct, the latter can be true even if the former is not.

If that is the case, then giving to international aid agencies in some of the world's poorest countries would be another example of a consequentialist Each/We Dilemma.

In his famous article, "Famine, Affluence, and Morality," Peter Singer implied that individuals of good conscience may have to do *more* than they otherwise would to aid the needy, given that not enough other people who are able to help actually do so. In holding this view, he never doubted that such people would be doing more good than harm both individually and collectively. Angus Deaton held the oppositive view. He believed that, in most cases, people who try to aid the needy in the world's poorest regions do more harm than good, both individually and collectively. However, we have seen that Deaton could accept Singer's view regarding what each of us ought to do individually, and still maintain that we, collectively, ought not to act as Singer thinks we should. Ironically, then, given Singer's contention, Deaton might claim that people of good conscience may, collectively, have to do *less* than they otherwise would to aid the needy in the world's poorest countries, given that so many other people are doing the same thing. Underlying this view is Deaton's belief that, *collectively*, the direct, indirect, and interaction effects of such efforts are undesirable.

12.8 Challenging Two Assumptions

In this section, I present reasons to question the two assumptions that I made, for the sake of argument, in Section 12.2. Recall that I made those assumptions, because they were favorable to the response to Deaton's worry that was offered in Section 12.1 to which this chapter has been responding. As we will see, Deaton's argument is only strengthened if one rejects those assumptions.[23]

I begin with the first assumption, that when one donates to an effective aid agency, one's particular donation *itself* has a major positive impact on one or more people; for example, by curing some particular person of some deadly disease, and thereby significantly extending that person's life by many years.

---

[23] I am grateful to Jeff McMahan and Shelly Kagan whose comments, in discussion and correspondence, led me to write this section.

Many international aid agencies convey this impression when soliciting donations. However, in fact, there are relatively few cases where this is true. As noted in Chapter 4, it is rarely, if ever, the case that one's donation is kept separate from other donations and used to address the dire predicament of any particular individual or small group of individuals. Rather, the funds that one donates typically go into a general operating budget, where they are mingled with everyone else's donations. So, as we saw in Section 4.3, it makes most sense to think that one's donation is helping to pay for a small portion of all of the agency's operating expenses—salaries, rent, utilities, stamps, advertising, food, transportation costs, etc.—and also for a small portion of each of the activities in which the agency is engaged. Accordingly, it also makes sense to think that one's contribution is aiding each of the many people that the aid agency is benefiting, albeit only by a very small amount.

For example, suppose that the total contributions that an aid agency receives in a year is, say, $50,000,000 dollars and, including all of its operating expenses, it is able to use those funds to prolong the lives of, say, 10,000 people by an average of 30 years, at an average cost of $5,000 per person. Then, arguably, if one contributes $5,000 to that aid agency, it makes more sense to think that your contribution has helped to prolong the lives of each of 10,000 people by 1.1 days, than to think that your contribution has prolonged the life of some particular person by 30 years.[24]

Accordingly, once one drops the first favorable assumption, it appears that one's choice might well involve helping many people a small amount, while also, if Deaton is right, harming a large number of people by a small amount (per Deaton, virtually the entire country's population will be negatively impacted by weakening the responsiveness of the government to its citizens). In that case, a principle like the Disperse Additional Burdens View would no longer be applicable. Instead, an additive-aggregationist approach to summing harms and benefits might seem more appropriate for assessing the overall desirability of one's action, and it would no longer be evident that one was,

---

[24] Assuming that your contribution was pooled with the other money received, so that, in essence, your contribution helps pay a small portion of all of the agency's efforts, one arrives at the figure of 1.1 days of life extension for 10,000 people as follows. Your contribution of $5,000 was one ten thousandth of the total $50,000,000 spent by the agency. With their expenditures, the agency was able to prolong the life of each of 10,000 people by 30 years, which comes to a total of 109,500,000 extra days lived due to the agency's efforts (10,000*30*365). Since your contribution was one ten thousandth of the agency's expenditures, you can be credited for one ten thousandth of the good done, which, given our assumptions, comes to 10,950 extra days lived (109,500,000/10,000). Spreading your share of the good out across the 10,000 people who were positively impacted by the agency's efforts, this comes to an average of 1.1 (rounding up from 1.095) extra days of life that your contribution made possible for each of the 10,000 people the agency helped (10,950/10,000).

individually, bringing about a better outcome by contributing to an aid agency. After all, even if, as per our example, one was helping as many as ten *thousand* people with one's contribution of $5,000, one might also be harming as many as 15, 17, 21, 43, 50, 81, or 105 *million* people if one's aid agency was operating in Somalia, Zambia, Niger, Uganda, Kenya, the Democratic Republic of Congo, or Ethiopia, respectively.

The numbers here are merely suggestive. Clearly, no definitive conclusions can be drawn until one fills in the details about precisely how many people would be benefited or harmed, and to what extent, by one's charitable contribution. However, is not hard to imagine that even quite small harms to millions of people might outweigh larger, though still fairly small, benefits to thousands of people. We see, then, that once one drops the first assumption, it becomes more plausible for Deaton to claim not merely that, *collectively*, we may be doing more harm than good, and bringing about a worse outcome, by contributing to aid agencies, but also that, *individually*, each of us may be doing more harm than good, and bringing about a worse outcome, by contributing to aid agencies. However, how often that is the case remains an open question that is, I believe, difficult to resolve.

Let us turn next to the second favorable assumption made in presenting the argument of Section 12.2; namely, that no individual donation to an effective aid agency will have more than a negligible negative impact on any particular individual's life, due to its reducing the responsiveness of a government to its citizens. On reflection, this assumption is also dubious.

Let us continue to assume that the impact of one's individual contribution on a government's responsiveness to its citizens will be small. It does not follow from that that there will be no significant impact on any individual citizens. Consider, for example, the many ways in which a responsive government provides for its citizens: infrastructure, energy, defense, healthcare, pest eradication, and so on. Assume that one's individual contribution leads an aid agency to take on a task that the government might otherwise have undertaken on its own. Suppose this leads the government to wonder whether other aid agencies will perform similar tasks, and to convene a meeting to discuss whether the government should leave such problems for outsiders to address. Suppose the meeting only lasts fifteen minutes, and that ultimately the government decides to proceed roughly as it was originally planning to. Surely, one might argue, this would be a case where one's negative impact on the responsiveness of a government to its citizens was very small.

Still, suppose that the meeting delayed the Prime Minister's signature on a host of bills, so that those bills were signed one day later. Again, this might appear to be a very slight impact on the government's responsiveness to its citizens. However, that could mean that a needed road improvement, energy grid, weapons system, vaccine delivery, pesticide spray, and so on were all delayed by a single day. That, in turn, could mean that individuals died, because one day short of interventions that would have prevented their demise. For example, perhaps they spun out of control on a dangerous curve, had a lifesaving machine fail in a blackout, were betrayed by an antiquated weapon, failed to receive a lifesaving vaccine, were bitten by a mosquito carrying malaria, and so on.

The reality is that tiny reductions in the responsiveness of a government to its citizens may only be correlated with tiny, perhaps imperceptible, harms for most of the population. However, such reductions in responsiveness can also have unpredictable harms of the largest magnitude on a few, unfortunate, people. In that case, if one continues to make the first favorable assumption, one's contribution to an aid agency may significantly benefit a few, but, due to reducing the responsiveness of the government to its citizens—even by only a very tiny amount—it may also *significantly* harm a few *as well as* insignificantly harm most of the population. It is just that those who are significantly benefited by the aid agency's actions are *readily identifiable* in a way that those who are significantly harmed are not.

This would again make Deaton's position stronger, as he could argue that, in fact, the Disperse Additional Burdens View does not apply in the real-world cases of aid, and that the negative impact that aid efforts have on government responsiveness opens up the real possibility that contributions to aid agencies may produce more harm than good, and bring about a worse outcome, individually, as well as collectively.

Moreover, if one rejects the first favorable assumption, then Deaton could appeal to the Disperse Additional Burdens View in support of the view that contributions to aid agencies are likely to bring about a worse outcome, individually, even if one grants that the sum total of benefits is greater than the sum total of harms. The thought, here, would be that one's individual contribution is likely to be helping a fairly large number of people by a small amount. However, it is also likely to have a significantly negative impact on a few people (due to the ripple effects on actual people of even tiny reductions in a government's responsiveness) and the relative distribution of dispersed benefits and concentrated harms is *itself* likely to be enough to make the outcome worse, not even counting the myriad of tiny ways in which the vast majority of the population may be negatively impacted by the government's being slightly less responsive to its citizens.

12.9 Summary

In this chapter, I have tried to illuminate Deaton's worry that contributors to on-the-ground international aid agencies may be acting undesirably. To do this, I first argued for the plausibility of anti-additive-aggregationist principles like the Disperse Additional Burdens View. I then showed that if such principles are correct, there can be consequentialist Each/We Dilemmas, and suggested that large-scale giving to international aid organizations might exemplify such a dilemma. In particular, I showed that Deaton could be correct in thinking that contributions to aid agencies could be doing more harm than good, and bringing about a worse outcome, collectively, *even if* each individual contribution was bringing about a better outcome.

In doing this, I assumed that Deaton could be right that, due to the negative impact on a government's responsiveness to its citizens, the total harms produced by all aid agencies might outweigh the total benefits produced by all aid agencies, both individually and collectively. However, I showed that even if this were the case, this would not entail, as Deaton may have thought, that each individual was bringing about a worse outcome in contributing to aid agencies, or even that any individuals were doing do, for that matter.

In developing my position, I made two assumptions favorable to the view of those who believe that surely individuals who contribute to effective aid agencies are producing morally desirable outcomes. The first assumption was that individual contributions produce a significant amount of good for particular individuals. The second assumption was that even if an individual contribution does weaken the responsiveness of a government to its citizens, it will only do this to a very slight extent and, as such, it will only have a tiny negative impact on any individual citizens.

I concluded the chapter by suggesting that both of the assumptions in question are dubious, and that this only strengthens Deaton's position. Rejecting the two assumptions does nothing to weaken the plausibility of the claim that we, collectively, may be bringing about a worse outcome by contributing to aid agencies, even if, individually, none of us is doing so. On the other hand, rejecting the two assumptions does weaken the plausibility of the claim that we can be confident that individual contributions to aid agencies are desirable, because of how the harms and benefits of such contributions are distributed in the world's poorest regions.

13

Further Objections to Deaton's Worry and Some Responses

In Chapter 11, I presented Angus Deaton's worry that contributions to on-the-ground international aid efforts may do more harm than good, by undermining a government's responsiveness to its citizens—a crucial component, Deaton believes, of long-term social and economic progress. In Chapter 12, I considered one natural response to Deaton's worry; namely, that even if there are *some* individual aid organizations whose overall impact is morally undesirable, surely there must be *others* whose overall impacts are morally desirable. Thus, we should concentrate on supporting those organizations in addressing global need. I suggested that this response fails to fully appreciate Deaton's claim. More particularly, I argued that even if each person, individually, only supported aid efforts that were morally desirable, it could still be the case, as Deaton believes, that the overall collective impact of such efforts was morally undesirable. In this chapter, I present further objections to Deaton's view, and the considerations I offered in support of it. I also offer some responses to those objections.

In Section 13.1, I discuss Peter Singer's suggestion that Effective Altruists can avoid my defense of Deaton's worry, because they should reject the Disperse Additional Burdens View. I contend that rejecting the Disperse Additional Burdens View will require "biting a bullet" that most people will find too big to swallow. More importantly, I show that Deaton's worry does not depend on the defense I offer of it. To the contrary, I show that Deaton's worry is even more compelling if, as Singer suggests, one rejects the Disperse Additional Burdens View. Moreover, this is especially true for those who follow Expected Utility Theory, as many Effective Altruists do.

In Section 13.2, I consider several views that challenge the scope of Deaton's worry. Some claim that there are charitable organizations that work directly to improve the responsiveness of governments to their citizens, and that those charities are worthy of our support. Others insist that even if Deaton's worry

Being Good in a World of Need. Larry S. Temkin, Oxford University Press. © Larry S. Temkin 2022.
DOI: 10.1093/oso/9780192849977.003.0013

applies to many, or even most, international aid organizations, it almost certainly does not apply to the top-rated aid organizations endorsed by Effective Altruists organizations like GiveWell. I note that such claims might be true, and express the hope that they are. However, I offer several reasons to take such claims with a grain of salt.

Among other things, I note that outside efforts to get governments to be more responsive to their people raise the issues of paternalism, autonomy, and respect discussed in Chapter 10. I also note that even if we can be confident that contributions to top-rated aid organizations have an overall *expected value* that is positive, that does not mean that we can be confident that contributions to such aid organizations will do more good than harm, or even that they will do any (substantial) good at all. In addition, I question whether we *can* be confident that the expected value of contributions to the top-ranked aid organizations is positive, given how many important questions have not yet been answered that are relevant to the matter. Finally, I suggest that the very success of some international aid organizations may prompt other aid organizations to arise which, though created with the best of intentions, may do more harm than good. In this way, effective aid organizations could inadvertently lead to overall negative outcomes in the world's poorest regions *even if* those organizations, considered just by themselves, did more good than harm, both individually and collectively.

In Section 13.3, I suggest that Deaton's worry raises deontological concerns that are distinct from the consequentialist concern of whether, together, we are doing more harm than good by contributing to international aid efforts. Echoing the remarks of Section 7.3, I suggest that contributions to aid efforts may be deontologically problematic, if, in essence, they involve harming some people—by undermining government responsiveness—for the sake of benefiting others.

In Section 13.4, I consider Deaton's worry from the perspective of this book's pluralistic approach to global need. I suggest that even if Deaton is right that, collectively, aid efforts do more harm than good, this does not settle the question of whether we should support such efforts, as Effective Altruists and most development economists—including Deaton—seem to presume.

Section 13.5 offers some final remarks regarding Deaton's worry, and the lessons to be learned from it.

This chapter is likely to be of particular interest to philosophers, Effective Altruists, and experts on global aid. Others may want to dip in and out of the various sections, depending on their interests, before continuing on to Chapter 14.

13.1 Singer's Response to My Defense of Deaton

Peter Singer questions the defense that I have offered of Deaton's worry, on the grounds that it depends on the Disperse Additional Burdens View. He suggests that even if Effective Altruists are not themselves classical total utilitarians, they should reject the Disperse Additional Burdens View, and so need not be concerned about my argument on Deaton's behalf.[1]

In response to this objection, I have two main points. First, I have been lecturing on the nature of the good for three decades now, to thousands of people in many different countries. In my experience, the vast majority of people—well over 95 percent of those I have informally polled about the matter—find anti-additive-aggregationist principles like the Disperse Additional Burdens View compelling for contexts like the ones I am discussing here. So, while Singer can claim that Effective Altruists should reject the Disperse Additional Burdens View, the fact is that doing so will require "biting a bullet" that most people will find deeply unpalatable and difficult to swallow.[2] Indeed, as the preceding discussion is intended to suggest, I believe that rejecting the anti-additive-aggregationist view that underlies the Disperse Additional Burdens View is akin to accepting Parfit's Repugnant Conclusion, and allowing one lollipop lick, for each of many people, to outweigh someone enduring an entire lifetime of pain and misery. I am not sure how many Effective Altruists will be comfortable doing that. More importantly, I think it would be a mistake for them to do so.

Second, and more significantly, while my defense of Deaton's position depends on the Disperse Additional Burdens View, Deaton's conclusion doesn't. To the contrary, if one rejects the anti-additive-aggregationist position, which underlies the Disperse Additional Burdens View, that creates a faster, easier route to Deaton's conclusion. Let me explain.

Deaton believes that, together, the actions of aid agencies undermine the responsiveness of certain governments in some of the world's poorest countries in ways that make those countries worse off, on balance, than they would be if those actions didn't obtain. The plausibility of Deaton's claim depends on the many ways in which a country's population may be substantially worse off if they have an unresponsive government (to which I will return in the concluding chapter). Notice, however, that a government may become

---

[1] Singer raised this objection in correspondence.
[2] See Temkin, Larry, *Rethinking the Good: Moral Ideals and the Nature of Practical Reasoning* (New York: Oxford University Press, 2012), especially Chapters 2, 3, 5, and 10.

significantly unresponsive to its citizens via numerous steps each of which, individually, only makes the government a tiny bit less responsive than it would otherwise have been; and likewise, the large majority of a population may be significantly worse off as a result of numerous steps each of which, individually, only decreases each person's level by a tiny amount. Notice, further, that even tiny losses in wellbeing can add up to very significant amounts if they are incurred by millions of people if one accepts the sort of additive-aggregationist-approach that Singer seemingly favors.

Thus, on Singer's view, even if my individual contribution to an aid agency does something as important as saving several people's lives, my contribution could easily lead to more harm than good. For that to happen, on Singer's view, it only needs to be the case that the actions of the aid agency in some ways, directly or indirectly, undermine the responsiveness of the government to its citizens, and that, as a result, a very large number of people has its overall wellbeing decreased, even if only slightly.

I add, here, that since most Effective Altruists focus on the *expected* value of actions, Deaton's argument may only require a fairly small possibility that my contributions to an aid agency will contribute to undermining the responsiveness of the government to its citizens. This could be so if the agency's actions positively impact a relatively small number of people, while a non-responsive government negatively impacts millions of people. In such cases, the expected disutility of the latter could well outweigh the expected utility of the former, even if the likelihood of the positive results is significantly greater than the likelihood of the negative results, and even if the likely size of the benefits for the few, if they are realized, would be much greater than the likely size of the losses for the many if they are realized.

In sum, Singer is right that my argument for the possibility of consequentialist Each/We Dilemmas turned on accepting an anti-additive-aggregationist position like the Disperse Addition Burdens View, for certain contexts. I showed how, on such a view, Deaton could be right that collectively, we might do more harm than good, even if, as most of us believe, each of us, individually, promotes a desirable outcome by contributing to aid agencies. However, Deaton's view does not turn on the Disperse Additional Burdens View. To the contrary, if one rejects the Disburse Additional Burdens View, as Singer claims that Effective Altruists should, this simply makes it more plausible for Deaton to claim that contributions to aid agencies will often do more harm than good *individually, as well as collectively*, because of the way that aid agencies undermine the responsiveness of governments to their citizens, and the vast numbers of people negatively impacted by unresponsive governments.

13.2 Challenging the Scope of Deaton's Worry

Let me turn, next, to a second line of criticism offered by Michelle Hutchinson.[3] Hutchinson doesn't deny that there is something to Deaton's position. However, she believes that it is limited in scope. In particular, she insists that there are certain, and perhaps many, effective aid organizations that do more good than bad, even in terms of the concerns that Deaton has. Thus, Hutchinson believes, there is good reason for Effective Altruists, and others, to support such organizations.

In support of her view, Hutchinson points out that some aid organizations focus their efforts on effecting positive political changes in countries where the current political situation is in desperate need of improvement. Some of these efforts aim to promote democracy. Others promote improvements in policing, the judicial system, and the rule of law. Others promote the protection of basic human rights. Others seek to reduce systemic corruption. And so on. Arguably, all of these efforts directly work towards *improving* the responsiveness of a government to its citizens' basic needs and fundamental rights.

Some of these efforts take place at the state or national levels. However, often the aid efforts that are most effective take place at the local level, where efforts are taken to try to ensure that local laws, leaders, and councils *are* responsive to the neediest people directly affected by their actions. Generally, these include the aged, young, poor, handicapped, ill, women, persecuted minorities, members of low castes, and so on.

Now, as it happens, Hutchinson believes that many of the aid organizations in question *are* highly successful in promoting the very goal that Deaton has argued is necessary for there to be substantial, long-term social, political, and economic progress. Correspondingly, Hutchinson believes that those organizations are highly likely to be doing more good than harm, and to be worthy of our support. She would also hold, I believe, that similar aid efforts should be replicated in other regions of great need. However, presumably Hutchinson would contend that even if (contrary to fact, in her judgment) none of the current aid organizations were effectively promoting the responsiveness of local, state, and national governments to their citizens, that would be no argument for abandoning the needy. At most, it would be a reason for spending our time, effort, and resources developing aid organizations that

---

[3] In correspondence, and also during the question period after my Third Uehiro Lecture (Oxford University, November 10, 2017).

would effectively promote the responsiveness of governments to the plight of their neediest citizens in the world's poorest regions.

A closely related position is echoed by others in the Effective Altruism community. Nick Beckstead, for example, thinks that even if Deaton and others are right that there are many aid efforts that collectively do more harm than good, he doubts that this is generally true. More particularly, his "intuition" is that even if there are subtle negative effects on governance, the overall collective effects of GiveWell's top-rated charities are positive. Accordingly, he believes that one can safely support giving to such charities, and that those who are concerned to aid the world's needy should do so.[4] Similarly, Holden Karnofsky, one of GiveWell's Co-Founders, has claimed that there is, and should be, a lack of controversy over well-targeted aid of the sort that GiveWell recommends, contending that "the arguments of aid critics—important though they may be in many contexts—[don't] provide grounds for . . . an argument" against contributing to GiveWell's top charities.[5]

Hutchinson, Beckstead, Karnofsky and others may be right about these claims. I hope they are. Moreover, I have no empirical evidence of my own to show that they are not. Even so, I think there are reasons to be cautious, and to take such claims, often expressed with unwavering confidence, with a grain of salt.

Let me begin with two worries about Hutchinson's conviction that we can safely support aid organizations whose very aim is to foster good governance. First, I do not doubt that there are some ways that "we" in the West can work to try to help foster conditions that are more conducive to good governance in some of the world's poorest regions. In fact, I shall try to develop this point further in my concluding chapter. However, it is not clear, to me anyway, that we can best do that, effectively, by working on the ground, in the world's poorest regions, to accomplish that goal, rather than, say, by changing the prevailing political, legal, and economic rules of international engagement.

For reasons already given in this book, when "we" in the West enter a region with a different social, political, cultural, religious, ethical, and historical

---

[4] Beckstead conveyed this position in correspondence. Many others sympathetic with the aims of Effective Altruism have also conveyed similar sentiments to me in conversations, including Peter Singer, Shelly Kagan, Jeff McMahan, Will MacAskill, Hilary Greaves, Theron Pummer, Tim Campbell, and Tyler John.

[5] "The lack of controversy over well-targeted aid," *The GiveWell Blog*, posted November 6, 2015, updated July 26, 2016, URL: https://blog.givewell.org/2015/11/06/the-lack-of-controversy-over-well-targeted-aid/, accessed July 10, 2019. I am grateful to Nick Beckstead for calling this blogpost to my attention.

context than our own, the possibility of serious misinterpretations, misunderstandings, and damaging meddling arises. This is especially likely to occur whenever "we" try to set up programs to push, cajole, entice, or "incentivize" "them" to be more like "us."

All the worries that I previously raised in Chapter 10 concerning paternalism, autonomy, and respect are relevant here. So, too, is the concern that if we genuinely want a government to be more responsive to its citizens, then *we* should not be dictating the terms, or trying to unduly influence or shape the manner and extent to which it does so. After all, thanks to a combination of carrots and sticks that an aid agency employs to promote its ends, there will always be the very real risk that, in essence, an aid agency's efforts to promote better responsiveness of a government to its citizens is likely to result in the government responding to the aid agency and *its* views about how the government should be responsive to their citizens, rather than to the citizens themselves, and *their* views about what the government needs to do to be responsive to their interests and needs.

My worry, here, is that there may be serious limits on the sort of things that "we," in the West, can do for non-Westerners. Distributing food and medicines to those who need them may lie squarely within those limits. But effectively promoting the terms of engagement between a government and its citizens, and the responsiveness of the government to its *citizens*, rather than to *us*, may, alas, lie beyond them. Unfortunately, there may be an asymmetry in the way that an on-the-ground international aid agency can impact the responsiveness of a government to its citizens. Having a negative impact may be all too common, even if wholly unintended, while having a positive impact may be difficult to achieve, even if one is assiduously aiming at it.

The preceding worry is defeasible. No doubt there have been some cases where one can point to concrete gains in the responsiveness of a government to its citizens thanks to the efforts of intervening aid agencies. However, whether such efforts can be generally scaled up, and effectively employed to promote more responsive governments throughout the regions of greatest need, and at the state and national, as well as local, levels is much less clear. Perhaps they can. But perhaps not.

This brings me to my second point. Like Hutchinson, I believe that there have been targeted efforts at the local level in some of the world's poorest regions, which have improved the responsiveness of local leaders to some of the neediest people in those regions. Still, those same efforts might indirectly weaken the responsiveness of state and national governments, even if only by a small amount. In that case, we might once again be in a situation where the actions of an aid agency directly lead to significant per person positive effects, at the local level, but which only impact a relatively small number of people; while at the same time indirectly leading to small per person negative effects, at the state or national levels, but which impact a vastly larger number of people. Unfortunately, we might be acutely aware of the former, significant effects, and oblivious, or only obscurely aware, of the latter, small effects.

If that occurs, we might confidently claim, as Hutchinson does, that the efforts of such an aid agency have been desirable. Correspondingly, we might also claim that each of us, individually, has strong moral reason to do so, and hence that each of us, individually, *should* support such agencies. Moreover, if a position like the Disperse Additional Burdens View were correct, we might be entirely correct in making such claims. Even so, as should be clear by now, if that is what is going on when we support such agencies, it could still be the case that, *collectively*, we and the agencies in question, are doing more harm than good.

So, it is not enough, to support Hutchinson's position, that we can point to aid agencies that directly aim at, and have made significant strides in, increasing the responsiveness of local governments to their citizens. We must be confident that those positive effects have not been offset elsewhere in the system, by decreases in the responsiveness of state or national governments impacting vastly larger numbers of people. It is unclear, to me anyway, that we have much evidence that bears on the latter question one way or the other. However, in the absence of such evidence, there is, I believe, reason to be cautious about the matter.

Let me turn, next, to Beckstead and Karnofsky's confidence that the aid efforts of GiveWell's top-rated charities are doing more good than harm. Again, they might be right. And I genuinely hope they are. But it is hard for me to see how they can be so sure of their position. Let me explain why.

Consider, for example, the case of *SCI Foundation* (formerly known as the Schistosomiasis Control Initiative), a deworming organization. The SCI Foundation has been one of GiveWell's top-rated charities since their first set of recommendations came out in 2008. I have, myself, contributed to SCI for a number of years, based on GiveWell's recommendation. Moreover, my confidence in the organization was only increased after I had the good fortune of meeting SCI's Founder, Professor Alan Fenwick OBE, at the launch of the Birmingham (United Kingdom) Chapter of Giving What We Can. Professor Fenwick is an impressive man. He is smart, hardworking, and clearly dedicated to helping the needy. He comes across as completely trustworthy, and his sincere belief in the importance of his work instills confidence in others. Still, as GiveWell itself makes plain, there are many reasons to worry about the effectiveness of deworming.

Here are a few worries that GiveWell calls attention to in its commendable transparency about the topic of deworming.

- There is strong evidence that administration of drugs reduces worm loads, but weaker evidence on the causal relationship between reducing worm loads and improved life outcomes.
- Evidence for the impact of deworming on short-term general health is thin. We would guess that deworming has small impacts on weight, but the evidence for its impact on other health outcomes is weak.
- A series of...experiment[s]...finds that reducing worm infection loads during childhood can have a significant later impact on income. We find these studies to constitute evidence that is suggestive, though not con-clusive or necessarily representative (the intensity of worm infections in this study was substantially heavier than the intensity of worm infections in most contexts where deworming is carried out today).
- Attempts to estimate the cost-effectiveness of deworming within the disability-adjusted life-year (DALY) framework have been problematic. In 2011, GiveWell found the figures published by the World Health Organization to be off by ~100x due to errors and flawed in other ways even once corrected.
- After school-based mass deworming in...Kenya, in the late 1990s, kids came to school more.... However, children did not do better on stand-ardized tests.
- Two respected organizations, Cochrane and the Campbell Collaboration, have systematically reviewed the relevant studies and found little reliable evidence that mass deworming does good. Indeed, more strongly, Cochrane's review of the deworming literature found "quite substantial evidence that deworming programmes do not show benefit."
- The evidence on deworming is complicated and ambiguous.[6]

---

[6] The first four bullet points are taken from "Combination Deworming (Mass Drug Administration Targeting Both Schistosomiasis and Soil-Transmitted Helminths)," *GiveWell*, posted December 2013, updated January 2018, URL: https://www.givewell.org/international/technical/programs/deworming, accessed, July 31, 2020. The last three bullet points are taken from David Roodman's "Why I Mostly Believe in Worms," *The GiveWell Blog*, posted December 6, 2016, updated February 14, 2020, URL: https://blog.givewell.org/2016/12/06/why-i-mostly-believe-in-worms/, accessed, July 31, 2020.

Despite all the above worries, GiveWell notes that "our best guess is that deworming is comparably cost-effective to our priority programs."[7] But, again, in a credit to their transparency, GiveWell cautions that "Cost-effectiveness calculations are extremely sensitive to many assumptions."[8] Indeed, in a separate blogpost on the topic they note the following:

- While cost-effectiveness analysis represents our best guess, it's also subject to substantial uncertainty; some of its results are a function of highly debatable, difficult-to-estimate inputs.
- Sometimes these inputs are largely subjective.... But even objective inputs are uncertain.
- Our deworming models are very uncertain, due to the complexity of the evidence base and the long time horizons over which we expect the potential benefits to be realized.
- We [GiveWell] make a "replicability adjustment" for deworming. To account for the fact that the consumption increase in a major study we rely on may not hold up if it were replicated. If you're skeptical that such a large income increase would occur, given the limited evidence for short-term health benefits and generally unexpected nature of the findings, you may think that the effect the study measured either wasn't real, wasn't driven by deworming, or relied on an atypical characteristic shared by the study population but not likely to be found among recipients of the intervention today. This adjustment is not well-grounded in data.[9]

In light of the preceding, one might wonder why SCI has always been one of GiveWell's top-rated charities. In brief, the answer is that one important study, which tracked down subjects ten years after they had received extra deworming treatments, "found that the average 2.4 years of extra deworming given to the treatment group led to 15% higher non-agricultural earnings.... The earnings gain appeared concentrated in wages...which rose 31%. That's a huge benefit for a few dollars of deworming, especially if it accrued for years. It is what drives GiveWell's recommendations of deworming charities."[10]

[7] "Combination Deworming."   [8] "Combination Deworming."
[9] These bullet points are taken from James Snowden's "How uncertain is our cost effectiveness analysis?" *The GiveWell Blog*, posted December 22, 2017, updated December 29, 2017, URL: https://blog.givewell.org/2017/12/22/uncertain-cost-effectiveness-analysis/, accessed July 31, 2020.
[10] Roodman, "Why I Mostly Believe in Worms."

To be sure, as GiveWell clearly recognizes, some respectable organizations later cast doubt on these results; there is little evidence for significant short-term gains due to deworming (for example, educational or health gains); it is hard to see how there can be significant long-term gains in the absence of significant short-term gains; and, more particularly, there is no clear causal mechanism that would explain how deworming might account for the reported income increases. Even so, deworming treatments are incredibly cheap (roughly fifty U.S. cents per treatment), they only need to be administered twice a year, they can be easily distributed to millions of people, and those treated experience few, if any, negative health effects from the treatment. Given all this, then, if there is *any* chance that deworming might lead to future earnings increases—increases which might persist over the course of someone's work life, perhaps another 30–45 years—then even if the earnings increases are not as robust as the key study suggested they might be, they might be well worth the cost of deworming programs.

This is straightforward cost-effectiveness reasoning. The costs of deworming are extremely low, and the downsides, seemingly, minuscule. But there are upsides, and possibly huge upsides—income gains for millions of people over the entire course of their working lives. So, even if there is only a small chance that deworming programs will positively impact people's lives, it seems a chance worth taking. This is why, despite all the uncertainty that GiveWell forthrightly acknowledges regarding the benefits of deworming, "deworming is comparably cost-effective to our [other] priority programs."

The preceding is an important reminder of what Beckstead and Karnofsky's confidence in GiveWell's top-rated charities amounts to. They are *not* saying that one can be confident that a contribution to SCI will do more good than harm. In fact, they are not even saying that one can be confident that a contribution to SCI will do *any good at all*. What they are saying is that one can be confident that the *expected value* of a contribution to SCI is positive, and comparable with other high priority aid programs. The latter, if true, may be important, but it is very different than the former.

Some aid proponents urge people to make substantial sacrifices of their own wellbeing, or that of their children, on behalf of those less fortunate. I understand the moral force of such appeals. In fact, I have made similar appeals, myself, many times over the years. Still, it is one thing to ask that such sacrifices be made, to support charities that we can be confident will save innocent lives with the contributions we make. It is another thing to ask that such sacrifices be made to support charities that *may*, ten years from now, increase some people's incomes, but which may also have *no* significant short-

or long-term effects whatsoever; and where the likelihood of the latter being true may be greater, and perhaps substantially so, than the likelihood of the former being true.

So far, I have suggested that, given GiveWell's own, forthright, analysis of the possible benefits and harms of deworming programs, one cannot be confident that a contribution to SCI, or any of the other deworming programs for that matter, will do any good at all. A fortiori, one cannot be confident that it will do more good than harm. However, can one at least be confident, with Beckstead and Karnofsky, that the *expected value* of deworming efforts is positive? Perhaps. But, again, perhaps not.

Are the deworming programs promoting brain or character drains? Are they operating in areas dominated by gangs, warlords, or tyrants? If so, is there a chance that corrupt leaders will find a way, directly or indirectly, to benefit from the aid operations of the deworming programs, in ways that strengthen them, and enable them to perpetuate rights violations or advance unsavory agendas? Is there a chance that the deworming programs will help undermine the responsiveness of the local or national governments to their citizens, in ways that may adversely affect the entire population over which they have control? In the absence of definitive answers to these questions, it is hard to see how one can be completely confident that the overall expected value of deworming programs is positive.

Let me next raise a worry which applies equally to Hutchinson's, Beckstead's, and Karnofsky's claims. As we have noted previously, the aid world is massive. It consists of innumerable organizations of every type and size including, for example: bilateral and multilateral government aid programs like *USAID* (U.S. Agency for International Development), *PEPFAR* (the President's Emergency Plan for AIDS Relief), *DAC* (the Development Assistance Committee) and the European Union's *OECD* (Organisation for Economic Co-operation and Development); international financial organizations like the World Bank, the International Monetary Fund, and the Islamic Development Bank; multi-national organizations and their agencies like *UNICEF* (the United Nations Children's Fund), *WFB* (the Word Food Program), *CARE* (the Cooperative for Assistance and Relief Everywhere), and *UNHCR* (the (Office of the) United Nations High Commissioner for Refugees); foundations like the Bill and Melinda Gates Foundation, the Stichting INGKA Foundation, the Ford Foundation, and the Rockefeller Foundation; large secular NGOs like Oxfam, Save the Children, Doctors Without Borders, the International Federation of Red Cross and Red Crescent Societies; large religious NGOs like Catholic Charities, *WCC* (the World Council of Churches), World Vision, Compassion International, and Food for the Poor; and countless small "mom and pop" NGOs.

Now serious criticisms have been leveled at many aid agencies of these different kinds. And Hutchinson, Beckstead, and Karnofsky are well aware of these criticisms. Moreover, I take it that all three are willing to grant that, unfortunately, some, and perhaps many, aid efforts backfire, in the long term, in the sense of doing more harm than good. Generally, when this happens, it is the result of some combination of arrogance, stupidity, ignorance, fraud, laziness, lack of coordination, mistakes, misunderstandings, intervening evil agents, bad luck, and/or indirect negative effects that were both unintended and unforeseen, such as the weakening of government responsiveness to its citizens.

However, as common as such failings may be, what Hutchinson, Beckstead, Karnofsky, and other Effective Altruists do not find even remotely plausible is that they beset *every* aid organization to *such* an extent that *every* one of them does more harm than good. More particularly, they believe that the serious criticisms that have been legitimately leveled at so many aid efforts entirely miss the mark when it comes to the *most effective* aid organizations, such as those recommended by GiveWell. Hence, they believe that Deaton is engaging in dangerous and wrongheaded hyperbole when he suggests that people like Peter Singer are doing more harm than good by urging people to give to the most effective aid agencies.

This view may seem obviously true. And perhaps it is. However, let's unpack it a bit further.

I take it that advocates of this line believe the following. First, the most effective aid organizations are doing more good than harm. Second, this is so by any reasonable criteria. Third, in particular, the most effective aid organizations will not only be doing more good than harm by the lights of anti-additive-aggregationist principles like the Disperse Additional Burdens View, they will be doing more good than harm by the lights of simple additive-aggregationist principles, of the sort that Singer favors.

This will be clearest in the cases where the aid agency is positively affecting a very large number of people, each to a very large extent, while only negatively affecting a very small number of people, if any, to a very small extent, if at all. But there are also other ways this might be true. Indeed, Effective Altruists are likely to point out that even if Deaton is right that there are many ways in which aid organizations might undermine the responsiveness of certain governments to their citizens, one cannot ignore the respects in which the reverse may also be true.

For example, arguably, such standard charitable goals as feeding the hungry, curing the sick, decreasing infant and maternal mortality, improving infrastructure, increasing employment, empowering women, and so on, will all contribute, in the long run, to an environment in which government officials can no longer safely ignore their citizens. This is because the more stable, prosperous, educated, and healthy a society's most disadvantaged members are, the more they will contribute to society, the more power and self-respect they will have, and the better position they will be in physically, psychologically, financially, and culturally to both expect more from their government, and to effectively pressure their government to be more responsive to their needs and desires.

Arguably, then, the most effective aid efforts will have indirect, long-term positive impacts on the responsiveness of governments to their citizens, that will fully or largely offset the indirect, long-term negative impacts on government responsiveness to which Deaton has pointed. Thus, when combined with the significant direct positive impact of the most effective aid efforts, the total amount of good produced by such efforts will outweigh the total amount of harms they produce, even on a simple additive model. If this is so, then those who restrict their charitable giving to the most effective aid agencies can be confident not only that each of them, individually, is doing more good than harm, and not only that each of the aid agencies to which each is contributing is doing more good than harm, but also that, collectively, they, together—meaning both all of the individual contributors to the most effective aid agencies and all of the most effective aid agencies themselves—will be doing more good than harm.

That is, on the assumptions in question, if one restricts one's focus to the most effective aid agencies, one can be confident that the members of that set of aid agencies will *not* face a consequentialist Each/We Dilemma. Hence, the argument concludes, Deaton has no basis for claiming that people like Peter Singer and other Effective Altruists are doing more harm than good in urging people to contribute to the most effective aid agencies, and individuals can, and should, safely and confidently do so.

For the sake of discussion, I want to accept all the premises of the preceding argument. Let us suppose that it is true that the most effective charities do more good than harm, even on an additive-aggregationist approach, so that, considered by themselves, the set of most effective charities, and the individuals contributing to them, will not face a consequentialist Each/We Dilemma. My question is whether, in thinking about Deaton's worries, it is legitimate to consider the group of most effective aid agencies *as if* they were operating alone, when *in fact* their aid efforts are undeniably embedded in a much larger context. I want to know what, if any, the *overall* impact of the most effective charities is on the larger environment of global giving. I have no answer to that question. However, let me suggest a reason for thinking that it requires an answer. I shall do this via two analogies.

Consider, first, the case of gambling. There are many people who believe that, overall, gambling does more harm than good in society. They recognize that there are many "social" gamblers who gamble for fun, who don't ever gamble more than they can afford to lose, and for whom gambling is a net positive. They also recognize that there are some successful gamblers for whom gambling is a major gain. Some of these are just plain lucky, but others are highly skilled. However, they also see that gambling is a major problem for certain people, who gamble far more than they can afford to lose. For many such people, gambling has a severely negative impact on their lives, those of their family and friends, and their contributions to society. Some end up deep in debt to loan sharks and lose everything they have to mobsters; others end up as criminals themselves; and others commit suicide, leaving their loved ones to deal with their debts and the mess they have left behind. Given all this, one can see how it could well be that, overall, gambling does more harm than good in society, and why some think that it would be good if gambling were banned entirely—if it could be done in such a way that doing so didn't cause even more problems than it prevented (recall the failed experiment of Prohibition, in the United States, from 1920 to 1933).

Recall, however, that gambling is not a problem for everyone. In fact, some people win. And some win big. The casinos love it when this happens. When someone wins a major payoff at a slot machine, bells and sirens go off throughout the casino, so that everyone knows there has been a big winner. And when individuals have a successful weekend of gambling, the casinos know that they will almost certainly tell all their friends about how much fun they had and how much money they won. This, of course, is the best kind of advertising the casinos can get. Because the excitement and enthusiasm are real, and it is coming from a friend or relative, and not some stale ad or scripted commercial.

The point, here, is that for gambling to thrive, there must be some genuine winners. If gamblers always lost, the institution would die out, or be a small fraction of the multi-billion-dollar industry that it is today. So, unfortunately, though it is not their intention to do so, successful gamblers become role models and, in effect, shills for a massive industry that could well be doing more harm than good.

Now suppose there were scientific studies that enabled us to accurately identify certain types who would flourish as gamblers, and others who could enjoy it without problems. One can imagine that someone keen to promote the good might strongly urge the first type to take up gambling and encourage the second group to give it a try, while vehemently insisting that, to be safe, everyone else should avoid gambling. They might even blanket all the major media outlets trumpeting the significant benefits to be gained from a life of gambling, but *only if one had the aptitude for it.* Such people might rightly claim that *as long as everyone followed their advice,* they would be doing more good than bad. However, I suspect that gambling opponents would not be impressed by such claims.

They would point out, quite plausibly, that if we live in a society where gambling is permitted, and the winners are highlighted, it is quite likely that many people who shouldn't be gambling will end up doing so. In this way, they might claim, even those who only trumpet the virtues of gambling for *certain* people will be part of the problem, not part of the solution. That is, even if it were true that *if* everyone followed one's advice that only a certain subset of identifiable people should gamble, one would be doing more good than harm, *the very successes one's advice leads to* might entice others to take up gambling who shouldn't. In this way, unfortunately, one's well-meaning intentions might backfire, and one might end up doing more harm than good, despite one's very best efforts to prevent that from happening.

Similar claims might be made, *mutatis mutandis*, about a wide array of other activities. Let us consider just one more example, the case of prescription pain killers in the U.S. In the U.S., opioids such as Percocet, Codeine, and Oxycodone, have long been prescribed by doctors to deal with pain management. They are extremely effective for dealing with all sorts of pain, including chronic pain, and millions have used them for many decades. However, in recent years, it has come to be recognized that opioids have been overprescribed, that a black market has arisen in opioids giving rise to many problems, and that opioid addiction is a serious problem.

Indeed, it is a striking fact that despite being one of the world's richest countries, and the country that spends more, per capita, on healthcare than any other, the average life expectancy in the U.S. has declined for three years in a row, with a large portion of that decline due to opioid overdoses.[11]

---

[11] Saiidi, Uptin. "Average life expectancy in the US has been declining for 3 consecutive years," CNBC, *USA Today*, July 9, 2019, URL: https://www.usatoday.com/story/money/2019/07/09/u-s-life-expectancy-decline-overdoses-liver-disease-suicide/1680854001/, accessed July 12, 2019.

This is the longest consecutive period of decline in U.S. life expectancy in 100 years—since the period from 1915 to 1918, when millions died globally due to World War I and the Spanish Flu.[12] It is estimated that in 2017, alone, opioids were involved in more than 47,000 U.S. overdose deaths.[13] To put that in perspective, there were "only" some 49,000 U.S. military combat deaths in the entire twenty-year period of the Vietnam War (1955–1975).[14]

In light of such facts, prescription pain medication in the U.S. has widely come to be regarded as an "opioid crisis," and many people believe that, overall, the use of opioids in the U.S. is now doing more harm than good. Suppose that is true. This doesn't change the fact that opioids can be extremely beneficial for certain people. Accordingly, one can imagine some people trying to scientifically identify the *most effective* uses of opioids, and arguing powerfully that opioids should be allowed in *such* cases, while readily granting that in many other cases opioid use does more harm than good, and should be avoided. Could those who maintained such a view be confident that they were doing more good than harm, on the basis of the claim that *if* opioids were only used in the very restricted ways for which they were advocating, opioid use would, indeed, do more good than harm?

I think not. Here, again, the actions and effects of those defending the restricted use of opioids don't take place in a vacuum. The very fact that the most effective uses of opioids will be highly successful at reducing severe pain, will make such uses highly visible exemplars of why opioids are in high demand. Many who are in pain, but not good candidates for opioids, will clamor for them, and plenty of good-hearted people will seek ways to supply them with opioids to ease their pain. And others who are not in pain will be willing to pay a pretty penny for the pharmacological effects of opioids, giving rise to a black market that contributes to bribery, theft, corruption, blackmail, adulteration, and so on, in hospitals and pharmacies.

Predictably, then, having helped keep opioids on the market, for good reasons and with the best of intentions, the defenders of a very restricted use of opioids may inadvertently be contributing to a much wider use of opioids than they, themselves, favor. In this way, then, they may be doing more harm than good, even though it is true that *if* everyone else followed their advice,

---

[12] Saiidi, "Average life expectancy in the US has been declining for 3 consecutive years."

[13] Saiidi, "Average life expectancy in the US has been declining for 3 consecutive years." Unfortunately, this number, significant as it is, now pales in comparison with the number of deaths in the U.S. due to Covid-19, a staggering number which ensures that the decline in U.S. life expectancy will continue to decline until an effective vaccine or cure for Covid is found.

[14] "Vietnam War U.S. Military Fatal Casualty Statistics," Military Records, *National Archives*, URL: https://www.archives.gov/research/military/vietnam-war/casualty-statistics, accessed July 12, 2019.

and opioids were *only* used in the ways they advocated, then they would, contrary to fact, be doing more good than harm.

I readily grant that the analogies between gambling, opioid use, and aiding the needy are not perfect. But I believe they are close enough, for our present purposes, to warrant consideration. I also grant that it is disputable whether gambling or opioid usage produces more harm than good, overall. It doesn't matter, for my purposes, whether they do or not. The point of the preceding is to remind people that it is not enough for Effective Altruists to absolve themselves of the charge that they might be doing more harm than good, to point out that they only advocate support for the most effective aid efforts, and that such aid efforts, considered just by themselves, are surely doing more good than harm. Even if the latter is true, their actions take place in a complex environment of global aid giving, where the very successes that they achieve may encourage countless others to engage in aid efforts that Effective Altruists, themselves, would roundly condemn.

In sum, if no individual aid efforts were successful, the institution of global aid giving might quickly come to a halt. However, if there are powerful exemplars of successful aid giving, such as those highlighted and strongly promoted by Effective Altruists, that can help sustain a global environment where countless well-meaning people are prepared to support endless aid efforts to help people desperately in need, even in the absence of hard evidence that doing so is effective, and even in environments where there are great risks that such efforts may backfire. In this way, the very successes of Effective Altruism may indirectly and inadvertently contribute to the much larger global aid environment in deleterious ways, even as Effective Altruists explicitly restrict their endorsement of aid efforts to those that are most effective. I fear, then, that Deaton could be right. Effective Altruists like Singer could be doing more harm than good, *even if* the particular aid efforts that they support are both individually and collectively doing more good than harm.

Let me conclude this section by reminding the reader of the heart of Deaton's view. Deaton isn't asking whether there are individual aid efforts that do more harm than good, considered just by themselves. He is asking whether aid efforts *as a whole* do more harm than good. Unfortunately, there are a host of ways in which individual aid efforts which, considered just by themselves, might do more good than harm, might nevertheless do more harm than good, in the real-world contexts in which aid efforts take place.

Here is a toy example to further illustrate this point. Suppose that the most adverse effects of climate change will only occur if a certain amount of carbon dioxide (CO_2) is released into the atmosphere. In addition, suppose that there is a certain form of carbon-based energy, A, that produces a whole lot of good, and releases only a relatively small amount of CO_2 into the air. Suppose, further, that if less than 1,000,000,000 people use A, and no other forms of carbon-based energy are used, then the Earth would remain safely below the CO_2 threshold which, if exceeded, would damage the Earth and its inhabitants. On the other hand, if more than 1,500,000,000 people use A, the resulting climate change would wreak havoc on the Earth's inhabitants. Moreover, let us presume, the greater the amount of CO_2 above the threshold, the worse the harm would be. One could then truthfully claim that any particular use of A, considered just by itself, was safe, desirable, and doing more good than harm. Clearly, however, that truth wouldn't be enough to support the view that *everyone* should start using A.

Likewise, suppose that many people were already using a different form of carbon-based energy, B, that was less clean, less efficient, and less desirable. Suppose that 1,000,000,000 people were using B, and that, together, the emissions from those uses were dangerously close to the level that would be reached if 1,500,000,000 people were using A. One might think it clear that one should advocate that people use A rather than B. After all, given our assumptions, it *would* be better if anyone using energy used A rather than B. Still, if such advocacy only led 200,000,000 people to switch from B to A, but led 500,000,000 people to start using A who weren't previously using any form of carbon-based energy, the result would be disastrous. Moreover, this is so even though it would still be true that if, contrary to fact, the *only* energy use was that of the 700,000,000 people using A, that use *would* be safe and desirable, and do much more good than harm.

The analogy is that there may be certain amounts of aid intervention in the world's poorest regions that are not enough to undermine the responsiveness of a government to such a degree that that the citizens subject to that government are substantially negatively affected. However, beyond a certain level, the reverse may be true. In that case, one can't assess the desirability of supporting certain aid interventions merely by focusing on the desirability of those interventions considered just by themselves. One must look at the larger context within which such aid will take place. An intervention which, by itself, would be wholly desirable, may nevertheless contribute to an undesirable outcome depending on what else is going on in the region. This is Deaton's point. And he is surely right.

This is why I think there is reason to be wary of any claims to the effect that one can be confident that contributions to GiveWell's top-rated charities will be doing more good than harm. How can one know this, in the absence of knowing the *overall* impact that aid in the region has on a government's responsiveness to its citizens; the overall impact that that, in turn, has on the wellbeing of the citizens; and the role, if any, that contributions to GiveWell's top-rated charities play in all that, given the wider context of which they are a part?

13.3 A Deontological Gloss on Deaton's Worry

In this chapter, I have been discussing various responses to Deaton's worry that, collectively, we may be doing more harm than good in contributing to on-the-ground international relief efforts in some of the world's poorest regions. This worry reflects a largely consequentialist framework that is common ground among many development economists and most Effective Altruists. However, throughout this work I have urged that we need to adopt a pluralistic approach in our response to the world's needy.

Accordingly, in thinking about Deaton's worries, it is important to bear in mind some of the observations previously presented in Chapters 7 and 11. If, as Deaton believes, our contributions to aid agencies help undermine the responsiveness of governments to their citizens and, thanks to Deaton, we are now aware of the ways in which this is so, then in making such contributions we are open to the charge of helping to victimize those who suffer due to the decrease in their government's responsiveness. Arguably, in some cases, individuals will suffer to an extent greater than they would be required to voluntarily incur for the sake of the benefits that our contributions promote. This is especially likely if, as suggested in Section 12.8, we believe that the positive impact on any particular person of our individual aid contribution is likely to be relatively small, while the negative impact on at least some individuals of even slightly undermining the government's responsiveness is likely to be relatively large.

In that case, we may believe that ultimately our contributions to aid agencies may be participating in the victimization of some people in a way that unjustifiably harms those people. If that is so, then our contributions to aid agencies may be impermissible for deontological reasons, even if, overall, those contributions do more good than harm, both individually and collectively.

This is, I believe, a legitimate worry prompted by Deaton's observations about the impact of giving on government responsiveness. Though, as indicated, the deontological basis of this worry is distinct from the consequentialist basis of Deaton's original worry.[15]

13.4 A Pluralist Response to Deaton's Worry

Let me next turn to some other concerns about Deaton's claim that significant amounts of international aid in the world's poorest countries may be counterproductive, as it may undermine the responsiveness of poor governments to their citizens, thereby stymieing long-term social and economic progress.

Recall the so-called Paradox of Aid, first introduced in Section 7.4, which holds that aid is unnecessary in countries with good governments, and unhelpful in countries with bad governments. Deaton's line appears to imply that we should not provide on-the-ground aid to the world's neediest people in the world's poorest countries, because doing so contributes to poor governance within such countries. However, it might be claimed that there is already poor governance in such countries, otherwise there wouldn't be so many desperate people in those countries needing help. So, it isn't as if withholding aid will prevent there from being poor governments in such countries. They are already there, with or without our interventions.[16]

Likewise, Deaton worries that outside funding from international agencies enables national governments to pursue their agendas, without having to rely on taxes from the local population. This is a problem, Deaton contends, because when governments must tax their populations, this sets up a dynamic between the governments and their citizens whereby the governments are more likely to have to be responsive to the basic needs and wishes of their citizens, since people will insist on having a say in how *their* money is spent. Still, one can't get blood from a turnip, and it is arguable that the world's neediest people won't have sufficient resources to be part of a country's tax base anyway. So, even if the governments did have to tax their citizens more in the absence of outside funds flowing into their country, that doesn't mean that they would need to be responsive to the basic needs and wants of their neediest citizens.

It appears, then, that our choices are between letting the neediest people suffer or die, while they are ruled by a poor government that is unresponsive to

---

[15] I am grateful to Frances Kamm for this important point (in discussion).

[16] Martin Ravallion holds such a view. Further, he has argued that the removal of aid often does little to promote "better" governance and may, in fact, contribute to a country's being in a "poor institutions trap" (see Ravallion's "On the Role of Aid in *The Great Escape*," *Review of Income and Wealth* 60 (2014): 967–84). For a similar view, see also, Jones, S. and F. Tarp, "Does Foreign Aid Harm Political Institutions?" *Journal of Development Economics* 118 (2016): 266–81.

their plight; or helping them out, while they are ruled by a poor government that is unresponsive to their plight. And if *those* are our choices, it may seem plain that we ought to do the latter, notwithstanding Deaton's possibly accurate claims about the ways in which outside aid funding can contribute to the unresponsiveness of poor governments.[17]

Here, Deaton *seems* to be suggesting that we should let people suffer or die now, on the *chance* that if we do so, that may lead to long-term changes in the responsiveness of the government, which in turn will eventually lead to substantial long-term social and economic progress. The thought is that sending aid to countries with poor governance enables such conditions to persist longer than they otherwise would, since without such outside aid unresponsive governments might have to change, or risk being ousted. That is, if poor governments couldn't count on outside funding resources, both to fund their political agendas, and to take care of their needy, perhaps they would have to adopt policies that would generate tax revenues within their countries to enable them to advance their agendas, remain in power, and deal with their countries' problems. Presumably, the best and most sustainable way to do this, long term, would involve adopting policies that would eventually transform their societies' neediest members from being drains on their societies' resources, to being productive members of their societies who are contributing to their tax bases.

In response, one might reasonably hold that this is a pretty risky approach to aiding the needy—as there are certainly no guarantees that our failing to aid those who are currently needy will lead to the necessary changes in governments and improvements in responsiveness that Deaton champions. Moreover, one might think that Deaton's approach smacks of cold-hearted utilitarian reasoning—as it seems prepared to sacrifice the lives and welfare of those who are currently needy, for the sake of presumably larger numbers of future people who would otherwise be needy, if the necessary changes in government that Deaton envisages fail to be realized.[18*]

---

[17] To be clear, Deaton believes that there are other actions we can take to help the world's needy, including actions we can take to try to help make governments more responsive to their citizens (see Deaton, Angus, *The Great Escape: Health, Wealth, and the Origins of Inequality* (Princeton: Princeton University Press, 2015), Chapter Seven). However, for the most part, these are long-term approaches to aiding the world's needy which do not change the basic dynamic of the choice we face when it comes to helping those most in need *now*.

[18*] No doubt some of Deaton's readers will be reminded of Thomas Malthus, who gave economics the moniker "the dismal science" when he argued, at the end of the 18th century, that countries had to be prepared to let many people starve, rather than grow more food to feed them, because he thought that increased food production would inevitably lead to population growth, and that this would inevitably lead to greater famines, and death, in the future (see Malthus's *An Essay on the Principle of Population* (London: J. Johnson, 1798)). Deaton acknowledges, in correspondence, that his approach

Notice, by the lights of Effective Altruism, Deaton may be entirely right to offer his somber advice. That is, if we are moved in our decisions about how best to aid the world's needy, solely on the basis of the expected benefits and burdens of alternative courses of action, it *could* turn out that the expected harms of letting many needy people die today, might be outweighed by the expected benefits of far larger numbers of people not having to be needy for many decades or even centuries to come, even if the expected harms are a virtual certainty, while the expected benefits are less likely to be realized than not. Still, even if we ultimately decide that Deaton's advice is warranted on the grounds of Expected Utility Theory, and so would also be prescribed by Effective Altruism, we might balk at following it. (For more on this, see Appendix A.)

Consider the standard deontological view that I ought to save my mom, rather than five strangers, even if saving five strangers would do more good; or that I ought not to break my promise, to stop five other people from breaking their promises. Furthermore, recall the discussion from Section 3.6, regarding dramatic rescues. We often believe that there is something uplifting, noble, and morally compelling about going to great lengths to perform dramatic rescues—for example, to continue to search through the rubble seven days after a major earthquake hits, on the off chance that we may still find someone alive, amidst all the death and destruction—even as we recognize that the costs involved in such rescues would almost never be justified solely on the grounds of cost-effectiveness.

These observations serve to remind us that there is much more to morality than merely doing the most expected good that we can. A thoroughly decent human being will be virtuous, and will give due weight to a host of deontological considerations that run counter to the simple dictate of maximizing the good. This is why many of us will feel queasy about Deaton's

---

may seem cold-hearted, but adds, in defense of his position, that "I don't see an alternative that doesn't harm them [the needy] more." Still, as the text makes plain, it is important to note that Deaton is not considering a choice between allowing one group of needy people to be harmed, to prevent those very same needy people from being harmed even more. Rather he is considering a choice between allowing one group of needy people to be harmed now, to prevent a larger group of similarly needy people from being harmed even more at some point in the future.

Also, as recognized in the previous note, Deaton is not suggesting that we abandon the needy. He just believes that the best ways of aiding the needy will involve international political, economic, and research efforts that take place outside of the world's poorest countries, rather than on-the-ground efforts of outside international aid organizations aimed at directly ameliorating the plight of the needy in the world's poorest regions; since, Deaton believes, the former is not likely to undermine the responsiveness of local governments to their citizens in the way that the latter do. (Some of Deaton's suggestions in this regard are noted in my concluding section, 16.4, but for a more detailed presentation of these suggestions see Chapter Seven of *The Great Escape*.)

recommendations, even if we accept that they might be supported by long-term, impartial, cost-effectiveness calculations.[19]

When we learn that people are suffering from the ravages of war, illness, or natural disasters, we are moved by a host of morally relevant considerations to ease their plight. We may recognize that we might be able to do more total good by husbanding our resources to achieve other, more cost-effective, long-term goals. However, for many of us, we are not prepared to sacrifice the current needy on the altar of need minimization. We would be fools, or worse, to ignore the sorts of considerations to which Deaton has rightly alerted us. However, we must balance those considerations against all the other morally relevant considerations that have a bearing on how a decent person responds to the plight of the needy.

13.5 Final Remarks Regarding Deaton's Worry

I have spent three chapters discussing Deaton's worry that Peter Singer, and others, might be doing more good than harm, by supporting on-the-ground international aid efforts. I have not taken a stand as to whether Deaton is ultimately right about this. There are opponents of aid who are convinced that he is right. There are proponents of aid who are convinced that he is not right. And there are others who are not sure what to believe.

As indicated earlier, I think that most development economists believe that the overall impact of international aid has been small, but positive (at least as far as the alleviation of poverty is concerned). However, as also indicated earlier, I, myself, fall into the agnostic camp. That is, with Riddell, I don't believe that we have all the evidence we need, about the direct and indirect short-term and long-term consequences of aid efforts, to definitively conclude whether past aid efforts have done more good than harm, or whether future aid efforts are likely to do so.[20]

Thus, the reason I have discussed Deaton's worry at length is not, ultimately, because I agree with him, but because he draws attention to a lack of nuance that permeates the field. Far too often, Effective Altruists, development economists, and supporters of international aid efforts possess an almost blind faith that surely the well-intentioned efforts of aid organizations (or at least

---

[19] Of course, Deaton, Effective Altruists, and consequentialists would contend that one should feel queasy about acting virtuously or fulfilling one's deontological commitments whenever doing so comes at the expense of others.

[20] See Section 1.9, for a brief presentation and discussion of Riddell's view.

those of the most effective aid organizations) have a positive overall impact on those in need. Yet, unfortunately, their confidence fails to take account of many of the worries raised in this book, including Deaton's.

It is certainly possible that Deaton is right, that aid efforts unwittingly undermine government responsiveness to its citizens, at least in certain contexts. It is also highly plausible that government responsiveness is a crucial component to long-term social and economic progress in the world's poorest regions. This is a position that must be taken seriously, since government policies impact virtually every meaningful aspect related to a population's wellbeing—e.g. infrastructure, energy policies, education, the economy, healthcare, the environment, reproductive policies, etc. Unfortunately, even small reductions in a government's responsiveness to its citizens may have far-reaching and lasting impacts on the wellbeing of a country's present and future generations.

In this chapter, I have presented numerous responses to Deaton's worry. I have raised concerns about most of those responses. I have also noted that Deaton's worry gives rise to deontological concerns that may cast doubt on the moral permissibility of aid efforts even if, contrary to what Deaton believes, those efforts succeed in promoting more good than harm. As importantly, I have suggested that even if Deaton is right that, overall, international aid efforts produce more harm than good, that doesn't settle the question of whether we should support such aid efforts. As I have argued throughout this book, there is much more to being good, and/or acting rightly, in a world of need, than merely doing the most (expected) good that one can, in aiding the needy.

Finally, let me end this chapter by returning to the lesson of Chapter 12. Conflicts between individual rationality and morality, and collective rationality and morality, are deeply puzzling and profoundly troubling. Arguably, they lie at the root of many of our most pressing social and political problems, and they can be particularly intractable.[21] The domain of obligations to the needy is no exception to this. Effective Altruists might well be right that we can identify many effective international aid agencies that are promoting morally desirable outcomes. Given this, it may well be true that each of us, individually, ought morally to support such agencies. Yet, despite that, there is the

---

[21] Climate change "stands out at the quintessential global-scale collective action problem" (Esty, Daniel C. and Anthony L.I. Moffa, "Why Climate Change Collective Action Has Failed and What Needs to be Done Within and Without the Trade Regime," *Journal of International Economic Law* 15 (2012): 777–91). A seminal discussion of collective action problems is Garrett Hardin's classic article "The Tragedy of the Commons," *Science*, New Series 162 (1968): 1243–8.

possibility that, collectively, we ought not to support such agencies, since if we do, we, together, will be bringing about a morally undesirable outcome. If that is the real-world situation that each of us, and we, together, find ourselves in, then it is very unclear what to say about it. More precisely, it will be very clear what each individual should do; and also very clear what we, collectively, should do. Unfortunately, however, what will be unclear is how to defensibly reconcile the two competing perspectives and prescriptions.

14

Responsibility and Fairness

Further Support for a Pluralistic Approach to Global Aid

In this chapter, I consider two further issues. These issues offer further support for the importance of adopting a pluralistic approach to the complex topic of global aid.

In Section 14.1, I briefly discuss Thomas Pogge's view that aiding the global needy is often a matter of duty, and not a matter of charity. Pogge thinks this because he believes that often those who are well-off are responsible for the plight of the needy. I argue that Pogge has called our attention to a very important, non-consequentialist, factor relevant to the topic of global aid. More importantly, for my purposes, I point out that Pogge's view raises a host of complex questions that are not easily answered, and that require a pluralistic approach to address.

In Section 14.2, I briefly discuss the topic of fairness. I note that a concern for fairness, and the related ideals of equality and justice, underlie the recent push for universal healthcare by the World Health Organization. They also underlie the efforts of VillageReach, an international aid organization that aims to provide high quality healthcare to remote villages. I argue that fairness, justice, and equality are important ideals that must be given due weight when responding to global need, but that such ideals often conflict with the utilitarian ideal of doing the most good (at least as that notion is often understood by Effective Altruists and others). This section is a further reminder of the complexity of the topic of global aid, and the necessity of adopting a pluralistic approach in addressing it.

Section 14.3 ends with a few final thoughts prompted by the chapter.

14.1 Pogge and the Importance of Responsibility

In this section, I want to briefly discuss a view championed by Thomas Pogge.[1] Pogge has argued that often affluent people must provide aid to the world's

---

[1] See Pogge's *World Poverty and Human Rights*, 2nd Edition (Cambridge: Polity Press, 2008), and also his *Politics as Usual: What Lies Behind the Pro-Poor Rhetoric* (Cambridge: Polity Press, 2010).

Being Good in a World of Need. Larry S. Temkin, Oxford University Press. © Larry S. Temkin 2022.
DOI: 10.1093/oso/9780192849977.003.0014

needy not merely as a matter of *charity*, or as an act of *supererogation*—an act that is above and beyond the call of duty—but as a matter of strict *duty*. Reflection on Pogge's view reminds us of the complexity of the topic of global aid, and the importance of adopting a pluralistic approach in addressing that complexity.

Pogge's argument for his view is lengthy, complex, and subtle. I won't try to reproduce it here. However, roughly, Pogge's contention is that the world is governed by a host of guidelines, statutes, laws, and policies which determine the rules of international commerce and the relations between different nations. Overwhelmingly, Pogge claims, these regulations have been written by governments, multi-national corporations, or international bodies in ways that work to the benefit of the most affluent people in the world's richest and most powerful countries, and to the detriment of the worst-off in the poorest countries. As citizens of rich and powerful countries whose governments make decisions in their name; as stockholders in multi-national companies which largely set the terms of international commerce and engage in global business practices that work for the benefit of their stockholders; and as the principal beneficiaries of the regulations that govern global interactions; affluent people in the world's richest and most powerful countries are complicit in, and at least partially responsible for, the decisions and practices that are made in their name, and from which they benefit. Accordingly, insofar as it is often those very decisions and practices that substantially contribute to the plight of the world's neediest people, affluent people in the world's richest and most powerful nations are at least partly responsible for their plight, and therefore have a direct obligation to rectify the situation.[2] More concretely, it is Pogge's view that the world's best-off actively engage in a host of economic and legal practices that harm the world's worst-off in ways that violate those people's rights or are otherwise unjust or immoral. Accordingly, Pogge says that we have a duty to stop committing such harms, and to rectify the harms we have done.

For example, history is replete with cases of rich and powerful governments installing puppet governments, or supporting repressive totalitarian or authoritarian regimes, in the name of national security or economic

---

[2] There is also the further issue of how previous decades of colonialism and imperialism helped set the stage for many of the most destructive social, political, and economic conditions that we see in some of the world's poorest regions today. Many development economists believe that European colonial powers had a significant part to play in the current state of poverty across much of Africa. See, for example, Rodney, Walter, *How Europe Underdeveloped Africa* (London: Bogle-L'Ouverture Publications, 1973). (I am grateful to Brian Oosterhuizen for prompting this note, and providing this reference.)

prosperity. Perhaps the regimes stand with "us" in the fight against commun-ism or jihadist terrorism. Or perhaps the governments provide "us" with oil, or other valuable resources that are vital to our economy. As Pogge has rightly pointed out, international law allows rich countries and big businesses to sign deals with a country's functioning government for the rights to its resources, in exchange for whatever goods and services the government in question deems appropriate. And, unfortunately, even if we recognize, in our heart of hearts, that in some sense a country's natural resources belong to its citizens, and should be used for *their* benefit, it will typically be hugely cost-effective, from the standpoint of the rich countries and businesses, for such deals to essentially buy off a few key government officials, their henchmen, and the local elites, rather than to provide for the basic needs of the country's populace.[3*]

The staunch supporting of authoritarian, totalitarian, or repressive regimes by rich and powerful countries for their own benefit has occurred, and continues to occur, throughout the world, including in many countries in the Middle East, Asia, Africa, Central America, South America, and the Caribbean. Often, such support includes massive amounts of military aid that enables repressive regimes to remain in power despite being opposed by the majority of their citizens. When the leaders of such regimes amass vast personal fortunes while many of their citizens starve or suffer from treatable or preventable illnesses, or when such leaders create humanitarian crises by engaging in genocide or other large-scale acts of oppression, war, and aggres-sion, those who have supported such regimes bear significant responsibility for the havoc they wreak. This helps explain why, according to Pogge, inter-national relief and development aid is often not merely a matter of *charity*, but a matter of *duty*—specifically, a duty of *rectification* that is *owed* to the world's needy by powerful countries and their citizens, in virtue of the role that the latter have played in fostering the conditions that have harmed the needy and produced much of their undeserved suffering.[4]

[3*] To mention just a few examples from recent U.S. history, this helps explain the U.S. support of autocrats, strongmen, or tyrants such as Mohammad Reza Shah Pahlavi of Iran, Saddam Hussein of Iraq, Ferdinand Marcos of the Philippines, Jorge Rafael Videla of Argentina, Generalissimo Francisco Franco of Spain, Augusto Pinochet of Chile, President Suharto of Indonesia, Mobutu Sese Seko of the Democratic Republic of the Congo, King Abdullah of Saudi Arabia, and the apartheid government of South Africa (often there were political, as well as economic, reasons for the U.S. support of these figures).

[4] Note, on my pluralistic approach, if we do have a deontological duty of rectification that underlies our obligation to aid the needy, then we might have compelling reason to do so even in some cases where doing so involved doing more harm than good (at least collectively). Given this, one might naturally wonder when, if at all, we should fulfill our duties of rectification to the needy, even when we

Pogge's position raises a host of thorny issues in the areas of individual and collective responsibility. How much responsibility does an individual citizen bear for the actions of her government? Does it matter to this question whether the citizen voted for, or in other ways supported, the members of the government and their harmful policies? Do individual citizens have personal duties of rectification for wrongful actions perpetrated by their government, or do they merely have political responsibilities to fight for changes to their government and its policies, and to try to make their government pay rectification for their harmful actions? How responsible are current governments and their citizens for the harmful policies of previous governments, and how far back in time does such responsibility extend? And so on.

I cannot address these thorny issues here. However, in thinking about Pogge's view, one is quickly reminded of how many complex questions must be addressed to get a full picture of the nature and extent of our obligations to the needy. Effective Altruism says that in considering which "charitable" organizations to support, we should focus on the single question of which organizations would do the most good with our support. This is a very important question. However, it totally leaves out of account the questions of individual and collective responsibility that Pogge has raised. On my preferred, pluralistic approach, we must pay attention to both sorts of considerations, as well as others, in considering what, if anything, we should do on behalf of others.

Let me say a bit more about the importance and complexity of such questions. Consider first the following case.

Distracted Driver: Fatima is driving to a jewelry store to sell her expensive watch. Her intention is to donate the proceeds from the sale to an effective international aid agency, which will then save two lives with the money she gives them. While daydreaming about the good that she will be producing, Fatima runs a red light, and crashes into a car that has legally entered the intersection. Unfortunately, the other car is damaged beyond repair, and its sole occupant is significantly hurt, though she does not suffer crippling or life-threatening injuries.

know that, collectively, doing so will be worse for the needy themselves. If there are such cases, they appear to commit us to prioritizing our interests—in this case the interest in acting rightly—over the pressing interests of those who are much worse off. Of course, like many others, Pogge has simply assumed that fulfilling our duties of rectification would, on balance, benefit rather than harm the needy. But if that isn't the case, as people like Deaton believe, would Pogge still urge that we fulfill such duties? This is an issue of great practical and theoretical importance.

In Distracted Driver, Fatima is personally responsible for the harm that she has caused to the other car and its occupant. Given this, she now has a duty of rectification that may trump the general duty that she has to aid the needy. Accordingly, while Fatima may still have a strong preference to sell her watch and send the proceeds to an effective charity, she may no longer have that option. That is, it may now be the case that Fatima ought, morally, to turn over the proceeds from the sale of her watch to the person that she has harmed, even though doing so may not produce as much good as saving two lives.

Similarly, consider the following case.

Broken Window: A group of people regularly get together to play baseball in a vacant lot. One day, a batted ball flies into a neighbor's yard and damages her expensive car.

In Broken Window, it could well be that everyone playing the game bears responsibility for the car's damage, and not just the person who happened to hit the ball. This may require each participant to help pay for the repairs, or for the deductible on the neighbor's insurance claim, or perhaps for any hike in her premiums that ensues when she submits a damage claim to her insurance company. It may even require any one of the players to bear the entire costs in question, if the other group members are unable to shoulder their share of the burden. Paying to repair the damaged car may require a participant, morally, to spend funds that she was planning to give to an effective aid agency. This is so, even if the effective aid agency would do more good with the money than will be done by getting the car repaired.

Distracted Driver and Broken Window remind us that fulfilling one's duties and responsibilities can be at odds with the aim of doing the most good that one can with one's resources. This, of course, is not surprising. However, it may lead in unexpected directions when applied to the area of international aid.

Consider the following example.

Bangladesh Fabrics: Nigel is the owner of a successful clothing company that acquires its fabrics from a company in Bangladesh. After many years, Nigel learns that the company in Bangladesh employs only female workers, whom it has been exploiting ruthlessly. The workers have had to work twelve-hour days, six days a week, but they have only been paid for forty-hour weeks. In addition, they have been paid substantially below-market wages. Nigel, and the owners of the Bangladesh company, have become very wealthy due to this exploitation.

In light of the considerations that Pogge adduces, many might think that Nigel has a special duty of rectification to the exploited workers in Bangladesh. And this sounds right. However, suppose that the Bangladesh workers still lead decent lives, especially in comparison with many of the world's needy. More particularly, suppose that they have steady jobs, and that their meager salaries are still enough for them to eke out decent lives for themselves and their families. Contrast their situation with the following one.

> *Refugee Camp*: The women in a refugee camp have been the brutal victims of rape as an instrument of war. Their husbands have been killed. They suffer from an assortment of debilitating illnesses. They have been forced into ongoing prostitution to feed themselves and their children. As it happens, neither Nigel nor his country is responsible for the sectarian violence that has led to the horrible plight of the women in the refugee camp.

As the owner of the profitable clothing company, who wants to aid the world's needy, should Nigel contribute to international aid organizations which will help the women in the refugee camp—whose needs, after all, are more compelling—or should he help the women who work in the Bangladesh fabric company, whose exploitation he is, at least partly, even if unwittingly, responsible for, and from which he has profited substantially?

There is, I believe, no easy answer to the preceding question. Rather, there are different bases, or kinds of moral reasons, for helping the different groups of women, which give rise to conflicting claims on Nigel's resources. How to adjudicate between such claims depends ultimately on the nature, relationship, and relative priority of their underlying moral bases, and this is by no means self-evident. (Recall that in Distracted Driver and Broken Window, personal responsibility for one's actions may prohibit people from using their resources to meet the most urgent claims, because others now have a rightful claim on those resources; so, in the morally relevant sense, the resources in questions are no longer "theirs" to do with as they see fit.)

One might say that Nigel has compelling moral reason to fulfill *both* sets of claims. And that may be right. But the reality is that every dollar that Nigel spends to aid the women in the refugee camp will be one less dollar available to aid the women in the fabric company, and vice versa. Thus, one must inevitably face a host of difficult questions in determining what to do.

What if the difference in quality of life between the women in the refugee camp and those in the Bangladesh fabric company is smaller than I have described, or perhaps even larger? What if Nigel is not the owner of the profitable clothing company, but only a shareholder in that company? And does it matter if Nigel is a large shareholder, or only a small shareholder? Or does it matter if Nigel's shareholdings contribute significantly to his income or wealth, or only insignificantly? And if significant contributions to Nigel's income or wealth do matter here, is it *absolute* or *relative* contributions that matter, or both? What if Nigel didn't own stock in the profitable clothing company itself, but owned stock in another company that profits from doing business with the clothing company? What if Nigel was merely a customer of the clothing company? Or merely a customer of the other company that does business with the clothing company? In other words, how far do the bases of responsibility extend, and how much weight do they have in comparison with the value of doing as much good as one can for those who are neediest?

My point, of course, is that if the pluralistic approach that I favor is correct, and if Pogge is right that we often have (deontological) duties of rectification towards people who are needy, this opens up the possibility that in some cases, at least, we might have most reason, all things considered, to fulfill our duties of rectification to some people who are needy, even if we could do more good for even needier people by not fulfilling that duty. More troubling still, given that deontology sometimes requires us to act in ways that produce more harm than good, the possibility arises that, if Pogge is right, there might be deonto-logical reason to fulfill our duties of rectification even when doing so did more harm than good for the very people to whom we had such duties, at least collectively.

If there are such cases, one might worry that, in so acting, we would, in essence, be prioritizing *our* interests—in this case our interests in acting rightly—over the pressing interests of others who are much worse off. Though, of course, the deontologist would balk at this description of the situation. She would claim, instead, that fulfilling one's duties is not a matter of acting in one's interest, but rather, a matter of doing what there is compel-ling moral reason to do. That is, for the deontologist, while it may (or may not) be in one's interest to act morally, that is not (typically) the *reason* for acting morally.

Like many others, Pogge has simply assumed that fulfilling our duties of rectification with respect to the needy would, on balance, *benefit* the needy. But if that isn't the case, at least collectively, as people like Deaton think, would Pogge still believe that we had such duties, and urge us to fulfill them? Alternatively, might Pogge suggest that in such cases we can assume hypo-thetical consent on the part of those who would be harmed if we fulfilled our duty to them, which would release us from the duty in question?

The issues that Pogge has raised about individual and collective responsibility for the plight of the world's needy are undeniably important. However,
as the preceding is intended to suggest, they raise a host of complex issues that
are not easily answered, yet are of great normative significance, both practically and theoretically. In thinking about these issues, we are reminded, once
again, that there are many important and often competing factors that have a
bearing on the nature, foundation, and extent of our obligations to the needy.

14.2 Fairness

Let me turn next to another important topic relevant to being good in a world
of need. The topic of fairness. As we will see, fairness concerns can conflict
with the goal of doing as much good as possible, in addressing global need.

To introduce this issue, it will be useful to start with an example from global
health. In recent years, there has been a strong push by the World Health
Organizations, and others, advocating universal health coverage throughout
the developing world.[5] Part of the impetus for this push stems from recognizing that in much of the developing world there are huge gaps in the availability
of supplies, health professionals, facilities, and quality care between urban and
rural populations.[6] For the World Health Organization, and other advocates of
the idea, universal health coverage holds out the promise that all citizens of a
country should have access to high quality healthcare regardless of where
they live.

Underlying this idea is a commitment to the fundamental values of equality,
fairness, and justice. Just as it seems deeply unfair or unjust for someone to die
from a readily preventable disease because of their race, sex, religion, nationality, or sexual orientation, so it seems deeply unfair or unjust for someone to
die from a readily preventable disease because they happen to have been born
in a remote area. Surely, a sick child living in the city is no more deserving of
adequate healthcare than her rural counterpart. Yet, in the developing world, a

---

[5] See the World Health Organization's 2005 World Health Assembly Resolution, 58.33,
URL: https://apps.who.int/iris/bitstream/handle/10665/20383/WHA58_33-en.pdf;sequence=1, accessed
September 2, 2019. See also, Thomas O'Connell's presentation for UNICEF, at the 2012 2nd Global
Symposium on Health Systems Research in Beijing, "Advancing equity through UHC: Are we
getting there?" URL: http://healthsystemsresearch.org/hsr2012/images/stories/media/1101/Afternoon/2%
20Plenary%20Advancing%20equity%20through%20UHC_Are%20we%20getting%20there-O'Connell_
UNICEF_Final-V2.pdf, accessed September 2, 2019. And see the special symposium on universal
health coverage in *The Lancet* 380 (2012): 859, 861–5.

[6] For a striking illustration of some of the relevant data on this in the context of Ethiopia, see slide
12 of Thomas O'Connell's presentation "Advancing equity through UHC: Are we getting there?"

sick urban child is often much more likely to be treated for a curable illness than her rural counterpart, in virtue of her greater proximity to hospitals, clinics, health professionals, and appropriate medical treatment.[7]

This is the well-known problem of "last mile" communities. The simple fact is that in the developing world, where medical and economic resources are scarce, where a large proportion of the medically needy typically live in just a few large cities, often in overcrowded slums, and where roads, electricity, clinics, hospitals, and other crucial elements of infrastructure, not to mention trained health professionals, may be poor or non-existent in outlying areas, it will often be terribly inefficient to cater to the medical needs of anyone living outside the major cities. Accordingly, as most global health experts are aware, in the developing world, the laudable goal of bringing equally high-quality health coverage to all people regardless of where they live is directly at odds with the goal of doing as much good as one can in terms of promoting good health states.

One international relief organization that is acutely aware of this problem, and dedicated to addressing it, is *VillageReach*. On their website, under the heading, *Reaching the Last Mile*, they write: "While tremendous investments have been made to bring new medicines, technologies, and other global health innovations to LMICs [Low and Middle Income Countries], barriers to delivering these innovations and providing basic health services remain a significant challenge, especially in the most rural and remote communities. Health systems simply don't have the capacity to effectively respond to demand through to the last mile . . . . Sustainable and scalable solutions in this setting require an integrated approach with a focus on last mile delivery. This is the cornerstone of our mission and work."[8]

For two years, VillageReach was the top-rated charity, out of more than 400 evaluated, by GiveWell, receiving the highest ranking, of "strong" for evidence of effectiveness, and also the highest rating of "excellent" for cost-effectiveness.[9] This is rather ironic, since GiveWell is supposed to be one of the most reliable sources for Effective Altruism, and yet it is almost certain that VillageReach, by its very nature, couldn't have been one of the most cost-

---

[7] This paragraph and the following one are taken from my article "Universal Health Coverage: Solution or Siren? Some Preliminary Thoughts," *Journal of Applied Philosophy* 31 (2014): 1–22; doi: 10.1111/japp.12050. This phenomenon is also prevalent in the developed world, though generally to a lesser extent.

[8] See http://www.villagereach.org/about/, accessed June 10, 2017.

[9] 2009, 2010. See, https://www.givewell.org/charities/top-charities/2009 and https://www.givewell. org/charities/top-charities/2010, accessed June 10, 2017.

effective charities in terms of doing the most good (at least, not in the welfarist terms favored by many Effective Altruists).[10]

Note, I am not questioning whether VillageReach delivered on its promises to its donors. That is, I am reasonably confident, given GiveWell's evaluation, that any money sent to VillageReach was used, as effectively as possible, to address pressing health needs in remote regions of the developing world. However, as VillageReach accurately recognizes, the hurdles for reaching ill people in remote regions are very high; too high for most health systems in the developing world to overcome. This is why, if one is concerned about the fundamental ideals of equality, fairness, and justice in addressing one of the most basic of all human needs, health, one needs to support NGOs like VillageReach. Still, it is important to recognize that in supporting such NGOs, one is doing so *despite* any concerns that one might have to maximize good health outcomes, not as a way of addressing such concerns.

As should be clear, my point here is not to denigrate the important work of NGOs like VillageReach. Quite the opposite. VillageReach embraces values— equality, fairness, and justice—that I have spent much of my life promoting and defending.[11] On the other hand, my point here is also not to say that we should give priority to the values that VillageReach promotes above all others, when seeking to aid the needy. Here, as throughout, I am arguing in favor of a pluralistic approach to aiding the needy.

---

[10] Peter Singer suggests, in correspondence, that I cannot argue this point a priori. He is correct about that. However, as the following discussion is intended to make clear, I am *not* arguing for my point a priori. I am arguing for it on the basis of VillageReach's own description of its aims, and the nature of the empirical difficulties that VillageReach itself recognizes have to be overcome to achieve those aims. See VillageReach's home website, available at https://www.villagereach.org/, accessed July 17, 2019.

[11] See, for example, *Inequality* (New York: Oxford University Press, 1993); "Equality as Comparative Fairness," *Journal of Applied Philosophy* 34 (2017): 43–60, doi: 10.1111/japp.12140; "Inequality and Health," in *Measurement and Ethical Evaluation of Health Inequalities*, edited by Ole Norheim, Nir Eyal, Samia Hurst, and Dan Wikler, Oxford: Oxford University Press, 2013, 13–26; "Justice, Equality, Fairness, Desert, Rights, Free Will, Responsibility, and Luck," in *Distributive Justice and Responsibility*, edited by Carl Knight and Zofia Stemplowska, Oxford: Oxford University Press, 2011, 51–76; "Egalitarianism Defended," *Ethics* 113 (2003): 764–82; "Inequality: A Complex, Individualistic, and Comparative Notion," in *Philosophical Issues* 11, edited by Ernie Sosa and Enriquea Villanueva, Oxford: Blackwell Publishers, 2001, 327–52; "Equality, Priority, and the Levelling Down Objection," in *The Ideal of Equality*, edited by Matthew Clayton and Andrew Williams, New York: St. Martin's Press, 2000, 126–61; "Equality, Priority, or What?" *Economics and Philosophy* 19 (2003): 61–88; "Illuminating Egalitarianism," in *Contemporary Debates in Political Philosophy*, edited by Thomas Christiano and John Christman, Oxford: Wiley-Blackwell Publishing, 2009, 155–78; "Equality and the Human Condition," *Theoria* (South Africa) 92 (1998): 15–45; "Intergenerational Inequality," in *Philosophy, Politics, and Society*, Sixth Series, edited by Peter Laslett and James Fishkin, New Haven: Yale University Press, 1992, 169–205; and "Inequality," *Philosophy and Public Affairs* 15 (1986): 99–121.

In thinking about our obligations to the needy, we do need to pay attention to the important value reflected by Effective Altruism—one that seeks to maximize good health outcomes, in choosing between health-related aid organizations. However, we *also* need to pay attention to other important values, including equality, fairness, and justice. Trade-offs between competing moral values are an extremely difficult, but ineliminable part of the equation for most significant moral issues; the pressing issue of obligations to the needy is no exception to this general and important truth.

14.3 Final Thoughts

This chapter introduced two further sets of concerns relevant to global aid. The first involves deontological issues of individual and collective responsibility for the plight of the world's needy. The second involves the ideals of fairness, justice, and equality. Both sets of concerns are at odds with the "do the most good" approach of Effective Altruism, at least as that is often understood; namely, in welfarist terms.

This chapter raises far more questions than it answers. To deal adequately with the complex issues related to individual and collective responsibility would require an entire book of its own. So, too, would dealing adequately with the complex issues related to fairness, justice, and equality. The point of this chapter, then, is mainly to identify some further, fundamentally important, normative factors that must be taken into account in thinking about global need.

In sum, taking this chapter's factors into account appropriately will, I believe, be extraordinarily difficult. This should not be surprising. It is a reminder of just how complex morality is, and why we need a pluralistic approach to capture that complexity. Unfortunately, it is extremely difficult to get clear on the many different factors that matter morally; and even more difficult to determine how much they matter vis-à-vis each other in different contexts. However, I believe this is a task that we must face squarely, if we truly hope to be good in a world of need.

15

Taking Stock, Clarifications, and Further Thoughts

This book has argued for a pluralistic approach to global need. In doing this, I have argued that we need to pay attention to *all* of the positive and negative factors—direct, indirect, short-term, and long-term—in assessing the overall impact of international aid efforts. I have also argued that there is much more to the question of how to be good in a world of need, than simply doing the most good in terms of improving welfare. In this chapter, I take stock of some of the book's key results, and offer some qualifications, implications, and further thoughts.

In Section 15.1, I take stock of this book's implications for Singer's famous article "Famine, Affluence, and Morality," and the key example and principles within it. I contend that while Singer's article has many virtues, it doesn't actually provide much guidance regarding how to respond to global need. Singer believes that his argument strongly supports the conclusion that we should be contributing to international aid organizations like Oxfam. This book challenges that view. Unfortunately, much more work need to be done, both empirically and normatively, before we can arrive at Singer's conclusion.

In Section 15.2, I take stock of this book's implications for (Global Aid) Effective Altruism. I acknowledge that most of this book's claims are fully compatible with Effective Altruism, at least in principle. However, I note three areas of difference between my approach and that of some Effective Altruists. Some of my remarks are particularly aimed at those Effective Altruists who are concerned to maximize the welfare of the global needy, who have a relatively narrow conception of welfare, and who, for a variety of reasons, tend to focus on global health interventions.

This book has employed (welfarist Global Aid) Effective Altruism as a foil, of sorts, to help present, develop, and clarify my own views. However, it remains true that I am on the same side as (Global Aid) Effective Altruism, in terms of our shared concern to aid the needy. So, while it is important not to understate our differences, it is also important not to overstate them.

Being Good in a World of Need. Larry S. Temkin, Oxford University Press. © Larry S. Temkin 2022.
DOI: 10.1093/oso/9780192849977.003.0015

Moreover, the differences between us shrink—though don't disappear—if Effective Altruism adopts a wide conception of the good; one which includes the many morally desirable ideals, other than welfare, appealed to in this book.

In Section 15.3, I note that, for many, Effective Altruism is supposed to be a *practical* movement, guiding people's behavior *now*. This is, I suggest, a laudable goal, but perhaps one that is premature. This book provides various reasons to worry that we may lack the information we need to fully assess the overall impact of aid interventions. I review three dangers associated with that worry.

In Section 15.4, I note several clarifications and caveats relevant to the scope of this book's worries. For example, I note that my worries about paternalism, freedom, and respect arise for certain aid efforts, but not others. I also note that some of the worries about perverse incentives that arise when aiding victims of social injustice may not arise when aiding certain victims of natural disasters. I further note that the worries I raise about aid efforts in countries headed by corrupt or unresponsive governments may not apply to aid efforts in countries with good governments that are responsive to their citizens. Relatedly, I note that many of the worries I raise about the corrosive effects of aid only arise in contexts where the aid represents a significant portion of a country's annual income, or a significant proportion of a government's annual expenditures. Thus, these worries can be avoided by focusing aid efforts in countries with strong economies, rather than in poor countries with weak economies. This is important, I suggest, since our goal should be to aid *people* who are poorly off, rather than *countries* which are poorly off, and since many people who are poorly off live in middle- and upper-income countries.

In Section 15.5, I discuss this book's implications for those who believe that they should follow Expected Utility Theory in evaluating aid organizations. This includes Effective Altruists, as well as many others who believe that doing the most good is relevant to which aid organizations to support. Although I have many reservations about Expected Utility Theory, I note that if one is going to rely on it when evaluating aid agencies, it is imperative that one does so properly. I argue that this requires taking seriously this book's worries.

I note that many people will think that this book's worries may be legitimate, theoretically, but that they can be largely ignored for practical purposes. I suggest that there are various psychological reasons why those working in the areas of global aid or development economics may hold such a position, that are unrelated to evidence for its truth. I further offer various reasons for thinking this attitude is mistaken. Most importantly, I argue that this response is incompatible with the proper use of Expected Utility Theory. Concretely,

I suggest that even if there is only a small chance that some of this book's worries are correct, that may be enough to alter the expected utility calculations that underlie the recommendations of Effective Altruist organizations like GiveWell.

Section 15.6 summarizes the chapter.

15.1 Reassessing Singer's Approach to Global Need

As indicated in Section 2.1, for many years, I taught the topic of obligations to the needy in my large ethics classes. In doing so, I often taught Peter Singer's "Famine, Affluence, and Morality," alongside Garrett Hardin's classic article, "The Tragedy of the Commons."[1] While Singer famously argued that we should all be supporting international aid organizations like Oxfam, Hardin famously argued that we ought not to support international relief efforts on the grounds that such efforts produced more harm than good.

I subjected Hardin's article to a litany of critical, and often scathing, objections. I treated Singer's article much more sympathetically. I thought Singer's article was a shining example of "applied philosophy done right." It illustrated to my students that philosophy could be genuinely relevant to the real world and that philosophers could actually have a substantial impact on the world. Predictably, many of my students were moved, after that section of the course, to contribute to international relief organizations. Some even went on to work for such organizations. I readily admit that I was pleased by such developments.

Looking back, I am now somewhat abashed about all this. I believe that I was not really giving Hardin's article a fair reading. I was looking for all the holes in his arguments, and was too quick to overlook any insights that he may have been onto. My reaction to Singer's article was just the reverse. I was looking for all the insights in his article, and was too quick to overlook any worries that might be raised about it.

I still believe that Singer's article has many of the virtues that I attributed to it. It *is* an outstanding example of applied philosophy; it *does* show that philosophy can have real-world relevance; and it clearly illustrates that philosophers *can* impact the world. However, I no longer believe, as I once did, that

---

[1] Singer, Peter, "Famine, Affluence, and Morality," *Philosophy and Public Affairs* 1 (1972): 229–43 and Hardin, Garrett, "The Tragedy of the Commons," *Science*, New Series 162 (1968): 1243–8.

there is a straight route from Singer's arguments to the conclusion that we ought to be supporting international development agencies that operate directly in the world's poorest regions.[2*] As we have seen, throughout this book, there are numerous disanalogies between Singer's Pond Example, and the complex realities that surround the plight of the needy in some of the world's poorest regions.

When we are confronted with Singer's Pond Example, we don't need to worry about whether: the victim is innocent or responsible for her plight; there are intervening agents with their own agendas; our lifesaving efforts may be diverted for other purposes; the drowning child is a victim of social injustice; others may stand to benefit from our intervention; our intervention may support, or incentivize, evil or corrupt regimes and evil or disastrous policies; our interventions may introduce marketplace incentives and distortions that cause problems elsewhere in society; our action could be replicated or scaled up; we are failing to respect the drowning child, her customs, ways of life, or autonomy; our intervention may undermine the responsiveness of a government to its citizens; our action, though it might be beneficial when considered by itself, might be one of a set of actions that, together, do more harm than good; and so on. Unfortunately, we need to be worried about *all* these possibilities when we consider supporting international development efforts in the world's poorest regions.

As noted in Chapter 3, Singer himself is careful not to claim more for his Pond Example than it might support. That is, officially, Singer's Pond Example is "merely" intended to exemplify the truth of one of two propositions, a strong principle:

Preventing Bad without Comparable Moral Loss: if it is in our power to prevent something very bad from happening, without thereby sacrificing anything of comparable moral significance, we ought, morally, to do it.[3]

[2*] Singer agrees. He notes, in correspondence, that "The path is more complicated than the article implies. But I think that it still leads to the same destination—or at least the expected value of heading down the path is greater than the expected value of not doing so." I'm less sure than Singer that the expected value of heading down the path *is* greater than the expected value of not doing so. At least, I'm less sure about this in many of the world's poorest regions that are controlled by warlords, dictators, and/or corrupt governments that are unresponsive to their citizens. But even where the expected value *is* greater by heading down the path, part of the point of this book is to urge that in this domain, as in most domains of practical ethics, there is more to consider if one wants to be good than the question of what will maximize the expected value of one's actions.

[3] "Famine, Affluence, and Morality," p. 231.

Or a weak principle:

Preventing Bad without Moral Loss: if it is in our power to prevent something very bad from happening, without thereby sacrificing anything morally significant, we ought, morally, to do it.[4]

Nevertheless, the reality is that Singer suggests that much follows about our obligations to the needy from the truth of either the strong or weak principles. Moreover, many of Singer's readers and followers clearly infer from his article that they ought to be supporting international development organizations that directly operate in the world's poorest regions to aid the needy.

The problem with this reasoning is that it seems to be focusing on whether the person making the contribution to aid the needy would *herself* be sacrificing anything morally significant, or anything of comparable moral significance, in doing so. But this is clearly a mistake. It is much too narrow of a focus. Surely, as Singer himself would accept, if the strong and weak principles are to have any claim to plausibility, their focus must extend to *everyone* who would be affected by our attempt to prevent something very bad from happening, both directly and indirectly, and in the long term as well as the short term.

However, once the scope of the weak principle is correctly extended, it is evident that nothing follows at all about whether we should be donating money to support international development organizations. Likewise, given the extraordinarily complex realities with which international aid organizations frequently must contend, it is clear that much more empirical work needs to be done about the total direct, indirect, and collective impacts of international development efforts, and much more normative work needs to be done on what sorts of impacts are, or are not, of comparable moral significance, before one can pass judgment on whether the strong principle, properly extended, would or would not require the funding of international development organizations.

Singer's pioneering article has an exalted place in the annals of applied philosophy. Rightly so, in my judgment, as it has launched a much greater awareness of the fundamentally important topic of our obligations to the needy. On reflection, however, I believe that Singer's article, and his Pond Example in particular, don't actually take us very far in answering the question of what we should do, all things considered, to aid the world's needy.

---

[4] "Famine, Affluence, and Morality," p. 231.

15.2 Reassessing Effective Altruism's Approach to Global Need

Let us next reconsider Effective Altruism's approach to global need, in light of this book's claims. Throughout this book, I have acknowledged that Effective Altruism reflects an important perspective that is relevant to our obligations to the needy. However, I have argued that, ultimately, one should adopt a broader, more pluralistic approach to thinking about the needy. Specifically, I have argued that there is much more to *being* good in a world of need, than *doing* the most good for the needy.

I shall return, again, to the importance of my pluralistic approach in my concluding chapter. Still, it is important to acknowledge that virtually all my worries regarding international aid efforts are compatible with Effective Altruism's approach. So, Effective Altruists might question whether my worries are *practically* significant, but they have no reason to deny their *theoretical* relevance to the topic of global aid.

There have, in fact, been only a few respects in which my arguments have been at odds with the thinking of some Effective Altruists. Let me mention three.

First, a pragmatic point. Although Effective Altruists are committed, in principle, to maximizing the welfare of the needy, in fact, I believe that some Effective Altruists (though certainly not all) have focused their aid efforts on global health. Those who share this focus believe that where the global needy are involved, the greatest return on investment is likely to come in the fields of health. On the view of these Effective Altruists, we should support those international efforts that have the greatest impact on extending people's lives, or ameliorating the health-related physical or mental effects of the most debilitating diseases, conditions, or events.

It is not surprising that some Effective Altruists have this focus, since arguably the greatest "successes" in international aid interventions have come in the health field: for example, the eradication of smallpox, the near eradication of polio, and significant reductions in mortality due to malaria. Moreover, the natural tendency to focus on health, and in particular on physical health, may largely reflect the tractability of dealing with adverse physical conditions, and the seeming intractability of dealing with many other deep-rooted social, political, and human problems. Still, in this book, I have adopted a much broader focus in thinking about how to respond to the plight of the needy.

I believe that there is an important kernel of truth to the old adage that "if you don't have your health you don't have anything." Correspondingly,

I believe that good physical and mental health is an important, and perhaps even essential, component of human wellbeing. Still, pluralist that I am, I believe that there are many important components to human wellbeing, including, but not limited to, freedom, autonomy, love, respect, rights, equality, justice, fairness, creativity, beauty, knowledge, understanding, friendship, good family relationships, achievement, meaningful work, virtue, spirituality, etc. Moreover, I believe there is significant value to many ideals—such as freedom, autonomy, equality, fairness, justice, perfection, virtue, duty, respect, beauty, knowledge, and truth—*beyond* the extent to which the realization of such ideals improves human wellbeing.[5] Thus, when I think about the overall impact of international relief efforts, both positively and negatively, I would give weight to *all* those factors, as well as others, in my evaluation of which international aid efforts, if any, to support, and not merely the health impacts of different aid efforts.

Now, in fact, most philosophers who are Effective Altruists would readily agree that there is much more to wellbeing than merely good health (though welfarist Effective Altruists will disagree with me that there can be value to promoting ideals when they do not benefit anyone—in the sense of improving someone's welfare). Still, for a variety of social, cultural, political, historical, and practical reasons, it all too easy to focus attention on health interventions in evaluating international relief efforts. As indicated, I believe this is a mistake.

Among other things, I suspect that the focus on health may help explain why some people have underestimated the significance of Angus Deaton's worries about undermining government responsiveness to its citizens; since much of the value of government responsiveness may lie in important human values and endeavors that lie outside the health domain. In particular, responsive well-functioning governments have a crucial role to play in fostering the conditions where such quintessential human ideals as freedom, autonomy, respect, fairness, equality, justice, rights, duty, virtue, and perfection can be realized. In my judgment, the values of such ideals are both extremely

⁵ See, for example, my "Harmful Goods, Harmless Bads," in *Value, Welfare, and Morality*, edited by Richard Frey and Christopher Morris, Cambridge: Cambridge University Press, 1993, 290–324; *Inequality*, New York: Oxford University Press, 1993, Chapter 9; "Personal versus Impersonal Principles: Reconsidering the Slogan," *Theoria* 69 (2003): 20–30; "Egalitarianism Defended," *Ethics* 113 (2003): 764–82; "Equality, Priority, and the Levelling Down Objection," in *The Ideal of Equality*, edited by Matthew Clayton and Andrew Williams, New York: St. Martin's Press, 2000, 126–61; "Illuminating Egalitarianism," in *Contemporary Debates in Political Philosophy*, edited by Thomas Christiano and John Christman, Oxford: Wiley-Blackwell Publishing, 2009, 155–78; and *Rethinking the Good: Moral Ideals and the Nature of Practical Reasoning*, New York: Oxford University Press, 2012.

important, and largely orthogonal to the value of being healthy. Moreover, this is so, I believe, even though it may be true that in conditions of poor health it may be difficult, or even impossible, to fully achieve, appreciate, or take advantage of such ideals.

Second, in Chapter 10, I raised a number of worries about whether international relief efforts might often be associated with demeaning or otherwise inappropriate attitudes towards the recipients of aid, and whether such efforts might involve forms of paternalism that fail to show sufficient respect for the people being aided, their ways of life, and their autonomy. Consequentialists can, in principle, attach weight to such concerns in a variety of ways. However, worries about respect, autonomy, and inappropriate attitudes are perhaps more naturally at home within the deontological tradition.

Even if Effective Altruists attach value to autonomy and respect, their "do the most good" approach implies paternalistic interventions on behalf of the needy are always morally permissible as long as they genuinely do the most good. For welfarist Effective Altruists, even if they see autonomy and respect as important components of welfare, they will still favor any paternalistic interventions that maximize overall welfare. Moreover, this will be so whether or not such interventions show respect for other people's autonomy, customs, and ways of life, and whether or not they reflect attitudes that some may find objectionable. I reject these positions.

As a pluralist who gives weight to deontological considerations, as well as consequentialist ones, I believe that in some cases, at least, we must refrain from acting paternalistically on behalf of others, even if our doing so would genuinely maximize their welfare, or the overall good. This might be so if our interventions involve inappropriate attitudes towards the needy, and/or a failure to show sufficient respect for them, their ways of life, or their autonomy. (And, I should add, since I am not an absolutist, if the consequentialist gains from such interventions are not so substantial as to outweigh the strong deontological considerations otherwise prohibiting such interventions. Deontological restrictions can place high barriers against maximizing the good; however, if *enough* good is at stake, even very high barriers can be crossed. So, unlike Kant, I think it would be morally permissible to imprison an innocent person if that were necessary to save an entire nation. However, granting that does not imply that it is morally permissible to imprison an innocent person *whenever* doing so would maximize the good.)

Third, I have worried that in some cases, at least, international development efforts might directly or indirectly strengthen the position of ruthless governments and support their actions and agendas. In some cases, I suggested, this may involve our being complicit in evil crimes that they perpetrate against innocent citizens or non-citizens. In those cases, I suggested, there may be deontological objections, or perhaps virtue-based objections, which could make it impermissible for us to be complicit in such activities, even if the total amount of good produce by the international relief efforts outweighed the total amount of bad produced by the ruthless governments due to the international relief effort's complicit behavior. This position, too, is at odds with the "do the most good" spirit of Effective Altruism.

There are, then, several important respects in which my arguments are at odds with Effective Altruism's approach. However, as already acknowledged, most of my arguments pose no objection to Effective Altruism, in principle. This is because most of my arguments raised worries about possible negative effects of international development efforts, and this reflects the consequentialist perspective that underlies Effective Altruism. Nevertheless, as I shall discuss next, the qualification "in principle" is important.

15.3 Effective Altruism as a Clarion Call to Practical Action

One of the qualities that I admire most about many of those in the Effective Altruism Movement is that they are not merely content to put forward Effective Altruism as a plausible theoretical philosophical position. To the contrary, they are very concerned that Effective Altruism itself be an effective practical movement. My worry is that in their efforts to make concrete practical suggestions, here and now, Effective Altruists do not, and perhaps cannot, adequately take account of many of this book's worries. Worries of which, by the lights of their own theory, they really need to take account.

In this book, I have given some of the many reasons for this. The positive effects of aid interventions are often direct, easily identified, and easily quantified. Moreover, there is every reason for international aid agencies to keep track of these and trumpet their successes. The negative effects of aid interventions are often indirect, difficult to identify, and hard to quantify. Moreover, there are reasons for aid agencies, and others, to fail to look for these, underreport them if they are spotted, or even cover them up. As a result, it is very easy for those who want to help the needy, including Effective Altruists, to receive, and convey, an overly rosy one-sided picture that distorts the benefits of supporting international relief organizations. There are several worries here, other than the obvious one that we might not be doing as much good as we think we are.

One worry, of course, is that we are not actually supporting the most effective international relief organizations, despite our best intentions. If we have much better information about our interventions' benefits, than we do about our interventions' harms, then we may well end up supporting agencies that produce great benefits, but also great harms, rather than agencies that only produce very good benefits, but almost no harms. However, in terms of what Effective Altruists care about, the second sort of agencies might be much better than the first.

A second worry is that we may be overlooking more important ways of aiding the needy. Perhaps our first priority should be to promote human rights; or to promote social, political, and economic reforms to reduce corruption and promote good governance; or to work for changes in international law, the rules of international commerce, patents and intellectual property rights, and so on, all of which are largely dictated by, and for the benefit of, the world's wealthiest and most powerful nations, and many of which have the effect of buttressing many of the world's most oppressive and corrupt governments and dictators.[6]

Undoubtedly, Effective Altruists are more than open to such possibilities, in theory. However, I fear that a focused attention on which of the many international aid organizations directly improve welfare outcomes may distract us from seriously considering and promoting alternative social, political, legal, and economic mechanisms that may ultimately be even more important for improving the plight of the needy. Moreover, this is especially likely to be so if we focus on the observable benefits of the international aid organizations that we are assessing, and fail to see the harms that may accompany those benefits elsewhere in the system.

A third worry—the worst-case scenario discussed in Chapters 11 through 13—is that if we mainly focus on the direct benefits and overlook the indirect harms of international aid organizations, we may, in some contexts at least, actually be doing more harm than good, either individually or collectively.[7*]

---

[6] A champion of the latter approach is Thomas Pogge, whose views I discussed in Section 14.1. See Pogge's seminal work on the topic in *Realizing Rawls* (Ithaca: Cornell University Press, 1989); "An Egalitarian Law of Peoples," *Philosophy and Public Affairs* 23 (1994): 195–224; *World Poverty and Human Rights*, 2nd Edition (Cambridge: Polity Press, 2008); and *Politics as Usual: What Lies Behind the Pro-Poor Rhetoric* (Cambridge: Polity Press, 2010). See, also, Leif Wenar's *Blood Oil: Tyrants, Violence, and the Rules that Run the World* (New York: Oxford University Press, 2017).

[7*] Interestingly, some leaders of the Effective Altruism movement share the concern expressed in this section, even if they were once associated with Effective Altruism being a practical movement. For example, Will MacAskill, the author of *Doing Good Better: How Effective Altruism Can Help You Help*

15.4 Important Clarifications and Caveats

In this book, I have raised a host of worries about possible indirect negative effects of international relief efforts. I have certainly not claimed that each of these worries is equally serious. Nor have I claimed that each of these worries is equally likely to obtain. Nor, importantly, have I claimed that all these worries arise in all contexts of need, and for all aid organizations.

For example, *GiveDirectly* is an international aid organization that gives unconditional cash transfers to poor people in the developing world.[8] Recipients of the cash can use it however they see fit. This is one international development organization that I believe largely, and perhaps wholly, avoids Chapter 10's worries about paternalism, respect, autonomy, and inappropriate attitudes towards aid recipients.

Similarly, as implied previously, some of the perverse incentives that may arise when aid is provided to victims of social injustice, don't arise in cases where aid is provided to victims of natural disasters that no one could have done anything to prevent, and where everything that could have been reasonably done in advance to mitigate the effect of such natural disasters had been done. Arguably, that will be the case for at least some of the many natural disasters that occurred during the months of August and September of 2017 as I was preparing my Uehiro Lectures: hurricanes, cyclones, and massive flooding throughout the Caribbean, portions of the U.S. and Mexico, Ghana, the Central Republic of Africa, Ethiopia, Nigeria, and South Sudan; substantial earthquakes in Mexico; mudslides and landslides in Sierra Leone and the Democratic Republic of Congo; Dengue outbreaks in Pakistan and Sri Lanka; major forest fires in Tunisia; and damaging volcanic eruptions in Indonesia.[9]

Others, Do Work that Matters, and Make Smarter Choices about Giving Back (New York: Avery, 2016) and one of the Co-Founders of the Effective Altruism group 80,000 Hours (which provides concrete suggestions for what avenues people should pursue if they want to do the most good) has told me in conversation that this book's worries are more relevant against the "practical" wing of Effective Altruism, identified with Peter Singer, than with the "theoretical" wing of Effective Altruism, with which he now aligns. That is, despite his widely influential work on the practical importance of Effective Altruism, MacAskill now believes that Effective Altruists should mainly focus on figuring out what actions would, in fact, have the greatest expected utility, rather than trying to act now before we have the information necessary to settle that question.

So, MacAskill shares my worries. However, we do not share the same view of how to proceed in light of those worries.

[8] For more information on GiveDirectly, see their website, "What We Do," *GiveDirectly*, 2018, URL: https://givedirectly.org/operating-model, accessed September 10, 2018.

[9] "Disasters, 2017/01/01 to 2018/01/01," ReliefWeb, *OCHA*, UHL: https://reliefweb.int/disasters?date=20,170,101–20,180,101#content, accessed September 26, 2017.

Many of these disasters required massive amounts of aid to deal with the most basic problems of food, safe water, shelter, and urgent medical care. Beyond that, however, massive infrastructure and construction efforts were required for months, and in some cases years, to rebuild and restore entire communities that were destroyed. Clearly, focusing on such aid efforts would avoid some of my worries, though not others. (Unfortunately, many of the natural disasters struck in areas with poor, corrupt, weak, or unresponsive governments, such that the worries raised in Chapters 6, 7, and 11 would come into play.)

Many of the worries I raised were specifically about ways in which international aid might indirectly support corrupt, evil, or unresponsive governments. And unfortunately, many of the world's needy live in nations that are headed by such governments. However, there are plenty of needy people across the globe who could benefit from international assistance who are living in nations with governments that are not corrupt, evil, or are unresponsive, or are much less so. Accordingly, one could avoid the worst of the problems associated with operating in countries headed by terrible governments by focusing on providing aid to needy people in nations headed by good governments, or at least decent governments. (Although if Deaton is right, there remains the worry that aid can have a destabilizing effect on decent or even good governments, leading to forms of corruption that weren't there previously; and also the worry that aid can undermine the responsiveness of governments that were previously responsive to the interests, needs, and wills of their citizens.)

Relatedly, some of my worries regarding marketplace distortions, and internal or external brain drain, may not arise in countries where there is a large, talented, highly motivated, well-educated workforce. Likewise, my worries about perverse incentives, indirectly supporting the evil activities of evil governments, and undermining the responsiveness of a government to its citizens are particularly acute in desperately poor countries where foreign aid represents a significant portion of the countries' annual incomes, and an even greater proportion of the governments' annual expenditures. Thus, for example, speaking about the argument that aid threatens institutions, Deaton observes, as noted previously, that this argument "depends on the amount of aid being large. In China, India, or South Africa, where ODA [Official Development Assistance] in recent years has been less than 0.5 percent of national income, and only occasionally more than 1 percent of total government expenditures, aid is not important in affecting government behavior or the development of institutions. The situation is quite different in much of Africa. Thirty-six (out of forty-nine) countries have received at least 10 percent of their national income as ODA for three decades or more . . . . [T]he ratio of aid to government expenditure is larger still. Benin, Burkina Faso, the DRC [Democratic Republic of Congo], Ethiopia, Madagascar, Niger, Sierra Leone, Togo, and Uganda are among the countries where aid has exceeded 75 percent of government expenditure for a run of recent years. In Kenya and Zambia, ODA is a quarter and a half of government expenditure, respectively."[10]

Now ODA are the funds donated by the governments of rich donor countries for the welfare and development of poor recipient countries, and in this book I have been mainly focusing on the effects of NGO efforts to aid the needy. However, it is important not to lose sight of the context in which NGOs are operating. If NGOs are operating in a context where a significant percentage of the national income or government expenditures stems from outside sources, then the worry about contributing to the undermining of government responsiveness and effective government institutions is significant, otherwise not.

It is a striking fact that most of the world's development aid is directed to the world's poorest countries. It may seem obvious that this is how it should be, except when one pauses to consider that millions of the world's poor live outside of such countries. For example, the World Bank notes that due to the impact of Covid-19, an estimated 88 million people will have been pushed into extreme poverty in 2020, alone, using an estimated global economic contraction rate of 5 percent due to Covid-19, and as many as 115 million with a contraction rate of 8 percent.[11] Strikingly, it is estimated that "overall, some 72 million of the projected new poor in the baseline scenario [5 percent contraction] will be in middle-income countries—more than four-fifths of the total new poor."[12] The estimates "suggest that South Asia will be the region hardest with 49 million (almost 57 million under the downside scenario [8 percent contraction rate])."[13] Further, these are the figures using the global poverty income rate of US$1.90 a day; when "applying the higher regional poverty thresholds appropriate for lower-middle-income countries (US$3.20 a day) and upper-middle-income countries (US$5.50 a day), the poverty impact of COVID-19 will be much greater."[14]

[10] Deaton, Angus, *The Great Escape: Health, Wealth, and the Origins of Inequality* (Princeton: Princeton University Press, 2013), p. 296.

[11] *Poverty and Shared Prosperity 2020: Reversals of Fortune*, pp. 5–6, World Bank Group, available at https://openknowledge.worldbank.org/bitstream/handle/10986/34496/9781464816024.pdf, accessed March 29, 2021.

[12] *Poverty and Shared Prosperity 2020*, pp. 5–6.   [13] *Poverty and Shared Prosperity 2020*, p. 5.

[14] *Poverty and Shared Prosperity 2020*, p. 6.

For that matter, there are many millions of poor, desperately ill, or badly-off people living in substandard conditions scattered throughout the world's most developed countries, including significant numbers of: migrant workers, immigrants, refugees, the unemployed and unemployable, the severely physically or mentally handicapped, servants, manual laborers, the elderly, slum dwellers, the rural poor, victims of severe bullying, abuse, or discrimination, de facto slaves, victims (often underage) of sexual predation, the homeless, members of the lowest castes, etc. In a 2018 *New York Times* Op-Ed essay, Angus Deaton pointed out that according to the World Bank, of the world's poorest people—those living "on less than [US]$1.90 a day in 2013, . . . 3.2 million live in the United States, and 3.3 million in other high-income countries (most in Italy, Japan, and Spain)."[15] Moreover, he notes that "When we compare absolute poverty in the United States with absolute poverty in India, or other poor countries, we should be using $4 in the United States and $1.90 in India. Once we do this, there are 5.3 million Americans who are absolutely poor by global standards. This . . . is more than in Sierra Leone (3.2 million) or Nepal (2.5 million), about the same as Senegal (5.3 million) and only one third less than Angola (7.4 million)."[16]

Here, Deaton is using World Bank data from 2013, and there were improvements in U.S. poverty numbers between 2013 and 2019. Unfortunately, with the disproportionate health and economic impact of Covid-19 on the disadvantaged, many of those gains have since been lost, and the general point Deaton was making remains true. While the proportion of people facing dire situations is much greater in the world's poorest countries than in the world's richest countries, it remains true that many people are very badly off even in the world's wealthiest countries, and even more so in middle-income countries.

One might believe, perhaps correctly, that such people are the responsibility of the rich countries that they inhabit. Further, the conventional wisdom tells us that one can produce far more good for far less money, by aiding people who are badly off in poor countries than one can by aiding people who are badly off in rich countries. Still, given that there are clearly badly-off people in rich countries who are not, in fact, adequately being taken care of by their governments or local communities, perhaps more attention should be paid

---

[15] Deaton, Angus, "The U.S. Can No Longer Hide From Its Deep Poverty Problem," *The New York Times*, January 24, 2018, URL: Opinion | The U.S. Can No Longer Hide From Its Deep Poverty Problem—The New York Times (nytimes.com), accessed June 5, 2019.

[16] Deaton, "The U.S. Can No Longer Hide From Its Deep Poverty Problem."

by international aid organizations to relieve the plight of the needy in middle- and high-income countries, on the grounds that ultimately it is needy *people* who matter, more than needy *countries*. (Note, *more* attention does not necessarily mean exclusive attention.)

Clearly, many of the worries that arise concerning the possible negative effects of relatively large expenditures in desperately poor countries will not arise if similar size expenditures are instead directed to aid needy people in India, China, France, the UK, Canada, Italy, Japan, the United States, Vietnam, Ukraine, Morocco, Egypt, the Philippines, and so on. Moreover, here, too, there are different ways one could go about trying to aid the needy in wealthy countries. One could seek ways of improving their lot directly. Alternatively, or additionally, one could seek social, cultural, and political changes within the more developed countries that would lead those countries to appropriately care for the neediest people within their borders.

15.5 Taking Expected Utility Theory Seriously

For reasons presented in my book *Rethinking the Good*, and touched on in Appendix A, I have serious doubts about putting too much weight on Expected Utility Theory. Nevertheless, I believe that Expected Utility Theory can be a valuable tool, if used wisely, and properly. In this section, I want to comment on the importance of my worries for anyone who takes Expected Utility Theory seriously. This applies to Effective Altruists, or anyone else who believes that efforts to aid the needy should be guided, at least in part, by the goal of doing as much good as one can.

As noted previously, most Effective Altruists are committed to following Expected Utility Theory in determining which international aid organizations are most effective (although if they are non-consequentialist Effective Altruists, their support of such organizations will be constrained by the requirement that the organizations not be acting wrongly in promoting their ends). But Expected Utility Theory requires that one consider *all* the possible effects of any action, both positive and negative, weighted by the probabilities of the different possible effects occurring. Given the understandable zeal to do *something* to aid the world's needy; the readily identifiable and quantifiable good effects that international aid agencies can point to; and the difficulty of identifying and quantifying any negative direct, indirect, short-term, long-term, and interaction effects to which international aid efforts give rise (not to mention the disincentive that international aid agencies have to look for such negative effects in the first place,[17] or to report those of which they are aware); I suspect that Effective Altruists have largely concentrated on the positive outcomes relative to expenditures of alternative aid organizations when they assess their effectiveness.

Clearly, to the extent that this unbalanced approach is occurring—whether or not anyone is intentionally responsible for it, or it is anyone's fault that this is how people have proceeded given the information at their disposal— Effective Altruists are abandoning the Expected Utility Theory approach that serves as the foundation for their position. In so doing, they open themselves to the real possibility that they are not identifying and supporting the most effective international aid organizations. Indeed, in the worst-case scenario, they may even be supporting efforts that are doing more harm than good, overall. Moreover, this may be so individually and/or collectively.

Let me make several further observations related to this. I have identified a number of worries about possible negative effects of certain international aid efforts. Experience informs me that some Effective Altruists and others will acknowledge that the negative effects I have discussed are, indeed, *possible*, but relatively unlikely to result from any particular international aid intervention, so that these worries can, and should, be ignored for practical purposes. But there are several responses to this, besides the fundamentally important one, already discussed in detail in Chapter 12, that even if no *particular* aid

---

[17] Jeff McMahan and Roger Crisp have suggested, in correspondence, that aid organizations and their well-intentioned members do have incentive to look for any negative effects to which their efforts might lead, to improve on their efforts and avoid such negative effects in the future. This is so even if, for the reasons noted earlier, they may lack incentive to *advertise* those negative effects to potential donors. I accept this point, in principle, and no doubt there are some aid workers who proceed just as McMahan and Crisp believe they should.

However, I fear that once an aid organization is actually up and running, the bureaucratic tendency for job preservation and self-perpetuation takes on a life of its own. This gives rise to substantial pressures to keep the organization running as easily, smoothly, and efficiently as possible, and to not rock the boat in ways that might seriously threaten the continued existence of the agency and its efforts. These pressures may well come to have greater impact on the operation of the agency than the moral considerations that led to its creation in the first place, though the agency's members may not see it in that light. They might just be extremely confident that their organization is, on balance, doing great things, and this might naturally lead them to want to protect its ability to continue to do its important work.

Further, there are a variety of complex psychological, practical, and financial reasons, why aid organizations and their members may not, in fact, see much point in looking hard for seriously negative effects from their efforts. First, looking for negative effects can be time consuming and costly. Second, psychologically, few people deeply invested in helping people really wants to find out that their efforts have backfired. Third, if one does find seriously negative effects it may be hard, practically, to keep such news "in house," and, of course, if word gets out it could have disastrous effects on future donations. Fourth, even if one *could* keep negative effects out of the news, that might require misleading, or lying to, outside evaluators and potential donors, and that would set up a dynamic between the organization and its backers that was unhealthy, awkward, and morally suspect. For these, and other reasons, I suspect that most aid organizations and their members will not think it a good idea, on balance, to go "looking for trouble," even if they really do see their mission as the noble one of aiding those in need.

intervention causes problems, by itself, the *collective* effects of a large *set* of interventions, may do so.

First, I wonder if there is empirical evidence to support the assumption that the negative results are unlikely to occur, or if this is just wishful thinking on behalf of those who are committed to helping the world's needy, or a byproduct of the fact that there isn't much incentive for people in the aid world to look for possible negative side-effects of their work. It is, I believe, telling that many development economists, whose business it is to traffic in the empirical realm, share many of the concerns that I have raised.[18]

To be sure, it is also the case that most development economists are pro aid, despite sharing many of my concerns. But one cannot help wondering, just a bit, how much of their pro aid stance is rooted in firm empirical evidence of the historical success of aid projects, and how much might be due to other factors. In light of a host of well-known psychological factors, such as cognitive dissonance, confirmation bias, and anchoring bias, one would expect it to be difficult for people whose temperament led them to enter the field of development economics, who trained in that field, and who have devoted their careers to the field, to come to the view that many and perhaps most of their efforts and those of their colleagues and students have been ineffective and/or counterproductive.[19*] The same is true for those who are committed to Effective Altruism, and has also been true for me.

---

[18] Admittedly, development economists are usually focusing their attention on Official Development Assistance (ODA), which is to say bilateral or multilateral foreign aid between governments, rather than aid from NGOs. Still, in my (admittedly limited) reading of the literature, I think most development economists would agree that although the problems associated with ODA and NGOs can differ both in degree and kind, there is also sufficient overlap between them that most of the problems I have discussed are pertinent to the latter, as well as the former.

[19*] Roughly, *cognitive dissonance* is the state of anxiety or distress that arises from simultaneously holding contradictory or otherwise incompatible attitudes or beliefs. It is well known that humans naturally tend to avoid cognitive dissonance. Thus, someone who entered the field of development economics with the firm conviction that the field could illuminate effective ways of aiding the needy and that by participating in the field they would be substantially helping the needy, would try to avoid unsettling results incompatible with those beliefs. This might include avoiding, discounting, or finding ways to "explain away" evidence or theories that were incompatible with their beliefs.

Similarly, *confirmation bias* is the well-known psychological tendency for humans to interpret new evidence as confirmation of one's existing beliefs or theories. Accordingly, someone who entered the field of development economics with the firm belief that the field could illuminate effective ways of aiding the needy and that by participating in the field they would be substantially helping the needy, would tend to interpret any new evidence about the effects of aid efforts in ways that confirmed their antecedent beliefs. And since much of the evidence in this domain is rough, complex, incomplete, and not definitive, there is ample room for those with optimistic pro-aid convictions to interpret the evidence in the field as supporting their beliefs.

Finally, *anchoring* is a common cognitive bias where individuals depend too heavily on an initial piece of information or belief (the anchor) when making decisions. Anchoring occurs when individuals allow their anchoring information or belief to influence their judgments about future information or evidence, in that those bits of information or evidence that are like the initial anchor are readily taken on board and accepted, while those that are at odds with the anchor are not taken on board. Thus, the

Second, even if the likelihood of any *particular* negative effect obtaining is relatively small, if there are many such possibilities, the overall likelihood that at least *one* of them will obtain might still be relatively high. This is easy to lose sight of.

Third, even if the possibility of a negative effect obtaining is small, if the negative effect is extremely bad—such as might be the case if international aid efforts indirectly further the agenda of a genocidal regime—that could have a significant impact on the expected utility of an international aid intervention.

Fourth, I suspect that many people in the international aid world start with the "obvious" assumption that *of course* they should be focusing their efforts on aiding those people in the world's poorest regions facing premature death or severely debilitating conditions due to poverty, famine, war, tyranny, ignorance, or disease. Accordingly, they may reason that many of the worries that I have raised, however, legitimate, will be faced by *any* international aid agency operating in those regions, so that, for practical purposes, they can be safely ignored in our expected utility calculations when evaluating the *comparative* effectiveness of different aid agencies seeking to promote the goal in question.

However, there are two problems with this. First, even if it is true that most of my worries will be faced by any international aid agency operating in the world's poorest regions, the particular probabilities and magnitudes of the negative effects in question will vary from context to context (where the magnitude of the negative effects will be a function of both the quality and quantity of any negative effects that obtain). Thus, one needs to do the best one can to estimate those for each unique context, if one is serious about determining the effectiveness of alternative aid efforts on the basis of Expected Utility Theory.

---

anchoring bias makes it difficult for new evidence to move one to a drastically different position than where one started out, on the basis of one's initial evidence or beliefs. Thus, again, if people started out with what they took to be clear evidence for the effectiveness of aid efforts—which might well have been formed under conditions that do not typically obtain with international aid efforts—they are likely to take on board any purported evidence for the effectiveness of aid efforts, and to be suspicious or dismissive of purported evidence for the ineffectiveness of aid efforts.

I am not claiming, of course, that the effects of cognitive dissonance, confirmation bias, and anchoring are the same for everyone, that they cannot be overcome, or that, ultimately, they offer the best explanation for the fact that most development economists are cautiously optimistic about the overall effects of international aid. Perhaps the evidence really does best support their cautiously optimistic position. However, it is worth bearing in mind that even the most brilliant of people are liable to such psychological phenomena. Thus, it would not be surprising if those who entered a field predisposed to believe that that field, and their participation in it, could substantially help the needy, might be persuaded that the evidence supported their position even if, in fact, objectively it did not.

Second, as noted previously, given that there are many desperately poor and badly-off people scattered throughout the world, it is a mistake to just assume, as one's starting point, that efforts to aid the world's needy should focus on the world's poorest regions. If, for example, one could help 1,000 needy people in the desperately poor region of sub-Saharan Africa, or 1,000 needy people in Australia, it *might* be better from the standpoint of Expected Utility Theory to focus one's aid efforts in Australia. This could be the case even if the expected benefits of aiding people in sub-Saharan Africa exceeded the expected benefits of aiding people in Australia. Whether or not this was so, of course, would depend on whether the expected harms of intervening in sub-Saharan Africa were *sufficiently* greater than the expected harms of intervening in Australia, as determined by both the probability and the magnitude of any negative effects that might arise from one's interventions in the different environments.

Many development economists believe that there is little concrete evidence to believe that, collectively, international aid efforts in the world's poorest regions have done much, if anything, to promote long-term social and economic progress; some, like Angus Deaton, believe that such efforts are likely to be doing more harm than good.[20] Even if we find such views intuitively difficult to believe, we cannot simply ignore such views if we are serious about employing the approach of Expected Utility Theory underlying Effective Altruism. Even if, after considering all the relevant facts, we ultimately decide that Deaton and others who share his view are more likely to be wrong than right, surely there is *some* chance that they are right. Is it 40 percent, or 25 percent, or 10 percent? Even if it were only 10 percent, I suspect that that would be high enough to have a substantial impact on the practical recommendations of Effective Altruism.

One thing that I have not done in this book is to offer concrete practical advice as to what one *should* do if one wants to be good in a world of need. It would be nice if I could provide such advice. However, I am a philosopher, not a social scientist. I have pointed out a host of considerations that I believe need to be taken into consideration, if one genuinely wants to be good in a world of need, and many of these will also have to be taken into consideration if one genuinely wants to make decisions based on the proper use of Expected Utility

---

[20] Easterly sides with Deaton. Riddell contends that the evidence is simply inconclusive to support an overall, general, conclusion. Glennie and Sumner believe that aid sometimes works, and sometimes not, but that, overall, aid has been effective, though perhaps not significantly so if measured in terms of long-term social, political, and economic growth. See, Easterly, William, *The White Man's Burden: Why the West's Efforts to Aid the Rest Have Done So Much Ill and So Little Good* (New York: Penguin Press, 2006); Riddell, Roger, *Does Foreign Aid Really Work?* (Oxford: Oxford University Press, 2007); and Glennie, Jonathan and Andy Sumner, *Aid, Growth and Poverty* (London: Palgrave Macmillan, 2016).

Theory. However, to get beyond that, one actually needs to do the difficult messy work of empirical social science, to gather and assess the relevant data that would enable us to make educated guesses as to the relevant probabilities and magnitudes of both benefits *and* harms of different possible aid efforts. Moreover, this needs to be done not only for health-related aid efforts, but for aid efforts along other important social, economic, and political dimensions (that is, one must give proper weight to the positive and negative effects of aid interventions on freedom, autonomy, rights, respect, fairness, justice, equality, beauty, perfection, love, duty, virtue, religion, friendships, and so on).

I am aware that good faith efforts have been made by many decent people to do exactly what I am seeking. I just believe that even more work needs to be done before we can rest content in this domain. (Happily, the people I know in the Effective Altruism community readily accept this.)

Consider, again, the case of GiveWell, which has arguably done as good a job as any organization—Effective Altruist or otherwise—of trying to take account of negative as well as positive, indirect as well as direct, and long-term as well as short-term effects in their evaluation of different aid agencies. I have not read everything that GiveWell has put on its site and blogs, which is by now a massive amount; however, I have read a great deal of it. So far as I can tell, GiveWell has no variable in its formula for ranking aid agencies that gives weight to the positive or negative ways in which an aid agency's efforts might impact a government's responsiveness to its citizens, either individually or in concert with other aid efforts. Yet, arguably, as Deaton has pointedly observed, the responsiveness of a government to its citizens is the single most important factor relevant to the long-term social, political, and economic progress of a country. If this is right, then one has to wonder about how much confidence one can have, at this stage, in any of the concrete recommendations of organizations like GiveWell.

Here, it might be useful to recall Section 13.2, where we saw that GiveWell has ranked deworming projects highly based on their cost-effectiveness.[21] This, despite only weak evidence, at best, of deworming having short- or long-term positive impacts on wellbeing; and despite there being no known causal mechanism that would explain the positive long-term income increases that some beneficiaries of deworming were found to have in one highly influential study. Does it not stand to reason that GiveWell's cost-effectiveness

[21] Although our discussion in Section 13.2 focused on GiveWell's evaluation of the SCI Foundation, it applies to other deworming agencies as well. Strikingly, given that discussion, of GiveWell's eight top-rated charities, in 2020, four were deworming agencies. See GiveWell's List of Top Charities, URL: https://www.givewell.org/charities/top-charities, accessed August 11, 2020.

calculation should change, if there were even a small possibility that the on-the-ground aid interventions of the deworming projects might undermine the responsiveness of a government to its citizens, even slightly, with negative impacts along multiple important dimensions for virtually an entire population?

In light of the preceding considerations, one has to wonder whether the default should be to follow the current recommendations of organizations like GiveWell until even more sophisticated and nuanced evaluation mechanisms are developed, whether the default should be to look for entirely different ways of benefiting the needy until that day arrives, or whether some other, in-between, approach is warranted. I shall return to this pressing question in the final chapter.

There is an old adage that one shouldn't go looking for trouble, because you might find it! The domain of global aid is one area where I fear that, intentionally or otherwise, many basically follow that adage. Like it or not, we need to look for trouble, or possible troubles, if we are serious about identifying and supporting the most effective international relief organizations by the lights of Expected Utility Theory. In this domain, as in so many others, the ostrich's approach of burying one's head in the sand is a recipe for disaster—or at least a recipe for doing much less good than we otherwise might.

15.6 Summary

This chapter has taken stock of some of this book's main lessons. It has also offered various clarifications, qualifications, and implications of my views.

I have noted that my original, one-sided approach to the topic of aid was misguided. I was too generous in my readings of pro-aid people like Singer, and too critical in my readings of aid skeptics like Hardin. In particular, this book has shown that despite its many virtues, Singer's classic article, "Famine, Affluence, and Morality," offers little actual guidance as to how we should respond to the plight of the needy. In particular, it doesn't support the conclusion that many, including Singer, seem to have thought it does: namely, that we should be donating to international aid organizations like Oxfam.

I have noted that most of this book's worries about international aid efforts are compatible with the theoretical approach of Effective Altruism. However, while we share a fundamental concern to aid the needy, my pluralistic approach to the issue is decidedly different from Effective Altruism's "do the most good" approach. This is especially so in the case of those Effective

Altruists who adopt a welfarist approach, and even more so where welfare is understood narrowly in terms of the quality of people's conscious mental states or the satisfaction of their preferences.

In assessing the overall impact of aid efforts, I believe that in addition to giving weight to both positive and negative impacts on the quality of conscious mental states, or preference satisfaction, one should also give weight to both positive and negative impacts on factors such as freedom, autonomy, love, respect, rights, equality, justice, fairness, creativity, beauty, knowledge, understanding, friendship, good family relationships, achievement, meaningful work, virtue, and spirituality. Moreover, I believe that many of these factors have some value that is independent of the extent to which they promote welfare. To the extent that Effective Altruists are willing to widen their conception of the good to embrace such claims the differences between us will be smaller. To the extent that Effective Altruists resist such claims, the gulf between us will be larger.

Regardless, I suggested that my pluralistic approach to global aid leads me to value deontological and virtue considerations, as well as ideals like freedom, autonomy, respect, equality, fairness, and justice, in ways that are not fully captured by the "do the most good" approach of Effective Altruism. This is so whether or not one accepts an expanded conception of the good.

I noted that this book's worries suggest that we lack the information needed to confidently assess the overall impact of current aid interventions. This raises important practical questions regarding the recommendations of Effective Altruist organizations like GiveWell. For one, it means that in following their recommendations we may not actually be supporting the most effective aid organizations. For another, it raises the possibility that in following their current recommendations, we may be overlooking even more important ways of aiding the world's needy; ways that might have emerged if we had a full picture of the possible negative impacts of current aid efforts. Further, as argued in Chapters 11 through 13, it opens the possibility that our contributions to current aid efforts may actually be doing more harm than good, individually or collectively.

This chapter also introduced some important clarifications and caveats regarding the scope of my arguments. For example, I noted that certain aid efforts, like those of GiveDirectly, may avoid many of the worries about paternalism, autonomy, and respect, raised in Chapter 10. I also noted that some of the perverse incentives that may arise when one tries to aid victims of social injustice may not arise in certain cases of aid to victims of natural disasters. I further noted that many of my worries regarding marketplace distortions, internal and external brain drain, perverse incentives, buttressing of corrupt regimes and their agendas, or undermining the responsiveness of a government to its citizens, are especially acute in poor countries, with weak economies, ruled by corrupt leaders. Thus, many of my worries would not apply to aid efforts in countries with large, successful economies, or responsive, well-functioning governments with substantial internal sources of income. Bearing in mind that millions of the world's poor live in middle- or high-income countries that are not riddled by corruption, I noted that one could avoid many of this book's worries by supporting aid efforts in those countries. Such an approach to global aid would fit with a focus on aiding poor *people*, rather than poor *countries*. (Whether or not one should adopt this approach is an issue I will return to in the following chapter.)

Finally, I noted that many people are likely to dismiss this book's worries as theoretically interesting, but not of much practical significance. I suggested that this attitude may be based on several psychological factors that are not grounded in the facts. Furthermore, I offered several reasons for thinking that this attitude is deeply problematic for anyone who takes Expected Utility Theory seriously. Thus, for Effective Altruists, ignoring this book's worries is not a defensible option. Indeed, this is so for anyone for whom doing as much good as one can is an important consideration—even if not the only one—in determining how to respond to the plight of the needy.

16

Conclusion

This has been a lengthy book. This concluding chapter presents its main claims, reflects on the possible dangers of a book like this, notes various paths that still need to be explored, and ends by considering where one should go from here if one believes, as I still do, that ignoring the needy is not a morally permissible option.

In Section 16.1, I summarize the book's main claims and arguments.

In Section 16.2, I address the worry that this book may hurt the very people I am concerned to help. Although I share that worry, I claim that there is a similar danger if I don't write this book. I also consider the objection that I don't offer much empirical evidence in support of my worries. I point out that part of my book's point is that we don't yet have the evidence we need to settle the important worries I raise. I also note that it is not my job to provide such evidence. That job falls to social scientists and others. My job, qua philosopher, is to illuminate the complex topic of global aid as clearly, carefully, and honestly as I can. I express the hope that if my worries can be laid to rest that will be readily shown. And if they cannot, they will lead us to a clearer, better, path in responding to the needy.

In Section 16.3, I note that this book has had to leave many important questions unanswered. However, the book offers guidance as to what considerations or paths still need to be pursued to answer those questions. In this section, I briefly canvas nine of the considerations, or paths, that need further exploration in determining how to be good in a world of need.

In Section 16.4, I address the question of how one should proceed in responding to global need in light of this book's arguments. I reiterate a point made at the end of Chapter 1, that although I am agnostic about the desirability of many on-the-ground aid efforts in the world's poorest regions, I am not anti-aid. I suggest ten important ways that we might be able to help people in need, without directly spending money in those countries.

I note my belief that in times of humanitarian crises we may have to intervene to help the needy even when doing so may not be our most effective aid alternative, or even, perhaps, when our intervention may do more harm than good. However, I express my view that far more mid-term and long-term

Being Good in a World of Need. Larry S. Temkin, Oxford University Press. © Larry S. Temkin 2022.
DOI: 10.1093/oso/9780192849977.003.0016

efforts need to be undertaken to significantly change the systematic social, political, legal, and institutional factors that give rise to so much global need.

Unfortunately, the issue of global need is extremely complex, and there are no easy, obvious, or straightforward solutions to it. However, that does not lessen our responsibility to search for solutions. I conclude that if we want to be good in a world of need, ignoring the needy is not an option, even if it is unclear what we should do in light of that truth.

16.1 Summary

In this section, I summarize the book's main arguments and conclusions, to this point.

In Chapter 1, I noted some basic facts concerning the prevalence and significance of global need. I discussed the audience for this book, offered several methodological remarks and preliminary comments, commented on the role that intuitions play in my arguments, and discussed why, for the most part, I focus on those who are innocent in discussing the needy. Among other things, I explained why, in this book, I was focusing on worries about global aid efforts.

I also introduced Effective Altruism, and noted that my discussion would be limited to that subset of Effective Altruism that focuses on helping the global needy. Roughly, on (Global Aid) Effective Altruism people ought to support the most effective charities doing the most important work, and they should do this in the most effective manner possible. Practically, it has been thought that this means identifying and supporting the most effective international relief and development organizations whose goals, typically, are to aid those people in the world's poorest countries facing premature death or severely debilitating conditions due to poverty, famine, war, tyranny, ignorance, or disease.

I noted that despite the many worries raised in this book, I am not an opponent of global aid. To the contrary, I am a strong proponent of global aid. I just believe that the topic of global aid is much more complex, and murkier, than most have realized.

In Chapter 2, I noted that I have long been concerned about aiding the world's needy, both personally and professionally. I then presented a synopsis of my previous views regarding the topic, claiming that there are powerful consequentialist-, virtue-, and deontological-based reasons to aid the needy.

Regarding outcome-based reasons, I claimed that surely an outcome in which affluent people eat out less, and have fewer toys, clothes, or appliances, is better than one in which many innocent people painfully die of easily avoidable causes. Regarding virtue-based reasons, I suggested that a person of good character would possess the virtues of beneficence, sympathy, compassion, and generosity, and that this would dictate giving priority to easily preventable hunger, illness, and suffering, over the acquisition of goods that one does not need, may hardly use, and would not miss if one didn't have. Regarding deontological-based reasons, I contended that we have a positive duty to aid the needy; that positive duties can be every bit as strong, or even stronger, than many negative duties; that our positive duty to aid the needy will often require us to give priority to addressing more urgent needs over less urgent needs; and that there can be strong reasons of justice to aid the needy even if failing to aid the needy need not involve our acting unjustly.[1]

I further claimed that absent special agent-relative duties, or our deepest projects and commitments being involved, our positive duty to aid others will require us to address the most urgent needs of others before we address other laudable, but less critical goals. I pointed out that most people in the developed world are incredibly well off by global standards, and I provided data regarding the extraordinary sums that people spend on such things as tobacco, alcohol, snack food, entertainment, and eating out. I claimed that the ability to help those less fortunate is not merely available to the rich or superrich; it is available to a large majority of ordinary citizens living in wealthy countries, including many ordinary people who think of themselves as poor, relative to their wealthy compatriots. I noted that there are countless ways in which most people in affluent countries could make small changes in their consumption patterns that, over time, could add up to fairly substantial amounts which could then be used to aid the needy. I further contended that many of the changes required to accomplish this would be such that there would not even *be* a difference in one's life in terms of the overall quality of one's experiences or the satisfaction of one's desires; or where, after a brief time, one wouldn't even *notice* the difference; or where the difference would actually be *better* for oneself. I concluded that most of us in the developed world could do vastly more than we do to help the needy, without making a dent in our affluent lifestyle. In the past, I concluded that our failure to do so was a serious moral failing. While I still believe that, I now believe the issue is much more complicated than

---

[1] On the nature of this distinction, and its importance, see my article "Thinking about the Needy, Justice, and International Organizations," *The Journal of Ethics* 8 (2004): 349–95; especially, Section 3.2, 368–70.

I previously recognized, and that much more work needs to be done to determine the true nature and extent of our obligations to the needy.

In Chapter 3, I presented Peter Singer's famous Pond Example. I noted that Singer's example has had a profound effect on many people's thinking about our obligations to the needy, and I suggested that a significant portion of the modern Effective Altruism Movement has its roots in Singer's example. I noted that while Singer's Pond Example is compatible with Effective Altruism, it is also compatible with other approaches to aiding the needy, including my own pluralistic approach.

I argued that while the Pond Example *seems* to support the conclusion that if we can directly help someone in need at little cost to ourselves, we should do so, that conclusion is much too quick. I offered several examples illustrating that we must take account of the impact of our actions on others, and also on whether aiding the needy would require us to violate the rights of others or to act immorally. These cases reminded us that there may be relevant moral considerations that constrain what it is permissible to do to aid the needy. This point, of which Singer himself was acutely aware, indicates that a number of considerations may be morally relevant to the morality of aiding the needy, besides the general utilitarian consideration of "doing the most good that one can."

I offered several examples in support of the view that in addition to the general agent-neutral duty to aid the needy, there may be various moral considerations that buttress our intuitive reaction to the Pond Example. These might include the virtues of sympathy, caring, kindness, compassion, and generosity. They might also include a special agent-relative duty to aid someone in need that can arise when someone comes into direct contact with another. In connection with this point, I suggested that there is something deeply important for morality about personal one-on-one interactions, where one is confronted, in a stark and undeniable form, with the reality, fragility, mortality, and humanity of another. It is, I claimed, largely in those moments where one's own character and humanity are formed and revealed.

Together, these various moral considerations would not only support our intuitive reaction to Singer's original Pond Example, they would also support the intuitive reaction that we should save a child who was drowning in a pond directly in front of us, rather than let the child drown in order to preserve the value of a watch so that we could save even more children, by later selling the watch and sending the proceeds to an effective charity. So, I argued, our intuitive reactions to variations of Singer's Pond Example favor a pluralistic approach to thinking about the needy, rather than the "do the most good" approach of Effective Altruism.

I next discussed cases of dramatic rescues and of certain global responses to many large-scale disasters. Such rescues and responses would often be condemned by Effective Altruists as tragically wasteful. And there is something to be said about their position. Yet, I contended, there is also something uplifting and noble about such rescues and responses. Among other things, they remind us of our common humanity, and prompt competing factions and countries to join together and act in light of that common humanity, in a way that few, if any, other events do. Echoing Williams, I suggested that, overall, human life would be sadder, bleaker, colder, less valuable, and less praiseworthy, if we lacked the virtues and spark of humanity that lead us to make costly dramatic rescues and respond to global disasters in the way that we often do, despite the massive inefficiencies of such actions.

Similarly, I addressed the view of some Effective Altruists who would advise those who can do so to pursue very lucrative jobs, and to be prepared to "cut corners" and leave one's moral scruples at the door in performing those jobs, and then to donate a significant portion of their income to effective aid organizations, rather than wasting time personally aiding the needy or keeping one's hands "clean" as a matter of personal integrity. I readily granted that there would be many cases where acting in the ways in question *would* do the most to benefit the needy. However, I contended that there are a host of other normatively significant factors that have a bearing on such cases, and that there is much more to being a genuinely good and decent human being than merely doing as much as one can to benefit the needy. I contended that there is something to be said for engaging in a morally praiseworthy life where one has the courage, at least at times, to directly confront other human beings in need, one-on-one, and to respond, appropriately, to their plight. I also contended that there is much to be said for living a life of great virtue and integrity. Someone who has abandoned the virtues of honesty, trustworthiness, dependability, reliability, and integrity for the sake of aiding the needy may produce a lot of good in her life; however, to my mind, she will not be leading a good life.

Chapter 3 also introduced the morally problematic relations that can arise when aiding the needy, a topic I discussed in greater depth in Chapter 10. It also noted a distinction between personal and political domains of aid giving, and suggested that while Singer's example lies squarely within the personal domain, many cases of global aid lie within the political domain.

Arguably, the two main lessons of Chapter 3 were: first, Singer's famous Pond Example does not actually take us very far in answering the question of what we should do, all things considered, to aid the world's needy; and second, we need to be responsive to the full range of moral factors that have a bearing on that question, including all of the factors that are relevant to leading a morally praiseworthy life.

Development economists have come to realize that they should refrain from making definitive judgments about whether aid "works" or not. This is because the world of development assistance is incredibly complex and multi-faceted, and any judgment about aid efficacy has to understand this as much as is possible.[2] Accordingly, as the development literature has amply shown, if aid efforts are to have any hope of success, by the lights of those being aided, as well as by the lights of those providing the aid, then those providing the aid have to be fully sensitive and responsive to the wide range of empirical factors that vary with each individual case of need, including variations in the social, cultural, political, religious, and economic environments occupied by those in need, and within which aid efforts must operate.[3]

Chapter 3 argues that the world of global aid is not merely empirically complex, it is normatively complex, and incredibly so. Those concerned about the global needy need to understand the normative complexity of the topic every bit as much as they need to understand its empirical complexity. The "act so as to do the most good" approach of Effective Altruism, especially insofar as it focuses on a narrow conception of welfare (quality of conscious mental states or preference satisfaction), reflects *one* very important factor that needs to be considered; but it is not, I argued, the only one.

In Chapter 4, I considered the worry that Singer's Pond Example is disanalogous from the case of giving to international relief organizations, in that in Singer's example it is natural to presume that the child we would save is a member of our own community, while those aided by international relief organizations are likely to be members of communities other than our own. I raised several doubts about the moral significance of the disanalogy in question. Ultimately, I granted that there may be some contexts where individuals or groups would have greater obligations to their own community members than to others. Even so, I offered several variations of Singer's Pond Example in support of the view that there would be powerful and compelling reason to save a drowning child that was not a member of our community.

---

[2] See, for example, Riddell, Roger, *Does Foreign Aid Really Work?* (Oxford: Oxford University Press, 2007); and Glennie, Jonathan and Andy Sumner, *Aid, Growth and Poverty* (London: Palgrave Macmillan, 2016); Acemoglu, D, and S. Johnson, "Disease and Development: The Effect of Life Expectancy on Economic Growth," *Journal of Political Economy* 115 (2007): 925–85; Ravallion, Martin, "On the Role of Aid in *The Great Escape*," *Review of Income and Wealth* 60 (2014): 967–84; and Rogerson, A., "What if Development Aid Were Truly 'Catalytic'?" Background Note. London: ODI, 2011, P1.

[3] On this point, see, again, the works cited in the previous note.

This is enough, I believe, to show that the disanalogy in question is not especially relevant to the cogency of Singer's argument.

I next considered Singer's quick dismissal of the view that "nearness or proximity" could be morally relevant in determining whom we should aid. In Appendix B, I suggested that this issue is much more complicated than Singer, and most others, have recognized. However, even if one grants that mere geographical differences are not *themselves* morally relevant, I argued that often there are a host of factors accompanying geographical differences that are of great normative significance. Such factors include social, political, historical, cultural, moral, and religious differences that often obtain between "distant" peoples. Unfortunately, the "instant communication and swift transportation" that make it easy to intervene in distant lands, also make it easy for international aid efforts to run roughshod over such differences. I noted that this can be morally problematic in a variety of ways; a topic I explored in greater depth in Chapters 9 and 10.

I next noted that Singer's Pond Example is disanalogous from the case of giving to an international development organization, in that in the former case one personally, and directly, brings about the goal one seeks through one's actions, while in the latter case, there are a host of intermediate agents who stand between one, one's gift, and the execution of one's intentions. Singer blithely assumes that this fact has little normative significance; but I suggested that in the real world this assumption is highly suspect. I noted that the more people that stand between me and the execution of my will, the more possibilities there are for something to go awry, whether intentionally or unintentionally, whether as the result of an accumulation of many small deviations or a few large ones, and whether as a result of morally laudable motives or morally objectionable ones.

I then noted another possible disanalogy between Singer's Pond Example and the case of giving to an international development organization. In the former case, one knows that one is saving someone's life, while in the latter case one's contribution may be going to help defray any of a large number of perfectly legitimate business expenses and perfectly laudable moral goals. I then gave a series of cases showing that, intuitively, we regard the moral obligation to save an innocent life as more compelling than the obligation to help pay for many of the perfectly respectable expenses that international relief organizations must incur. My examples implied that while there may be many reasons to give to international relief organizations, and some overlap between those reasons and the reasons to save a life, one should not pretend that the two sets of reasons are the same, much less that they are of equal strength.

Correspondingly, I argued that one cannot plausibly infer that there is a powerful obligation to contribute to international relief organizations, based on the intuitive conviction that there is a powerful obligation to save a drowning child.

In Chapter 5, I discussed the dark side of human nature, and worries about internal corruption to which it gives rise. I noted that many people are corruptible, and capable of acting basely depending on the circumstances. In the Pond Example, there is no one who stands between the child who needs saving, and the person passing by who can save her. However, when one gives to an international relief organization, many people within the organization may have an opportunity to divert one's gift for their own benefit, and some may do so. This points to another disanalogy between the Pond Example and giving to international relief organizations. In the former, there is no need to worry about corruption. In the latter, there is.

I next considered, and rejected, the view that people who work for aid organizations are a special breed, so that we don't have to worry about corruption within such organizations. I also considered the view that we could set our minds to rest regarding corruption, by only giving to effective charities that have been approved by independent evaluating agencies. I granted that this response might work in principle, but that in the real world it would not succeed in entirely allaying our worries about corruption within aid organizations. I noted several reasons for this, including the fact that most evaluating organizations, perforce, base their evaluations on data provided to them by the charities themselves. But then, anyone who has embezzled funds from the organization will cook the books to cover their tracks, to the extent they are able to do so. Moreover, even people who are not themselves corrupt will have strong reason to protect the reputation of the organization to avoid losing the support of loyal or potential donors. Thus, those responsible for preparing the organization's annual reports will have every reason to highlight its accomplishments and to minimize its shortcomings, providing strong incentive not to look too carefully for any malfeasance within the organization, or even to cover up any malfeasance of which they become aware. Further, I noted that worries can be raised about the true independence and impartiality of outside evaluating agencies who, over time, increasingly get to know an organization's members, and that the problem of corruption can be re-raised at the level of the independent evaluating agencies themselves.

Having raised these worries, I acknowledged that concerns about corruptibility and weakness of will apply to any large organization, and not merely to international relief organizations. Thus, unless one is prepared to restrict one's charitable contributions to small local charities with which one is personally involved, the worry about internal corruption may be one with which one must simply learn to live.

However flawed and imperfect people may be, for most people who hope to help make the world a better place, giving to a major charity will likely be their best means of doing so. This is so notwithstanding the legitimate possibility that there may be some corruption within whatever organization they choose to support, so that their aid assistance might not be as effective as perhaps they would hope.

In Chapter 6, I discussed a deeper worry about corruption that many share. This is the worry that there may be corruption *external* to an aid organization with which that organization might become enmeshed. The sad reality is that in many of the world's poorest countries, where the need is greatest, what many in the West regard as bribery, graft, and corruption is very much part of the normal course of doing business. I noted that this worry about external sources of corruption helps explain why many are more concerned with the possibility of corruption when giving to international relief organizations, than they are with the possibility of corruption when giving to large charities in developed countries where institutional corruption is less endemic to many aspects of social and business intercourse. (But again, it is important to bear in mind the particularities of each circumstance. No doubt there are many places in the U.S., Russia, China, Italy, or other developed countries, where the corruption may be somewhat different in kind (or not), yet every bit as bad, or worse, than in many places in the world's poorest countries.)

I considered three responses to the worry about external corruption siphoning away resources from promoting the laudable goals of international aid agencies. The first response is to claim that corruption is much less rampant, and so much less of a concern, than those who raise the worry presuppose. The second is to acknowledge that the worry is a serious one that affects government-to-government foreign aid, but that NGOs can largely avoid entanglement with corrupt individuals or agencies by dealing directly with those in need. The third is to recognize that corruption is sometimes prevalent, but that one can, and in some circumstances should, simply learn to live with it, for the sake of the good that international aid agencies accomplish.

I expressed some doubts about the first two responses. However, I offered several considerations in support of the third. I suggested that allowing corrupt individuals to flourish may be a cost worth bearing if it enables us save innocent lives, and that in the global economy most people have learned to live with the prospect that their purchases may benefit unsavory people for far more trivial reasons than saving innocent lives. Accordingly, I questioned why many people seem to hold international relief organizations, which seek to promote laudable ends, to a higher standard regarding corruption than they hold other international organizations that provide them with consumer products such as coffee, sneakers, clothing, and appliances. I also suggested that sometimes we should favor an alternative in which we support greater corruption but also save more innocent lives, over one in which we avoid or support less corruption, but at the cost of saving fewer innocent lives.

In Chapter 7, I noted several other disanalogies between Singer's Pond Example, as naturally interpreted, and many cases involving the global needy. I noted that Singer's Pond Example is naturally interpreted as involving a terrible accident, for which no one is responsible. While this is analogous to some cases involving the global needy—for example, those due to certain diseases or natural disasters—it is disanalogous from many others—for example, those due to grave social injustices perpetrated by responsible evil agents. I also noted that unlike in Singer's drowning child case, some of the global needy will not be innocent, and some will be responsible for their plight. In addition, I noted that in Singer's Pond Example no one stands to profit or otherwise benefit from one's intervention, other than the drowning child herself, and that she will be no better off due to one's intervention than she would have been had she not been drowning in the first place. The case is often otherwise in situations where international agencies intervene to aid the global needy.

I argued that just as it will often be wrong to give in to extortionist threats, it will also often be wrong to reward people for committing grave social injustices. I then suggested that, in a variety of direct and indirect ways, international development organizations may often benefit the very people responsible for the plight of the needy, and in so doing this may enable them to continue to perpetrate grave social injustices against the very people we aim to help, or against other innocent people in the future. It may also incentivize others to commit similar social injustices elsewhere, thereby increasing the number of needy people.

I rejected the view that we have no duty to help people with whom we do not stand in special relations. I also rejected the view that we have no duty to aid people in need unless we are responsible for their plight. In addition, I rejected the view that we have no duty to aid someone in need if some other rational agent, or group, is responsible for their plight. I claimed that there may be a variety of duties of varying strengths to aid the needy, but that our duty to aid a stranger in need is not lessened by the fact that others may have an even stronger duty to aid such a person, and that their duty may take precedence over ours. If someone else fulfills their duty to aid the needy, and thereby removes the need, then we will be off the moral hook, as it were; but otherwise not.

I next discussed the so-called "problem of dirty hands." I considered, and rejected, the view that I cannot be held responsible for the actions of others if I don't share their goals or in any way intend to support their actions. I suggested that, other things equal, I can be at least partly responsible for the evil actions of others if I could have easily and safely intervened to prevent them from doing what they did, but failed to do so. Similarly, I suggested that I can be at least partly responsible for the evil actions of others, if I knowingly provide them with support that enables them to perpetrate their evil deeds, or have good reason to believe that what I am doing will likely support their endeavors. Moreover, I claimed, this is so even if I don't share their intentions, and I strongly disavow their actions. In sum, I suggested that there may be deontological, as well as consequentialist, objections to acting in ways that can be reasonably predicted to support the evil actions of other agents, even if I only do so for the sake of accomplishing some important, or greater, good, such as saving, or relieving the suffering of innocent people.

I also noted how similar worries can arise in cases of natural diseases or disasters, where no one is responsible for the plight of the needy. A crucial question that needs considering is whether evil agents may benefit from our interventions and what the consequences are if, indeed, that is the case. Unfortunately, there are a host of direct and indirect ways in which local and national leaders can take advantage of international aid to boost their own wealth, status, and power, thereby taking advantage of the plight of their compatriots to further their own political agendas. Where these agendas involve grave unjust wars, brutal acts of aggression and repression, and other social injustices, these effects cannot be ignored.

I further observed that the distinction between diseases and natural disasters, on the one hand, and social injustices, on the other, is not always a clean one. In reality, many calamities are a hybrid of natural/man-made disasters. This is relevant to whether we should, in fact, simply learn to live with corruption when it "merely" goes to line the pockets of the greedy. The problem is that often corrupt leaders adopt policies that line their own pockets, rather than policies that might help prevent or mitigate the effects of disease outbreaks or natural disasters. If, in fact, such leaders can siphon off funds from international relief efforts into their own coffers, then they will have two perverse incentives not to change their policies. After all, doing so will curtail their income from their original, corrupt, policies, and it will also curtail the income from the international resources that flow into the region due to the ensuing calamities that their policies help spark. Sadly, then, international aid efforts may provide corrupt leaders with the perverse incentives to retain or adopt policies that help promote hybrid natural/man-made disasters, and to undermine the long-term development efforts of international aid organizations aimed at preventing similar calamities in the future.

I concluded Chapter 7 by presenting some details of what happened at Goma. At Goma, virtually all of this book's worries about how international aid efforts can go awry were realized, with horrifying, tragic, results. Goma is a stark reminder that the issues raised in this book are not mere abstract possibilities—philosophical bogeymen with no real-world implications. To ignore what has happened at Goma, and elsewhere, is not merely irresponsible, it is deeply wrong. The point of supporting aid agencies is not to feel good about ourselves, but to help people in need. We must be sure that our aid efforts don't harm the very people we intend to aid, or other innocent people, elsewhere.

The upshot of my discussions of the dark side of humanity, in Chapters 5 through 7, is that in giving to international aid organizations, we must be keenly attuned to the many direct or indirect ways in which our aid may inadvertently benefit the perpetrators of grave social injustices, and how this may, in turn, enable them and incentivize others to continue to perpetrate similar injustices against the same people we are aiming to help, or against other innocents. Moreover, international aid resources may end up rewarding corrupt leaders whose policies have helped contribute to hybrid natural/man-made disasters, and in so doing incentivize them and other corrupt leaders to continue with, or adopt, such policies. Complicating matters is the fact that international aid organizations have every incentive to emphasize the good that they accomplish, and to not look for, ignore, or even cover up any bad effects that may result from their interventions. Furthermore, agencies tasked with assessing aid effectiveness may lack the resources necessary to determine the perverse incentives, or other direct or indirect negative effects, to which international aid efforts may inadvertently give rise.

Singer, and Effective Altruists, could fully accept everything I presented in these chapters. Still, the many worries raised remind us how disanalogous Singer's Pond Example is from the realities that international aid agencies must contend with in aiding the world's needy. However compelling Singer's example is, much more needs to be considered before one can pass judgment on the overall merits of giving to international aid organizations. A duty to do the latter does not follow, in any straightforward way, from the duty to save a drowning child.[4*]

In Chapter 8, I discussed an often-overlooked problem of aid efforts in the world's poorest regions. This is the problem of marketplace distortions in human capital that can lead to both internal and external brain and character drains. I pointed out that human capital is the greatest natural resource, and that an efficient use of the most valuable human resources is imperative for social, political, and economic development. This is especially so in the world's poorest regions.

I then pointed out that high paying jobs in the aid sector can lead to marketplace distortions in human capital that are highly inefficient. So, for example, highly talented people of great character may be lured away from crucially important public sector positions, to take much less crucial positions with an aid agency where their talents are underutilized. I noted that this can have a significantly deleterious effect on the efficiency and success of the government, the economy, and public projects in ways that will often be difficult to identify and quantify.

Similarly, I suggested that highly talented people of great character who work with international aid agencies may develop skills and connections that will enable them to leave their countries for higher paying jobs and better working conditions outside of their country. Unfortunately, however, their skills and character may be underutilized, and have far less of a significant impact in a highly developed country than they would have had in their home country. This kind of external brain and character drain can also have deleterious effects on a country's development. I acknowledged, however, that the issue of external brain and character drain cuts both ways, as it often has positive as well as negative impacts on the countries most affected by it. In particular, I noted that poor countries often benefit substantially from remittances sent back to families from successful workers abroad, and that

---

[4*] In correspondence, Singer notes that in his more recent work he is careful to eschew any such general claim. For example, in *The Life You Can Save* (New York: Random House, 2009) and *The Most Good You Can Do* (New Haven: Yale University Press, 2015), Singer is quite clear that we need to do a lot of hard work to determine the best organizations for helping people in extreme poverty. About this we are in complete agreement. Still, Singer's books are quite optimistic, both in tone and content, about the prospects for success in this regard. And while I am, by temperament an optimist myself, I think it is important not to brush aside the worries this book raises. The urge to do *something* to help the needy can be overwhelming. However, it is important to bear in mind that this deadly serious matter is *not* about us feeling good about ourselves, but about our responding appropriately to the plight of the needy, taking account of *all* of the factors that are morally relevant to this extraordinarily difficult issue.

often such workers eventually return to their native countries with valuable knowledge, skills, and capital acquired abroad.

The gist of this discussion was that aid agencies readily look for every benefit produced by their efforts; however, they tend not to identify any losses that may occur elsewhere in the system due to their hiring local workers who contribute to their success. Clearly, however, any such losses are relevant to the overall impact of an agency's aid efforts. Furthermore, there is every reason to believe that in some cases, at least, the losses elsewhere in the system, due to internal or external brain or character brain, could be substantial. This is especially so, when one considers the collective impact of internal and external brain and character drains wrought by the many thousands of aid agencies operating in the world's poorest regions.

In Chapter 9, I took up several issues relevant to Effective Altruism's goal of finding aid organizations that can be counted on to have (expected) future success, based on proven past successes. I pointed out that each aid context is unique, with its own social, cultural, political, and historical background. This makes it problematic to believe that just because a given aid effort was a great success in one location, similar efforts will meet with similar successes elsewhere.

I also pointed out that it is often difficult to predict what the long-term effects of aid interventions will be. I gave various examples where highly touted aid efforts that appeared to be great successes in the short run, proved to be disasters in the long run, for unforeseen reasons.

I next pointed out that there are often problems of scaling up. Unfortunately, for a variety of reasons, the success of a few small model projects at the local level is no guarantee that similar success will be met if the models are replicated countless times at the national or international level.

I offered an example from a field outside of global aid to illustrate many of these worries. The Rice School was a classic example of where the best laid plans of highly motivated, highly talented, highly financed, well-intentioned, people went badly awry, for reasons that few foresaw. It was also an example where, even if everything had gone very well, it would have been extremely difficult to replicate its success on a larger scale.

I suggested that what happened with the Rice School should serve as a cautionary tale for those who believe that "surely" well-financed, carefully-crafted, well-intentioned aid interventions can be counted on to meet with success. Indeed, if a model project that has virtually unlimited financial, political, and intellectual resources behind it, and that literally takes place in one's own neighborhood can spectacularly fail, should we really be surprised if aid efforts that take place in distant regions that are drastically different than ours socially, politically, economically, culturally, historically, and ethically often fail to achieve the success one might hope for them? It is extremely hard for "outsiders" to get things right, when there are so many unanticipated ways in which even the best laid plans can go astray.

I next considered the response of some Effective Altruists, who believe that Chapter 9's worries are genuine, and may apply to many aid efforts, but that they don't apply to the top-rated charities of Effective Altruist organizations like GiveWell. I suggested that there is something to be said for this response, but that, even for the top-rated charities, there is reason to take the rosy picture it portrays with a grain of salt.

In Chapter 10, I discussed the worry that international aid efforts promote ethical imperialism and the hegemony of Western values. I argued that even if aid efforts lack the reprehensible attitude that the needy are inferior to their benefactors, there are often other unsavory aspects of the attitudes and actions of international aid organizations that are reminiscent of colonialism. I pointed out that often, in the name of *progress* and *benefiting* those in need, aid organizations work to undermine longstanding social, cultural, and economic practices—practices often viewed as backward, ignorant, primitive, stunting, immoral, and, in some cases, barbaric. I argued that even if one believes that, ultimately, the aid organizations are correct in their value assessments, their actions and attitudes can often have consequences that are both morally and practically problematic. I further argued that even in the absence of any objectionable attitudes, outside pressures and financial induce-ments can lead locals to shift their priorities in ways that alienate them from important aspects of their social, cultural, historical, and religious traditions. I suggested that this can be unsettling at the individual level, and worrisome at the collective level.

Ultimately, I argued that international aid efforts often involve paternalistic interventions that raise worries about autonomy, and our failing to properly respect the values and ways of life of those whom we are seeking to aid.

In Chapter 11, I presented a surprising, and controversial claim of Angus Deaton's—that people like Peter Singer and his followers are doing more harm than good, by urging that we support international relief organizations like Oxfam. At the heart of Deaton's claim are two views. First, that good govern-ance is crucial for social and economic development, and the long-term well-being of a country's citizens. Second, that in the world's poorest countries, international aid efforts undermine good governance, by undermining the responsiveness of a government to its citizens. For Deaton, then, however successful international aid organizations may be in achieving their immediate ends, ultimately, they often do more harm than good for the citizens in the poorest countries in which they operate.

I argued that Deaton's first view is plausible, that genuinely substantial and long-lasting social and economic gains require a well-functioning government which can effectively formulate and pursue plans to develop infrastructure, energy, food production, schools, the health system, etc. That is, it is plausible to believe that the large-scale systematic social and economic institutions that allow for human flourishing are not the sort of things that outside development organizations, no matter how well-intentioned or well-funded, can accomplish, or impose, on their own.

I then argued that Deaton's second view is also plausible. In particular, I highlighted various ways in which outside aid could undermine a government's responsiveness to its citizens. These included the facts that: there are many ways, both direct and indirect, that corrupt governments can take advantage of outside resources to strengthen their own internal positions and further their own agendas; that local governments can abdicate their responsibilities to provide for the basic needs of their citizens, leaving that task to outside agencies, and then shift the blame to outside agencies if basic needs remain unmet; that outside infusions of funds can lessen the need for local governments to raise money through taxation, weakening the government's need to be responsive to its citizens for how their hard-earned tax money is spent; that aid resources can be akin to natural resources, and give rise to a similar "resource curse," whereby significant resources over which a government has control encourages tyrants to take control and use those resources to control the powers of the state (e.g. the army and police), to provide for their followers, and to advance their goals without much regard for the citizenry as a whole; and finally, since "he who pays the piper calls the tune," significant outside resources are likely to lead governments to be responsive to the interests and values of the outside institutions providing those resources, which is not the same as being responsive to the aims and values of their citizens.

In Chapter 11, I also discussed Jeffrey Sachs's approach to global poverty, and discussed the Millennium Villages Project. I noted that the results of the Millennium Villages Project were mixed, at best. I further noted that Sachs's selection process for Millennium Villages revealed his acute awareness of the significance of well-functioning and stable governments being responsive to their citizens and committed to their wellbeing for sustainable long-term development in the regions where need is greatest. Given this, I argued that Sachs and his followers need to take Deaton's worries seriously.

I concluded Chapter 11 by offering some suggestive empirical data supporting—though not conclusively—Deaton's claim that substantial social and economic progress is more likely to be correlated with a well-functioning government that is responsive to its citizens, than it is to outside aid efforts.

In Chapter 12, I noted that many people find it almost impossible to believe that they could be doing more harm than good by contributing to effective aid organizations. I argued that given two natural assumptions, this response is perfectly understandable. The two assumptions are: first, by contributing to an international aid organization one is likely to be having a substantial positive impact on the quality of someone's life—for example, one may actually be saving someone from an early death from hunger or disease; and second, the extent to which one's individual contribution to an international aid agency undermines the responsiveness of a government to its citizens is likely to be incredibly small, and hence, the negative impact that one's contribution has on any given individual is also likely to be incredibly small.

I argued that given the two assumptions in question, it is plausible to think that donating to effective aid agencies will be desirable. However, I argued that that does not settle the question of whether or not Deaton may be right. This, I suggested, is because Deaton's real concern is with the *overall* impact of aid efforts in the world's poorest countries. This, I argued, could be undesirable, *even if* the impact of each *individual* contribution to an aid agency were desirable.

The key to understanding this puzzle is that there can be genuine conflicts between *individual* rationality and morality, and *collective* rationality and morality. Specifically, it can be the case that even if each of us, individually, acts rationally or morally, it can still be the case that we, together, act in a way that is, collectively, irrational or immoral. Game theorists established that there can be conflicts between individual and collective rationality with the classical Prisoner's Dilemmas. Derek Parfit established that there can be conflicts between individual and collective morality for deontological moralities, with moral analogues of classical Prisoner's Dilemmas. And I showed that there can be conflicts between individual and collective morality for consequentialist moralities.

I noted that most people, including most consequentialists, accept principles like the Disperse Additional Burdens View, and presented various examples in support of such principles (for example, Parfit's Repugnant Conclusion and my Lollipops for Lives). I then showed that given these results, Deaton could well be right. It could be that even if each of us, individually, is doing something that is morally desirable when contributing to international aid agencies, it could still be the case that we, together, are doing something that is morally undesirable. Specifically, it is possible for each of us, individually, to be bringing about a better outcome, by supporting aid efforts, and yet for all of us, collectively, to be doing more harm than good by our doing so.

I noted that conflicts between individual and collective rationality and morality are deeply troubling, both theoretically and practically, and argued that this is especially so in the case of individual versus collective conflicts of the sort that would obtain if Deaton is right. In such cases, each of us will know what he ought to do, morally, as an individual; and we will also know what we ought to do, collectively; but there is no apparent way to resolve the conflict that confronts each/us.

My analysis helped illuminate both the power of Deaton's view, and why so many people have been loath to accept it. However, I argued that there are probably good reasons to reject both of the natural assumptions that I employed in my argument. I then showed that if one does reject either or both of the assumptions, that only strengthens Deaton's position. Without those assumptions, it is more plausible to believe that contributions to aid efforts might be both collectively and individually undesirable, if, in fact, such contributions help to undermine, even slightly, a government's responsiveness to its citizens.

In Chapter 13, I presented several objections to Deaton's view, and the considerations I offered in support of it. These included the claim that we should reject anti-additive-aggregationist principles like the Disperse Additional Burdens View; that we should support aid organizations that effectively work to promote good governance; and that Deaton's worry almost certainly doesn't apply to GiveWell's top-rated charities.

In response, I noted that rejecting the Disperse Additional Burdens View will be hard for most people to accept, and that Deaton's argument does not depend on that view. To the contrary, I noted that Deaton's position will be more plausible if one rejects anti-additive-aggregationist principles. I also noted that while there is something to be said in favor of aid organizations that seek to improve local governmental responsiveness, such organizations may raise worries about paternalism, autonomy, and respect, as discussed in Chapter 10. Further, such organizations still may do more harm than good, if they increase government responsiveness at the local level, but undermine it at the national level.

Looking closely at the case of a deworming charity, I pointed out that even if we can be confident that contributions to top-rated aid organizations have an overall *expected value* that is positive, that does *not* mean that we can be confident that contributions to such aid organizations will do more good than harm, or even that they will do any (substantial) good at all. I noted that this is especially important to bear in mind, for those who urge people to make substantial sacrifices of their own welfare, or that of their loved ones, to benefit the needy. I expressed my skepticism about the view that there is compelling reason for someone to make steep sacrifices to support programs that are unlikely to significantly benefit anyone, just because the expected utility of doing so is positive. In addition, I questioned whether we really *can* be confident about the expected value of contributions to top-ranked aid organizations, given how many important questions have not yet been answered that are relevant to those values.

Employing an analogy with successful instances of gambling or opioid use, I further suggested that the very successes of some international aid organizations may prompt other aid organizations to arise which, though created with the best of intentions, may do more harm than good. In this way, effective aid organizations could inadvertently lead to overall negative outcomes in the world's poorest regions, even if those organizations, considered just by themselves, did more good than harm, both individually and collectively.

I pointed out that in addition to Deaton's consequentialist worry, regarding the overall net impact of aid efforts, contributions to aid efforts may be deontologically problematic. This will be so if they harm some people—by undermining government responsiveness—for the sake of benefiting others.

Notwithstanding my previous arguments, I pointed out that even if Deaton is right, this does not settle the question of whether we should support aid efforts, as Effective Altruists and most development economists—including Deaton—presume. In accordance with this book's pluralistic approach, I argued that it may be that we ought to aid the needy in the world's poorest regions *even if* our doing so is not the most effective use of our resources, or *even if* our efforts ultimately lead to more harm than good.

In Chapter 14, I considered two further issues related to global aid. First, I discussed Pogge's view that aiding the global needy is often a matter of duty, and not a matter of charity, because often the well-off are at least partly responsible for the needy's plight. I argued that Pogge's view reflects a very important, non-consequentialist, factor relevant to the topic of global aid.

I next argued that the ideals of fairness, equality, and justice are also important to the topic of global aid. I pointed out that such ideals underlie the push for universal healthcare by the World Health Organization, and that they also underlie the efforts of VillageReach, an international aid organization that aims to provide high quality healthcare to remote "last mile" villages.

I argued that the ideals of fairness, justice, and equality often conflict with the "do the most good" approach of welfarist utilitarians and Effective Altruists.

I noted that there are a host of extremely complex and difficult questions about how to parse out individual responsibility for one's role in a collective enterprise; and also difficult unresolved questions about how best to understand the notions of fairness, equality, and justice. In addition, there are a host of extremely difficult issues regarding how to weigh these different values against each other, and against other normatively significant factors. This chapter served as a further reminder of the complexity of the topic of global aid, and the necessity of adopting a pluralistic approach in addressing it. It also served as a reminder of the complexity of morality, itself, and of how much normative work still needs to be done before we can truly hope to know how to be good in a world of need.

In Chapter 15, I took stock of some of the book's key results, and offered some qualifications, implications, and further thoughts. I noted that the book shows that, for all its many virtues, Singer's famous Pond Example, and the larger argument of which it is a part, offers precious little guidance regarding how to respond to global need. More specifically, Singer's argument does not show, as many have thought, that the well-off should be contributing to international aid organizations like Oxfam. Unfortunately, much more work need to be done, both empirically and normatively, to arrive at that conclusion.

I noted that while most of this book's claims are compatible with (Global Aid) Effective Altruism, at least in principle, there are three areas of difference between my approach and that of Effective Altruism—at least, the "do the most good" version that accepts a welfarist conception of the good, and has a relatively narrow conception of welfare (quality of mental states or desire satisfaction). In assessing the desirability and impact of aid efforts, I emphasized that we need to consider a wide range of factors, including, but not limited to: deontological considerations, virtue considerations, equality, justice, fairness, freedom, autonomy, rights, respect, love, friendship, beauty, and perfection. I noted that while it is important not to understate the differences between my view and Effective Altruism, it is also important not to overstate them. I further noted that the differences between us shrink—though do not disappear—if Effective Altruism adopts a wide conception of the good; one which includes the many morally desirable ideals, other than welfare, appealed to in this book.

I claimed that Effective Altruism's goal of being a practical movement that tells us which aid organizations to support is laudable, but probably premature. The worries raised in this book suggest that we currently lack the information needed to fully assess the overall impact of aid interventions, and I presented three dangers associated with ignoring that fact.

I also noted several important clarifications and caveats regarding the scope of my worries. For example, I noted that my worries about paternalism, freedom, and respect arise for certain aid efforts, but not others. I also note that some of the worries about perverse incentives that arise when aiding victims of social injustice, may not arise when aiding victims of certain natural disasters. I further noted that many of my worries about aid efforts in countries with corrupt governments will not apply to aid efforts in countries with good governments. Relatedly, I noted that many of my worries about the corrosive effects of aid only arise in contexts involving poor countries with weak economies. Thus, those worries can be avoided by concentrating aid efforts in countries with large, or strong, economies. This is important, I suggested, since our goal should be to aid *people* who are badly off, rather than *countries* which are badly off, and since many people who are badly off live in relatively well-off countries.

I noted that many people grant that my worries may be legitimate, theoretically, but doubt that they are practically significant. I offered various reasons for thinking that this view is mistaken, and incompatible with the proper use of Expected Utility Theory. Concretely, I suggested that even if there is only a small chance that some of this book's worries are correct, that may be enough to alter the expected utility calculations that underlie the recommendations of Effective Altruist organizations like GiveWell—including, for example, the four deworming programs that are among GiveWell's eight top-rated charities.

16.2 How Dare I Write This Book

Some people will be puzzled by this book. Others frustrated or even angry. Their reactions may be summed up as follows. There you sit, in the comfort of your armchair, speculating about all sorts of possible negative effects that international relief efforts may, or may not, produce. In raising the worries that you do, you provide ammunition for all those people who are perfectly content to selfishly pursue materialistic lifestyles of conspicuous, wasteful, consumption.

Thanks to you, such people may believe it is perfectly fine to do nothing to aid those less fortunate than they. Worse yet, you haven't offered much empirical evidence to support the philosophical bogeymen that you have conjured up.

Meanwhile, millions of real flesh and blood innocent people, many of whom are women, children, or elderly, are dying or suffering from easily preventable hunger and disease. Don't you worry that by even raising these worries you may be contributing to the suffering of the world's needy? You should be *ashamed* of yourself for engaging in such irresponsible philosophical speculations where people's very lives and wellbeing are at stake!

I understand such reactions. Indeed, I confess that I have lain awake many nights with these very same concerns. In the end, however, I decided to proceed; hopeful that in those cases where my worries can be laid to rest, that will be shown quickly, and in those cases where my worries cannot be laid to rest, people will be motivated to rethink their assumptions regarding how to respond to the needy, and will proceed along a clearer, better, path.[5]

Throughout this book, I have cited literature in support of many of my claims. However, I readily admit that part of the gist of this book is that we don't yet have sufficient empirical evidence to determine the full impact of on-the-ground aid efforts in the world's poorest regions. Unfortunately, in the absence of such evidence, we can't even be confident that our aid interventions are doing more good than harm, much less doing the most good we can. I believe this is often true individually, but even more so collectively.

I also readily admit that I have not done the empirical research necessary to settle the empirical questions raised here. However, that isn't my job. My job, as a philosopher, is to help identify some of the important empirical and normative issues that are relevant to how we should respond to the needy. But as for gathering and assessing any relevant empirical data, I must leave that to the economists, sociologists, political scientists, anthropologists, and other social scientists, as well as to aid agencies, aid evaluators, and governments.

I only add, in this connection, that there seems to be something of a consensus among development economists that many of the empirical worries raised here must be taken much more seriously than most philosophers, and advocates of international relief efforts, have so far taken them. More particularly, development economists on all sides of the debate regarding aid efficacy agree that there are a host of legitimate empirical worries about aid. The difference is that those who fall on the optimistic side of the debate believe that there are cases where aid does work, or where it would work if it were

---

[5] Such a path will need to take account of the enormous complexity and many nuances that I have noted throughout this book, both normatively and empirically. For outstanding discussion of the empirical complexity surrounding this topic, and the need for nuance in addressing it, see Riddell's *Does Foreign Aid Really Work?* and Ben Ramalingam's *Aid on the Edge of Chaos* (Oxford: Oxford University Press, 2013).

done "properly." And they believe that to make aid more effective, generally, we "merely" need to avoid or improve on the empirical conditions that can make aid problematic. Aid pessimists, on the other hand, believe that in many cases where the need is greatest, the empirical conditions that make aid problematic are present, and extremely difficult to remedy, so that *in fact* on-the-ground aid interventions in such cases are likely to be ineffective, at best, or to do more harm than good, at worst.[6]

I should also add that while I deeply worry about the possibility that this book may do more harm than good regarding the world's needy; it is also possible that I would do more harm than good if I didn't write this book, and continued the one-sided optimistic approach to thinking about the needy that was characteristic of my earlier writings on this topic. Indeed, it is at least arguable that the charge of acting selfishly—for one's own edification, or because it makes one feel good about oneself—could be leveled at anyone who donates to international aid agencies without giving a second thought to the legitimate worries that have been raised as to whether such efforts might be producing more harm than good for the world's needy, either individually or collectively.

There are practical dangers in taking up any complex topic that is morally important. There are also practical dangers in failing to take up such topics, and leaving people's views about them to be shaped by society's dominant social mores. The philosopher's job, I believe, is to examine such topics as clearly, carefully, and honestly as she can, and see where the arguments lead. That is what I have tried to do in this book.

16.3 Paths Needing Further Exploration

This book has covered a lot of ground. Although it has had to leave many questions open, the book suggests numerous considerations to bear in mind, and paths that need further exploration, in thinking about the needy. In this section, I briefly note some of these.

First, we must consider the full range of morally relevant factors for aiding the needy. So, in addition to paying attention to welfare-based reasons, we must pay attention to deontological-, virtue-, egalitarian-, fairness-, and justice-based reasons for aiding the needy. Among other things, this will require us to come to terms with a host of questions related to issues of

---

[6] The last half of this paragraph is indebted to a thoughtful suggestion of Brian Oosterhuizen's.

individual and collective responsibility. This will include coming to a better understanding of the conditions under which, and the extent to which, we are partially responsible for, and have duties of rectification towards, people who are needy, in virtue of the fact that we are complicit in, partially responsible for, or the beneficiaries of the events that led to their being needy.

Second, we must come to terms with the fact that what each of us, individually, has most practical or moral reason to do, may be different from what we, together, have most practical or moral reason to do. Tragically, it is, I have suggested, a very real possibility that if each of us, individually, does what he or she ought to do, morally, on behalf of the needy, that collectively, we will not be doing what we ought to do, morally, on behalf of the needy.

Third, there might be important reasons to get personally involved in aiding the needy, even when doing so may not be the way of doing the most good that one can to aid people in need. Similarly, there may be compelling moral reasons to refrain from participating in certain jobs or actions that would most benefit the needy.

Fourth, insofar as one wants to do as much good as one can, it is important to focus on *people* who are badly off, rather than *countries* that are badly off. From the Expected Utility Theory perspective of Effective Altruism, it could be that one will maximize the expected value of one's aid efforts by focusing on providing aid to people in countries with good governance, rather than on providing aid to people in countries with poor governance. Sadly, this may be so even if the latter people are every bit as needy as—and perhaps even needier than—and no less deserving than the former people. Thus, though it may seem counterintuitive, it may be that a more effective way of aiding the needy will focus on aiding the neediest members of middle-income countries, or perhaps even high-income countries, rather than on aiding the neediest members of some of the world's poorest countries.

Fifth, while there are some reasons to favor giving aid to needy people in countries with good governance rather than to needy people in countries with poor governance, one must remain acutely aware of the many ways in which outside aid interventions can, under certain circumstances, undermine the responsiveness of a government to its people or entice people who would not be responsive to the needs of their people to take control of the reins of government. As Deaton puts this point, "An ocean of aid from abroad can corrupt even potentially good leaders and good political systems."[7] Thus, one

---

[7] Deaton, Angus, *The Great Escape: Health, Wealth, and the Origins of Inequality* (Princeton: Princeton University Press, 2015), p. 313.

must be vigilant about engaging in aid efforts that either individually or collectively might destabilize governments that currently are responsive to their citizens. Such efforts might be beneficial in the short run, yet have devastating long-term consequences.

Sixth, notwithstanding the previous two points, we should not lose sight of the fact that there are a host of important moral considerations that might support aiding people who are urgently in need *now*, even if they live in countries with poor governance, or in countries with good governance that is precarious, and other available efforts might have greater total expected value. Indeed, it is possible that sometimes we must come to the aid of those in dire predicaments, even if we have good reason to believe that our doing so may ultimately do more harm than good.[8]

Seventh, we need a serious commitment from social scientists, aid activists, Effective Altruists, governments, and others, to actively seek and identify any possible negative effects of aid efforts, and the probability of such negative effects. In doing this, one must be attuned to indirect as well as direct effects, interaction effects, and long-term as well as short-term effects. Nothing short of clear-eyed honesty in this domain is acceptable if we hope to answer the critics of international aid efforts and, more importantly, if we are to have any hope of actually doing as much good as we can (consistent with all other morally relevant considerations) on behalf of the world's needy.

Eighth, ultimately our aim is not merely to help a never-ending supply of needy people as much as we are able to, but to break the cycles of poverty, war, repression, hunger, ignorance, prejudice, and illness that cause people to be in need in the first place. This is why we need to be sure that our efforts to aid the needy are not indirectly contributing to such cycles by buttressing evil gangsters, warlords, or tribal leaders, or repressive or unresponsive governments. This is also why we need more serious efforts to identify substantial, effective, and long-lasting approaches to undermining the root causes of hunger, poverty, and disease. This will need to include not only efforts to address problems of infrastructure, education, healthcare, energy production, and such. It will also require serious efforts to address local, national, and international inequality and injustice, the promotion of human rights and the rule of law, and fundamental changes in the rules and policies that govern national and

---

[8] Not everyone accepts this of course. It would be rejected by Effective Altruists, consequentialists, and many development economists. But it is a straightforward implication of the pluralistic approach to morality that I have taken throughout this work. The pluralistic approach is, I believe, the only one that can remotely hope to do justice to the complexity of the normative domain, and the full range of reasons in that domain.

international social, political, and economic interactions. (More on this in section 16.4.)

Ninth, it should also be noted that while development has long been, and remains, the main focus of international aid efforts, it is not uncontroversial. If the point of development is to set up conditions that remove people from poverty, and development efforts are expensive, fraught with problematic attitudes and power relationships, by no means guaranteed to succeed, and may even backfire (in the sense of ultimately doing more harm than good), then some have thought that it may make more sense to aim to lift people directly out of poverty by a direct transfer of resources to them.

This way of thinking aligns with that of the basic income movement, which seeks to guarantee a minimum basic income for everyone sufficient for them to live a minimally comfortable life of their own choosing. Having been supplied with sufficient income to live a minimally decent life, it is then up to each individual, rather than their government or some charitable organization, to determine whether, and how best, to pursue any other avenue than those available to them given their basic income.[9] The charitable organization GiveDirectly, discussed in Section 15.4, reflects this approach to aid, giving no-strings-attached cash to needy recipients, and leaving it to them to decide how best to use that cash to further their own interests.

16.4 Whither from Here?

This book has been mostly negative. However, though I am largely agnostic on the question of whether current on-the-ground aid efforts in many of the poorest regions are, overall, desirable, that does not put me in the anti-aid camp. To the contrary, I remain, firmly, in the pro-aid camp. Thus, let me end this book by emphasizing, one last time, that *nothing* in this book supports the view that a good person can just abandon the needy. Even the needy in the world's poorest regions.

In my judgment, there will almost always (but only *almost* always) be compelling reason to respond to genuine humanitarian disasters whenever, and wherever, they occur. Additionally, as the economist Jagdish Bhagwati

---

[9] For important arguments in support of the basic income approach to government and international aid, see Philippe Van Parijs's seminal work, *Real Freedom for All: What (If Anything) Can Justify Capitalism?* (Oxford: Clarendon Press, 1995), and James Ferguson's excellent book *Give a Man a Fish: Reflections on the New Politics of Distribution* (Durham, NC: Duke University Press, 2015). (I am grateful to Angus Deaton for calling my attention to this paragraph's point.)

once noted, "it is hard to think of substantial increases in aid being spent effectively *in* Africa. But it is not so hard to think of more aid being spent productively elsewhere *for* Africa."[10] This is an important truth that generalizes to all of the world's poorest regions.

I have no special advice to offer in this regard that others have not offered before. Still, it is perhaps worth noting some of the more promising paths one might pursue for helping the needy in the world's poorest regions, without supporting on-the-ground aid efforts in those regions.[11] In no particular order, these include the following suggestions.

1. One might support basic research in the STEM fields (Science, Technology, Engineering, and Medicine). Significant advances in these areas often lead to improvement in the lives of the least well off. Especially promising areas of research might include those that might promote: the prevention and treatment of diseases to which the neediest in the world's poorest regions are especially prone; innovations in agricultural methods, fish farming, reforestation techniques, etc.; safer, cleaner, low-cost, renewable, energy; lighter, cheaper, and longer-lasting materials for infrastructure projects; and improvements in computer and communication technologies.

2. One might support efforts to promote safer, cheaper, and more efficient methods of disseminating medical and technological know-how, treatments, and innovations, as well as educational opportunities throughout the developing world. Of particular importance, in this regard, one might work to change the World Trade Organization's TRIPS Agreement (the Agreement on Trade-Related Aspects of Intellectual Property Rights), which overwhelmingly benefits the world's most powerful businesses and their stockholders and the world's wealthiest countries and their citizens, and which often makes the widespread use of crucial advances in medicine and technology prohibitively expensive for the world's poorest countries.

3. More generally, one might seek changes in the rules and operations of such international organizations as the World Bank, the International Monetary Fund, and the World Trade Organization, whose rules and policies are all-too-often skewed to benefit the world's wealthiest

---

[10] Quoted in Abhijit Vinayak Banerjee's *Making Aid Work* (Cambridge, MA: MIT Press, 2007), pp. 95–6.

[11] Many of these are noted and developed further by Deaton in *The Great Escape* (see pp. 319–24).

countries, corporations, shareholders, and citizens, rather than the neediest people in the world's poorest countries. Indeed, if one is serious about aiding the world's needy, one should seek changes in the rules and operations of such organizations that don't merely *level* the playing field between the haves and the have nots, but which *tilt* the field to benefit the have nots.

4. Related to the previous point, one should seek to abolish tariffs and other protectionist trade policies of national and multi-national organizations that protect and promote the interest of well-to-do citizens in middle- and high-income countries, and replace them with trade-policies that would most benefit poor citizens in low-income countries.

5. One rule of international trade and law is so important that it deserves separate mention. This is the legal rule of "effectiveness." As Leif Wenar observes, in effect the international rule of "effectiveness" "says that coercive control over a population ('might') will result in legal control over that population's resources ('right'). 'Might makes right' is as much true for an autocrat in control of an oil-rich country as it is for a band of militants who seize a mine by force. In both cases, the alchemy of effectiveness transmutes the iron of coercion into the gold of legal title. Whoever can gain coercive control sends resources down through the sale chain to consumers, and consumers' cash flows back up to the coercive actors to help them maintain their power. Effectiveness puts consumers into business with bad actors abroad."[12]

6. One might work to strengthen the international rule of law, the International Court of Justice, the United Nations, the enforcement of international agreements such as the Geneva Convention, and so on. For example, one might seek to establish stronger, more effective, and more just social, political, economic, and, if necessary, even military options, in order to prevent, or bring to an end, genocides, and other substantial violations of fundamental human rights.

7. One might work to end human trafficking in all its nefarious forms. (Please do not misinterpret the brevity of this remark, as reflecting a relative lack of importance. That is far from the case.)

---

[12] Wenar, Leif, *Blood Oil: Tyrants, Violence, and the Rules that Run the World* (New York: Oxford University Press, 2017), p. xlv.

8. One can work to end the sale, or at least reduce the proliferation, of arms to ruthless dictators or unstable regimes, especially in war-torn regions. Globally, such sales contribute to injury, maiming, and death on a massive scale, as well as attempted genocides.

9. One can work to end or reduce the sale of cigarettes and other noxious, toxic, or carcinogenic products in the developing world, whenever one knows that such products are associated with significant increases in morbidity and mortality rates.

10. In lieu of bringing money to people, one can work to bring people to money. That is, one can fight to stem the xenophobic tide that has spread across much of the developed world, and work for political changes that will open the borders of the developed world as much as possible. As noted in Section 8.3, such a policy will often benefit not only the immigrants themselves (as well as, typically, their new country), but also needy members in the country they are emigrating from, if they send remittances back to their homelands, or if they eventually return to their countries with greater knowledge, more valuable skills, and other resources that they previously lacked.

Before proceeding, let me say a bit more about the rule of effectiveness, and then the desirability of open borders. The rule of effectiveness essentially affords the legal right to dispose of a country's assets to whomever comes to have effective control over those assets, regardless of how they came to attain that control. The rule greatly benefits wealthy businesses and rich consumers, but it is largely responsible for the so-called Resource Curse. It often encourages the rise of ruthless dictators and ongoing sectarian violence, with devastating consequences for untold millions, including many of the world's neediest people. If one is keen to improve the plight of many of the world's neediest people, there is compelling reason to try to abolish the rule of effectiveness, and replace it, if possible, with a rule that would make a country's citizens—and especially its neediest citizens—the ultimate beneficiaries of any valuable resources possessed by that country.[13]

---

[13] For an eye-opening account of this topic, its impact on the world's economy, and its importance for relieving global misery, see Leif Wenar's powerful, and chilling, *Blood Oil*. See also, Thomas Pogge's pioneering work on this issue, and the more general issue of how to develop an egalitarian approach to the world's resources, so that their consumption benefits everyone: in *Realizing Rawls* (Ithaca: Cornell University Press, 1989); "An Egalitarian Law of Peoples," *Philosophy and Public Affairs* 23 (1994): 195–224; *World Poverty and Human Rights*, 2nd Edition (Cambridge: Polity Press, 2008); and *Politics as Usual: What Lies Behind the Pro-Poor Rhetoric* (Cambridge: Polity Press, 2010).

Regarding open borders, ideally, borders would not only be open to displaced persons and refugees—those fleeing persecution or other human rights abuses in their home countries, and those fleeing war, sectarian, or criminal violence—but also to those simply seeking a better life for themselves or their families. There are, I believe, strong moral reasons to open one's borders to any decent law-abiding person seeking social, political, economic, or personal security regardless of their "ability to pay" or likely contributions to society.

To be sure, pluralist that I am, I recognize that there are considerations that would dictate against a policy of totally open borders for every non-threatening person who wishes to enter a country. However, my own view is that powerful reasons must be offered for any restrictions on an open-border policy, and that such restrictions must meet strong requirements of fairness and justice both in their formulation and implementation.

Finally, I readily acknowledge that while immigrants generally benefit their host countries, there will often be upfront costs associated with admitting poor people into one's country; including costs of education, housing, healthcare, and other social services, as well as costs to certain members of society in terms of competition for jobs and downward wage pressure. Insofar as one advocates for open borders, one should also work to ensure that any such costs are fairly shared, and that, in particular, the brunt of the costs are borne by those most able to bear them; namely, society's wealthiest members, rather than its poorest members. (Society's wealthiest members also typically benefit the most from immigrants who provide them with services as maids, caregivers, gardeners, cooks, personal aides, and so on.)

The preceding is just a partial laundry list of ten ideas concerning how one might conceivably help people in the world's poorest regions, while hopefully avoiding the damaging effects that often accompany on-the-ground aid efforts in those regions. The list is by no means intended to be complete. No doubt other effective mechanisms for aiding the needy in the world's poorest reasons are feasible and should be added to this list. Likewise, it is possible that, upon closer inspection, some of the suggested approaches should ultimately be removed.

Most of the suggested approaches are only likely to be effective, if at all, in the medium or long run. Correspondingly, the list provides no concrete guidance about what, if anything, one should do to help people who are in need *now*. In addition, the list does not tell us which of the suggested approaches are most important or most likely to succeed, nor does it tell us how best to pursue them. Hence, the list provides no concrete guidance as to what someone should do *now* even if one is willing to take a medium- or long-term approach to aiding the needy.

I have already indicated my general support of urgent humanitarian aid efforts, as well as aid efforts in countries where the ill effects described in this work are unlikely to arise (for example, fostering corruption, internal or external brain drain, or government unresponsiveness). However, beyond that, what one needs, before more concrete guidance can be offered, is a close examination of the most effective methods of implementing or advancing each of the proposals noted above, as well as any others that might be suggested. Such an examination must include a thorough assessment of the direct and indirect, short- and long-term costs and benefits of any proposed method for aiding the needy. It is crucial for those in a position to accurately do so to take up this task, including development economists, other social scientists, Effective Altruists, and government officials. It is also crucial that any proposed method for benefiting the needy is appraised in light of the *full* range of normative factors that are relevant to aiding the needy, and not just the narrow question of what will do the most good from a welfarist perspective. Perhaps some on-the-ground aid efforts in the world's poorest regions will be among the best of those methods. But perhaps not. Perhaps the best ways of helping the world's needy will involve pursuing some of the preceding suggestions, or some other creative approaches that have yet to be developed.

Some people will dismiss the preceding claims as being too abstract and theoretical or, even worse, as banal, impractical, and unrealistic. We know how to provide people with mosquito nets, and we can get a general consensus to work towards the eradication of malaria. However, seeking substantial changes in the global political and economic order is another matter, with too many powerful interests lined up against it, for it to ever be feasible. Perhaps that is so.

I am fully aware that only a few very powerful individuals or groups have much of a chance at significantly impacting the current rules of international law and trade.[14] For most "ordinary" citizens, it may not make sense for them to devote too much time, effort, and resources to attacking the deepest roots of global misery. Perhaps their efforts are better spent elsewhere if they want to effectively aid people in need. I am not a Pollyanna about this. Yet, one must also guard against defeatist attitudes that are self-fulfilling. Ordinary citizens *can* band together in global writing campaigns, in electing or pressuring their representatives to change the international rules that favor the world's rich and powerful, in adopting consumer practices that support efforts to even the international economic playing field, and so on.

---

[14] I am grateful to Leif Wenar for comments that prompted the writing of this paragraph.

As the old Chinese adage states, a journey of a thousand miles begins with a single step.[15] It is imperative, if we hope to one day attack the roots of the problem of global need, and not merely its symptoms, that we clearly identify both the thousand-mile journey that we need to take, and the most important first steps of that journey. Absent that, there is no hope of ever arriving at our ultimate destination, where global need is no longer a prominent feature of the human condition.

The point about attacking the roots of the problem of global need, and not merely its symptoms is, of course, a familiar one. International aid organizations have long trumpeted the virtues, and necessity, of focusing on international *development* efforts, and not merely international *relief* efforts. In doing so, they often refer to another famous adage: feed a man a fish, and he eats for a day; teach a man to fish and he eats for a lifetime. Still, my own sense is that international development efforts have tended to focus on such things as improving water supplies, farming techniques, education, infrastructure, empowering women, etc.

I do not mean to suggest that aid activists have ignored the importance of the social, political, and economic contexts in which such changes take place. However, I believe that many have, quite naturally and understandably, focused on the problems which they deemed more readily tractable via the efforts of outside intervention. In addition, perhaps they have hoped that eventually social, political, and economic changes would accompany the improvements that they sought to achieve. Such hopes are not unreasonable, especially as they are attached to advances in education and the empowerment of women. Still, I believe that even more effort must be expended to identify ways of effectively addressing the many systemic factors that give rise to global need, including the many institutions, rules, and laws that regulate international political and economic relations.

* * * * *

In choosing which, if any, approaches to aiding the needy to support, one will inevitably have to make trade-offs. One could devote one's resources to humanitarian relief efforts. Or, one could devote one's resources to on-the-ground development efforts. Alternatively, one could devote one's resources to mid- and long-term social, political, and economic changes. A fourth

---

[15] The actual quote, attributed to the Chinese sage Laozi, is "A journey of a thousand Chinese miles starts beneath one's feet." See, Laozi and D. Lau, *Tao Te Ching* (London: Penguin Books, 1963), Chapter 64.

alternative would be to devote different portions of one's resources to each of the three aims.

It is possible that, individually, it doesn't matter which of these four approaches one adopts. I'm not sure about that. I once thought that each of the four approaches were clearly permissible. However, I am now much less confident than I once was about the second approach, and I find myself leaning towards the view that, individually, one should adopt some combination of the first and third approaches.

Collectively, the arguments are even stronger for favoring some combination of the first and third approaches. Yet, despite all the worries this book raises regarding the second approach, it is hard not to think that, ultimately, we, together, should be pursuing the fourth approach. The hope underlying this view is that if we are sufficiently careful in focusing on the collective impact of our aid efforts, we will be able to identify on-the-ground relief and development efforts that will produce more good than harm, especially if those efforts are combined with other policies that improve the social, political, and economic environments within which such efforts take place.

I also believe that in adopting the fourth approach, we must be attuned to all the factors that are relevant to aiding the needy, and not solely focus on bringing about the best outcome in terms of welfare. Thus, in particular, I believe there will be some cases where, all things considered, there will be decisive moral reason to provide relief efforts to desperately needy people who need our help now, even though, from a purely cost-effective welfarist perspective, that money could be better spent elsewhere. I have not shown this to be true, of course. However, I believe that it follows straightforwardly from the pluralistic approach that this book advocates.

I remain convinced, as I have been throughout my life, that those who are well off are open to serious moral criticism if they ignore the world's needy. Unfortunately, however, what one should do in light of that truth is much more complex, and murkier, than most have realized.

How Expected Utility Theory Can Drive Us Off the Rails

In my book, *Rethinking the Good*,[1] I provided numerous reasons to be worried about Expected Utility Theory. Among other things, I challenged many of the key axioms underlying the theory, including: the *Axiom of Completeness*—that for any two alternatives A and B, either A is better than B, B is better than A, or A and B are equally good; the *Axiom of Continuity*—that for any three alternatives A, B, and C, if A is better than B, and B is better than C, then there must be some probability, p, such that we should be rationally indifferent between getting alternative B for sure, and taking a gamble of getting A with probability p, or C with probability (1 − p); and various axioms of transitivity, including the *Axiom of Transitivity for All Things Considered Better Than*—that for any three alternatives A, B, and C, if, all things considered, A is better than B, and, all things considered, B is better than C, then, all things considered A is (must be) better than C. I shall not repeat any of the arguments of *Rethinking the Good* here. Instead, I want to stress that Expected Utility Theory is a valuable tool, but it is only that. We should employ it to guide us in those cases where it is most applicable, but we should not allow ourselves to become slaves to its dictates.

When Toby Ord and Will MacAskill founded Effective Altruism, they were originally concerned with determining the most effective means of helping the world's needy. This was also Nick Beckstead's original concern, when, following in Ord's footsteps, he co-founded the first U.S. chapter of the Effective Altruist organization Giving What We Can at Rutgers University. Strikingly, however, all three of those key figures in the Effective Altruism Movement have shifted the focus of their attention. All three now think that those who want to do the most good should focus on issues of existential risk. To put the point roughly, and tendentiously, all three have *abandoned* the needy to focus on humans continuing to exist far into the future.

Those of us who continue to be deeply concerned to ameliorate the conditions of the world's neediest people may feel betrayed by the shift in focus of Ord, MacAskill, Beckstead, and others, who previously trod the same path as us. However, we should not be surprised by their shift in focus. It followed, straightforwardly, from their commitment to the "do the most good" approach of Effective Altruism, where this is understood in terms of doing the most *expected* good, as determined by Expected Utility Theory.

The actual details underlying their shift can get rather weedy. But the basic line of reasoning is easy to grasp. I shall illustrate it with a toy example involving some numbers. In doing this, I want to emphasize that the numbers I have chosen are purely for illustrative purposes. I am not claiming that they are realistic. Whether they are, or not, is irrelevant to my point.

---

[1] *Rethinking the Good: Moral Ideals and the Nature of Practical Reasoning*, New York: Oxford University Press, 2012.

Suppose that we have some funds with which we want to do good. We have two ways of spending those funds: option one, *Poverty Elimination*; or option two, *Asteroid Deflector*. Suppose that if we do Poverty Elimination, we will, with certainty, significantly improve the quality of life of one hundred million people in desperate need. More particularly, we would transform their lives from ones that would be short, and filled with great misery, into ones that would be long, and very well off. So, for the sake of the example, let us say that if we don't do Poverty Elimination, each person will live only 15 years, at level -50 (utiles, meaning that their lives would be significantly below the level at which life ceases to be worth living), while if we do Poverty Elimination, each person will live for 75 years at level 100 (utiles, meaning that their lives would be well worth living). We can calculate the expected value of Poverty Elimination as 825 billion years of utility. ((50(utiles)*15(years) *100 million(people)) + (100(utiles)*75(years)*100 million(people)).) Undeniably, that is a *lot* of expected good.

In the real world, of course, there may be all sorts of further consequences from lifting 100 million people out of poverty, and keeping them alive for 75 years, rather than having them all die before their fifteenth birthday. Many of these effects will be positive, others may be negative. However, for the purposes of keeping this example as clean, and clear, as possible, let us suppose that there are no other effects, positive or negative, from adopting Poverty Elimination, other than those described above. So, as stated, in this example, the total amount of expected value of Poverty Elimination is 825 billion years of utility.

Next, suppose that scientists have calculated that in any given year, there is a one in 50 million chance that all life on Earth will be wiped out due to collision with a giant asteroid. This means that there is a one in 250,000 chance that life will be wiped out by an asteroid collision sometime in the next 200 years. If one spends one's funds on Asteroid Deflector, there is only a one in a thousand chance that it will work. Is it worth spending money on Asteroid Deflector, which would only reduce the odds of human extinction due to an asteroid collision from one in 250,000 sometime in the next 200 years (0.000004 percent chance) to one in 250,250 sometime in the next 200 years (~0.000003996 percent chance)? That is, is spending the money on Asteroid Deflector worth increasing the odds of our surviving for the next 200 years by a mere four billionths (0.000000004)?

The answer to the preceding question depends on all sorts of factors that are difficult to accurately estimate. However, if we assume that the likelihood of our going extinct in the next 200 years due to an asteroid collision is not connected to the likelihood of our going extinct from other causes, and also assume, more controversially, that reducing the chance of extinction from any given type of extinction event by n percent reduces the total chance of extinction by n percent, then one might think about this issue along the following lines.

It is reasonable to suppose that if we manage to survive the next 200 years, there will be an explosion of developments in knowledge, creativity, morality, politics, technology, medicine, and so on. This explosion will enable humans to live vastly longer lives and, as importantly, vastly better lives. It will also allow humans to explore other planets, and possibly other galaxies, and hence to live in vastly greater numbers. It will also allow humans to effectively anticipate and avoid future existential risks, so members of our species will be able to continue to exist, perhaps spread throughout the solar system or galaxies, for a very long time into the future. Given how bright the future might be for us as a species, it might seem extremely important to try to ensure that we manage to attain that future. How important?

Well, for the sake of the example, let us suppose that the following were true. If we manage to avoid destroying ourselves in the next 200 years, or being destroyed by a virus, asteroid, or some other cataclysmic disaster, then there is at least a 90 percent probability that the future will include at least 100 billion humans, living an average of 200 years each, at a very high quality of, say, 200 utiles throughout their lives, for a total of at least 500 million years. The expected value of that outcome would be at least 9,000 billion billion years of utility (0.9(the probability of the desirable future)*100 billion(people who would be living in that future at any given time)*200(utiles, the quality of each person's life at each moment of their life)*500 million(years of existence such humans would live)). That is an extraordinary amount of utility which, by hypothesis, hangs in the balance, depending on whether we survive the next 200 years.

So, even if funding Asteroid Deflector only increases the chances of our attaining that golden future by 0.000000004, that would still have an expected value of 3.6 million million years of utility, or 36,000 billion years of utility. That, of course, is considerably more than the expected value of Poverty Elimination, which we calculated at 825 billion people years of utility. In fact, given these figures, the expected value of Asteroid Deflector would be over 43 times greater than the expected value of Poverty Elimination. Therefore, in accordance with Expected Utility Theory, we should fund Asteroid Deflector.

Suppose, next, that further funds become available that we could use to help the one billion people with terrible life prospects. However, we also learn that there is a one in 20 chance that a crucial component in Asteroid Deflector will fail, and that if we fund Backup Machine One we can protect against this failure. By the lights of Expected Utility Theory, we should fund Backup Machine One, rather than Poverty Elimination, since the expected value of funding the former will be 1,800 billion years of utility (0.05 (the chance that we will need Backup Machine One)*36,000 billion years of utility(the amount of good that is at stake if Asteroid Deflector fails and we don't have Backup Machine One)), while the expected utility of funding the latter will still "only" be 825 billion years of utility.

Next, suppose that we once again find ourselves with additional resources that would enable us to fund Poverty Elimination. However, we now learn that there is a 50 percent chance that Backup Machine One will fail, and that we could build Backup Machine Two to protect against this. By the lights of Expected Utility Theory, we should then fund Backup Machine Two, rather than Poverty Elimination, since the expected value of funding the former will be 900 billion years of utility (0.5(the chance that we will need Backup Machine Two)*1,800 billion years of utility(the amount of good that is at stake if both Asteroid Deflector fails and Backup Machine One fail, and we don't have Backup Machine Two)), while the expected utility of funding the latter will still "only" be 825 billion people years of utility.

This toy example helps illustrate how considerations of vast numbers of possible future people, all of whom might live much better, longer, lives than anyone alive today, can utterly swamp the urgent claims of very large numbers of actual people who are suffering terribly. This can happen if one allows one's judgments about which endeavors to support to be driven by the "do the most (expected) good" approach of Effective Altruism, and if one follows Expected Utility Theory in determining the expected good (or value, or utility) of one's actions.

Effective Altruists who believe that we should focus on existential risk may quibble with the details of my example, or the way that I have put some of my claims, but they should not, I think, object to the gist of my claims. To the contrary, they should insist that the sorts of considerations I have offered here are no objection to their views, but rather an explanation, and vindication, of their views.

With all due respect, however—and I really *do* respect the people who advocate the position in question—I can't, myself, accept such a view. I do believe, and have argued in print, that it is very important to try to ensure that high quality life exist as far into the future as possible.[2] In addition, I readily accept that in thinking about such issues, there is much to be said for considering the expected value of one's different alternatives. Even so, in my judgment, Expected Utility Theory is a tool, nothing more, which needs to be employed carefully. It can generate a mathematical truth about the relevant amounts of an artificial construct—expected utility—that we can attach to different options. But it cannot tell us how much weight, if any, to attach to that mathematical truth in deciding what we ought to do.

To be clear, and fair, real-world Effective Altruists who believe we should focus on existential risk are *not* arguing that we should be spending money on projects like Asteroid Deflector. Indeed, they would argue, as Nick Beckstead pointed out in correspondence, that Asteroid Deflector "may be among the least effective of existential risk interventions, and that the Effective Altruist community thinks that it's possible to get thousands or millions of times better [expected] returns by focusing on nuclear weapons policy, artificial intelligence, and threats to liberal democracy." Indeed, it is worth recalling, as previously noted in Section 1.7, that Will MacAskill believes that thoughtful efforts to reduce global catastrophic risks "have a better cost-effectiveness than organizations like AMF [*Against Malaria Foundation*, long rated as one of the top global aid charities by GiveWell and The Life You Can Save], *even if we just consider the potential deaths of people over the next 100 years* (emphasis added)." If true, this is important. However, it does not undermine the point of this appendix.

I am not disputing whether there is good reason to devote significant resources to reducing existential risks. There is. Nor am I disputing whether considerations of Expected Utility Theory have an important role to play in our thinking about how to distribute our resources. They do. However, none of this changes the fact that if we let our thinking about such issues be driven by Expected Utility Theory, rather than merely partly guided by it, then even after we have addressed all of the vastly more cost-effective approaches to reducing existential risk, we should still be spending money on projects like Asteroid Deflector, rather than Poverty Elimination, because the former has a greater expected utility than the latter. At this point, I believe, we have, in the name of Expected Utility Theory, effectively abandoned the needy, for the sake of a far-flung future filled with well-off individuals; a future whose contours may or may not look anything like we now hope it will, and whose realization may or may not turn on the decisions we now make.

My own view is that adherence to Expected Utility Theory will drive us off the rails if, based on it, we choose to fund Asteroid Deflector rather than Poverty Elimination. Moreover, in my judgment, we go further off the rails if we later fund Backup Machine One, and still further off the rails if we subsequently fund Backup Machine Two. Faced with the choice of substantially helping one hundred million people who are desperately in need now, or supporting a one in a thousand chance to prevent an occurrence of something which would itself only have a one in 250,000 chance of occurring, so as to thereby ever-so-slightly increase the possibility of lots of distantly future people living incredibly great lives, I prioritize the former over the latter. And if I did postpone meeting the urgent needs of

---

[2] See Chapter 10 of *Rethinking the Good*; "Rationality with Respect to People, Places, and Times," *Canadian Journal of Philosophy* 45 (2005): 576–606; "Neutrality and the Relations between Different Possible Locations of the Good," *Croatian Journal of Philosophy* 18 (2019): 1–13; and "Population Ethics Forty Years On: Some Lessons Learned from 'Box Ethics,'" in *Ethics and Existence: The Legacy of Derek Parfit*, edited by Jeff McMahan, Tim Campbell, James Goodrich, and Ketan Ramakrishnan, Oxford: Oxford University Press, 2022.

some of the world's worst-off, to ever-so-slightly increase the possibility of a future, lengthy, Eden for our descendants, I certainly wouldn't do this a second time, let alone a third time.

This is not, I believe, because I fail to understand how the math works out. I simply fail to accept that what we ought to do, in such cases, is determined by the math. There is, as I argue throughout this book, so much more to being good in a world of need, than merely "doing the most expected good" that one can.[3]

---

[3] This appendix was largely prompted by Nick Beckstead's outstanding PhD thesis, "On the Overwhelming Importance of Shaping the Far Future" (Rutgers, The State University of New Jersey, 2013), available at https://rucore.libraries.edu/rutgers-lib/40469/PDF/1/play/, accessed September 4, 2020. Beckstead's thesis has had a substantial impact within the Effective Altruist community. It is regarded by many as providing theoretical justification for the view, of some Effective Altruists, that we should focus our altruistic efforts on reducing existential risk. I am grateful to Beckstead for his useful feedback on this appendix.

On the Irrelevance of Proximity
or Distance for Morality

In this appendix, I discuss the widely-accepted view that proximity or distance is morally irrelevant from a normative point of view. Although regarded as a truism by most philosophers, I now believe that the issue is much more complicated than I, or most others, have previously recognized.

In "Famine, Affluence and Morality," Singer considers, and quickly dismisses, the view that proximity or distance could have moral significance in an important passage worth quoting in detail. He writes:

> I do not think I need to say much in defense of the refusal to take proximity and distance into account . . . . If we accept any principle of impartiality, universalizability, equality, or whatever, we cannot discriminate against someone merely because he is far away from us . . . . Admittedly, it is possible that we are in a better position to judge what needs to be done to help a person near to us than one far away, and perhaps also to provide the assistance we judge to be necessary . . . . This may have once been a justification for being more concerned with the poor in one's own town than with famine victims in India . . . . [However] instant communication and swift transportation have changed the situation . . . . Expert observers and supervisors sent out by famine relief organizations or permanently stationed in famine prone areas, can direct our aid to a refugee in Bengal almost as effectively as we could get it to someone on our own block. There would seem, therefore, to be no possible justification for discriminating on geographical grounds.[1]

Singer's claims here are representative of many people's views regarding the moral irrelevance of proximity and distance. However, as I will try to show next, such claims are hardly conclusive.

Unfortunately, in assessing the plausibility of Singer's claim about the moral irrelevance of proximity and distance, there are several distinct views that might be conflated. They might be framed as follows:

Spatial Neutrality Principle: mere difference in spatial location is not itself morally relevant.

Persons Neutrality Principle: from the moral point of view, we ought to treat all people equally, to be impartial between people, and to act in accordance with principles that are universalizable, other things equal (note, this clause allows for the moral relevance of certain special relations between different people).

Spatial Relations Neutrality Principle: spatial relations such as "nearness" or "farness" are themselves morally irrelevant.

For some, Singer's claim that there would seem to be "no possible justification for discriminating on geographical grounds" may simply seem to reflect the Spatial Neutrality Principle.

---

[1] "Famine, Affluence, and Morality," *Philosophy and Public Affairs* 1 (1972), p. 232.

That principle tells us, in essence, that if the only difference between two possible events, E_1 and E_2, is that E_1 would occur at one spatial location, S_1, while E_2 would occur at a different spatial location, S_2, then E_1 and E_2 would have the exact same moral status. On the other hand, Singer defends his "refusal to take proximity and distance into account" by asserting that "if we accept any principle of impartiality, universalizability, equality, or whatever, we cannot discriminate against someone merely because he is far away from us." This assertion seems to infer the truth of the Spatial Relations Neutrality Principle from the Persons Neutrality Principle. However, while there is great plausibility to both the Spatial Neutrality Principle and the Persons Neutrality Principle, those principles do not entail, either individually or jointly, the Spatial Relations Neutrality Principle.

To see this, notice that anyone who rejects the Spatial Relations Neutrality Principle could nevertheless accept, and indeed insist on, the truth of both the Spatial Neutrality Principle and the Persons Neutrality Principle. Thus, someone could consistently hold the following constellation of views. First, rejecting the Spatial Relations Neutrality Principle, one might hold that one person's obligation to another is, in part, a function of their proximity to or distance from each other. So, for example, one might hold that the closer someone is to me, the greater my obligation to help them if they are in need. Second, accepting the Spatial Neutrality Principle, one might insist that the truth of that view does not depend on where, in space, one is located. So, the strength of one's obligation to help someone in need will decrease with the distance that he or she is from you, and the extent to which this is so will be exactly the same no matter where in space one is located. Third, barring special relations, the strength of one's obligation to help someone in need will decrease with the distance that he or she is from you, and the extent to which this is so will be exactly the same no matter who you are and no matter who the other person is. In other words, on the constellation of views in question, we must be neutral with respect to both people and places when giving due weight to the *relational* role that proximity and distance play in one's obligations to others.

Consider an analogy from science. The Universal Law of Gravitation is neutral with respect to all spatial locations. That is, an object of any given mass will exert the same gravitational pull no matter where in space it is located. The Universal Law of Gravitation is also completely "impartial" in the way that it applies to objects in the universe. That is, nature is "blind" in the way that its laws apply—the notions of prejudice, favoritism, or unequal treatment simply have no application concerning nature's laws. Yet proximity and distance *are* relevant to the gravitational force that one object exerts on another. In fact, not only does the gravitational force between objects decrease with the distance between them, but it does so exponentially.[2]

Similarly, it might be suggested, the fact that someone is in need gives others a reason to help that person. However, perhaps the reason-giving force which that person's need gives rise to decreases, as it were, with the distance that that person is from someone who would be in a position to help, just as the gravitational force that a body of mass exerts throughout the universe decreases as that force extends further and further away from the center of the mass.

Now I am not claiming that the moral laws governing the normative realm are, in fact, analogous to those governing the empirical realm. But the analogy with the Universal Law of Gravitation illustrates that there is nothing incoherent about a combination of views that

---

[2] The Universal Law of Gravitation is an inverse square law which holds that the gravitational pull of two objects with mass decreases as a function of the square of the distance between the center points of the masses.

involves a principle of neutrality with respect to space, a principle of neutrality (or impartiality) with respect to entities in the universe, and a principle that recognizes spatial relations as important.

Elsewhere, I have argued that while there are important respects in which we ought, morally, to be neutral with respect to people, spaces, and times, it is not clear what, exactly, this entails, and that many common assumptions regarding this are mistaken.[3] In a similar vein, Frances Kamm has offered a series of ingenious arguments that challenge standard assumptions regarding the irrelevance of different temporal locations,[4] and another series of ingenious arguments in support of the view that distance *is* morally significant, though not in the ways that most people assume.[5]

In light of all this, though I am still inclined to believe that proximity and distance are not, themselves, normatively significant, I believe that much more thought needs to be given to this issue than most have assumed.

[3] See Chapter 10 of *Rethinking the Good: Moral Ideals and the Nature of Practical Reasoning* (New York: Oxford University Press, 2012), pp. 313–62; "Rationality with Respect to People, Places, and Times," *Canadian Journal of Philosophy* 45 (2005): 576–606; "Neutrality and the Relations between Different Possible Locations of the Good," *Croatian Journal of Philosophy* 18 (2019): 1–13; and "Population Ethics Forty Years On: Some Lessons Learned from 'Box Ethics,'" in *Ethics and Existence: The Legacy of Derek Parfit*, edited by Jeff McMahan, Tim Campbell, James Goodrich, and Ketan Ramakrishnan, Oxford: Oxford University Press, 2022.

[4] See Chapter 3, "Accounting for Asymmetry?" in *Morality, Mortality: Volume I, Death and Whom to Save from It* (New York: Oxford University Press, 1993), pp. 39–55.

[5] See Chapter 11 "Does Distance Matter Morally to the Duty to Rescue?" and Chapter 12 "The New Problem of Distance in Morality" in *Intricate Ethics: Rights, Responsibilities, and Permissible Harms* (New York: Oxford University Press, 2007), pp. 345–97.

Bibliography

"About Us." *VillageReach*, URL: https://web.archive.org/web/20190225081419/http://www.villagereach.org/about/, accessed October 6, 2007.

Acemoglu, D. and S. Johnson. "Disease and Development: The Effect of Life Expectancy on Economic Growth." *Journal of Political Economy* 115 (2007): 925–85.

Adams, Robert. "Motive Utilitarianism." *Journal of Philosophy* 73 (1976): 467–81.

Addison, T., O. Morrissey, and F. Tarp. "The Macroeconomics of Aid: Overview." *The Journal of Development Studies* 53 (2017): 987–97.

Alcos, Carlos. "50 Nonprofits making a world of difference." *Matador Network*, November 2, 2011, URL: https://web.archive.org/web/20200824014624/https://matadornetwork.com/change/50-nonprofits-making-a-world-of-difference/, accessed September 14, 2017.

Alkire, Sabina and Maria Emma Santos. "Multidimensional Poverty Index." Oxford Poverty and Human Development Initiative (OPHI), Department of International Development, Oxford University, July 2010, URL: https://www.ophi.org.uk/wp-content/uploads/OPHI-MPI-Brief.pdf, accessed September 6, 2018.

Arendt, Hannah. *Eichmann in Jerusalem: A Report on the Banality of Evil*. New York: Viking Press, 1963.

Aristotle. *Nicomachean Ethics*. In *The Basic Works of Aristotle*, edited by Richard McKeon. New York: Random House, 1941.

Attanasio, Orazio et al. "Human development and poverty reduction in developing countries: Full Research Report." Department for International Development, ESRC End of Award Report, RES-167-25-0124, ESRC, Swindon, UK, January 1, 2009, URL: https://www.gov.uk/research-for-development-outputs/human-development-and-poverty-reduction-in-developing-countries-full-research-report, accessed September 12, 2017.

Atun, Rifat A., S. Bennett, and A. Duran. "When Do Vertical (Stand-Alone) Programmes Have a Place in Health Systems?" World Health Organization, 2008, URL: https://web.archive.org/web/20200824010850/https://www.who.int/management/district/services/WhenDoVerticalProgrammesPlaceHealthSystems.pdf, accessed July 19, 2019.

Banerjee, Abhijit V. *Making Aid Work*. Cambridge, MA: MIT Press, 2007.

Barnett, Chris. "Thumbs up or thumbs down? Did the Millennium Villages Project work?" *From Poverty to Power*, Oxfam blog, September 20, 2018, URL: https://oxfamblogs.org/fp2p/thumbs-up-or-thumbs-down-did-the-millennium-villages-project-work/, accessed March 30, 2021.

Bar-Yam, Yaneer. "General Features of Complex Systems." *Encyclopedia of Life Support Systems*. Oxford: Encyclopedia of Life Support Systems/UNESCO, 2002.

Bauer, P. "Dissent on Development." *Scottish Journal of Political Economy* 16 (1969): 75–94.

Bauer, P. *Dissent on Development*. London: Weidenfeld & Nicolson, 1971.

Beckstead, Nick. "On the Overwhelming Importance of Shaping the Far Future." PhD diss., Rutgers, The State University of New Jersey, 2013.

Bendavid, Eran. "The fog of development: evaluating the Millennium Villages Project." *The Lancet*, May, 2018. doi: https://doi.org/10.1016/S2214–109X(18)30196–7. URL: https://www.thelancet.com/journals/langlo/article/PIIS2214-109X(18)30196–7/fulltext#back-bib1, accessed March 29, 2021.

Bermeo, Sarah. "Foreign Aid and Regime Change: Assessing the Impact of Different Donors." Prepared for conference: Aid Transparency and Development Finance: Lessons and Insights from AidData, University College, Oxford, March 22–25, 2010.

Black, Maggie. *International Development: Illusions and Realities*. Oxford: New Internationalist Publications, 2015.

Bloom, David E. and Matthew J. McKenna. "Population, Labour Force, and Unemployment: Implications for the Creation of (Decent) Jobs, 1990–2030." UNDP Human Development Report Office Background Paper, 2015, URL: http://hdr.undp.org/sites/default/files/bloom_hdr_2015_final.pdf, accessed September 10, 2018.

Buber, Martin. *I and Thou*. Mansfield Centre: Martino Publishing, 2010.

Burnside, C. and D. Dollar. "Aid, Policies, and Growth." *American Economic Review* 90 (2000): 847–68.

Burnside, C. and D. Dollar. "Aid, Policies, and Growth: Revisiting the Evidence." World Bank Policy Research Paper No. 0–2834, Washington, DC: World Bank, 2004.

"CAF World Giving Index 2018: A Global View of Giving Trends." Charities Aid Foundation, URL: https://www.cafonline.org/docs/default-source/about-us-publications/caf_wgi2018_report_webnopw_2379a_261018.pdf, accessed August 24, 2019.

Carey, Ryan, ed. *The Effective Altruism Handbook*. Oxford: Centre for Effective Altruism, 2015.

Carson, Rachel Louise. *Silent Spring*. New York: Houghton Mifflin, 1962.

Cartwright, Nancy and Jeremy Hardie. *Evidence-Based Policy: A Practical Guide to Doing It Better*. New York: Oxford University Press, 2012.

Casal, Paula. "Sexual Dimorphism and Human Enhancement." *Journal of Medical Ethics* 39 (2013): 722–8.

Chaib, Fadela, Sabrina Sidhu, and Anugraha Palan. "A child under 15 dies every 5 seconds around the world." *World Health Organization Newsroom*, September 18, 2018, URL: https://www.who.int/news-room/detail/18-09-2018-a-child-under-15-dies-every-5-seconds-around-the-world-, accessed May 28, 2020.

Charusheela, S. "Social Analysis and the Capabilities Approach: A Limit to Martha Nussbaum's Universalist Ethics." *Cambridge Journal of Economics* 33 (2008): 1135–52.

Clemens, Michael. "New Documents Reveal the Cost of 'Ending Poverty' in a Millennium Village: At Least $12,000 Per Household." *Center for Global Development*, March 30, 2012, URL: https://www.cgdev.org/blog/new-documents-reveal-cost-%E2%80%9Cending-poverty%E2%80%9D-millennium-village-least-12000-household#:~:text=%E2%80%809CThe%20Millennium%20Village%20aims%20to,up%20to%E2%80%9D%202%2C250%20households, accessed March 28, 2021.

Clemens, M.A., S. Radlett, and R. Bhavnani. *Counting Chickens When They Hatch: The Short Term Effect of Aid on Growth*. CGD Working Paper No. 44, Washington, DC: CGD, 2004.

Coffey, Diane and Dean Spears. *Where India Goes*. Noida: HarperCollins, 2017.

Collier, P. and D. Dollar. "Aid Allocation and Poverty Reduction." *European Economic Review* 45 (2002): 1–26.

Collier, P., and A. Hoeffler. "Aid, Policy and Growth in Post-Conflict Societies." *European Economic Review* 48 (2004): 1125–45.

"Combination Deworming (Mass Drug Administration Targeting Both Schistosomiasis and Soil-Transmitted Helminths)." *GiveWell*, December 2013, updated January 2018, URL: https://www.givewell.org/international/technical/programs/deworming, accessed July 31, 2020.

"Corruption Perceptions Index." *Transparency International—What We Do.* Transparency International, n.d., URL: https://web.archive.org/web/20200721103509/https://www.transparency.org/en/cpi, accessed July 21, 2020.

"Cost-Effectiveness." *GiveWell*, updated November 2017, URL: https://web.archive.org/web/20181215120714/https://www.givewell.org/how-we-work/our-criteria/cost-effectiveness, accessed December 17, 2018.

"COVID-19 Coronavirus Pandemic." *Worldometers*, URL: https://web.archive.org/web/20200527132552/https://www.worldometers.info/coronavirus/, accessed May 27, 2020.

"COVID-19 Coronavirus Pandemic: United States." *Worldometers*, URL: https://web.archive.org/web/20200527135239/https://www.worldometers.info/coronavirus/country/us/, accessed May 27, 2020.

Dalgaard, C.-J., H. Hansen, and F. Tarp. "On the Empirics of Foreign Aid and Growth." *The Economic Journal* 114 (2004): F191–F216.

Dancy, Jonathan. *Ethics Without Principles.* Oxford: Clarendon Press, 2006.

Deaton, Angus. *The Great Escape: Health, Wealth, and the Origins of Inequality.* Princeton: Princeton University Press, 2015.

Deaton, Angus. "The U.S. Can No Longer Hide From Its Deep Poverty Problem." *New York Times*, January 24, 2018, URL: Opinion |The U.S. Can No Longer Hide From Its Deep Poverty Problem – The New York Times (nytimes.com), accessed June 5, 2019.

Deaton, Angus and Nancy Cartwright. "Understanding and Misunderstanding Randomized Controlled Trials." *Social Science & Medicine* 210 (2018): 2–21.

Degnbol-Martinusses, John and Poul Engberg-Pedersen. *Aid: Understanding International Development Cooperation.* London: Zed Books, 2003.

Descartes, René. *Meditations on First Philosophy.* Translated by Donald A. Cress, 2nd Edition. Indianapolis: Hackett Publishing Company, 1988.

"Development aid rises again in 2016 but flows to poorest countries dip." *Organisation for Economic Co-operation and Development*, 2016, URL: http://www.oecd.org/dac/development-aid-rises-again-in-2016-but-flows-to-poorest-countries-dip.htm, accessed September 6, 2018.

de Waal, Alex. *Famine Crimes: Politics & the Disaster Relief Industry in Africa.* Oxford: James Currey and Bloomington: Indiana University Press, 1997.

"The Diary of Angelina Jolie and Dr. Jeffrey Sachs in Africa." *MTV*, 2005, URL: https://www.youtube.com/watch?v=_kv0VdBkkno, accessed April 5, 2021.

Dichter, Thomas W. *Despite Good Intentions: Why Development Assistance to the Third World Has Failed.* Amherst: University of Massachusetts Press, 2003.

"Disasters, 2017/01/01 to 2018/01/01." *ReliefWeb*, OCHA, URL: https://web.archive.org/web/20200824160908/https://reliefweb.int/disasters?date=20170101–20180101, accessed September 26, 2017.

Domonoske, C. "50 Years Ago, Sugar Industry Quietly Paid Scientists to Point Blame at Fat." The Two Way, *NPR*, September 13, 2016, URL: https://www.npr.org/sections/thetwo-way/2016/09/13/493739074/50-years-ago-sugar-industry-quietly-paid-scientists-to-point-blame-at-fat, accessed September 1, 2019.

"Donating to the Somalia Famine." *GiveWell*, The Clear Fund, August 11, 2011, URL: https://web.archive.org/web/20200611235440/https://www.givewell.org/donate-to-somalia, accessed June 11, 2020.

Dost, A.N. and H.A. Khan. "Explaining NGO-State Wage Differentials in Afghanistan: Empirical Findings and New Theoretical Models with Policy Implications in General Equilibrium." MPRA Paper 66639, 2015, URL: https://mpra.ub.uni-muenchen.de/66639/1/MPRA_paper_66639.pdf, accessed October 9, 2018.

Duff-Brown, Beth. "A Look at the Millennium Project." *Scope*. Stanford Medicine, April 24, 2018, URL: https://scopeblog.stanford.edu/2018/04/24/a-look-at-the-millennium-villages-project/#:~:text=The%20authors%20concluded%20that%20the,the%20project%20sites%2C%20they%20wrote, accessed March 29, 2021.

Easterly, William. *The White Man's Burden: Why the West's Efforts to Aid the Rest Have Done So Much Ill and So Little Good*. New York: Penguin Press, 2006.

Epstein, Helen. *Another Fine Mess: America, Uganda, and the War on Terror*. New York: Columbia Global Reports, 2017.

Esty, D.C. and A. Moffa. "Why Climate Change Collective Action Has Failed and What Needs to be Done Within and Without the Trade Regime." *Journal of International Economic Law* 15 (2012): 777–91.

Fallon, J., C. Sugden, and L. Pieper. "The Contribution of Australian Aid to Papua New Guinea's Development 1975–2000." AusAID Evaluation and Review Series No. 34. Canberra: AusAID, 2003.

Fengler, W. and H. Kharas. "Overview: Delivering Aid Differently." Brookings Institution, 2016, URL: https://www.brookings.edu/wp-content/uploads/2016/07/deliveringaiddifferently_chapter.pdf, accessed June 9, 2018.

Ferguson, J. *Give a Man a Fish: Reflections on the New Politics of Distribution*. Durham, NC: Duke University Press, 2015.

Fiennes, C. "Help the homeless—don't give them spare change." *The Financial Times*, April 19, 2017, URL: https://web.archive.org/web/20190102192611/https://www.ft.com/content/f2e25252-1b8b-11e7-a266-12672483791a, accessed December 18, 2018.

Fleck, T. "What Went Wrong at the Rice School?" *Houston Press*, Houston Press LP, August 21, 1997, URL: http://www.houstonpress.com/news/what-went-wrong-at-the-rice-school-6570776, accessed August 30, 2017.

Foot, Philippa. "The Problem of Abortion and the Doctrine of Double Effect." *Oxford Review* 5 (1967): 5–15.

Gayfer, J. "An Independent Evaluation of SDC Nepal Country Programmes 1993–2004: Building Bridges in Nepal—Dealing with Deep Divides." Bern: Swiss Agency for Development and Cooperation, 2005.

Glennie, Jonathan and Andy Sumner. *Aid, Growth and Poverty*. London: Palgrave Macmillan, 2016.

"Global malaria spending $2 billion short of WHO target, stifling progress toward eliminating disease." *Institute for Health Metrics and Evaluation*, April 24, 2019, URL: https://web.archive.org/web/20190426002903/http://www.healthdata.org/news-release/global-malaria-spending-2-billion-short-who-target-stifling-progress-toward-eliminating, accessed May 27, 2020.

Glover, Jonathan. *Humanity: A Moral History of the Twentieth Century*. New Haven: Yale University Press, 2001.

Goldberg, D.T. "Liberalism's Limits: Carlyle and Mill on 'the negro question.'" *Nineteenth-Century Contexts: An Interdisciplinary Journal* 22 (2000): 203–16, doi:10.1080/08905490008583508.

Golding, William. *Lord of the Flies*. London: Faber and Faber, 1954.

"Grants by private agencies and NGOs." *Organisation for Economic Co-operation and Development*, 2016, URL: https://data.oecd.org/drf/grants-by-private-agencies-and-ngos.htm#indicator-chart, accessed September 6, 2018.

Green, Duncan. "The Idealist: a brilliant, gripping, disturbing portrait of Jeffrey Sachs." *From Poverty to Power*, October 31, 2013, URL: https://oxfamblogs.org/fp2p/the-idealist-a-brilliant-gripping-disturbing-portrait-of-jeffrey-sachs/, accessed March 28, 2021.

Green, M. "Oxfam and the dark side of the aid industry." *Financial Times*, Nikkei, February 15, 2018, URL: https://web.archive.org/web/20200621013909/https://www.ft.com/con tent/8799725c-123c-11e8-8cb6-b9ccc4c4dbbb, accessed June 20, 2019.

Hansen, H. and F. Tarp. "The Effectiveness of Foreign Aid and Cross-Country Growth Regressions." Mimeo, 1999.

Hardin, Garett. "Lifeboat Ethics: The Case Against Helping the Poor." *Psychology Today Magazine*, Ziff-Davis Publishing Company, 1974.

Hardin, Garrett. "The Tragedy of the Commons." *Science*, New Series 162 (1968): 1243–8.

Harris, Al. "John Stuart Mill: Servant of the East India Company." *The Canadian Journal of Economics and Political Science* 30 (1964): 185–202.

Hobbes, Thomas. *Leviathan*. London: Printed for A. Crooke, 1651.

The Holy Scriptures. Philadelphia: The Jewish Publication Society of America, 1955.

"Home." *VillageReach*, URL: http://www.villagereach.org/about/, accessed July 17, 2019.

Hoque, Mofidul. "Bangladesh 1971: A Forgotten Genocide." *Bangladesh—Audacity of Hope*, March 5, 2013, URL: https://mygoldenbengal.wordpress.com/2013/03/05/bangla desh-1971-a-forgotten-genocide/, accessed September 4, 2016.

Horvath, Mark. "Giving Money to Homeless People is Okay." *Huffpost*, March 31, 2017, URL: https://web.archive.org/web/20170912175455/http://www.huffingtonpost.com/entry/ giving-money-to-homeless-people-is-okay_us_58de9ef7e4b0ca889ba1a57b, accessed December 18, 2018.

Hume, David. *A Treatise of Human Nature*. Edited by L.A. Selby-Bigge. Oxford: Clarendon Press, 1896.

Jack, C.Y. "J.S. Mill's Career at the East India Company." *The Victorian Web*, URL: https:// web.archive.org/web/20190811055352/http://www.victorianweb.org/philosophy/mill/car eer.html, accessed August 8, 2019.

Jaeger, David A. and M.D. Paserman. "Israel, the Palestinian Factions, and the Cycle of Violence." *AEA Papers and Proceedings: The Economics of National Security* 96 (2006): 45–9.

"John 8.7." *BibleGateway*, URL: https://www.biblegateway.com/passage/?search=John% 208:7&version=KJV, accessed August 31, 2020.

Jones, Philip P. and Thomas T. Poleman. "Communes and the Agricultural Crisis in Communist China." *Food Research Institute Studies* 3 (1962): 3–22.

Jones, Sam and F. Tarp. "Does Foreign Aid Harm Political Institutions?" *Journal of Development Economics* 118 (2016): 266–81.

Kagan, Shelly. "The Additive Fallacy." *Ethics* 99 (1988): 5–31.

Kagan, Shelly. *The Limits of Morality*. Oxford: Clarendon Press, 1989.

Kagy, Gisella. "Long Run Impacts of Famine Exposure: A Study of the 1974–1975 Bangladesh Famine." Preliminary Draft, University of Colorado, 2012.

Kamm, F.M. *Intricate Ethics: Rights, Responsibilities, and Permissible Harms*. New York: Oxford University Press, 2007.

Kamm, F.M. *Morality, Mortality: Volume I, Death and Whom to Save from It*. New York: Oxford University Press, 1993.

Kamm, F.M. *Morality, Mortality: Volume II, Rights, Duties, and Status*. New York: Oxford University Press, 1996.

Kant, Immanuel. *Groundwork of the Metaphysics of Morals.* Edited by Mary J. Gregor. Cambridge: Cambridge University Press, 1998.

Kant, Immanuel. *The Metaphysics of Morals.* Edited by Mary J. Gregor. Cambridge: Cambridge University Press, 2013.

Kaul, I., P. Conceicao, K. Le Goulven, and R.U. Mendoza. *Providing Global Public Goods: Managing Globalization.* Oxford: Oxford University Press, 2003.

Kearns, C.E., L.A. Schmidt, and S.A. Glantz. "Sugar Industry and Coronary Heart Disease Research: A Historical Analysis of Internal Industry Documents." *JAMA Internal Medicine* 176 (2016): 1680–85, doi:10.1001/jamainternmed.2016.5394.

Kharas, H. "Trends and Issues in Development Aid." Wolfensohn Center for Development, Working Paper 1. Washington, DC: Brookings Institution, 2007.

"Kidnap for Ransom, Global Trends 2017." *AIG*, NYA24, April 2018, URL: https://web.archive.org/web/20200727032450/https://www.aig.dk/content/dam/aig/emea/denmark/documents/k-r-trends2017-nya.pdf, accessed August 31, 2019.

Kim, James H. and Anthony R. Scialli. "Thalidomide: The Tragedy of Birth Defects and the Effective Treatment of Disease." *Toxicological Sciences* 122 (2011): 1–6, URL: https://academic.oup.com/toxsci/article/122/1/1/1672454, accessed July 1, 2019.

"The lack of controversy over well-targeted aid." *The GiveWell Blog*, November 6, 2015, updated July 26, 2016, URL: https://blog.givewell.org/2015/11/06/the-lack-of-controversy-over-well-targeted-aid/, accessed July 10, 2019.

Laderchi, C.R., R. Saith, and F. Stewart. "Does it Matter that we do not Agree on the Definition of Poverty? A Comparison of Four Approaches." *Oxford Development Studies* 31 (2003): 243–74, URL: https://www.academia.edu/8302026/Livelihoods_and_Poverty_Approved_Public_Version_of_Chapter_13_of_the_Working_Group_II_contribution_to_the_IPCC_Fifth_Assessment_Report, accessed August 24, 2019.

The Lancet 380 (2012): 859, 861–5.

Laozi and D. Lau. *Tao Te Ching.* London: Penguin Books, 1963.

Leitenberg, Milton. "Deaths in Wars and Conflicts in the 20th Century." Cornell University Peace Studies Program, 3rd Edition, 2006, URL: https://www.clingendael.org/sites/default/files/pdfs/20060800_cdsp_occ_leitenberg.pdf, accessed June 15, 2020.

Lensink, R. and O. Morrissey. "Uncertainty of Aid Flows and the Aid-Growth Relationship." Mimeo, University of Nottingham, 1999.

Lensink, R. and H. White. "Assessing Aid: A Manifesto for Aid in the 21st Century." GESPA Working Paper 15, March 1999.

Levinas, Emmanuel. *Ethics and Infinity: Conversations with Phillipe Nemo.* Pittsburgh: Duquesne University Press, 1995.

Levine, Ruth and the What Works Working Group. *Millions Saved: Proven Successes in Global Health.* Sudbury, MA: Jones and Bartlett Learning, 2004.

Lubold, Gordon and Dustin Volz. "U.S. Says Chinese, Iranian Hackers Seek to Steal Coronavirus Research." *The Wall Street Journal*, Dow Jones & Company Inc., May 14, 2020, URL: https://web.archive.org/web/20200528110146/https://www.wsj.com/articles/chinese-iranian-hacking-may-be-hampering-search-for-coronavirus-vaccine-officials-say-11589362205, accessed May 28, 2020.

MacAskill, William. "80,000 Hours thinks that only a small proportion of people should earn to give long term." *80,000 Hours*, July 6, 2015, URL: https://80000hours.org/2015/07/80000-hours-thinks-that-only-a-small-proportion-of-people-should-earn-to-give-long-term/#:~:text=give%20long%20term,80%2C000%20Hours%20thinks%20that%20only%20a%20small%20proportion%20of,earn%20to%20give%20long%20term&text=N, accessed June 17, 2019.

MacAskill, William. *Doing Good Better: How Effective Altruism Can Help You Help Others, Do Work that Matters, and Make Smarter Choices about Giving Back.* New York: Avery, 2016.

McBride, J. "How Does the U.S. Spend Its Foreign Aid?" *Council on Foreign Relations,* October 1, 2018, URL: https://www.cfr.org/backgrounder/how-does-us-spend-its-foreign-aid, accessed June 3, 2019.

McCormick, E. "EA Survey 2017 Series: Cause Area Preferences." *Rethink Charity,* URL: https://web.archive.org/web/20190428220550/https://forum.effectivealtruism.org/posts/xeduPnHfCQ9m9f3go/ea-survey-2017-series-cause-area-preferences, accessed December 18, 2018.

McKay, A. and B. Baulch. "How Many Chronically Poor People are There in the World? Some Preliminary Estimates." Chronic Poverty Research Centre Working Paper No. 45. Manchester: University of Manchester, 2004.

McMahan, J. *The Ethics of Killing: Problems at the Margin of Life.* New York: Oxford University Press, 2002.

Malthus, T. *An Essay on the Principle of Population.* London: J. Johnson, 1798.

Maren, Michael. *The Road to Hell: The Ravaging Effects of Foreign Aid and International Charity.* New York: The Free Press, 1997.

Martiner, Ramon. "Causes of Death in the World. 1990, 2005, 2010." *Health Intelligence,* May 18, 2013, URL: http://publichealthintelligence.org/content/causes-death-world-1990-2005-2010, accessed August 31, 2020.

"Mega-charities." *GiveWell,* The Clear Fund, June 13, 2013, URL: https://web.archive.org/web/20200519190341/https://blog.givewell.org/2011/12/28/mega-charities/, accessed June 28, 2019.

Milgram, Stanley. "Behavioural Study of Obedience." *Journal of Abnormal and Social Psychology* 67 (1963): 371–8.

Mill, John Stuart. *Dissertations and Discussions: Political, Philosophical, and Historical,* Vol. 3. New York: H. Holt & Co., 1874.

Mill, John Stuart. *On Liberty.* London: Longman, Roberts & Green, 1869.

Mill, John Stuart. *Utilitarianism.* Indianapolis: Hackett Publishing Company, 1979.

Miller, Ronnie. *From Lebanon to Intifada.* Lanham: University Press of America, 1991.

Mitchell, S., A. Gelman, R. Ross, J. Chen, S. Bari, U.K. Huynh, et al. "The Millennium Villages Project: a retrospective, observational, endline evaluation." *The Lancet* 6, Issue 5, E500–E513, May 1, 2018. doi:https://doi.org/10.1016/S2214-109X(18)30065-2, URL: https://www.thelancet.com/journals/langlo/article/PIIS2214-109X(18)30065-2/fulltext, accessed March 28, 2021.

Morgenstern, Oscar. *On the Accuracy of Economic Observations,* 2nd Edition. Princeton: Princeton University Press, 1963.

Morrissey, O. "Why do Economists Disagree so much on Aid Effectiveness? Aid Works (in Mysterious Ways)." Initial draft paper for presentation at the IMF-CFD Conference on Financing for Development. Geneva, 2015.

Mosley, P. "Aid-effectiveness: The Micro-Macro Paradox." *IDS Bulletin* 17 (1986).

"Most Corrupt Countries 2020." *World Population Review,* n.d., URL: https://web.archive.org/web/20200502153652/https://worldpopulationreview.com/countries/most-corrupt-countries/, accessed August 30, 2020.

Moyo, Dambisa. *Dead Aid: Why Aid Is Not Working and How There Is a Better Way for Africa.* New York: Farrar, Straus and Giroux, 2009.

Munk, Nina. *The Idealist: Jeffrey Sachs and the Quest to End Poverty.* New York: Doubleday, 2013.

Murphy, Liam B. *Moral Demands in Nonideal Theory*. New York: Oxford University Press, 2000.

Nagel, Thomas. *Equality and Partiality*. New York: Oxford University Press, 1991.

Narveson, J. "Is World Poverty a Moral Problem for the Wealthy?" *The Journal of Ethics* 8 (2004): 397–408.

Narveson, J. "Welfare and Wealth, Poverty and Justice in Today's World." *The Journal of Ethics* 8 (2004): 305–48.

The New Testament. Edited by William Beck. Saint Louis, MO: Concordia Publishing House, 1964.

Nozick, Robert. *Anarchy, State, and Utopia*. New York: Basic Books, 1974.

Nunnenkamp, P. and H. Öhler. "Funding, Competition and the Efficiency of NGOs: An Empirical Analysis of Non-charitable Expenditure of US NGOs Engaged in Foreign Aid." Kiel Institute for the World Economy Working Papers 1640 (2010).

Nussbaum, Martha C. *Creating Capabilities: The Human Development Approach*. Cambridge, MA: Harvard University Press, 2011.

Nussbaum, Martha C. "Non-Relative Virtues: An Aristotelian Approach." In *The Quality of Life*. Edited by Martha Nussbaum and Amartya Sen. Oxford: Oxford University Press, 1993.

Obadare, E. "Religious NGOs, Civil Society and the Quest for a Public Sphere in Nigeria." *African Identities* 5 (2007): 135–53.

O'Connell, Thomas O. "Advancing equity through UHC: Are we getting there?" Presented for UNICEF at the 2012 2nd Global Symposium on Health Systems Research in Beijing, URL: http://healthsystemsresearch.org/hsr2012/images/stories/media/1101/Afternoon/2%20Plenary%20Advancing%20equity%20through%20UHC_Are%20we%20getting%20there-O'Connell_UNICEF_Final-V2.pdf, accessed September 2, 2019.

O'Connor, A. "How the Sugar Industry Shifted Blame to Fat." *The New York Times*, September 12, 2016, URL: https://web.archive.org/web/20190909073501/https://www.nytimes.com/2016/09/13/well/eat/how-the-sugar-industry-shifted-blame-to-fat.html, accessed September 1, 2019.

"On the Ground Support for Farming Communities." *Starbucks*, Starbucks Coffee Company, n.d., URL: https://web.archive.org/web/20200314224325/https://www.starbucks.com/responsibility/community/farmer-support/farmer-support-centers, accessed August 30, 2019.

O'Neill, O. *Bounds of Justice*. Cambridge: Cambridge University Press, 2000.

O'Neill, Sean. "Oxfam Scandal: staff still offering aid for sex, report claims." *The Times*, Times Newspapers Limited, June 28, 2019, URL: https://web.archive.org/web/20191031164528/https://www.thetimes.co.uk/article/oxfam-scandal-staff-still-offering-aid-for-sex-report-claims-pbx32xctw, accessed June 28, 2019.

O'Neill, Sean. "Top Oxfam staff paid Haiti survivor for sex." *Word & Action*, Word & Action, Inc., February 9, 2018, URL: http://web.archive.org/web/20200723025447/https://www.wordandaction.org/single-post/2018/02/08/Top-Oxfam-staff-paid-Haiti-quake-survivors-for-sex, accessed June 28, 2019.

"Operating Model." *GiveDirectly*, 2018, URL: https://web.archive.org/web/20200824160538/https://www.givedirectly.org/operating-model/, accessed October 9, 2018.

Ord, Toby. *The Precipice: Existential Risk and the Future of Humanity*. New York: Hachette Books, 2020.

"Oxfam Haiti allegations: How the scandal unfolded." *BBC*, February 21, 2018, URL: https://www.bbc.com/news/uk-43112200, accessed June 28, 2019.

Parfit, Derek. "Can We Avoid the Repugnant Conclusion?" *Theoria* 82 (2016): 110–27.

Parfit, Derek. *On What Matters*, Vols. 1 and 2. Oxford: Oxford University Press, 2011.

Parfit, Derek. *Reasons and Persons*. Oxford: Clarendon Press, 1984.

Passell, Peter. "Dr. Jeffrey Sachs, Shock Therapist." *New York Times*, June 27, 1993, URL: https://www.nytimes.com/1993/06/27/magazine/dr-jeffrey-sachs-shock-therapist.html?pagewanted=all&src=pm, accessed April 7, 2021.

Pinker, Steven. *The Better Angels of Our Nature: Why Violence Has Declined*. New York: Viking Books, 2011.

Pinker, Steven. *Enlightenment Now: The Case for Reason, Science, Humanism, and Progress*. New York: Penguin Books, 2018.

Plato. *The Republic*, 3rd Edition. Translated by B. Jowett. London: Oxford University Press, 1892.

Pogge, Thomas. "An Egalitarian Law of Peoples." *Philosophy and Public Affairs* 23 (1994): 195–224.

Pogge, Thomas. *Politics as Usual: What Lies Behind the Pro-Poor Rhetoric*. Cambridge: Polity Press, 2010.

Pogge, Thomas. *Realizing Rawls*. Ithaca: Cornell University Press, 1989.

Pogge, Thomas. *World Poverty and Human Rights*, 2nd Edition. Cambridge: Polity Press, 2008.

Polman, Linda. *The Crisis Caravan: What's Wrong with Humanitarian Aid?* Translated by L. Waters. New York: Metropolitan Books, 2010.

Pope, Alexander. "An Essay on Criticism." *Poetry Foundation*, URL: https://web.archive.org/web/20200901022554/https://www.poetryfoundation.org/articles/69379/an-essay-on-criticism, accessed August 31, 2020.

"Process for Identifying Top Charities." *GiveWell*, The Clear Fund, n.d., URL: https://web.archive.org/web/20200723024411/https://www.givewell.org/how-we-work/process, accessed June 28, 2019.

Putnam, Hilary. "The Meaning of 'Meaning.'" In *Language, Mind, and Knowledge: Minnesota Studies in the Philosophy of Science*, Vol. 7. Edited by Keith Gunderson, 131–93. Minneapolis: University of Minnesota Press, 1975.

Qian, N. "Making Progress on Foreign Aid." *Annual Review of Economics* 3 (2014).

Ramalingam, Ben. *Aid on the Edge of Chaos*. Oxford: Oxford University Press, 2013.

Ravallion, M. "On the Role of Aid in *The Great Escape*." *Review of Income and Wealth* 60 (2014): 967–84.

Rawls, John. *A Theory of Justice*. Cambridge, MA: Harvard University Press, 1971.

Raz, Joseph. *The Morality of Freedom*. Oxford: Clarendon Press, 1986.

"The Rice School." *Niche*, URL: https://web.archive.org/save/https://www.niche.com/k12/the-rice-school—la-escuela-rice-houston-tx/, accessed July 1, 2019.

Riddell, Roger. *Does Foreign Aid Really Work?* Oxford: Oxford University Press, 2007.

Rieff, David. *The Reproach of Hunger: Food, Justice, and Money in the Twenty-First Century*. New York: Simon & Schuster, 2015.

Rodney, Walter. *How Europe Underdeveloped Africa*. London: Bogle-L'Ouverture Publications, 1973.

Rodrik, Dani. "Diagnostics Before Prescriptions." *Journal of Economic Perspectives* 24 (2010): 33–44.

Rogerson, A. "What if Development Aid Were Truly 'Catalytic?'" Background note. London: ODI, 2011.

Romans 3:23–24. *The Bible*, URL: https://www.bible.com/bible/compare/ROM.3.23–24, accessed August 31, 2020.

Roodman, D. "Why I Mostly Believe in Worms." *GiveWell Blog*, December 6, 2016, updated February 14, 2020, URL: https://web.archive.org/web/20200824034709/https://blog.givewell.org/2016/12/06/why-i-mostly-believe-in-worms/, accessed July 31, 2020.

Roser, Max and Hannah Ritchie. "Malaria." *Our World in Data*, November, 2015, URL: https://web.archive.org/web/20200527132259/https://ourworldindata.org/malaria, accessed May 27, 2020.

Ruggeri Laderchi, C., R. Saith, and F. Stewart. *Does It Matter That We Don't Agree on the Definition of Poverty? A Comparison of Four Approaches*. QEH Working Paper No. 107. Oxford: Queen Elizabeth House, 2003.

Rummel, R.J. *Death By Government*. New Brunswick, NJ: Transaction Publishers, 1994.

Sachs, Jeffrey D. *The End of Poverty*. New York: Penguin Books, 2005. Reprinted with a new preface 2015.

Sachs, Jeffrey D. "Lessons from the Millennium Villages Project: a personal perspective." *The Lancet* 6, E472–E474, May 1, 2018. doi:https://doi.org/10.1016/S2214–109X(18)30199–2, URL: https://www.thelancet.com/journals/langlo/article/PIIS2214-109X(18)30199–2/fulltext, accessed March 28, 2021.

Saiidi, Uptin. "Average life expectancy in the US has been declining for 3 consecutive years." *USA Today*, July 9, 2019, URL: https://web.archive.org/web/20200824035902/https://www.usatoday.com/story/money/2019/07/09/u-s-life-expectancy-decline-overdoses-liver-disease-suicide/1680854001/, accessed July 12, 2019.

Scheffler, Sam. *The Rejection of Consequentialism*. Oxford: Clarendon Press, 1982.

Seo, H.-J. "Politics of Aid: A Closer Look at the Motives Behind Foreign Assistance." *Harvard International Review* 38 (2017): 42–7.

Shah, Anup. "Poverty Facts and Stats." *Global Issues: Social, Political, Economic and Environmental Issues That Affect Us All*, URL: https://web.archive.org/web/20200901010445/https://www.globalissues.org/article/26/poverty-facts-and-stats, accessed August 31, 2020.

Sidgwick, Henry. *The Methods of Ethics*, 7th Edition. London: Macmillan, 1907.

Singer, Peter. "Famine, Affluence, and Morality." *Philosophy and Public Affairs* 1 (1972): 229–43.

Singer, Peter. *The Life You Can Save*. New York: Random House, 2009.

Singer, Peter. *The Most Good You Can Do*. New Haven: Yale University Press, 2015.

Smith, Adam. *The Theory of Moral Sentiments*. Edited by Knud Haakonssen. Cambridge: Cambridge University Press, 2012.

Snowden, James "How uncertain is our cost effectiveness analysis?" *The GiveWell Blog*, December 22, 2017, updated December 29, 2017, URL: https://blog.givewell.org/2017/12/22/uncertain-cost-effectiveness-analysis/, accessed July 31, 2020.

"Starbucks Social Impact." *Starbucks*, Starbucks Coffee Company, n.d., URL: https://web.archive.org/web/20200727031325/https://www.starbucks.com/responsibility, accessed August 30, 2019.

Starobin, Paul. "Does It Take a Village?" *FP [Foreign Policy]*, June 24, 2013, URL: https://foreignpolicy.com/2013/06/24/does-it-take-a-village/, accessed March 30, 2021.

Stevenson, Robert Louis and Hiram Albert Vance. *Treasure Island*. New York and London: The Macmillan Company, 1902.

Szekely, M., N. Lustig, J.A. Meijia, and M. Cumpa. *Do We Know How Much Poverty There Is?* Washington, DC: Inter-American Development Bank, 2000.

Tavares, J. "Does Foreign Aid Corrupt?" *Economics Letters* 79 (2003): 99–106.

Temkin, Larry. "Being Good in a World of Need: Some Empirical Worries and an Uncomfortable Philosophical Possibility." *Journal of Practical Ethics* 7 (2019): 1–23.

Temkin, Larry. "Egalitarianism Defended." *Ethics* 113 (2003): 764–82.

Temkin, Larry. "Equality as Comparative Fairness." *Journal of Applied Philosophy* 34 (2017): 43–60.

Temkin, Larry. "Equality and the Human Condition." *Theoria* 92 (1998): 15–45.

Temkin, Larry. "Equality, Priority, and the Levelling Down Objection." In *The Ideal of Equality*. Edited by Matthew Clayton and Andrew Williams, 129–61. New York: St. Martin's Press, 2000.

Temkin, Larry. "Equality, Priority, or What?" *Economics and Philosophy* 19 (2003): 61–88.

Temkin, Larry. "Harmful Goods, Harmless Bads." In *Value, Welfare, and Morality*. Edited by Richard Frey and Christopher Morris, 290–324. Cambridge: Cambridge University Press, 1993.

Temkin, Larry. "Illuminating Egalitarianism." In *Contemporary Debates in Political Philosophy*. Edited by Thomas Christiano and John Christman, 155–78. Oxford: Wiley-Blackwell Publishing, 2009.

Temkin, Larry. "Inequality." *Philosophy and Public Affairs* 15 (1986): 99–121.

Temkin, Larry. *Inequality*. New York: Oxford University Press, 1993.

Temkin, Larry. "Inequality: A Complex, Individualistic, and Comparative Notion." In *Philosophical Issues* 11. Edited by Ernie Sosa and Enriquea Villanueva, 327–52. Oxford: Blackwell Publishers, 2001.

Temkin, Larry. "Inequality and Health." In *Measurement and Ethical Evaluation of Health Inequalities*. Edited by Ole Norheim, Nir Eyal, Samia Hurst, and Dan Wikler, 13–26. Oxford: Oxford University Press, 2013.

Temkin, Larry. "Intergenerational Inequality." In *Philosophy, Politics, and Society*, Sixth Series. Edited by Peter Laslett and James Fishkin, 169–205. New Haven: Yale University Press, 1992.

Temkin, Larry. "Justice and Equality: Some Questions about Scope." *Social Philosophy & Policy* 12 (1995): 72–104.

Temkin, Larry. "Justice, Equality, Fairness, Desert, Rights, Free Will, Responsibility, and Luck." In *Distributive Justice and Responsibility*. Edited by Carl Knight and Zofia Stemplowska, 51–76. Oxford: Oxford University Press, 2011.

Temkin, Larry. "Neutrality and the Relations between Different Possible Locations of the Good." *Croatian Journal of Philosophy* 18 (2019): 1–13.

Temkin, Larry. "Personal versus Impersonal Principles: Reconsidering the Slogan." *Theoria* 69 (2003): 20–30.

Temkin, Larry. "Population Ethics Forty Years On: Some Lessons Learned from 'Box Ethics.'" In *Ethics and Existence: The Legacy of Derek Parfit*. Edited by Jeff McMahan, Tim Campbell, James Goodrich, and Ketan Ramakrishnan. Oxford: Oxford University Press, 2022.

Temkin, Larry. "Rationality with Respect to People, Places, and Times." *Canadian Journal of Philosophy* 45 (2015): 576–606.

Temkin, Larry. *Rethinking the Good: Moral Ideals and the Nature of Practical Reasoning*. New York: Oxford University Press, 2012.

Temkin, Larry. "Thinking about the Needy, Justice, and International Organizations." *The Journal of Ethics* 8 (2004): 349–95.

Temkin, Larry. "Thinking about the Needy: A Reprise." *The Journal of Ethics* 8 (2004): 409–58.

Temkin, Larry. "Universal Health Care Coverage: Solution or Siren? Some Preliminary Thoughts." *Journal of Applied Philosophy* 31 (2014): 1–22.

Temkin, Larry. "Welfare, Poverty, and the Needy: A Pluralistic Approach." In *Philosophie und/als Wissenschaft* (*Philosophy-Science-Scientific Philosophy: Main Lectures and Colloquia of GAP.5*). Edited by Christian Nimtz and Ansgar Beckermann, 147–63. Paderborn: Mentis Press, 2005.

Temkin, Larry. "What do we owe those in need?" *The Minefield*, interviewed by Waleed Aly and Scott Stephens, Australian Broadcasting Corporation, URL: https://www.abc.net.au/radionational/programs/theminefield/what-do-we-owe-those-in-need/10774518, accessed September 5, 2020.

Temkin, Larry. "Why Should America Care?" *Ag Bioethics Forum* 11 (June 1999): 9–15.

Thomson, Judith Jarvis. "A Defense of Abortion." *Philosophy and Public Affairs* 1 (1971): 47–66.

Thomson, Judith Jarvis. "Killing, Letting Die, and the Trolley Problem." *The Monist* 59 (1976): 204–17.

Todd, Benjamin J. *80,000 Hours: Find A Fulfilling Career That Does Good.* Oxford: Centre for Effective Altruism.

"Top-Rated Charities – 2009 Archived Version." *GiveWell Blog*, 2009, URL: https://web.archive.org/web/20200824043459/https://www.givewell.org/charities/top-charities/2009, accessed October 6, 2017.

"Top-Rated Charities – 2010 Archived Version." *GiveWell Blog*, 2010, URL: https://web.archive.org/web/20170831200820/http://www.givewell.org/charities/top-charities/2010, accessed October 6, 2017.

Unger, Peter K. *Living High & Letting Die: Our Illusions of Innocence.* New York: Oxford University Press, 1996.

United Nations Development Programme. "Millennium Development Goals," 2021, URL: https://www.undp.org/content/undp/en/home/sdgoverview/mdg_goals.html, accessed April 1, 2021.

United States Agency for International Development. "US Foreign Aid: Meeting the Challenges of the Twenty-first Century." Washington, DC: USAID, 2004.

U.S. Census Bureau. "Table No. 1313. U.S. Foreign Economic and Military Aid Programs: 1970–1996." *U.S. Census Bureau, the Official Statistics^{TM}*, Statistical Abstract of the United States: 1998, September 25, 1998, URL: https://www2.census.gov/library/publica tions/1998/compendia/statab/118ed/tables/sasec28.pdf#, accessed July 3, 2019.

Van Parijs, P. *Real Freedom for All: What (If Anything) Can Justify Capitalism?* Oxford: Clarendon Press, 1995.

Viens, Ashley. "Ranked: The Richest Countries in the World." *Visual Capitalist*, May 24, 2019, URL: https://web.archive.org/web/20200522064226/https://www.visualcapitalist.com/richest-countries-in-world/, accessed May 27, 2020.

The Vietnam War: A Film by Ken Burns & Lynn Novick. Directed by Ken Burns and Lynn Novick. Florentine Films and WETA, 2017.

"Vietnam War U.S. Military Fatal Casualty Statistics." Military Records, National Archives, URL: https://web.archive.org/web/20200824040358/https://www.archives.gov/research/military/vietnam-war/casualty-statistics, accessed July 12, 2019.

Wenar, Leif. *Blood Oil: Tyrants, Violence, and the Rules that Run the World.* New York: Oxford University Press, 2017.

Wenar, Leif. "Poverty is No Pond: Challenges for the Affluent." In *Giving Well: The Ethics of Philanthropy.* Edited by P. Illingworth, T. Pogge, and L. Wenar, 104–32. New York: Oxford University Press, 2011.

"What we do." *GiveDirectly*, GiveDirectly Inc., 2018, URL: https://givedirectly.org/operat ing-model, accessed September 10, 2018.

White, H. "The Case for Doubling Aid." *IDS Bulletin* 36 (2005): 8–13.

Wikipedia Contributors. "Edward John Eyre." *Wikipedia*, Wikimedia Foundation, URL: https://web.archive.org/web/20200824003413/https://en.wikipedia.org/wiki/Edward_John_Eyre, accessed August 8, 2019.

Wikipedia Contributors. "Jamaica Committee." *Wikipedia*, Wikimedia Foundation, URL: https://web.archive.org/web/20200824003743/https://en.wikipedia.org/wiki/Jamaica_Committee, accessed August 8, 2019.

Wikipedia Contributors. "List of Important Publications in Philosophy." *Wikipedia*, Wikimedia Foundation, URL: https://web.archive.org/web/20200815053514/https://en.wikipedia.org/wiki/List_of_important_publications_in_philosophy, accessed June 21, 2020.

Wikipedia Contributors. "The Rice School." *Wikipedia*, Wikimedia Foundation, URL: https://en.wikipedia.org/w/index.php?title=The_Rice_School&oldid=787761043, accessed August 30, 2017.

Wikipedia Contributors. "Walkathon." *Wikipedia*, Wikimedia Foundation, URL: https://web.archive.org/save/https://en.wikipedia.org/wiki/Walkathon, accessed August 23, 2020.

Williams, Bernard. "A Critique of Utilitarianism." In Smart, J.J.C. and Bernard Williams, *Utilitarianism For and Against*. London: Cambridge University Press, 1973.

Williams, Bernard. *Ethics and the Limits of Philosophy*. Cambridge, MA: Harvard University Press, 1985.

Williams, Bernard. "Persons, Character, and Morality." In *Moral Luck: Philosophical Papers 1973–1980*. Cambridge: Cambridge University Press, 1981.

Wolf, Susan. "Moral Saints." *The Journal of Philosophy* 79 (1982): 419–39.

The World Bank. "GDP per capita (current US$)—Hong Kong SAR, China, Guinea-Bissau." URL: https://web.archive.org/save/https://data.worldbank.org/indicator/NY.GDP.PCAP.CD?end=2015&locations=HK-GW&most_recent_year_desc=true&start=1960, accessed July 5, 2019.

The World Bank. "Net official development assistance and official aid received (current US$)." 1960–2017, URL: https://web.archive.org/save/https://data.worldbank.org/indicator/DT.ODA.ALLD.CD?locations=CN-HK-CF-CG-SG-NE-MG-MY-GQ-GW-KR-HT-NI-TH, accessed July 5, 2019.

The World Bank Group. "Poverty and Shared Prosperity 2020: Reversals of Fortune.", URL: https://openknowledge.worldbank.org/bitstream/handle/10986/34496/9781464816024.pdf, accessed March 29, 2021.

World Health Organization. World Health Assembly Resolution 58.33, 2005, URL: https://apps.who.int/iris/bitstream/handle/10665/20383/WHA58_33-en.pdf;sequence=1, accessed September 2, 2019.

World Health Organization. *The World Health Report 2006: Working Together for Health*. Geneva: WHO, 2006.

World Population Review. "Most Corrupt Countries." August 20, 2019, URL: https://web.archive.org/web/*/https://worldpopulationreview.com/country-rankings/most-corrupt-countries, accessed August 30, 2019.

"Zimbabwe: One Year On, Reform a Failure." *Human Rights Watch*, February 12, 2010, URL: https://web.archive.org/web/20190928025038/https://www.hrw.org/news/2010/02/12/zimbabwe-one-year-reform-failure, accessed August 27, 2019.

Z., W. "How to do the most good possible: The 'effective altruism' movement thinks it has some answers." The Economist Explains, *The Economist*, 2018, URL: https://web.archive.org/save/https://www.economist.com/the-economist-explains/2018/06/07/how-to-do-the-most-good-possible, accessed September 6, 2018.

Index

List of Principles and Examples